CORAL & CLUB FUNGI

JELLY FUNGI

FALSE MORELS

EARTH TONGUES

MORELS & RELATIVES

CUP FUNGI

MUSHROOMS
of the SOUTHEAST

Todd F. Elliott and
Steven L. Stephenson

TIMBER PRESS FIELD GUIDE

Published in 2018 by Timber Press, Inc.

Photo and illustration credits appear on page 389.

Half title page: *Parasola plicatilis*

Title page: *Mycena leaiana*

The information in this book is accurate and complete to the best of our knowledge. All recommendations are made without guarantee on the part of the authors or Timber Press. The authors and publisher disclaim any liability in connection with the use of this information. In particular, eating wild mushrooms is inherently risky. Mushrooms can be easily mistaken, and individuals vary in their physiological reactions to mushrooms that are touched or consumed.

Timber Press
The Haseltine Building
133 S.W. Second Avenue, Suite 450
Portland, Oregon 97204-3527
timberpress.com

Printed in China

Series design by Susan Applegate.

Library of Congress Cataloging-in-Publication Data

ISBN 13: 978-1-60469-730-8

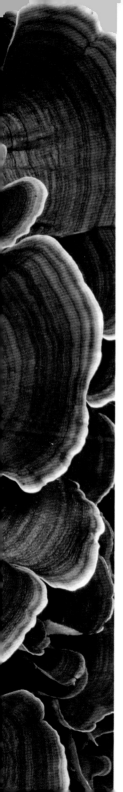

Contents

ACKNOWLEDGMENTS

Many individuals helped to make this book possible, both through the writing process and in the years preceding its publication. We are jointly and especially grateful to a number of individuals for editing taxonomy and providing detailed input on specific groups: Rich Baird, Alan Bessette, Michael Beug, Hal Burdsall, Michael Castellano, Efrén Cázares, Cathy Cripps, Roy Halling, Jay Justice, Brian Looney, Roz Lowen, Brandon Matheny, Steve Miller, Kerry O'Donnell, Walt Sturgeon, Larissa Vasilyeva, and Rytas Vilgalys. Species lists from forays within our region that assisted with species selection were provided by Charlotte Caplan (Asheville Mushroom Club forays); Patrick Leacock, Glenda O'Neal, and Gabrielle Zeiger (North American Mycological Association forays); and Mycol Stevens (northern Florida species lists). Several contributing photographers (see "Photo and Illustration Credits") provided images that were used in this field guide. Todd is particularly grateful for the inspiration, joint field excursions, friendship, and mentorship provided during this project by Cornelia Cho, Olga and Tradd Cotter, Carter Edgerton, Doug Elliott, Yanna Fishman, Tramell Forney, Tony Heffner, Sam Landes, Kate and Peter Marshall, Kelsey Myers, Allein Stanley, Babs and Bob Strickland, Samuel Thayer, Jim Trappe, Camille Truong, and Armin Weise. Steve is forever indebted to the late Orson K. Miller, Jr., for introducing him to the fungi. Over the years, he has benefited from the expertise and assistance in the field provided by a number of other individuals, not all of whom are mycologists. These include Denise Binion, Jerry Cooper, Marie Farr, Peter Johnston, Thida Win Ko Ko, Gary Laursen, Eric McKenzie, Richard Leschen, Yura Novozhilov, David Orlovich, Bill Roody, Martin Schnittler, Rod Seppelt, Barbara Stephenson, and Hanh Tran. We are grateful to Franni Farrell of Timber Press for editing our manuscript.

INTRODUCTION

For the purpose of this field guide, the Southeast is defined as extending from northern Florida to Maryland and encompassing the states of Alabama, Arkansas, Georgia, Kentucky, Louisiana, Mississippi, North Carolina, South Carolina, Tennessee, Virginia, and West Virginia. This region includes portions of seven different physiographic provinces in eastern North America. A physiographic province is defined as a geographic region with a characteristic type of landscape and usually a different type of subsurface rock (e.g., sandstone or limestone). Both landscape and subsurface rock contribute to the development of what is often a distinctive type of vegetation.

The Coastal Plain makes up the largest land area of the Southeast, extending from eastern Maryland southward to northern Florida and west to Louisiana. Virtually all of Louisiana and Mississippi, as well as major portions of southern and eastern Arkansas, Georgia, South Carolina, North Carolina, and Virginia, fall within this province. The Coastal Plain is characterized by a relatively flat landscape and sometimes poorly drained areas.

Located west of the Coastal Plain is a second physiographic province, the Piedmont, which extends from eastern Alabama northward through Georgia, South Carolina, North Carolina, and Virginia to central Maryland. The Piedmont is composed of more rolling hills than the Coastal Plain.

The southern Appalachian Mountains occupy portions of nine states in the Southeast and include three physiographic provinces. The Appalachian Plateau (or Cumberland Plateau, as it is known in Kentucky) occurs from western Maryland to northern Alabama; this dissected tableland is broadest in West Virginia, where it occupies more than half the state. Located just east of the Appalachian Plateau is the Valley and Ridge, which also extends from western Maryland to northern Alabama; this region consists of a series of well-defined alternating ridges and valleys trending from north to south. The Blue Ridge, situated between the Piedmont and the Valley and Ridge, occurs from Maryland to northern Georgia. The highest mountains in the Southeast are part of the Blue Ridge, with numerous peaks reaching elevations of 4,000 feet and several exceeding 5,000 feet in southwestern Virginia, western North Carolina, and eastern Tennessee.

The Interior Low Plateaus of Kentucky, western Tennessee, and far northern Alabama occur to the west of the Appalachian Mountains and consist of rolling hills. In central and northern Arkansas, the Ouachita-Ozark Highlands province contains two relatively low-elevation mountain ranges (Boston and Ouachita) separated by the broad, flat Arkansas River Valley.

Overview of the Region

The Southeast is characterized by diverse topography, climate, and vegetation. In southern portions of the Coastal Plain, the landscape is rather flat, the climate is almost subtropical (with warm, humid summers and mild winters), and the forests are commonly dominated by pine or oak hammocks. At higher elevations in the northern portion of the Southeast, the landscape is often exceedingly rugged; the climate is much cooler, and the forests are dominated by red spruce and resemble those found in southern Canada. Other major forest types found in the Southeast include oak-hickory, southern mixed hardwood, northern hardwood, mixed mesophytic, and mixed oak. Mixed oak forests are particularly common throughout the Appalachian Mountains. The mixed forests of the Great Smoky Mountains in eastern Tennessee and western North Carolina are the most biodiverse temperate forests in the world, with more tree species than all of Europe!

Unlike other regions of North America, fire plays a minimal role in most southeastern forests. The longleaf pine forests are an exception because this species and other affiliated organisms depend on fire for their continued existence. Some regions in the Carolina foothills are believed to have had irregular fire regimes. Some of the spruce forests that once covered large areas in the mountains of Virginia and West Virginia were burned following logging operations in the late 19th and early 20th century. Prescribed burning is now carried out in portions of the Southeast.

The patterns of vegetation in the Southeast are a result of changes that have taken place since the end of the last major glaciation, which ended about 20,000 years ago. Except for a small area of Kentucky, the Southeast was not directly glaciated, but the environmental effect of the glaciers that occupied much of the northern United States was profound. For example,

High-elevation forests in the northern portion of our region are dominated by red spruce.

Oak-hickory forest, another major forest type found in the Southeast.

Typical southern mixed hardwood forest.

Typical northern hardwood forest.

Mixed oak forests are particularly common throughout the Appalachian Mountains.

Longleaf pine forests depend upon fire for their continued existence.

extensive areas of tundra, a vegetation type no longer present in the region, occurred in the Appalachian Mountains, and many northern tree species were present far south of where they now occur.

The diversity in vegetation and habitat just described is reflected in a correspondingly high diversity in the associated mushrooms and other fungi. The Southeast is one of the most mycologically diverse regions in the world. This diversity presents both an extraordinary opportunity and an immense identification challenge for anyone interested in collecting and studying fungi.

Southeastern Fungi and Their Role in the Environment

What is a mushroom?
The term "mushroom" can have a variety of meanings, but in this context we use the term to refer to the fruiting body of any fungus (plural: fungi) large enough to be observed in the field. The vast majority of fungi are microscopic, so the groups of mushrooms we cover in this field guide actually represent a relatively small subset of a group of organisms whose species diversity is estimated to be several million. Fungi are abundant in nature, but they are often overlooked, usually underappreciated, and frequently misunderstood. Their ecological importance is vital to the functioning of the Earth, as will be discussed later in this section.

Mycology (the formal study of mushrooms and other fungi) had its origin in botany, since fungi were once considered to be members of the plant kingdom. Fungi lack chlorophyll, making them unable to photosynthesize. Instead, they obtain their food either by using enzymes to break down organic matter or by forming associations with other living organisms, including certain algae, animals, bacteria, invertebrates, slime molds, plants, and sometimes other fungi. The relationships fungi have with other living organisms range from parasitism to mutualism and are often complex. Some fungi are opportunists who cause disease if a tree's health is already compromised, while others kill the host plant and then continue growing as they decompose the organic material. Other groups of fungi parasitize insects, killing and then consuming them. Some fungi specialize in parasitizing only other fungi or slime molds.

Decomposition

Fungi compete with each other for nutrients, and it is easiest to observe this phenomenon by looking for spalted decomposing wood. Spalted wood can be found in firewood piles, decomposing stumps, and artisan woodworking pieces. It is highly desired by fine woodworkers for its irregular dark lines; ecologically, these lines serve as "territory boundaries" for different fungi. Each individual fungus puts up a black line as a barrier between sexually incompatible neighbors, serving as a way for fungi to partition resources in a piece of wood. Some spalting depends on animals for transmission. Two such examples are the ichneumon wasp–transmitted *Cerrena unicolor* (mossy maze polypore) and the complex symbiosis between ambrosia beetles and a diversity of ambrosia fungi. Whether found in firewood, a woodworker's spalted burl, or in a naturalist's examination of a decomposing stump, these black lines provide a fascinating display of complex lives of fungi.

Fungi that depend upon dead organic matter for nutrients are termed saprotrophs, and they are absolutely essential for the decomposition and cycling of much of the Earth's organic material. Many fungi are very adept at producing enzymes to break down and access nutrients from cellulose and lignin, which are the major chemical components of woody plant material. Some fungi are very specialized and only decompose the leaves of certain

plants, whereas others can utilize a wide range of substrates. There are three commonly encountered types of rots, and each has its own way of accessing nutrients.

Brown rot is a very common type of wood decomposition. It is common to find old logs and stumps that are dark brown in color and are broken up into small cubical sections. This type of rot is caused by a diverse array of fungi, including many polypores. These fungi primarily break down hemicellulose and cellulose, leaving the lignin behind. The loss of these compounds compromises the structural integrity of the wood, causing it to shrink and break up into small cube-shaped pieces.

White rot is another major group of decomposers. There are many white rot fungi, including shiitake (*Lentinula edodes*). White rot fungi generally cause wood to become pale in color and stringy in texture. They represent one of the few groups of organisms capable of breaking down lignin. This occurs through a

A decomposer—in the substrate of a house.

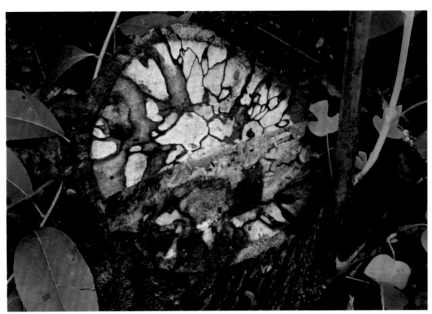

Beautifully spalted wood on a rotting stump.

complex process in which the fungus uses multiple enzymes that essentially oxidize the lignin.

Soft rot is a third type of decomposer, but most species in this group are beyond the scope of this field guide. Like brown rots, these fungi access the cellulose in wood through enzymes, but their mechanisms differ; they are particularly resilient and able to grow in aquatic or marine environments.

Mutualisms and symbiosis

The vast majority of plants worldwide depend upon fungi in order to grow and flourish. The roots of most plants are relatively inefficient at nutrient uptake and need to be colonized by the underground portion of a mushroom. The bulk of the biomass of fungi that form this type of association is in the soil. The fruiting body we typically find above ground is just the reproductive portion of a mushroom.

The below-ground portion of the fungus consists of hyphae (singular: hypha), an intricate network of very finely branched, microscopic, thread-like structures. An entire mass of hyphae is referred to as a mycelium (plural: mycelia). Hyphae are only a cell wide, but they can be very dense in healthy soils. There are reports that a cubic inch of soil can contain several miles of these fungal threads, leading to the belief that some mushrooms are the largest living organisms in the world. This vast "wood wide web" connects with tree roots on a cellular level and establishes a nutrient exchange that is essential for the plants involved, the fungi themselves, and the health of the ecosystem. This mutually beneficial relationship is more formally known as a mycorrhizal association. The fungus enables the plant to access nutrients and water that would otherwise be unavailable, and the plant provides the fungus with sugars that are produced by photosynthesis. This network of mycelia

Ectomycorrhizal hyphae form a vital below-ground network with the roots of trees and other plants.

An entire mass of hyphae, or mycelium, visible on a decorticated log.

not only connects plants within the same species but sometimes connects plants of different genera, thus serving as a biological network that can send nutrients and chemical signals.

Lichens are among the most conspicuous examples of a mutualism involving a fungus and another type of organism.

Lichens are "composite" organisms; historically, they were believed to be made up of an ascomycete fungus (or very rarely a basidiomycete) and an alga and/or blue-green alga (more formally called a cyanobacterium). Recent research has shown that yeasts are also involved in this association. The vegetative body (or thallus) that results from the combination of these organisms is a remarkable structure that looks completely unlike any of the individual organisms. Lichens have an enormous diversity of shapes, sizes, and colors. The majority of the lichen thallus consists of fungal hyphae. Only a few mushroom-like lichens are covered in this field guide, but this very diverse and adaptable group of organisms is truly ubiquitous in our region and found in nearly all habitats.

Mushrooms as Medicine, Food, and Nutrition

The medicinal properties of fungi are underutilized in the United States; not only have we lost traditional knowledge of their uses, but clinical trials of new compounds take decades to be approved for application in a western medical setting. Nevertheless, extensive research supports the application of fungi in both traditional folk medicine and in western clinical medicine. Many compounds currently in use or in clinical trials have been extracted from fungi, including cordycepin (a promising compound for leukemia and other cancer treatments), cyclosporine (an immunosuppressant that makes organ transplants possible), ganoderic acids (a promising group that has shown anticancer properties), lentinan (used in some cancer treatments), penicillin (one of the key early antibiotics), and some statins (a group of medications that are essential for fighting cardiovascular disease). Most of these, along with many other compounds, have been found in fungi that occur in our region.

The ultimate question: How can you access and utilize these and other medicinal compounds from fungi if you are not a chemist? Without a laboratory, you typically cannot use any of these compounds in isolation; in many cases, however, they can be as or more effective in their natural

states, which are accessible through home extractions. The best extraction process varies depending on the fungus with which you are working and what compounds are desired. The three most common types of extractions involve hot water, cold water, and alcohol. If you are trying to extract specific compounds, we suggest further reading in a medicinal mushroom or herbal medicine book. The chemical extraction process can be complex and can vary among different fungi.

Many of the medicinal polypore fungi in our region have compounds that can positively impact the immune system, and many of these compounds can be accessed simply by soaking the fungi in cold water or by simmering them over low heat. The resulting tea-like beverages are purported to help prevent sickness by optimizing the immune system's function. We do not claim that any of these compounds will cure particular diseases or conditions, and we encourage anyone interested in utilizing these promising compounds to consult

Humans and mushrooms go back a long way. Western North Carolina mountain man and forager Tony Heffner picks chanterelles (*Cantharellus lateritius*).

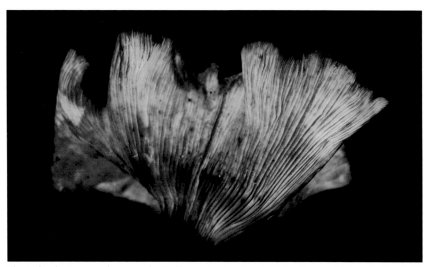

The jack-o-lantern mushroom, a look-alike to chanterelles, is bioluminescent (glows in the dark) when fresh (see page 220). Some wood colonized by certain fungi will also glow at night; this phenomenon is referred to as foxfire.

a health professional or the medicinal mushroom literature to learn more.

Many people are at first motivated to learn about fungi so they can find a gourmet meal in nature, and certainly—whether you are a four-star chef, a survivalist, a nature lover, or something in between—learning to identify edible and medicinal mushrooms can be a useful life skill. During the appropriate seasons, mushrooms can provide a substantial quantity of high-quality and nutritious food. This food source is generally underutilized in the Southeast in comparison to other parts of the world. Without a cultural context or the availability of mentors, it can be difficult to learn which mushrooms are safe to eat. In many parts of the world, among cultures with ancient traditions of mushroom hunting, much of the harvesting and identifying of the edible species is even done by children. Here in the United States, traditional mushroom hunting skills have been mostly lost. Sometimes, even seasoned wild food foragers make unfortunate mistakes in identification. One of the best ways to learn mushrooms is to join a regional mushroom club, where you can meet people who know the edible mushrooms in your area.

Mushrooms are such a large and diverse group of organisms that unfortunately there are no general rules to determine if a mushroom is good to eat or toxic. We can only advise users of this field guide who intend to eat wild mushrooms to take great care and not only learn the edible species but also carefully study and learn all of the look-alikes with which an edible species could be confused. We also suggest getting several field guides to see how different authors differentiate among similar species. Start slowly, learning only one or two edible species at a time and methodically studying them so that all their distinguishing features become apparent. If you are in doubt, throw it out! Sloppy taxonomy can lead to very sick and occasionally dead mushroom consumers.

Please read the next section to learn about the different types of fungal toxins.

Keep in mind that there is also the chance of an allergic reaction to a particular species. It is important to eat small quantities and not mix species when you are eating any mushroom for the first time. Just like peanut allergies, fungal reactions can be specific to certain people, and if one person has a reaction to a certain mushroom, it does not mean that this species is toxic or that this person will get sick from eating other mushrooms. Know too that certain species have compounds that can react negatively with alcohol consumption.

Some favorite edible mushrooms can be bioaccumulators, meaning that they absorb heavy metals and other undesirable compounds. Take care not to pick mushrooms for food from potentially toxic environments, such as close to busy roads, golf courses, downstream of parking lots, and in the vicinity of creosote-treated wood. Do not store mushrooms in plastic; if mushrooms are kept in nonpermeable bags or containers, various molds, bacteria, and other potentially harmful secondary organisms can spoil them for human consumption. For short-term storage, it is best to keep mushrooms in paper bags or open containers in a refrigerator; drying, freezing, or canning are good options for long-term storage. Despite the risks just described, many cautious people around the world and in the Southeast eat wild mushrooms for their entire life without any issues.

To make mushrooms most nutritious for human consumption, they should be cooked. This even includes the store-bought button mushrooms, which are commonly served raw. Some widely eaten mushrooms—morels, for example—can be dangerous if eaten raw. Mushrooms consist primarily of water and chitin but also have many other nutritious components, including amino acids, proteins,

chromium, vanadium, and selenium. The specific composition varies by species, so eating a diversity of mushrooms helps to maintain a balanced diet. Fungi can have high levels of vitamin D if exposed to the sun, including vitamins D2, D3, and D4. Exposure of the gill surface to sunlight after the fruiting bodies have been harvested has been shown to increase available vitamin D in shiitake mushrooms (and likely other mushrooms as well). Most vitamin D3 is derived from animal products or by spending time in the sun; Americans currently have record low levels of vitamin D because people spend less time outside and most animals are raised indoors. If you are concerned about maintaining healthy levels of vitamin D, spend more time out in the forests and fields, first hunting mushrooms and then eating big mushroom dinners!

A squirrel has hung this mushroom out to dry.

Caught in the act. This box turtle is a slow and steady mycophagist.

Humans are not the only animals that feast on fungi. A wide variety of organisms, from microscopic invertebrates to bears, use mushrooms as a food source. Some insects spend the majority of their lives in the center of a mushroom stalk or boring into the fruiting body of a polypore. The majority of the diets of some small rodents are composed of truffles, which have evolved to release pungent aromas once they are mature in order to entice animals to eat them. By digging for below-ground truffles, animals provide an essential ecosystem service of aerating the soil. Once the animal digests the fungi, the fungal spores will be dispersed throughout the forest in the animal's scat. It is common to find where squirrels have cached mushrooms in the forks of trees to dry, and if you pay close attention, you may just find a half-eaten deer truffle (*Elaphomyces*) or a pile of their powdery blackish spores atop a log or at the base of a stump. Many vertebrates in our region have been reported to eat fungi, including armadillos, bears, birds, chipmunks, flying squirrels, foxes, gray squirrels, mice, moles, opossums, rats, red squirrels, shrews, terrestrial turtles, voles, white-tailed deer, wild pigs, and wood rats. Just because an animal is observed eating a fungus does not mean that humans should do it too. Many animals actually consume species of mushrooms that are very toxic to humans.

Mushroom Toxins

Very few mushrooms in our region will kill you, but many can induce very unpleasant symptoms. Most mushroom poisonings could be avoided if mycophagists were more cautious, understood all the relevant characters used to distinguish among different mushrooms, and thoroughly studied look-alikes. Individuals who have learned to eat mushrooms in other regions must be aware that what may be a safe and easily identifiable species in one place could actually be a different and toxic species somewhere else. If you or someone you know suspects that they have eaten a poisonous mushroom, seek immediate medical help! In addition, we recommend contacting the North American Mycological Association (NAMA), which has skilled mycologists in regions all over North America who respond to poisoning emergencies by assisting with identification. It is important to keep a sample of what you ate, particularly if it is a new species for you. Positive identification can help determine the type of toxin, what symptoms are likely to occur, the possibility of allergic reactions, the likelihood of survival, and treatment options. In addition, one should file a report on the NAMA website (namyco.org) of any recent or past poisonings. The national database of poisonings maintained by NAMA is a valuable source of information relating to the edibility and toxicity of fungi.

Mycologists estimate that there are approximately fourteen different groups of fungal toxins worldwide, ten of which have been reported from North America. There are still many species of mushrooms whose toxicity has yet to be studied. Toxins produce a number of different symptoms, ranging from mild gastrointestinal discomfort to a painful death. The vast majority of fungal toxins are not fatal, but they can produce symptoms such as nausea, vomiting, diarrhea, sweating, and hallucinations. Symptom intensity and survival varies based on the quantity eaten, an individual's sensitivity, pre-existing health issues, age of the victim, and the presence of other substances (e.g., alcohol) in the body. Most nonfatal fungal toxins cause symptoms relatively quickly (in less than four hours); deadly toxins generally take six hours or longer to become evident. In the following section, we outline the eight most significant groups of fungal toxins in our region, along with the most common symptoms.

Amatoxins

Amatoxins are one of the major causes of fatalities from mushrooms. Individuals who have ingested a fungus containing amatoxins generally show symptoms in six to twenty-four hours. During this time, the amatoxins become absorbed in the body and circulate through the bloodstream, inhibiting protein synthesis. The first set of symptoms is excruciating pain, low energy, abdominal cramps, visual distortion, diarrhea, and vomiting. In some cases, the diarrhea will be bloody. Typically, these initial symptoms will pass and the victim often feels much better, sometimes leading to a mistaken diagnosis and release from medical care. Usually, in twenty-four hours to several days, symptoms return and signs of liver and kidney damage become apparent. Victims can die of organ failure or excessive blood thinning. Most individuals survive if they receive prompt and aggressive medical care, but they typically have lasting organ damage. In serious situations, emergency organ transplants, aggressive applications of IV fluid to flush the system, and silibinin (an extract from milk thistle) are used. Historically, activated charcoal and large doses of penicillin were suggested, but current research has shown this to be ineffective. In North America, some members of the genera *Amanita*, *Conocybe*, *Galeria*, and *Lepiota* have been documented to contain amatoxins.

Gyromitrin and monomethylhydrazine (MMH)

Gyromitrin and MMH are strong toxins that typically take five to twelve hours after consumption to produce symptoms. Symptoms include lingering headaches, nausea, vomiting, abdominal pain, a feeling of being bloated, diarrhea, muscle spasms, cramps, and a loss of coordination. These toxins sometimes cause fatal liver damage. MMH is a rocket propellant, and in the industries that use MMH, it is classified and regulated as a carcinogenic substance. How carcinogenic this substance is when found in mushrooms is not well understood, but studies with mice indicate that *Gyromitra esculenta* is highly carcinogenic. The effect of this group of toxins varies widely, partially because MMH is water soluble and volatile. Because of the chemical complexity and carcinogenic aspects of this group of toxins, we discourage people from eating fungi containing these compounds; however, many people in North America and Europe have traditions of eating species containing gyromitrin and MMH. Cooking these species in several different pots of water may remove some of the toxins (chefs have reportedly become ill from breathing steam containing the toxins), but it is not known if it changes the carcinogenic properties. The exact type and quantity of toxin present depends upon the species involved. Taxonomy in the groups of fungi that contain these toxins is undergoing revisions, so the level of toxins present in particular species is unclear. MMH and gyromitrin have been reported from some members of the genera *Gyromitra* and *Cudonia*. Historically, *Helvella*, *Verpa*, and uncooked morels (*Morchella*) were assumed to contain these toxins, but neither gyromitrin nor MMH has been confirmed in these three genera, indicating that a different neurotoxin may be involved.

Orellanine

Orellanine is a very potent toxin; however, it is known to occur in only a few species of fungi. The symptoms from this toxin are generally delayed for about eight days after consumption, but there are reports of symptoms manifesting after only two days and as long as three weeks later. Symptoms include chills and shivering (typically without a fever), headaches, nausea, vomiting, sweating, burning thirst, lethargy, loss of appetite,

Orellanine is believed to be restricted to the family Cortinariaceae, primarily *Cortinarius* species, which have a cobwebby protective covering (a cortina) when young.

and frequent urination. This toxin is often fatal because it causes kidney failure, but in some cases where low levels of the toxin are consumed, partial recovery is possible. It is currently believed that this toxin is restricted to the family Cortinariaceae, primarily members of the genus *Cortinarius*. This genus is very large, and the toxicity and taxonomy of many of its species are not well studied. It is unclear how many species contain this toxin and which of these are found in our region. Orellanine and the fungi that contain it are fluorescent under ultraviolet light—typically blue, but the color can change substantially with oxidation. This is not a positive identification character since other substances in some fungi can exhibit fluorescence; and the absence of fluorescence does not rule out the presence of other non-fluorescent fungal toxins.

Muscarine

Muscarine is a fast-acting toxin, and victims typically show symptoms in under an hour after consuming a mushroom in which it is present. Typically, recovery happens within twenty-four hours. The toxin impacts the involuntary nervous system.

A few fatalities due to respiratory failure have occurred, but this is uncommon. Symptoms typically include excessive sweating, excessive salivation, excessive lactation (if pregnant or nursing), teary eyes, blurred vision, constricted (pinpoint) pupils, lowered blood pressure, irregular or reduced heart rate, diarrhea, difficulty breathing or bronchial asthma, and urgent urination. Some, but not all North American members of the genera *Amanita, Clitocybe, Inocybe, Mycena,* and *Omphalotus* contain muscarine, as do a handful of red-pored members of the family Boletaceae.

Isoxazole derivatives

This group of toxins, including muscimol and ibotenic acid, affects the central nervous system, and the symptoms they produce can be complex. They are rarely found by themselves and may interact with other toxins (often muscarine), so both symptoms and treatments can be confusing. Symptoms manifest themselves approximately half an hour to two hours after consumption and rarely last for more than four hours (although a few people have become comatose for up to six days); additionally, there may be the sensation of a hangover the following day. Symptoms frequently include delirious and manic behaviors, confusion, dilated pupils, visions and visual distortion (especially a tendency to perceive small objects as very large), sleepiness, a feeling of increased strength, poor coordination, a desire for intense physical exertion, muscle spasms, and vomiting. This group of toxins is found primarily in the genus *Amanita* and in at least one species of *Tricholoma*. People who experiment recreationally with *Amanita muscaria* and its varieties often fall victim to these symptoms. These toxins have not been reliably reported to be fatal (aside from one or two situations as a result of complications); patients primarily need moral support.

Psilocybin, psilocin, and indole derivatives

Psilocybin and psilocin are likely the most widely consumed fungal toxins. Unlike most fungal poisonings, ingestion of these substances is typically purposeful and not a result of poor taxonomy. These toxins can be potent and impact the central nervous system, resulting in mild to severe hallucinations. Symptoms generally become apparent within a few minutes to an hour. The intensity of the symptoms varies greatly among individuals, but typically symptoms include visions of brilliant colors (including sound-generated visuals), visual distortion, difficulty concentrating, major changes in perception of object size, anxiety, depression, excessive excitement, uncontrolled laughter, nausea, vomiting, and seizures. These substances produce symptoms very similar to LSD (lysergic acid diethylamide) and are believed to bind to the same sites in the brain. Fatalities are very rare, with only one or two reports of small children dying; however, among adults, there are sometimes lasting psychological effects. Cultures around the world use mushrooms containing these substances in traditional ceremonies and for religious purposes; however, these fungi and the substances they contain are currently illegal in the United States.

Most of the fungi containing these substances do not look like the more commonly eaten mushrooms. Generally, people who consume examples of this group of fungi do so deliberately and are at least partially aware of the consequences legally, psychologically, and physiologically. The effects vary greatly depending on the quantity ingested, the species of fungus involved, and the pre-consumption psychological condition of the person. People regularly go to the hospital as a result of consuming these fungal toxins, but little can be done medically unless there are complications or if the individual involved is a small child. In general, simply talking calmly, not making sudden movements, avoiding bright lights, and keeping noise levels low are the best way to stabilize and help someone who is suffering undesired symptoms from these toxins. Some fungi that contain these toxins also contain other substances, and this can complicate reactions. The greatest danger is that someone intending to eat a mushroom for a hallucinogenic result instead consumes a species of *Galerina* (see amatoxins); this mistake is deadly and has led to at least one fatality.

There is promising research about the use of this group of toxins in treatment/management of post-traumatic stress disorder and in helping to ease end-of-life anxiety. Some, but not all, North American members of the genera *Conocybe*, *Gymnopilus*, *Inocybe*, *Mycena*, *Panaeolus*, *Pluteus*, and *Psilocybe* contain these toxins.

Coprine

Some would argue that coprine is not actually a toxin because it becomes an issue only if the fungus has been consumed before drinking alcohol. Coprine increases the potency of the negative effects of alcohol and produces symptoms very similar to those associated with the drugs antabuse or antabus, which are used to fight alcoholism. There is typically a delay of thirty minutes to two hours before the onset of symptoms, which generally include rapid breathing, increased pulse, salivation, tingling or heavy limbs, headaches, disorientation, flushing of the skin, nausea, and vomiting. Coprine can stay in the system for as many as five days after consumption. Some recent studies have shown that coprine is carcinogenic in animals, indicating that any fungus containing this compound should likely be avoided. Coprine is present in the fungus *Coprinopsis atramentaria*. Many other fungi are occasionally problematic if consumed in combination with alcohol;

the substances responsible are not always clear, and the symptoms induced may be related to allergic reactions.

Gastrointestinal irritants

The term "gastrointestinal irritant" describes the effect of one or many different toxins found in a wide range of fungi (most of them poorly studied); aside from acute symptoms, not much is known about their potential long-term impacts. Consumption of fungi that contain gastrointestinal irritants is almost never fatal, but the symptoms can be very unpleasant. Symptoms typically manifest twenty minutes to four hours after consumption and may include nausea, vomiting, intestinal or stomach cramps, and diarrhea. Some, but not all, North American species of *Agaricus*, *Chlorophyllum*, *Clitocybe*, *Entoloma*, *Gomphus*, *Gymnopus*, *Hebeloma*, *Hypholoma*, *Lactarius*, *Omphalotus*, *Paxillus*, *Ramaria*, *Russula*, *Scleroderma*, *Tricholoma*, and *Verpa*, along with some members of the Boletaceae, can induce these symptoms, which normally pass after the substance has been expelled from the body.

Morphology of Mushrooms

Mushrooms fulfill many ecological roles and are characterized by a large diversity of shapes, sizes, and colors. They also have characters that can only be observed with a microscope. Consideration of different characters makes it possible to identify a particular species or can help to narrow down mushrooms to certain taxonomic groups. Molecular evidence has in some instances confirmed traditional morphology-based classifications and in other instances has completely altered taxonomic classifications. For example, some puffball-shaped mushrooms are more closely related to mushrooms that form stalks and caps than they are to other puffball-shaped mushrooms; in the past, all these puffball-shaped mushrooms would have been placed together in the same group.

What's in a Mushroom Name?

Two types of names are used for mushrooms; one of these is the common name, and the other is the Latin (or scientific) name. Many common names are general and do not necessarily refer to a specific type of mushroom. This can be both useful and confusing. For example, the name "chanterelle," commonly used by chefs and mushroom foragers, refers to several hundred species in two genera found on six continents. Common names are of little taxonomic use; however, they make gourmet groups of mushrooms easily accessible to the public (particularly for culinary purposes). The most commonly encountered mushrooms usually have many common names that vary between regions and languages, and this can lead to confusion when discussing taxonomy. This potential confusion is why standardized Latin names are used. These scientific names are the basis of the Linnaean hierarchical classification system, whose levels—species, genus, family, order, class, phylum, kingdom, and domain—help us understand how different organisms are related to one another and to other groups of organisms. As their name indicates, fungi belong to the kingdom Fungi.

Although families are given, most of the focus in the taxonomic sections of this field guide is placed on binomial names. These consist of two parts, the first being the genus (plural: genera) and the second a specific epithet; together, they refer to a species. Ultimately, these two parts indicate the placement of a particular

organism in the Linnaean system. For example, the classic mushroom with a red cap and white spots, commonly called the fly agaric, is *Amanita muscaria*. The first part of the scientific binomial, *Amanita*, is the genus, which includes several hundred related species that share similar characters. The specific epithet, *muscaria*, is used only for a single species. Sometimes, taxonomists recognize subspecies or varieties of a particular species, and these are added after the binomial.

Binomial names must be published with a complete description of the organism in question before they are considered valid. Each name is followed by the name or an abbreviation of the name of the person (or persons) who first described the species. This is called the authority. Taxonomic concepts are always subject to change, and technological advances (e.g., microscopes and DNA sequencing) have led to many significant changes in fungal classification. A species is sometimes originally described in one genus and then transferred to another, even one in an entirely different family. When this happens, the name of the person who proposed the change is added to the authority and the original author's name is placed in parentheses. For example, *Amanita muscaria* (Linnaeus) Lamarck was originally described as *Agaricus muscarius* by Carl Linnaeus in 1753, and in 1783 it was moved to the genus *Amanita* by French naturalist Jean-Baptiste Lamarck. We call it *Amanita muscaria* to this day.

Taxonomy can seem confusing and arbitrary at times, and some have argued that it is the last art in the sciences. The need to classify is one of the few shared traits common to all humans. The very survival of our ancestors depended on their ability to distinguish subtle differences between the living things around them. Mistaken identifications resulted in the consumption of toxins, bites from venomous snakes, and the misapplication of natural medicines. Good taxonomy is in our genes and is a major reason that the lineage of anyone using this field guide has survived the gauntlet of natural selection. Learning to identify mushrooms or any other organisms is just a matter of honing your observation skills and awakening the discretion that your DNA has been perfecting since the dawn of the human race.

Taxonomists will likely continue to struggle with how to define a species, genus, family, or any other taxonomic category. It may seem obvious to some of us that a hummingbird, a deer, an oak tree, and a mushroom are different from each other. But how different are each of these things? Who is most closely related to whom? These types of questions are at the root of taxonomy. Early taxonomists could use only macroscopic character-istics that could be readily observed to distinguish among different organisms. In mushrooms, the characteristics used were such things as the basic shape of the fruiting body, presence or absence of a stalk, whether or not there were gills, and the color of the spores in mass. With the invention of the microscope, a large number of previously unknown characters became apparent and made taxonomy both clearer and more complex.

Over the past couple decades, the application of molecular-based studies to compare the DNA sequences of differ-ent mushrooms has both clarified and complicated taxonomy. These studies have revealed that many mushrooms previously believed to be closely related based on morphological characters are only distantly related and have simply evolved similar characters. This has led to ongoing changes in reclassification and has required major changes in the nomenclature used for mushrooms. If you compare this field guide with older mush-room books, you will likely notice different names for some of the same fungi. We

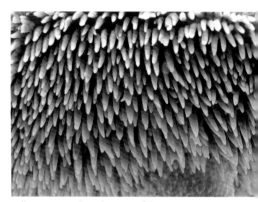

Gills, pores, and teeth are useful macroscopic identification characters.

Present or absent? Gills are a key macroscopic morphological character.

herein provide what we feel to be the most appropriate classification based on our evaluation of current nomenclature in the mycological community.

Collecting and Studying Mushrooms

It is easy to collect a mushroom, but learn-ing to identify it can be more of a chal-lenge. Some species are so distinctive that it is possible to recognize them instantly in the field, but others are difficult to identify even for highly trained mycologists. In many situations, it is necessary to collect fruiting bodies and subject them to more detailed study in a home laboratory. The latter can be rather simple, consisting of a working space, a compound microscope, and a few minimal supplies. If you are primarily interested in learning to identify mushrooms for food, most of the commonly eaten species can be identified without a microscope; however, if you desire to delve deeper into the study of mushrooms, learning to use a microscope will open your eyes to another world!

Making a tentative identification in the field is possible in many instances, but conducting a more in-depth and thorough examination of a mushroom requires microscopic or possibly even genetic study. It is important to record basic information about the fruiting body—for example, where it occurred (e.g., on the ground, on decomposing wood, or associated with dead leaves on the forest floor). For potentially mycorrhizal fungi, the types of trees in the immediate vicinity of the fruiting body should be recorded. Whenever possible, multiple fruiting bodies of the species in question should be collected, and ideally different developmental stages (e.g., mature as well as immature). Take care to collect only those fruiting bodies that appear to represent the same population of the mushroom, because making a mixed collection of several similar species can cause great confusion later on. To mycologists, the term "collection" refers to one or more fruiting bodies that are from the same location and believed to be the same species. A collection of multiple fruiting bodies at different developmental stages can provide valuable taxonomic information. If you carry a camera, photograph the fruiting bodies in the field before they have been damaged in transport; take photos of all the different features and/

or use several fruiting bodies to show all the characters in a single image. Consider carrying a tripod to obtain high-quality images, since mushrooms often fruit in low-light environments.

Be sure to collect the entire fruiting body. For some mushrooms (e.g., *Amanita* spp.), it is important to know what the base of the stalk and associated structures (e.g., volva and presence or absence of rhizomorphs) look like in order to identify it to species. Fruiting bodies should be loosely wrapped in wax paper or tin foil and placed in a basket or other container with rigid sides. Fishing tackle boxes are particularly well suited for carrying small fruiting bodies. The goal is to transport specimens intended for additional study from the field to the laboratory while keeping them as intact as possible.

For agarics, boletes, and many other mushrooms, the first step in identification is making a spore print. To make a spore print, cut off the cap at the top of the stalk (if the specimen has a stalk). Place the cap with the lower surface downward on a piece of white paper or tin foil, and cover this with a drinking glass, a bowl, or some other container for several hours or overnight. Placing the cap on the paper or foil in a plastic sealable bag also works. It is possible to begin obtaining a spore print in the field if a cap is removed, placed on a piece of paper, wrapped up, and placed in a collecting container with the lower surface pointing downward. It is sometimes possible to find a "natural" spore print that has been deposited on leaves, wood, or caps of other mushrooms directly beneath the fertile surface of a mature mushroom. Mushrooms with small fruiting bodies and thin caps often do not yield a lot of spores; in these cases, placing the cap directly on a glass microscope slide can be an effective way of obtaining a spore print.

Some mycologists make all their spore prints on microscope slides, because the spores are immediately ready to have a mounting medium applied and a cover-slip added for microscopic examination. Sometimes, if a cap is left on a table over-night, a spore print will be apparent the following morning. Not all caps will yield a good spore print, often because of matu-rity or moisture. Since many agarics have white spores, it can be hard to see them on a white piece of paper until it is exam-ined closely. Spore prints are the best way to determine the color of the spores in mass. This feature is particularly useful to differentiate between different groups of agarics. The spore print also provides easy access to mature spores for exam-ination under a microscope to determine their size and ornamentation.

Once spore prints have been made, fresh odors and/or tastes recorded, and good notes/photos obtained, the specimen can be dried. It is important to air-dry mushrooms that are intended for scientific purposes. You can use a food drier as long as it can be set at low heat. Mushrooms that have been dried at too high a tempera-ture often have their DNA damaged, mak-ing it difficult to obtain a usable genetic sequence. Temperature is not important in drying for culinary purposes. Once the specimen is dried, it should be placed in an airtight container to prevent dam-age from molds or invertebrates. If you combine your dried specimen with your images and notes on habitat, location, date, etc., it is possible to deposit the col-lection in a fungarium/herbarium (usu-ally associated with a college, university, research institution, or museum), and/or you can work on identifying the species under a microscope at a later date.

To make a microscope mount of the spores from a spore print, place a drop of water or other mounting solution on a microscope slide, scrape a few spores onto the drop, and then add a coverslip. This method will show only spores. In some situations, it is necessary to examine other microscopic characters, and this requires

A white spore print in nature.

slicing sections of different tissues. Obser-vation of these characters also requires the use of a compound microscope. These microscopes can be purchased on the Internet, from scientific supply compa-nies, or when a local school or university upgrades its laboratory equipment. The cost of a microscope varies greatly depend-ing on the age and capabilities; however, a relatively simple compound microscope is all that is needed to identify most mush-rooms. Purchasing a new microscope can be expensive, so generally a used one is the best way to start out.

The ideal microscope should be equipped with an oil immersion lens and an eyepiece with an ocular micrometer. The oil immersion lens allows the micro-scope to magnify objects about 1,000 times, which is necessary to discern characters such as spore ornamentation. Once the ocular micrometer has been calibrated, it is used to measure different characters. A mechanical stage and electric light source are very useful features on a microscope. With proper care, a good microscope is likely to remain fully functional for decades. Many mycologists have a favorite microscope that they will use throughout their entire career.

Setting up a home mushroom laboratory requires little special equipment aside from a microscope. Other essential items are glass slides and coverslips, a small plastic ruler (for determining such things as the diameter of the cap and length of the stalk), a razor blade, a pair of forceps, tissue paper, and several small dropper bottles for the liquids used as mounting media. These items can be purchased in a specialty store, from a company that sells biological laboratory supplies, or on the Internet.

Water and Melzer's reagent are the liquids used most often for studying mushrooms. Melzer's reagent causes a staining reaction in some of the microscopic structures in mushrooms, making it useful to distinguish among certain species. If a drop of Melzer's is added to a slide containing mushroom spores or tissue, three different color reactions are possible. If the tissue or spores turn a bluish black, the reaction is amyloid; if the tissues or spores turn dark reddish brown, the reaction is dextrinoid; if the spores or tissue stay the same pale reddish color as the Melzer's reagent (i.e., there is no reaction), the reaction is nonamyloid.

In this field guide, we focus on macroscopic characters wherever possible, and we do our best to restrict the microscopic characters to the color, size, shape, and ornamentation of spores; however, many other microscopic features are very useful for identifying mushrooms. For example, cystidia (singular: cystidium) are special cells often associated with the hymenium (spore-producing layer) in many fungi. These special cells vary considerably in size and shape, and some have surprisingly elaborate ornamentation. Cystidia can be very useful characters when identifying different species of mushrooms. The two types of cystidia most often considered in descriptions of agarics are pleurocystidia and cheilocystidia. The former occurs on the faces (or sides) of the gills, while the latter is found on the edges of the gills. Both can be observed if a small portion of a gill is removed with forceps, placed on a slide in a drop of mounting medium, a coverslip added, and then enough pressure placed on the coverslip to crush the sample, making what is called a "crush mount."

For a fresh fruiting body, a small portion of the gill can be placed directly in a drop of water on the slide. If the fruiting body has been dried, it is necessary to break off a small piece of the gill and transfer it to a large drop of alcohol (either 70% or 90% will work) on the slide. Allow the tissue to soak for a few minutes; the alcohol will evaporate, so it may be necessary to replenish the drop once or twice. Afterward, add a drop of water and a coverslip. The slide should be ready to observe under the microscope. It is possible to make this type of mount without alcohol, but it requires waiting longer for the water to be absorbed or adding a small amount of 3% KOH (potassium hydroxide). KOH is widely used in this manner because it typically causes the structures in dried specimens to expand to their full size. Lactophenol is sometimes used as mounting medium for spores when preserving a slide for an extended period of time. Slides prepared with lactophenol are semi-permanent, while those prepared with water, KOH, or Melzer's reagent are only temporary.

THE MUSHROOMS

Since the current estimate of fungal diversity is approximately 5.1 million species worldwide and fewer than 100,000 are described, it can be overwhelming to learn to identify a fungus; however, through the process of elimination, you can narrow down your search relatively quickly. For example, many fungi are microscopic or aquatic species and thus unlikely to be knowingly encountered on a hike in the woods. One of the best ways to narrow down your search is by using a key. Keys are sometimes intimidating, but they are intended to be useful tools to aid in the identification process. Find a quiet spot, sit down with the specimen in question, and read through the key. It may surprise you that it can often be quicker than flipping through pictures to identify your species. Because of the high level of fungal diversity, it is not possible for this field guide or any other book on fungi to comprehensively describe all fungal diversity, so a key is very useful in helping to

narrow down your search. Even if you can make it through only a few couplets in a key, you will have eliminated thousands, if not millions, of species that your fungus is not. Once at the correct group, you can then study the illustrated species and the comments about related or look-alike fungi. If you are still unsatisfied with what you have found, you can turn to technical books or look for monographs on specific groups. Some of these books and articles are expensive collectables, long out of print, but many have now been digitized and can be found on the Internet.

The keys in this field guide use minimal technical terms and rely primarily on features that can be seen in the field. In some of the later couplets, where genera become very similar, a spore print is required; only one couplet requires a microscope. Spore color is one of the first characters used in most field guide keys, and this is very helpful in identifying mushrooms; however, it is seldom possible to determine spore color in the field. Fortunately, making a spore print is easy to do at home (see page 25).

This field guide uses dichotomous keys, which means that there are two brief descriptions of features that contrast with each other. You select the one that most closely matches what you have found and follow the instructions at the end of the sentence. It is easy to have preconceived notions when attempting to key something out; however, it is important to focus on what is written and how it compares to the organism you are trying to identify. Nature is unpredictable,so sometimes characters of a specimen will fit into both couplets. If this happens, follow it in both directions until only one makes sense. Because fungi change throughout development, it is important to study a range of samples. Remember that some fruiting bodies can be atypical, and if one specimen has half a cap or has a second mushroom arising from its cap, it does not mean this is typical. Fungi are variable, and that is part of what makes them fascinating. Learning to key out and identify fungi should ultimately be fun, so do not let it frustrate you! Even professional mycologists who have studied mushrooms their entire careers

often get stumped. Take it as a challenge, and enjoy the learning process!

Fungi belong to two major groups, the ascomycetes and the basidiomycetes. This field guide also includes a few species of myxomycetes (slime molds) in the final section. Myxomycetes are not true fungi (they are more closely related to protozoans); however, they typically occur in the same ecological situations as mushrooms. Historically, they were thought to be fungi, and some species are still confused with fungi today.

In the context of this field guide, we apply the term "mushroom" to any type of fungal fruiting body that is large enough to be seen with the naked eye. Other guides use the term only in reference to species whose fruiting bodies consist of an expanded cap-shaped structure that is held aloft on a stalk. Many of the latter have gills (blade-like structures that radiate out from the stalk) on the underside of the cap; these fungi are often called gilled mushrooms, or more formally agarics. "Toadstool" is also used by some authors, but this non-technical term has a wide variety of meanings (including being reserved for poisonous species), so we have refrained from using it.

KEY TO FUNGI SUBSECTIONS

1. Fruiting body cup-shaped, mound-shaped, elongated and sometimes with a distinct head or a sponge-like structure on a stalk, or ball-shaped and then occurring in the soil; fruiting body never with a cap; microscopic spores produced inside of a sac-like structure (an ascus) . . . . **Ascomycetes** (page 30)
1. Fruiting body usually with a stalk and a cap or shaped like a shelf, ball (then occurring in or above the soil), jelly-like, star-like, phallus-like, coral-like, club-like, or taking the form of a crust-like layer; microscopic spores produced on the end of a club-like structure (a basidium) . . . . **Basidiomycetes** (page 112)

Note: Since slime molds are not true fungi, the eight species of myxomycetes described and illustrated in the final section of this field guide are not included in this key. Nevertheless, myxomycetes are commonly found in the same habitats as fungi and thus are likely to be encountered by anyone who uses this field guide. Please refer to the **Slime Molds (Myxomycetes)** section (page 375).

Ascomycetes

Ascomycetes make up approximately 75% of all known fungi. Many are microscopic and fulfill very specialized roles, such as forming microscopic leaf spots on certain plant species. Others inhabit aquatic environments, spending their entire lives in ponds, lakes, and streams. This field guide includes representatives of many of the largest, most common, and most interesting ascomycete fungi found in the Southeast.

Ascomycetes typically have at least two reproductive stages (some species have more). In their sexual (teleomorphic) stage, the spores (ascospores) are produced inside of a special cell called an ascus (plural: asci). Typically, two to eight spores are produced per ascus, and they often line up like peas in a pod or are scattered like marbles in a bag. In their asexual (anamorphic) stage, fruiting bodies can look entirely different. The fruiting body is often covered in powdery spores (conidia), and these are typically produced in structures that resemble the beads on a necklace. Some ascomycete fungi are known only from the asexual stage, and others only from the sexual stage, but with the aid of genetics it has become more feasible to link the two. Since spores are typically several micrometers long, identifying some species will require examining the spores under a microscope at a magnification of 1,000×.

The most widely known ascomycetes are the morels, but there are many other common and interesting species. Many ascomycete fruiting bodies are shaped like cups, bowls, clubs, or globular truffles.

KEY TO THE ASCOMYCETES

1. Fruiting body clearly associated with or arising from another fungus, slime mold, living plant, insect, or spider 2
1. Fruiting body occurring on or in the ground or directly associated with dead plant material (litter, fruits and nuts, dung, dead wood or bark). 4

2. Fruiting body arising directly from an insect or spider
. . . . ■ **Entomopathogenic Fungi** (page 31)
2. Fruiting body associated with a living plant, slime mold, or another fungus 3

3. Fruiting body arising from a living plant . . . . ■ **Plant Pathogens** (page 86)
3. Fruiting body arising from slime mold or another fungus . . . . . ■ **Mycoparasites** (page 98)

4. Fruiting body occurring in the ground but also sometimes partially emergent
. . . . ■ **Truffles** (page 89)
4. Fruiting body occurring on the surface of the ground or directly associated with some type of dead plant material 5

5. Fruiting body consisting of a stalk and a clearly distinct head, the latter expanded and brainlike, mound-like, pitted, convoluted, or sponge-like
. . . . ■ **Morels and Relatives** (page 42)
5. Fruiting body cup-shaped, club-shaped, or mound-shaped 6

6. Fruiting body club-shaped (but not arising from an insect or other fungus)
. . . . ■ **Club Fungi** (page 71)
6. Fruiting body not as above 7

7. Fruiting body more or less cup-shaped, saucer-shaped, or goblet-shaped, the entire structure sometimes irregular . . . . ■ **Cup Fungi** (page 50)
7. Fruiting body mound-like or ball-shaped. . . . . ■ **Wood Mounds** (page 108)

Entomopathogenic Fungi

Entomopathogenic—the word may seem excessively long, but it is easier to understand if you consider its etymology. It derives from the ancient Greek, *entomon* ("insect"), *pathos* ("disease"); hence, entomopathogenic ("insect-disease"). Entomopathogenic fungi are ascomycetes that are parasites of insects and spiders. As a group, they show promise in western medical applications. The rare white *Elaphocordyceps subsessilis* (syn. *Cordyceps subsessilis*), which we have encountered at high elevation in our region growing from beetle larvae in decomposing logs, was the original source of cyclosporine, an immunosuppressant that makes organ transplants possible. Another compound, cordycepin, with potential applications against leukemia and other cancers, was first found in an Asian species, *Ophiocordyceps sinensis* (syn. *C. sinensis*); current research indicates that some of the species found in the Southeast may share similar compounds. Entomopathogenic fungi are being used in some parts of the world as a biocontrol (mycoinsecticide) for some pest insects. Releasing organisms to kill other organisms is complex and controversial; however, a strong argument can be made that with careful research, the use of these species of fungi is more environmentally friendly than most chemical insecticides.

Outside of Asia, the mountains of the southeastern United States are home to the greatest known diversity of entomopathogenic fungi in the temperate world. In tropical regions, these fungi become even more prevalent and diverse. Entomopathogenic fungi have a wide range of morphologies and host preferences, ranging from microscopic parasites of aphids and scale insects to more substantial club-like fungi arising from large beetle larvae. Many mushroom guide books consider this group of fungi very rare and illustrate very few species. In the Southeast, these fungi are not as rare as typically reported. The primary reason they are seldom seen is because most mushroom hunters and naturalists are not aware of how to look for them. Since these fungi have actually killed and grown out of an insect or spider, you must look in habitats where the host would be before it died. Likely habitats are the undersides of living leaves, decomposing logs, sheltered spots at the edge of small rock overhangs, road banks, edges of streams, and small branches on hollies or other shrubs. Slowing down and studying the environment around you will increase your awareness of these fungi as well as countless other natural history phenomena.

Take care to collect the entire specimen of this type of fungus from the ground or decomposing wood without separating the insect host from the fruiting body. If the host is lost and was not identified, it can be more difficult to determine just what species of fungus is represented. In mid- to late summer of moist years, if you know how to find these fungi, it is possible to find half a dozen or more fruiting bodies of several species in an afternoon hike. Just as with disease outbreaks in humans, when you find one parasitized insect, it is likely you will find more in the same area, particularly if the host is a species that lives in colonies or dense populations. Also see *Septobasidium ramorum* (page 333), which is the only non-ascomycete entomopathogenic fungus in this field guide. Enjoy hunting for and identifying the elusive and fascinating entomopathogenic fungi!

Akanthomyces aculeatus
Lebert

MOTH AKANTHOMYCES

FAMILY Cordycipitaceae

Thin, rod-like structure with an expanded to club-like apex, 1–8 mm long and 0.1–0.5 mm wide, white, arising from white mycelium that partially or completely covers the body of a dead moth and usually extends to the substrate upon which the moth occurs; spores (conidia) hyaline in mass, 3–6 × 2–3 μm, broadly elliptical or egg-shaped, smooth.

Habitat/Biological Role: Parasitizing and emerging from the bodies of moths, with multiple rod-like structures arising from a single moth; usually appearing during the summer but can linger into winter. Parasite of insects (in this case, moths).

Distribution: Frequent in our region during wet years and widely distributed throughout eastern North America and elsewhere in the world, most frequently in the tropics.

Comments: The host is often attached to a branch or leaf above the ground. *Cordyceps tuberculata* also occurs on adult moths but differs in having several stalks with several prominent yellow to pale brown perithecia near apices. The anamorphic stage of *C. sphingum* (syn. *Hymenostilbe sphingum*) is similar, but the conidia are solitary, whereas the conidia of *Akanthomyces aculeatus* are chain-like. Other *Akanthomyces* species found in our region are not reported to parasitize adult moths. The distinctive *A. aranearum* parasitizes spiders; it has multiple thin club-like stroma arising from the host with white upper portion when young and is pale brown with age or at base. Edibility is unknown, but if dried with care, specimens keep well and are great for conversation pieces or teaching tools. In our region, a very common parasite of the Carolina leaf roller cricket (*Camptonotus carolinensis*) looks very similar but currently seems to be an undescribed species of fungus.

Beauveria bassiana (Balsamo-Crivelli) Vuillemin

PATHOGENIC INSECT MOLD

FAMILY Cordycipitaceae

Layer of white mycelium that covers portions of the body of a dead insect or other arthropod (e.g., spider), powdery due to the presence of masses of spores; frequently fruiting at the exoskeletal joints; spores (conidia) white in mass, 2–3 × 3 µm, more or less globose, smooth.

Habitat/Biological Role: Colonizing the bodies of insects, both adults and larvae; parasitized insects are most commonly encountered in summer but can be found throughout the entire year. Parasite of insects and other arthropods.

Distribution: Found throughout the world in soils but evident macroscopically only when colonizing the body of an insect or other arthropod.

Comments: This exceedingly common fungus can infect a broad range of insects and other arthropods. In the Southeast we have observed it occasionally parasitizing spiders but primarily on a wide diversity of insect hosts, including beetles (Coleoptera); cicadas and treehoppers (Hemiptera); ants, bumblebees, and hornets (Hymenoptera); praying mantis (Mantodea); and grasshoppers (Orthoptera). When the spores of this fungus come into contact with a suitable host, they germinate, penetrate the body, and kill the host within a few days. Afterward, the masses of spores (which have a cottony appearance) emerge from the joints in the exoskeleton. *Entomophthora sepulchralis* is a similar fungus in our region that parasitizes crane flies (Diptera); the fruitings of this species are common around the edges of swampy riparian areas, and the flies are usually attached to moist rocks and logs by a translucent white mold. The edibility of these fungi is not known, but moldy insects do not typically top the list of gourmet items. There is a potential application for them as insecticides.

Cordyceps militaris (Linnaeus) Link

ORANGE CLUB

FAMILY Cordycipitaceae

Cylindrical to club-shaped structure with a clearly distinct head and stalk, total height 2–5 cm, bright orange to orange-red or pale orange; head 1–2 cm long and up to 5 mm wide; surface roughened with numerous raised dots; stalk 0.5–3 cm long, tapering slightly downward, reddish orange, emerging from moth pupae; spores colorless in mass, 2–4.5 × 1–1.5 µm, segmented and breaking apart in elliptical fragments.

Habitat/Biological Role: Occurring on the ground among dead leaves or sometimes emerging from well-decomposed wood; appearing in early summer to fall. Parasite of moth pupae.

Distribution: Found throughout North America but most common east of the Rocky Mountains.

Comments: The fruiting bodies of *Cordyceps militaris* may appear to be arising directly from the ground or decomposing wood, but careful examination of the base of an individual fruiting body will reveal its attachment to the pupa of a moth. Occasionally several fruiting bodies are observed to arise from a single pupa. *Cordyceps militaris* has been shown to have many beneficial medicinal properties similar to those of the valuable Asian *Ophiocordyceps sinensis* (syn. *C. sinensis*). *Cordyceps cardinalis* is nearly identical to *C. militaris* but is a parasite on the larval (caterpillar) stage of moths and has genetic as well as subtle microscopic differences. *Trichoderma alutaceum* (syn. *Podostroma alutaceum*) is very similar in appearance but grows on wood (not insects) and has a more yellowish to pale brown fertile portion and a whitish stalk.

Cordyceps tuberculata
(Lebert) Maire

PERITHECIAL MOTH CORDYCEPS

FAMILY Cordycipitaceae

Cylindrical structures arising from the white mycelium that partially or completely covers the body of a dead moth, 1–11 mm long and 1.5–2 mm wide, usually narrowing somewhat toward the apex, the latter with a cluster or row of tiny, flask-shaped to pimple-like projections present, these yellow to yellowish brown; spores (ascospores) hyaline in mass, initially thread-like and with multiple crosswalls but breaking up into smaller portions (termed part-spores), these 2–6 × 0.5–1 µm, smooth.

Habitat/Biological Role: Parasitizing and emerging from the bodies of dead moths, with multiple cylindrical structures arising from a single host; usually observed during the summer. Parasite of moths.

Distribution: Most common in the Southeast during wet years and widely distributed throughout eastern North America and elsewhere in the world, most frequently in the tropics.

Comments: *Akanthomyces aculeatus* is similar, but the structures arising from the body of the dead moth are not as robust, and there are no flask-like to pimple-like projections at the apex. Neither the edibility nor the medicinal properties of *Cordyceps tuberculata* are known; however, many *Cordyceps* species have been shown to have the latter.

Isaria farinosa (Holmskjold) Fries

POWDERY ISARIA

SYNONYMS *Coremium gracile, Paecilomyces farinosus, Penicillium farinosum*

FAMILY Cordycipitaceae

Tree-like or club-shaped structure, variable in size, 0.5–6 cm tall and 0.2–2 cm wide, sometimes with multiple stalks arising from one host; upper portion forked and densely branched or sometimes consisting of just a solitary club, white to pale grayish, powdery, usually releasing cloud of white spores if brushed or moved suddenly; stalk smooth, equal to irregular, very variable in length, sometimes nearly absent or making up the majority of the length of the entire fruiting body, if present usually 1–5 mm wide, stalk very variable in color, ranging from white to pale grayish or cream to lemon yellow, rarely bright orange, stalk attached to the body of a dead insect host; spores (conidia) white to hyaline in mass, 1–2.5 × 1–1.5 µm, oval to subglobose, smooth.

Habitat/Biological Role: Usually emerging from the soil, leaf litter, or decomposing wood where the hosts are located; appearing from summer to fall, sometimes in winter. Primarily a parasite of moth pupae or rarely moth caterpillars, but reported occasionally from other insects.

Distribution: Most common in the Southeast and East but widely distributed in North America.

Comments: Despite extensive research, the teleomorphic (sexual) stage of this fungus has not yet been determined; however, it is likely to be something related to the genus *Cordyceps*. The taxonomic history of *Isaria farinosa* is complex, and when the diversity of morphological characters and host species are considered, it is certainly possible that *I. farinosa* is a species complex; however, some mycologists report that based on molecular evidence, there is primarily one species in our region. We have collected specimens in the Southeast that are very similar morphologically to *I. japonica*, but it is unclear if the Southeast is within the range of this fungus. *Isaria* species are not eaten, but some contain interesting medicinal compounds, and many have shown potential as insecticides.

Ophiocordyceps melolonthae (Tulasne & C. Tulasne) G. H. Sung, J. M. Sung, Hywel-Jones & Spatafora

BEETLE CORDYCEPS, RHINOCEROUS-BEETLE CORDYCEPS

SYNONYM *Cordyceps melolonthae*

FAMILY Ophiocordycipitaceae

Stalk-like structure, 5–8 cm long and 3–10 mm wide, equal, smooth, sometimes forking, base attached to a soft-bodied beetle larva, pale whitish yellow to bright yellow; with maturation enlarging irregularly toward apex, developing perithecia, apex sometimes remaining sterile, perithecia giving the surface a punctuate appearance, similar to or darker than the stalk in color; spores hyaline in mass, forming filament-like chains and breaking apart into shorter partial spores, 4–10 × 1–1.5 µm, smooth.

Habitat/Biological Role: Emerging from the soil and leaf litter where the host beetle larvae are found; fruiting summer to fall. Parasite of beetle (Coleoptera) larvae.

Distribution: Found throughout eastern North America.

Comments: This is one of the largest species of insect pathogens likely to be encountered in our region and one of the few associated with soft-bodied beetle larvae. *Cordyceps cardinalis* and *C. militaris* are the most morphologically similar species; however, they are generally smaller, orange in color, and associated with moth pupae or larvae. To our knowledge, *Ophiocordyceps melolonthae* has not been evaluated for edibility or tested for medicinal properties.

Ophiocordyceps sphecocephala (Klotzsch ex Berkeley) G. H. Sung, J. M. Sung, Hywel-Jones & Spatafora

YELLOW-HEADED HYMENOPTERA CORDYCEPS

SYNONYM *Cordyceps sphecocephala*

FAMILY Ophiocordycipitaceae

Slender vine-like structure, 2–10 cm long and 0.5–1.5 mm wide, sometimes straight but more often curving downward near the apex and in other instances curving multiple times, usually irregularly at hairpin angles, sometimes with multiple stalks from single host, smooth, base of the stalk attached to a wasp, hornet, bee, or bumblebee, stalk at first pale yellow-brown but becoming bright yellow or pale yellow; prominent head at the apex, 2–8 mm long and 1.5–2 mm wide, perithecia mostly embedded, resulting in smooth to slightly bumpy surface, similar to or paler than stalk in color; spores white to hyaline in mass, forming long filament-like chains and breaking into shorter partial spores, 8–14 × 1.5–2 µm, smooth.

Habitat/Biological Role: Emerging from leaf litter or occasionally decomposing logs (the fungus can parasitize wood-boring bees), with several fruiting bodies sometimes found in one area; appearing from midsummer to fall. Parasite of adult members of the Hymenoptera, including wasps, hornets, bees, or bumblebees.

Distribution: Most common in the Southeast but found throughout eastern North America.

Comments: This fungus can be regionally common and in certain years prolific; once it occurs in a locality, it will sometimes become common for a few years and then suddenly become rare. Since many of its hosts are social insects and diseases are easily spread by social organisms, infections of this fungus may follow the typical disease patterns observed in a human society! This fungus often turns the eyes of its host the same yellow color as the fruiting body. We have collected it on a wide diversity of hosts in the order Hymenoptera but never on species of ants. It can be challenging to extract the host intact, but it is an important identification character. *Ophiocordyceps myrmecophila* (syn. *Cordyceps myrmecophila*) is very similar, but it is rare in our region, smaller, and parasitizes only ants. *Ophiocordyceps unilateralis* (syn. *C. unilateralis*) is a species complex of multiple undescribed taxa, all of which parasitize ants; one or more representatives of this complex occur in our region, but they are smaller, gray to brown in color, and typically have the fertile head only part of the way up the stalk, not at the apex. *Ophiocordyceps dipterigena* (syn. *C. dipterigena*) has similar yellowish capitate heads but is rare in our region and parasitizes flies. No information on edibility or medicinal properties is available for any of these species.

Ophiocordyceps stylophora
(Berkeley & Broome) G. H. Sung, J. M. Sung, Hywel-Jones & Spatafora

GRAY-BROWN BEETLE LARVA CORDYCEPS

SYNONYM *Cordyceps stylophora*

FAMILY Ophiocordycipitaceae

Slender stalk-like structure, 1–3 cm long and 0.5–1 mm wide, straight to curved and rarely forking, base of stalk attached to a segmented beetle larva host, whitish to gray at the apex and gray to brown at the base, sometimes becoming completely brown with age; fruiting bodies rarely maturing, if mature retaining a sterile tip, fertile portion composed of densely packed perithecia and located approximately halfway up the stalk, pale to dark brown or sometimes grayish; spores hyaline in mass, forming long filament-like chains and breaking into shorter partial spores, 6–10 × 2 µm, smooth.

Habitat/Biological Role: Emerging from decomposing logs where the host beetle larvae occur; sometimes several fruiting bodies can be found in one log; appearing throughout the year. Parasite of beetle (Coleoptera) larvae.

Distribution: Most common in the Southeast but found throughout eastern North America.

Comments: This fungus is regionally common and in certain years prolific, but it is uncommon to find a mature specimen. In part, this may be because it frequently overwinters; however, we have observed specimens for nearly a year (throughout the winter) and not observed them to mature. *Ophiocordyceps superficialis* (syn. *Cordyceps superficialis*) and *O. michiganensis* (syn. *C. michiganensis*) are the most morphologically similar species; they are much less common, with fruiting bodies that are generally longer, often multiple from one host, and the perithecia are free (easily rubbed off) and usually scattered irregularly, not densely packed. *Ophiocordyceps stylophora* is too small to be of any culinary interest and has not to our knowledge been tested for medicinal properties.

Ophiocordyceps variabilis
(Petch) G. H. Sung, J. M. Sung, Hywel-Jones & Spatafora

FLY LARVA CORDYCEPS

SYNONYMS *Cordyceps variabilis, C. viperina*

FAMILY Ophiocordycipitaceae

Slender stalk-like structure, 5–17 mm long and 0.5–1 mm wide, straight to curved or sometimes forking; surface smooth to finely powdery, base of stalk attached to segmented fly larvae, stalk yellowish orange to reddish orange; fertile portion irregular in shape, consisting of clusters of perithecia, sometimes as few as ten perithecia in a cluster, clusters variable in shape and sometimes forming a cushion-like structure that wraps halfway around stalk midway up and at other times forming capitate head at the apex of the stalk, fertile portion similar to the stalk in color or sometimes darker; spores hyaline in mass, forming filament-like chains and breaking into shorter partial spores, 5–10 × 1.5–2 µm, smooth.

Habitat/Biological Role: Emerging from decomposing logs where the host fly larvae occur; sometimes several fruiting bodies can be found on one log; appearing from summer to late fall. Parasite of the larvae of flies (Diptera), particularly members of the family Xylophagidae.

Distribution: Most common in the Southeast and East but found throughout North America and south to Central America.

Comments: This small fungus can be distinguished from other members of the genera *Ophiocordyceps* and *Cordyceps* on the basis of its small size, type of host, and the variable shape of its fertile structures. *Cordyceps cardinalis* and *C. militaris* are somewhat similar in color, but these two species are generally much larger, have embedded perithecia, and are associated with moth pupae or larvae that only rarely occur in logs. The reddish color and obvious exoskeletal segments of *O. variabilis*'s host frequently cause it to be misidentified as a beetle larva. This fungus is too small to be of culinary value, and we do not know of any tests of its medicinal properties. Its asexual stage is *Syngiocladium tetanopsis*.

Torrubiella arachnophila var. *leiopus* (J. R. Johnston) Mains

SPIDER CORDYCEPS

SYNONYMS *Torrubiella gibellulae*, *Cordyceps arachnophila*

FAMILY Cordycipitaceae

Thin, rod-like structures, tapering from the base toward the apex, length varying and related to the size of the host, 0.5–7 mm long and 0.1–0.5 mm wide, white to yellowish to pale pinkish, arising from a white mycelium that partially or completely covers the body of a dead spider and usually extends to the substrate upon which the spider occurs; spores (conidia) hyaline in mass, 2.5–6 × 1.5–2.5 µm, fusoid-elliptical, smooth; ascospores 450–650 × 1.5–2 µm, thread-like, breaking into segments (4–10 µm long).

Habitat/Biological Role: Parasitizing and forming fruiting bodies that arise from the bodies of spiders, the latter generally attached to the undersides of leaves; fruiting during moist summer weather. Parasite of spiders.

Distribution: Widely distributed throughout eastern North America and elsewhere in the world, most frequently in the tropics.

Comments: The asexual (anamorphic) stage of this fungus, *Gibellula leiopus* (pictured), is more common than the sexual (teleomorphic) stage. *Torrubiella arachnophila* var. *pulchra* is most easily differentiated by its anamorph, *G. pulchra*. *Gibellula pulchra* occurs in our region but is less frequently encountered; it is very distinctive in having minute (less than 1 mm long) structures with small heads at the apex that cover the erect stalks, which are attached to the body of the spider. *Akanthomyces aranearum* is similar in that it parasitizes spiders; however, the parasitized host usually is not attached to the underside of a leaf and the lower portion of the fruiting body is typically orangish brown. All these fungi are too small to be of culinary interest. Some related species have displayed potential medicinal properties; however, to our knowledge, none of these species have been tested.

Morels and Relatives

Because of their culinary value, morels are among the best-known groups of fungi. In some parts of western North America, people make their living as migratory morel pickers, following where the previous year's fires have been; they often start in the mountains of California and follow the season north, all the way through Canada and into Alaska. Most of the morels picked commercially in these burned sites are blackish to brownish in color; they are not the species we have here in the Southeast. In eastern North America, we find some black to brown morels, but the yellowish or blond morels tend to be more common. The eastern species of morels do not seem to be fire-affiliated and are usually found among the early spring wildflowers, making it challenging to spot their well-camouflaged fruiting bodies.

The true morels (*Morchella*) are variable in color but always have a head-like structure with distinct pits and ridges at the apex of a hollow stalk. Morels are some of the best-tasting and easily identified edible mushrooms; however, they should never be consumed raw or with alcohol, and there are a handful of reports of a rare food allergy leading to mild gastrointestinal issues for some people who consume a member of this genus. Some of the poisonous false morels can resemble the genus *Morchella*; however, a careful study of the following descriptions should alleviate any concern of misidentification. The ecology of these groups is not well understood.

Eastern morels have many different folk names, particularly within the Appalachian Mountains. The common names we have most frequently encountered are molly moochers, dry land fish, haystack, muggies, sponge mushroom, honeycomb mushroom, and snake head mushroom. Whatever you call them, it is always an enjoyable challenge to go out into the spring woods and hunt for these elusive and tasty mushrooms.

Gyromitra korfii (Raitviir)
Harmaja

BULL-NOSE FALSE MOREL
SYNONYM *Discina korfii*

FAMILY Discinaceae

Contorted to brain-like structure, stalked, the upper portion cap-like, 2–12 cm wide and folded downward, irregularly folded, sometimes divided into folded lobes; upper surface smooth, with irregular wrinkles, the margin usually curving up away from stalk or sometimes fused with it, pale to dark brown or sometimes dull yellowish brown; lower surface finely granular, dingy whitish yellow or pale grayish; stalk 1–7 cm long and 2–7 cm wide, equal to enlarged toward the base, sometimes covered by dirt, usually ribbed, white to grayish, stalk interior stuffed with cottony white hyphae; spores hyaline in mass, 24–36 × 10–15 µm, elliptical to spindle-shaped, smooth to finely reticulate and in mature spores sometimes having blunt terminal projections.

Habitat/Biological Role: Occurring as solitary fruiting bodies or in small groups on soil in broadleaf or mixed broad-leaf-conifer forests; fruiting from early spring to early summer. The ecology of this fungus is not fully understood; it is possibly mycorrhizal or a decomposer of organic material.

Distribution: Widely distributed in eastern and midwestern North America, with the total range yet to be determined; however, it is rarely found south of Tennessee or the Carolinas.

Comments: Many species formerly assigned to the genus *Gyromitra* have been transferred to the genus *Discina*. Some mycologists believe that *G. korfii* and its western cousin *G. montana* are better referred to by the European name *G. gigas*, while others believe all three fungi are distinct species. The genus *Gyromitra/Discina* is diverse in North America but uncommon in our region. *Gyromitra brunnea* (syn. *G. fastigiata*) is found in our region but differs in having a less wrinkled brain-like cap that is usually folded on itself. *Gyromitra caroliniana* (syn. *D. caroliniana*) is rare but produces the largest and most striking fruiting body of any similar fungus in our region. The fruiting body has a vibrant reddish brown, cross-ribbed cap that can be up to 18 cm wide and a white stalk up to 16 cm long and 8 cm wide. *Gyromitra esculenta* is uncommon in our region but generally has a more prominent and slender stalk, a more brain-like cap, and smaller (16–28 × 7–13 µm) smooth spores. Some people eat members of this genus, but this group has been shown to contain toxic and/or carcinogenic compounds and should not be eaten (see pages 19–20).

Helvella latispora Boudier

SLENDER HELVELLA

SYNONYM *Helvella stevensii*

FAMILY Helvellaceae

Contorted cap-like structure on a slender stalk, 3–20 mm wide and folded downward, 5–20 mm high, saddle-shaped or irregularly lobed; upper surface smooth, irregularly undulate, margin usually curving up away from the stalk, pale gray-brown to dull yellowish brown; lower surface smooth to finely pubescent or with fine granules, dingy whitish yellow or pale grayish brown; stalk 6–20 mm long and 1–5 mm wide, equal to enlarged toward the base, finely pubescent, white to cream; spores hyaline in mass, 16–21 × 10–12.5 μm, elliptical, smooth.

Habitat/Biological Role: Occurring as solitary fruiting bodies or in small groups on soil or occasionally organic material in many different types of forests; fruiting from spring to summer. The ecology of this fungus is not fully understood; it is possibly mycorrhizal or a decomposer of organic material.

Distribution: Found primarily in eastern North America but widely distributed on the continent.

Comments: *Helvella* is a large genus of morel-like fungi. *Helvella albella* is morphologically similar but less common in our region; the upper surface of its cap is generally darker in color and the spores are larger (20–24 × 12–15 μm). *Helvella elastica* is similar, but the margin of the cap usually curves toward the stalk and the lower surface of the cap and stalk are smooth. *Helvella crispa* is somewhat similar but differs in usually being nearly white and having a stalk that is ribbed, chambered, and pitted. *Helvella atra* and *H. pezizoides* are considered distinct species by some mycologists and synonyms by others; both are dark gray to grayish black in color and are unlikely to be confused with *H. latispora* based on color alone, although they do share a similar growth form. None of these species should be consumed.

Helvella macropus (Fries) Karsten

LONG-STALKED GRAY CUP

SYNONYMS *Macroscyphus macropus, Peziza macropus*

FAMILY Helvellaceae

Cap 1.5–4 cm wide, at first shallow-cup-shaped but sometimes becoming nearly flat with age; upper fertile surface gray-brown to yellow-brown, smooth to slightly wrinkled; lower sterile surface gray to gray-brown, densely pubescent especially near the margin; stalk 2–5 cm long and 1–5 mm wide, rounded, somewhat enlarged downward, solid, gray to gray-brown with a whitish base; spores hyaline in mass, $18–25 \times 11–12$ µm, fusiform, smooth to minutely warted, with a large central oil droplet, nonamyloid.

Habitat/Biological Role: Occurring on the ground or sometimes on decomposing wood in broadleaf or conifer forests; solitary or scattered and often associated with mosses; typically fruiting from midsummer through fall. Thought to form mycorrhizal associations with trees, at least under some circumstances.

Distribution: Widely distributed throughout North America.

Comments: Typical specimens of *Helvella macropus* usually can be recognized by their gray color, shallow-cup-shaped cap, and relatively long stalk. This species looks more like a cup fungus than the false morel it is. *Helvella cupuliformis* is very similar but often darker in color and generally has substantially larger asci ($300–350 \times 17–20$ µm); the asci of *H. macropus* are generally $175–250 \times 14–18$ µm. The edibility of both these fungi is unknown.

Morchella americana Clowez & Matherly

COMMON MOREL, YELLOW MOREL

FAMILY Morchellaceae

Cap honeycomb- or sponge-like, held aloft on a cylindrical stalk, total height 5–20 cm; cap 1.5–5 × 2.5–11 cm, oval to more often elongated, yellow-brown to tan with the pits in the cap lighter in color; stalk 2–12 cm long and 1.5–4 cm wide, with distinct ribs or furrows overall and somewhat enlarged at the base, hollow, white to pale yellow-brown; spores buff to orange-buff in mass, 17–24 × 11–15 µm, elliptical, smooth.

Habitat/Biological Role: Occurring on the ground in broadleaf forests as solitary fruiting bodies or in small or large groups, particularly in areas of bottomland near rivers and streams; fruiting in spring. Often listed as a decomposer of litter and humus, but there is evidence that morels can form mycorrhizal associations with trees.

Distribution: Found throughout North America.

Comments: Unlike most of the larger fungi, morels fruit in the spring. Numbers of fruiting bodies vary considerably between regions and from year to year, but in some years they can be abundant. Several similar *Morchella* species occur in eastern North America, and their taxonomy is challenging and undergoing revisions. Morels are some of the best-tasting and easily identified edible mushrooms, but they should never be consumed raw or with alcohol.

Morchella angusticeps Peck

BLACK MOREL, EASTERN BLACK MOREL

FAMILY Morchellaceae

Cap honeycomb- or sponge-like, held aloft on a cylindrical stalk, total height 7.5–15 cm; cap 2–3 × 5–10 cm, conical to more often elongated, dark brown to black with the pits in the cap yellow-brown, pits elongated and longitudinally arranged; stalk 2.5–7.5 cm long and 1.5–2.5 cm wide, smooth to slightly furrowed, hollow, white to pale yellow; spores cream to light buff in mass, 22–28 × 11–15 µm, long-elliptical, smooth.

Habitat/Biological Role: Occurring as solitary fruiting bodies or in small or large groups on the ground in broadleaf or conifer forests; fruiting in early spring. Although often listed as decomposers of litter and humus, there is evidence that morels can form mycorrhizal associations with trees.

Distribution: Black morels are found all over the world, but this species is considered to be restricted to eastern North America.

Comments: *Morchella elata* is the name most often applied to the commonly encountered black morel, but this is a complex consisting of many different species. Black morels are often the first morels to appear in the spring. In the Appalachian Mountains, unlike other species of morels, *M. angusticeps* is more commonly found in the coves higher on mountainsides than down in the bottom-land and river valleys. *Morchella punctipes* is one of the most similar species; however, its honeycomb-like "cap" is not attached to the stalk. Morels are some of the best-tasting and easily identified edible mushrooms, but they should never be consumed raw or with alcohol.

Morchella diminutiva
M. Kuo, Dewsbury, Moncalvo & S. L. Stephenson

WHITE MOREL, TULIP MOREL

FAMILY Morchellaceae

Elongated structure with an expanded "head" supported by a stalk of approximately the same length, total height 2–10 cm, head 1.5–5 cm long and 1–3 cm broad, usually conic to pointed but sometimes curved or blunt-rounded, attached to the stalk, irregularly honeycombed, with vertical or curved ribs and numerous cross ribs, head grayish when young but becoming more yellow to whitish with age, ridges generally paler in color than the pits; stalk 1.5–7 cm long and 0.5–2 cm wide, equal or enlarged at the base, smooth or sometimes having fine granules present, white to pale yellowish tan; spores 19–25 × 11–17 µm, elliptical, smooth.

Habitat/Biological Role: Occurring on the ground as solitary fruiting bodies or in groups in broadleaf forests, particularly common in forests located on floodplains or at low elevations under tulip poplars; fruiting in spring. Our understanding of the ecology of morels is incomplete, and it is not known for certain if they are decomposers or possibly form mycorrhizal associations with trees.

Distribution: Particularly common in the foothills of the Appalachians Mountains and in the Piedmont and widely distributed in eastern North America.

Comments: Several similar pale yellowish to whitish morels occur in our region, and identifying them can be very challenging, partly because morel taxonomy is only recently beginning to be sorted out and also because there may be several undescribed species. *Morchella sceptriformis* (syn. *M. virginiana*), common at low elevations from Virginia to Mississippi, is very similar in appearance and nearly impossible to separate without molecular data. Small individuals of *M. americana* are also extremely similar. The good news for those of us interested in hunting morels for food is that all species of yellow morels are tasty (many were previously lumped together under the name *M. deliciosa*), and we can leave the finer points of their identities to be determined by morel taxonomists! Just don't eat them raw or with alcohol.

Morchella punctipes Peck

EASTERN HALF-FREE MOREL

FAMILY Morchellaceae

Elongated structure with a distinct "head" at the apex of a stalk, total height 5–18 cm, the head 1.5–4.5 cm wide and 1–4 cm high, irregularly conic, stalk attached about halfway up the inside of the head, the lower portion of the latter often flaring out from stalk and thus becoming skirt-like; surface irregularly honeycombed, typically with fifteen to twenty-five major vertical ridges that are longitudinally parallel, sometimes with cross ridges present, surface between the ridges pale to dark brown, ridges at first brown but darkening to black with age; stalk 2–15 cm long and 1–4.5 cm wide, irregularly equal or enlarged toward the base, hollow, surface sometimes having irregular longitudinal wrinkles, granular, whitish; spores pale orange to yellowish cream in mass, 22–28 × 12–18 µm, broadly elliptical, smooth.

Habitat/Biological Role: Occurring on the ground as solitary fruiting bodies or in small or large groups in broadleaf forests; fruiting during spring. Our understanding of the ecology of morels is incomplete, and it is not known for certain if they are decomposers or possibly form mycorrhizal associations with trees.

Distribution: Widely distributed in eastern North America.

Comments: The heads of all other *Morchella* species in our region are attached to the stalk at the margin of the head. *Verpa bohemica* and *V. conica* are the most morphologically similar fungi; however, these two species are found primarily in the western and northeastern United States, and whether either one occurs as far south as the northern portion of our region is questionable. In any case, we advise against using either of these species for culinary purposes because they are poisonous to some people. *Verpa bohemica* has a similar irregularly honeycombed head, but the head is attached only at the apex of the stalk (instead of halfway up the head as in *M. punctipes*), the stalk is not fully hollow, and the spores are larger (55–58 × 15–22 µm). *Verpa conica* has a smooth head that is attached only at the apex of the stalk. *Morchella punctipes* is edible but should never be consumed raw or with alcohol. Many field guides misapply the name of the European half-free morel, *M. semilibera*, to this species; however, molecular studies have shown them to be different.

Cup Fungi

As their name suggests, this large and diverse group of ascomycetes typically resemble cups, saucers, goblets, or bowls. A few species produce relatively large fruiting bodies, but those of most species are small. Cup fungi are diverse in color and ecological roles; some are plant pathogens, many are decomposers, and some species form mycorrhizal associations with trees. An amazing feature visible in many of the larger cup fungi is that when weather conditions are right, if you carefully blow into the fruiting body or use a small stick to "tickle" the inner surface, a cloud of powdery spores will likely shoot into the air! This trick can be a great teaching tool and helps a cup fungus disperse its spores. There are a few edible species in this group, but most are too small or poorly understood to be of culinary value, so they are best left for tickling or blowing as a way to mycologically entertain and amaze your friends.

Bisporella citrina (Batsch) Korf & S. E. Carpenter

YELLOW FAIRY CUP

FAMILY Helotiaceae

Cup-shaped structure, 1.5–3 mm across, lower portion narrowing to a small base; surface smooth, bright lemon yellow; spores white, cream, or pale yellow in mass, 9–14 × 3–5 μm, elliptical, smooth, with a prominent oil droplet at each end.

Habitat/Biological Role: Occurring in often dense clusters on decorticated logs or stumps; fruiting throughout the summer. Decomposer of wood.

Distribution: Found throughout North America.

Comments: This fungus is often exceedingly common. Although small, the bright yellow color of the fruiting bodies causes them to stand out against the darker substrates upon which they occur. This and related species are too small to be of any culinary interest. *Bisporella subpallida* is similar but has shorter spores (6–9 × 2.5–3 μm); *Calycina claroflava*

(syn. *B. sulfurina*) is similar but has more narrow spores (9–10 × 2 μm). *Lanzia luteovirescens* is similar in color but has long stalks and occurs on small twigs and the petioles of leaves.

Bulgaria inquinans (Persoon) Fries

RUBBER BUTTONS, BLACK JELLY DROPS

FAMILY Bulgariaceae

Shallow cup- or saucer-shaped structure with an incurved margin, 10–40 cm wide, at first somewhat turbinate before becoming saucer-shaped with age, sessile or attached to the substrate by a short stalk-like base, rubbery gelatinous; outer surface dark brown, scurfy; inner fertile surface consisting of a thin brownish black layer, shiny when wet; spores very dark brown to almost black in mass, 9–17 × 6–7 µm, elliptical to somewhat kidney-shaped, smooth, eight spores occurring in each ascus, four of these typically dark brown to black and the others hyaline.

Habitat/Biological Role: Occurring in small to large clusters on fallen branches and logs of broadleaf trees; typically fruiting in late summer and fall. Decomposer of wood.

Distribution: Widely distributed throughout North America.

Comments: Typical fruitings of *Bulgaria inquinans* are unlikely to be confused with any other fungus. Although their rubbery gelatinous texture is similar to that of some jelly fungi, the overall shape of the fruiting body clearly indicates this species is a cup fungus. Its edibility is not known. Also see *Galiella rufa*.

Chlorencoelia versiformis
(Persoon) R. Dixon

OLIVE-BROWN CUP

FAMILY Hemiphacidiaceae

Shallow, irregularly cup-shaped structure (but becoming more or less flat with age), 1–3 cm wide; upper surface olive-green to olive-brown or orange-brown; lower surface dull reddish brown, somewhat velvety; stalk 3–6 mm long and 1–2 mm wide, tapering downward toward the base, dull reddish brown; spores hyaline in mass, 9–16 × 2–4 µm, fusiform to almost cylindrical, smooth.

Habitat/Biological Role: Occurring as scattered fruiting bodies or in small groups on decorticated logs of broadleaf trees; fruiting during summer and fall. Decomposer of wood.

Distribution: Widely distributed throughout eastern North America.

Comments: The major distinguishing features of the fruiting bodies of *Chlorencoelia versiformis* are the olive-green to orange-brown color of the upper surface and their occurrence on the decorticated wood of broadleaf trees. The specific epithet refers to the somewhat irregular shape of the fruiting bodies. *Chlorencoelia torta* is identical macroscopically but differs microscopically in having slightly smaller and more elliptical spores (6–11.5 × 2–4 µm). *Chlorosplenium chlora* is somewhat similar but differs in being more brightly colored and having smaller fruiting bodies (1–3 mm) and smaller spores (7–9 × 1.5–2 µm). The edibility of these fungi is unknown.

Chlorociboria aeruginascens
(Nylander) Kanouse ex C. S.
Ramamurthi, Korf & L. R. Batra

GREEN STAIN FUNGUS

SYNONYMS *Chlorosplenium aeruginascens,*
Peziza aeruginascens

FAMILY Helotiaceae

Cup-shaped structure, 3–13 mm across,
becoming flattened in age, base narrowing to form a short stalk, bright green to
blue-green; upper surface smooth and
more vividly colored than lower surface;
lower surface somewhat roughened;
spores essentially colorless in mass, 6–8
× 1–2 μm, subfusiform to nearly cylindrical, smooth.

Habitat/Biological Role: Occurring
in small clusters on decorticated logs
or stumps of broadleaf trees; fruiting
throughout the year. Decomposer of wood.

Distribution: Found throughout
North America.

Comments: As the common name indicates, the vegetative body (mycelium) of
this fungus causes wood to turn green in
color. The fruiting bodies are encountered
much less often than the green-stained
wood. Some woodworkers have found
ways to use the naturally dyed wood; however, it is usually too decomposed to have
sufficient integrity for much other than
inlay. *Chlorociboria aeruginosa* is pretty
much identical except that it has larger
spores (8–15 × 2–4 μm) and possibly a
more centrally located stalk. These fungi
are too small to be of culinary interest.

Dumontinia tuberosa
(Hedwig) L. M. Kohn

ANEMONE CUP

SYNONYM *Sclerotinia tuberosa*

FAMILY Sclerotiniaceae

Cup-shaped structure, 1–3 cm wide, usually becoming flattened with age, arising from a yellowish brown to black sclerotium, the latter sometimes 2–4 cm in diameter; inner surface of cup tan to chestnut brown; outer surface the same color or slightly paler, smooth; stalk variable in length, up to 10 cm long (depending on the depth of the below-ground sclerotium), slender, brown, smooth; spores white to cream-colored or yellowish in mass, 12–17 × 6–9 µm, elliptical, smooth.

Habitat/Biological Role: Occurring on the ground in broadleaf or mixed broadleaf-conifer forests, always in association with the rhizomes (underground stems) of various members of the plant genus *Anemone*, solitary or more commonly occurring in a small cluster; fruiting in early spring. Probably best regarded as a parasite of *Anemone*, but a more complex relationship may exist between the two organisms.

Distribution: Widely distributed throughout eastern North America and also known from Europe but found only where the host plants occur.

Comments: Its association with members of the genus *Anemone*, which are common spring wildflowers in eastern North America, makes this an easy fungus to identify. Because *Dumontinia tuberosa* fruits so early in the year, the brown color of its fruiting bodies often cause them to blend in with dead leaves on the forest floor. There are other species of brown cup fungi that arise from fruits, roots, or sclerotia in our region. *Stromatinia rapulum* is very similar; however, it is not associated with anemones. *Monilinia vaccinii-corymbosi* is similar but occurs on the fallen fruits of blueberries. *Ciboria carunculoides* produces a similar brown cup that contorts the fruits of mulberry.

Galiella rufa (Schweinitz) Nannfeldt & Korf

HAIRY RUBBER CUP

SYNONYM *Bulgaria rufa*

FAMILY Sarcosomataceae

Globose to top-shaped structure when young but opening to become a shallow cup with incurved edges, 20–30 mm wide and 5–10 mm thick, gelatinous texture, tissue clear and jello-like; outer surface blackish brown, covered with clusters of fine hairs; inner fertile surface tan to pale orange-brown or reddish brown; stalk lacking or present and up to 10 mm long; spores hyaline in mass 17–21 × 8–10 μm, ellipsoid or occasionally nearly subfusiform, very finely pitted.

Habitat/Biological Role: Occurring on the fallen branches and woody debris of broadleaf trees, usually in small groups; fruiting from early spring to late summer. Decomposer of wood.

Distribution: Widely distributed throughout eastern North America.

Comments: Because of its rather dull color, *Galiella rufa* often tends to blend in with the leaf litter on the forest floor. Inner tissue is composed of clear jelly-like material (only visible if cut). No other similar cup fungus produces fruiting bodies with an inner surface that is orange-brown or reddish brown and has a somewhat gelatinous texture. Also see *Bulgaria inquinans*. Not much is known about the edibility of *Galiella rufa*.

Humaria hemisphaerica
(F. H. Wiggers) Fuckel

BROWN-HAIRED WHITE CUP

FAMILY Pyronemataceae

Cup-like structure with an incurved margin, 1–3 cm wide and 1–2 cm high; inner (fertile) surface smooth, whitish to grayish; outer surface covered with an erect to appressed mat of brownish yellow hairs; stalk absent; spores hyaline in mass, 22–27 × 10–13 μm, elliptical, finely but prominently warted.

Habitat/Biological Role: Usually occurring in small clusters or groups on bare soil, patches of moss, or sometimes decomposing wood; fruiting from spring to fall. Decomposer of organic material.

Distribution: Frequent in our region and widely distributed in North America.

Comments: This small hairy mushroom is one of the most common cup fungi in our region. *Hypomyces stephanomatis*, a gray mold-like fungus, sometimes parasitizes it. *Genea hispidula*, with its hairy surface, can appear similar, but it usually occurs below the surface of the soil and has very small apical openings and larger spores (30–42 × 25–35 μm) that are broadly warted. The edibility of *Humaria hemisphaerica* is not known, but it is too small to be of much culinary interest.

Hymenoscyphus fructigenus
(Bulliard) Gray

ACORN CUP FUNGUS

SYNONYM *Ciboria fructigena*

FAMILY Helotiaceae

Cup-like to flat structure, 1–5 mm wide; upper (fertile) surface smooth, whitish to pale yellow; lower surface smooth, similar in color to the upper surface; stalk up to 15 mm long and 1 mm wide, sometimes much shorter, equal, smooth, similar in color to the upper surface; spores 12–18 × 3–5 µm, irregularly spindle-shaped, smooth, usually containing oil droplets.

Habitat/Biological Role: Occurring in clusters on old, decomposing hickory nuts, acorns, or beechnuts; fruiting summer to fall. Decomposer of nuts.

Distribution: Common in our region and found primarily in eastern North America.

Comments: Many species of small white cup fungi are similar, but the association of *Hymenoscyphus fructigenus* with nuts makes it easy to identify. In our region, it is most common on hickory nuts. *Lachnum virgineum* occasionally fruits on beechnuts and other organic debris but differs in having smaller spores (6–10 × 1.5–2.5 µm) and a dense layer of white hairs on its outer surface. These fungi are too small to be of any culinary interest.

Lachnum pudibundum
(Quélet) J. Schröter

DECIDUOUS WOOD STALKED HAIRY FAIRY CUP

SYNONYM *Dasyscyphus pudibundus*

FAMILY Lachnaceae

Goblet- to cup-shaped structure, 1.5–4 mm wide and 2–6 mm tall; inner surface of the cup smooth and white; margin and outer surface completely covered by a dense layer of white hairs; stalk distinct and also covered by white to pale brown hairs; spores hyaline in mass, 7–9 × 1.5–2.5 µm, club- to spindle-shaped, smooth.

Habitat/Biological Role: Occurring in dense clusters or small groups on decomposing wood from broadleaf trees, sometimes found on the undersides of logs; fruiting summer to fall. Decomposer of wood.

Distribution: Widely distributed in North America.

Comments: Many *Lachnum* species are morphologically very similar and challenging to identify. *Lachnum virgineum* (syn. *Dasyscyphus virgineus*) is essentially identical to *L. pudibundum*, even with respect to spore size; it differs only in occurring on the wood from conifers (as well as on certain other types of plant debris, such as cones and beechnut burs) and having slightly longer hairs. *Lachnum bicolor* (syn. *Dasyscypha bicolor*, *Lachnella bicolor*) is similar in size, shape, and the presence of a hairy outer surface, but the inner surface of its cup is yellow to orange. All the aforementioned species are so small that they are of little or no culinary interest.

Microstoma floccosum
(Schweinitz) Raitviir

SHAGGY SCARLET CUP
FAMILY Sarcoscyphaceae

Cup-shaped structure, 3–10 mm wide; outer surface bright red and covered with prominent white hairs; inner surface smooth, scarlet; stalk 20–35 mm long and 1–5 mm wide, hairy, white; spores hyaline in mass, 20–35 × 15–17 μm, elliptical with extremely narrow ends, smooth.

Habitat/Biological Role: Occurring on decomposing twigs and branches of broadleaf trees; solitary or more commonly occurring in clusters; fruiting during summer and early fall. Decomposer of wood.

Distribution: Most common in the Southeast but found throughout eastern North America.

Comments: The bright color of its fruiting bodies makes *Microstoma floccosum* easy to spot despite its small size. In the southernmost portion of our region there are occasional reports of *Cookeina tricholoma* and *C. sulcipes*; these two species are members of a genus that is very common in the tropics but rarely occurs in temperate regions. *Cookeina sulcipes* has a prominent white stalk and a red to pinkish cup with only a scattering of short sparse hairs around the rim of the cup; it is most similar to *M. floccosum* but differs in having longer clear hairs that are less dense and more erect. Other red cup fungi (e.g., *Sarcoscypha austriaca*) occur in our region, but these lack the conspicuous white hairs on the outer surface. These fungi are so small that their edibility is not known.

Otidea unicisa (Peck) Harmaja

BROWN OTIDEA

SYNONYM *Otidea grandis*

FAMILY Pyronemataceae

Irregularly cup-shaped structure, 10–40 mm wide and 10–20 mm tall, cup turned up on one side and split to the base on the other; margin of cup inrolled; inner surface pale vinaceous fawn to yellowish brown with some pinkish tints, sometimes forming wrinkles at the bottom; outer surface brown to reddish brown; stalk short to nearly absent, stout, yellowish, 0.5–1.5 mm wide; spores hyaline in mass, 14–17 × 6–7 μm, long-elliptical to slightly fusoid, appearing smooth but minutely roughened when viewed under high magnification, nonamyloid.

Habitat/Biological Role: Occurring on the ground in broadleaf or mixed broadleaf-conifer forests, fruiting bodies solitary or in groups, sometimes associated with mosses; fruiting in summer and fall. Decomposer of litter and humus.

Distribution: Apparently most common in the more northern portion of our region but widely distributed in North America.

Comments: It is usually possible to distinguish *Otidea unicisa* from other brown cup fungi that occur on the ground by the split in the fruiting body, which extends to the base on one side. Many *Otidea* species are similar, but most of these are found outside our region. Not much is known about the edibility of this group, but they are not recommended.

Peziza michelii (Boudier) Dennis

MILKING LILAC CUP

SYNONYM *Galactinia michelii*

FAMILY Pezizaceae

Cup-shaped structure, 1–4 cm wide, lacking a stalk, expanding to nearly flat with age, margin inrolled; inner surface smooth, usually with a dimple at the bottom of the cup, lilac to purple in color, exuding a whitish to clear liquid if broken or cut; outer/lower surface smooth to covered by fine granules, at first pale yellowish white but becoming yellowish orange with age or staining; spores hyaline in mass, 14–17 × 7–9 μm, ellipsoid, finely warted at maturity.

Habitat/Biological Role: Occurring in small groups or as solitary fruiting bodies, typically from compacted soil; fruiting summer to fall. Either a decomposer of organic material or possibly mycorrhizal.

Distribution: Widely distributed in eastern North America.

Comments: *Peziza succosa* is similar but much paler in color and has larger (16–22 × 8–12 μm) more prominently warted spores. *Peziza vesiculosa* is somewhat similar but generally larger, brown in color, and does not exude a whitish to clear liquid if broken or cut. *Peziza griseorosea* can be similar in color, but its outer surface is paler, the spores are smooth, and it does not exude a whitish to clear liquid when broken. The edibility of this species is not known.

Peziza phyllogena Cooke

COMMON BROWN CUP

FAMILY Pezizaceae

Cup-shaped structure, 3–14 cm wide, cup shallow to deep, usually somewhat irregular, especially when occurring in clusters, margin generally turned inward; inner surface smooth, reddish brown to olive-brown; outer surface rough, pale reddish brown; stalk lacking; spores hyaline in mass, 17–21 × 8–10 µm, elliptical, finely warted.

Habitat/Biological Role: Occurring on the ground in broadleaf or conifer forests, fruiting bodies typically occurring in small clusters and near decomposing wood; fruiting in late spring and early summer. Decomposer of wood and humus.

Distribution: Apparently more common in the northern portion of our region but widely distributed throughout North America.

Comments: *Peziza phyllogena* can be challenging to identify. Some authors consider *P. badioconfusa* to be the same as this species, but others consider it to be a different, more northern species not found in our region. It is nearly impossible to separate the two, even with the use of microscopic characters. *Peziza badia* is morphologically almost identical but differs in fruiting in the fall; moreover, it has irregularly reticulate spores. Some authors report *P. badioconfusa* to be edible, but given the taxonomic confusion surrounding these two species and reports of problems with other members of this genus, eating these cup fungi is not recommended.

Peziza vesiculosa Bulliard

BLADDER CUP

FAMILY Pezizaceae

Cup-shaped structure, 2–10 cm wide, the cup shallow to deep, usually somewhat irregular, especially if occurring in clusters; cup margin entire when young but splitting irregularly with age; inner surface smooth, pale reddish brown to yellowish brown, sometimes forming blister-like bumps in the center of the cup; outer surface rough, usually lighter in color than inner surface, pale brown, rough with irregular wart-like bumps; stalk lacking; spores hyaline in mass, 19–23 × 11–13 µm, elliptical, smooth.

Habitat/Biological Role: Occurring in clusters on manure piles or the sawdust/ wood chips used in horse stalls, also sometimes fruiting from garden beds where manure has been added; fruiting from spring until fall. Decomposer of wood and humus.

Distribution: Widely distributed throughout North America but found most frequently on small farms and in gardens.

Comments: *Peziza* is a large genus of cup fungi, and it is often challenging to identify a particular specimen to species. However, since *P. vesiculosa* occurs in close proximity to manure, and the fruiting bodies have an outer surface covered by rough wart-like bumps, it can be identified rather easily. The edibility of this species is not known.

Sarcoscypha austriaca (Beck ex Saccardo) Boudier

SCARLET CUP

FAMILY Sarcoscyphaceae

Cup-shaped structure, at first rounded and deeply cup-shaped but becoming more shallow and irregular in shape with age, 2–7 cm wide and 2–3 cm high, margin incurved; outer surface white, frequently wrinkled, covered by fine curly hairs; inner surface smooth, at first scarlet to red but fading to reddish orange; stalk 5–30 mm long and 3–5 mm wide, white, sometimes very short or essentially lacking and in other instances prominent; spores hyaline in mass, 20–38 × 9–16 μm, elliptical to slightly oblong and almost all truncate (less than 3 μm at end), with multiple internal oil droplets, smooth.

Habitat/Biological Role: Occurring on decomposing twigs and branches on the forest floor in broadleaf and mixed forests, fruiting bodies solitary or occurring in small groups; fruiting early to late spring. Decomposer of wood.

Distribution: Widely distributed in eastern North America.

Comments: Some eastern North American field guides list this fungus under the name *Sarcoscypha coccinea*, which is a similar species now known to be restricted to western North America. In our region we often encounter *S. austriaca* while hunting morels in the Appalachian Mountains. *Sarcoscypha dudleyi* is nearly identical but differs in having truncate spores that almost always have two internal oil drops and one oil droplet that is 5–7.5 μm broad. The fruiting bodies of *S. occidentalis* are similar in color but smaller, almost always have a prominent stalk that is more slender, typically appear from late spring through summer, and have smaller spores (18–22 × 10–12 μm).

Scutellinia scutellata
(Linnaeus) Lambotte

EYELASH CUP

FAMILY Pyronemataceae

Shallow saucer-shaped structure, 0.5–2 cm wide; upper surface reddish orange to orange; lower surface light orange to pale brown with fine hairs, margin with dark brown to black, eyelash-like hairs extending outward; stalk very short or lacking; spores white in mass, 17–23 × 10.5–14 µm, elliptical, smooth when immature but becoming warted, nonamyloid.

Habitat/Biological Role: Occurring on decomposing wood or less commonly on moist soil, often found in clusters; fruiting throughout the year. Decomposer of wood.

Distribution: Found throughout most of North America.

Comments: If the fruiting bodies of *Scutellinia scutellata* are examined with a hand lens, the eyelash-like structures (hence the common name) are readily apparent. This fungus is often exceedingly common on large, moist, well-decomposed logs and stumps, sometimes occurring in large groups. *Scutellinia pennsylvanica* is very similar but tends to be lighter in color and lacks the fine hairs on the lower surface. *Scutellinia erinaceus* is morphologically similar but tends to be more yellowish in color. These fungi are too small to be a significant food source for humans.

Tarzetta catinus (Holmskjold) Korf & J. K. Rogers

STALKED ELF CUP

FAMILY Pyronemataceae

Urn-shaped or deeply cup-shaped structure, sometimes splitting into lobes or expanding outward with age, 1–5 cm wide, margin minutely toothed or notched; inner surface cream to brownish tan; outer surface downy or felt-like, the same color as the inner surface or paler; stalk usually short but sometimes relatively long, gradually expanding upward from a narrow base, typically buried in the substrate upon which the fruiting bodies occur; spores hyaline in mass, 18–24 × 10–13 µm, elliptical, smooth.

Habitat/Biological Role: Occurring on the ground in broadleaf or conifer forests, usually found in small groups; fruiting from spring to fall. Generally considered to be a decomposer of humus and litter but some closely related species are thought to possibly form mycorrhizal associations.

Distribution: Widely distributed throughout North America.

Comments: The distinguishing features of the fruiting body of *Tarzetta catinus* are the minutely toothed margin of the cup, the felt-like upper surface, and a stalk that is buried in the substrate and thus not readily apparent. *Tarzetta cupularis* is similar; however, it has a veil covering the inner surface of the cup when young. *Tarzetta bronca* is also very similar but lacks a prominent stalk at the base. Not much is known about the edibility of these fungi.

Tatraea macrospora (Peck) Baral

GRAY STALKED CUP

SYNONYMS *Calycina macrospora, Ciboria peckiana, Rutstroemia macrospora*

FAMILY Helotiaceae

Cup-like to flat structure, 5–15 mm wide; upper (fertile) surface smooth, pale gray to grayish white; lower surface finely scurfy, similar in color to the upper surface; stalk up to 15 mm long and 1.5 mm wide, sometimes much shorter, equal, smooth to finely scurfy, similar in color to upper surface; spores 22–34 × 6–8 µm, narrow oblong to tapering in the middle, smooth, sometimes containing oil droplets.

Habitat/Biological Role: Occurring in small to large groups or occasionally found as solitary fruiting bodies on decomposing wood from broadleaf trees or conifers; fruiting summer to fall. Decomposer of wood.

Distribution: Widely distributed in North America.

Comments: This small but common fungus is frequently overlooked because of its dull color and size. Some cup fungi are similar, but most of these species have amyloid asci, and *Tatraea macrospora* does not share this character with them. The edibility of *T. macrospora* is not known, but it is too small to be of much interest as food.

Urnula craterium (Schweinitz) Fries

DEVIL'S URN

FAMILY Sarcosomataceae

Club-shaped structure when young but opening and expanding to become urn-shaped, 3–6.5 × 4–6.5 cm, tough and leathery; inner surface dark brown to black and smooth; outer surface dark brown and scruffy, margin notched or ragged; stalk 1–2.5 cm long, approximately 5 mm wide, black; spores hyaline in mass, 24–36 × 10–15 μm, elliptical to spindle-shaped, smooth.

Habitat/Biological Role: Occurring on decomposing branches and the buried wood of broadleaf trees, especially oak, usually found in groups; fruiting in the spring as one of the first mushrooms to appear. Both a decomposer of wood and a parasite of oak and other trees.

Distribution: Found throughout North America and other regions of the northern hemisphere.

Comments: This is one of the first relatively large fungi to appear in the spring, but it is often overlooked because of its brown to black color, which blends in with the decomposing wood upon which the fruiting bodies occur. This fungus is listed in most field guides as inedible, nonpoisonous, unknown, or too tough; however, we have met some mushroom hunters who consider it a tasty early spring edible! During that time of year in the Southeast, there is almost nothing with which this fungus could be confused.

Wolfina aurantiopsis (Ellis) Seaver

YELLOW AND BLACK HAIRY CUP

FAMILY Chorioactidaceae

Irregularly globose cup-shaped structure when young but the apex expanding with age to become a firm shallow cup, up to 7 cm wide, stalk lacking, edge of cup incurved and whitish; cup interior (fertile surface) smooth, pale yellowish to nearly white or sometimes pale orangish; outer surface even to broadly lobed, firm, surface covered with dense matted to erect brown to black hairs, sometimes appearing almost woolly; spores hyaline to faintly yellow in mass, 24–33 × 13–18 µm, broadly elliptical, smooth or minutely longitudinally ridged.

Habitat/Biological Role: Occurring in small groups or as solitary fruiting bodies on decomposing wood or occasionally soil; fruiting from summer to early winter. Decomposer of wood.

Distribution: Widely distributed throughout eastern North America.

Comments: The color, firm texture, and hairy exterior make this a very distinctive fungus. *Galiella rufa* is morphologically similar but has a fertile surface that is darker in color, a gelatinous base, and lacks the hairy outer surface. *Wolfina aurantiopsis* is related to a group of rare cup fungi, including the distinctive and very rare *Chorioactis geaster*. The latter looks somewhat like an earthstar but lacks the spore case at the center. The edibility of *W. aurantiopsis* is not known.

Wynnea americana Thaxter

MOOSE ANTLERS, RABBIT EARS

FAMILY Sarcoscyphaceae

Elongated cup-shaped structure, 2.5–10 cm wide and 6–13 cm tall, occurring in cespitose clusters with all the individual cups arising from the same stalk; outer surface rough and sometimes wrinkled, blackish brown to reddish brown; inner surface smooth, pinkish orange to brownish orange; stalk tough, solid, dark brown, 1–2 cm long, attached to a below-ground brown irregular knobby sclerotium; sclerotium 4–10 cm wide; spores brown in mass, 32–40 × 15–16 µm, elliptical, pointed at each end and with longitudinal lines on the surface.

Habitat/Biological Role: Occurring on the ground in broadleaf forests, usually solitary; fruiting from midsummer until fall. Decomposer of litter and humus.

Distribution: Found throughout eastern North America but not particularly common.

Comments: The cluster of elongated brown cups that somewhat resembles a collection of rabbit ears is distinctive enough to be easily identified. *Wynnea sparassoides* is a rare but closely related species that also fruits in cespitose clusters, but its cups differ in being small and joined together, thus creating an unusual-looking fruiting body that somewhat resembles a brain. Some authors have reported *W. sparassoides* as not arising from a sclerotium, but we have collected it directly attached to a black sclerotium similar to the one produced by *W. americana*. Edibility not known for either species.

Club Fungi

The club fungi are a group of ascomycetes that produce club-shaped fruiting bodies. Most species are either decomposers or form mycorrhizal associations with trees; some species occur only on the seed pods of certain plants. The ascomycete club fungi are of little culinary interest.

Several species of ascomycete club fungi (*Tolypocladium* page 107) parasitize deer truffles (*Elaphomyces*) that fruit below ground. If the arthropod host of some of the Entomopathogenic Fungi (page 31) is lost, it would be possible to confuse clubs with members of that group. Clubs are also somewhat similar to the basidiomycete coral fungi (Coral Fungi and Relatives page 273).

Dibaeis baeomyces (Linnaeus f.) Rambold & Hertel

PINK EARTH LICHEN

FAMILY Icmadophilaceae

Tiny stalked structure with a spherical or slightly depressed cap-like upper portion, the latter 1–4 mm wide, pink; stalk 2–6 mm tall, smooth or fissured, white, arising from a white to gray (sometimes with a pinkish tinge) thallus on the surface of otherwise bare soil; spores hyaline in mass, 12–26 × 2.5–3 µm, fusiform, smooth, usually one-celled but occasionally two-celled.

Habitat/Biological Role: Occurring on bare soil in open, often disturbed areas, frequently on road banks and most common on acid soils with a high clay content, fruiting structures occurring together in small or sometimes rather extensive clusters. This organism is a lichen, found throughout the entire year.

Distribution: Widely distributed throughout eastern North America, particularly in the Southeast, and uncommon elsewhere.

Comments: Although the fruiting structures produced by *Dibaeis baeomyces* look like miniature mushrooms, this species is actually a member of a large genus of lichens. Some species of *Cladonia* (British soldier lichens) or *Pilophorus* (matchstick lichens) are similar in appearance; however, these are generally smaller and do not have the pink apex. Too small to be of culinary interest.

Geoglossum difforme Fries

COMMON EARTH TONGUE

FAMILY Geoglossaceae

Club-shaped structure, 3–7 cm tall, upper portion (head) 2–4 cm long and 4–10 mm wide at the broadest point and tapering at the apex and downward, tongue-shaped or sometimes spoon-shaped, older specimens often having a central longitudinal groove; surface smooth to shiny, dark brown to black; stalk 2.5–4.5 cm long and 1.5–6 mm wide, equal or sometimes enlarging toward the base or apex, smooth to rough; spores brown in mass, 90–120 × 6–7 μm, needle- or thread-like, smooth.

Habitat/Biological Role: Occurring as solitary fruiting bodies or in small groups on well-decomposed wood or on the ground; fruiting summer and fall.

The ecology of this fungus is unclear; it is likely a decomposer of organic material.

Distribution: Widely distributed in eastern North America.

Comments: *Geoglossum glutinosum* is nearly identical but has shorter spores (58–95 × 4–6 μm). Both *Geoglossum* and *Trichoglossum* have many species in North America that are morphologically similar to one another (see the description of *T. hirsutum*, for example). These species are not eaten.

Leotia lubrica (Scopoli) Persoon

JELLY CLUB

FAMILY Leotiaceae

Mushroom-like structure, rubbery, total height 1.5–7.5 cm; cap-like head 1–2.5 cm wide, variable in shape but usually more or less convex and somewhat convoluted; upper surface smooth or slightly wrinkled, buff, yellowish brown or dull yellow, sticky when moist, margin inrolled; lower surface of head smooth, pale yellow; stalk 2–6 cm wide and 5–10 mm wide, pale buff to yellow, minutely scaly; spores white in mass, 16–25 × 4–6 µm, narrowly ellipsoid to subfusiform, smooth.

Habitat/Biological Role: Occurring on the ground as solitary fruiting bodies, scattered or found in clusters in broadleaf or conifer forests; fruiting summer to fall. Typically reported to be a decomposer of litter and humus; however, recent evidence suggests this fungus might actually be forming mycorrhizal associations with plants.

Distribution: Widely distributed throughout North America.

Comments: In terms of overall shape, *Leotia lubrica* can resemble a small immature agaric or bolete, but this fungus is actually an ascomycete. The spores are produced on the upper surface of what appears to be the cap, and the lower surface is sterile. *Leotia viscosa* is similar in appearance but has an olive to dark green cap and a yellowish to buff-colored stalk. Some members of the genus *Cudonia* are macroscopically very similar to *L. lubrica*, particularly *C. circinans* and *C. lutea*; however, these species are not as gelatinous, and their spores are much larger (30–45 × 1.8–2.5 µm). The edibility of these species is not known. Occasionally *L. lubrica* is parasitized by *Hypomyces leotiicola*, a white mold-like fungus.

Microglossum rufum
(Schweinitz) Underwood

ORANGE EARTH TONGUE

FAMILY Geoglossaceae

Club- to paddle-shaped structure, up to 6 cm tall, stalk 1.5–5 mm wide at the base and abruptly enlarging in the uppermost portion to 3–16 mm wide to form a paddle-shaped head, sometimes with a central fold; upper fertile portion smooth and dark vibrant yellow; lower sterile stalk similar or paler in color and surface covered in pale yellow granules; spores colorless in mass, 18–38 × 4–6 µm, curved and sausage-shaped but sometimes tapering in the middle, smooth when young, forming crosswalls (usually five to ten) with age.

Habitat/Biological Role: Occurring as solitary fruiting bodies or in small groups on well-decomposed wood, frequently found among mosses; fruiting summer and fall. Believed to be a decomposer of organic material.

Distribution: Widely distributed in North America.

Comments: Its bright yellow color makes this one of the most striking species of earth tongues, and it is common in our region. *Microglossum longisporum* can appear similar but has fruiting bodies that are brown. *Microglossum fumosum* is similar but is found only in the northern edge of our region or at high elevations, and its fruiting bodies are smoky yellow in color and typically have a stalk that is substantially darker in color than the fertile surface. *Microglossum olivaceum* is another similar species, but it is very rare in our region and would likely be encountered only at high elevations; it differs in being duller in color, lacks granules on stalk, and has smaller spores (12–18 × 4–6 µm). *Microglossum rufum* should also be compared with species in *Spathulariopsis* and *Spathularia*. None of these species are known to be edible.

Mitrula elegans (Berkeley) Fries

SWAMP BEACON

FAMILY Sclerotiniaceae

Club-shaped structure, 20–50 mm tall, upper portion club-shaped, 3–10 mm wide and 5–15 mm tall, elliptical to pear-shaped sometimes elongated; surface smooth or slightly wrinkled, shiny, clear yellow to pale orange; lower portion (stalk) 10–40 mm tall and 1.5–5 mm wide, expanding slightly downward, white to pink-tinted, smooth, translucent; spores hyaline in mass, 11–17.5 × 2–3 µm, narrowly elliptical to somewhat cylindrical, smooth.

Habitat/Biological Role: Occurring on decomposing twigs, leaves, and other types of plant debris in shallow standing or slowly flowing water at the edges of bogs, springs, seeps, and temporary pools, sometimes scattered but often occurring in small groups; fruiting from late spring to midsummer. Decomposer of plant debris.

Distribution: Widely distributed in North America.

Comments: The fruiting bodies of *Mitrula elegans* occur in the water and somewhat resemble small yellow matchsticks. Some North American field guides list this species as *M. paludosa*, which is now believed to occur only in Europe and northeastern Canada. *Mitrula lunulatospora* is reported from some localities in eastern North America, but it is infrequently encountered, differs in being paler yellow to pinkish in color, and its spores typically have a gelatinous sheath. *Vibrissea truncorum* is similar but smaller; it is found only in small high-elevation mountain streams, has a more capitate head and longer spores (120–250 ×1–1.5 µm), and is generally fully submerged under water on decomposing branches.

Neolecta irregularis (Peck) Korf & J. K. Rogers

IRREGULAR EARTH TONGUE

SYNONYM *Mitrula irregularis*

FAMILY Neolectaceae

Irregular club-like to fan-shaped structure up to 6 cm long and up to 2.5 cm wide, often contorted or seeming deformed, sometimes irregularly lobed, having longitudinal ridges; the fertile surface located on the upper two-thirds of the fruiting body, tapering downward below the fertile zone to form a stalk; fertile surface smooth (not bumpy from perithecia), pale yellow to bright yellow; stalk smooth, whitish to pale yellow; spores hyaline in mass, 5.5–10 × 3.5–5 µm, elliptical to broadly kidney-shaped, smooth, nonamyloid.

Habitat/Biological Role: Occurring as solitary fruiting bodies or in clusters under conifers; fruiting summer to fall. It is unclear if this fungus is parasitic, saprotrophic, or mycorrhizal—or involved in some combination of these biological relationships.

Distribution: Infrequent south of the Carolinas but very common in other portions of the East and found throughout North America.

Comments: *Neolecta irregularis* is an unusual fungus that is believed to be a living relic more closely related to the ancestors of many modern ascomycete fungi than it is to current taxa. *Neolecta vitellina* is the most similar species; however, it has a more northern distribution and thus is unlikely to be encountered in our region. Moreover, it differs in having regularly club-shaped fruiting bodies that are much narrower and asci that are shorter (53–75 µm) than those found in *N. irregularis*, which are 100–135 µm. *Mitrula elegans* can be similar in appearance but is much smaller, more slender, and occurs on organic material in aquatic or swampy environments. *Microglossum rufum* is yet another similar species, but it differs in having a longer stalk that is yellow, circular rings of granules on the stalk, and much larger (18–38 × 4–6 µm) sausage- to spindle-shaped spores. *Neolecta irregularis* is edible but not recommended.

Spathulariopsis velutipes
(Cooke & Farlow) Maas Geesteranus

VELVET-FOOT FAIRY FAN

SYNONYM *Spathularia velutipes*

FAMILY Cudoniaceae

Fan- to spoon-shaped structure, 1–3 cm wide and 2–5 cm tall; upper portion smooth, frequently with irregular broad lobes, whitish yellow to pale yellow; stalk equal, smooth, sterile, extending upward into the middle of the fertile portion, often with longitudinal indentations or ribs, reddish brown, with a mass of orange mycelia at the base of the stalk and in the surrounding decomposing wood; spores hyaline in mass, 32–43 × 1.5–2.5 µm, thread-like, smooth.

Habitat/Biological Role: Occurring as solitary fruiting bodies or in small groups from very decomposed wood; summer to fall. Decomposer of wood.

Distribution: Widely distributed but found primarily in eastern North America.

Comments: *Spathularia flavida* is the most morphologically similar species in our region, but it has white, not orange, mycelia at the base of the stalk. *Neolecta irregularis* is similar in appearance but more rounded, brilliant yellow in color, and has a white stalk. *Microglossum rufum* is a brighter yellow-orange, more club-shaped, and has a stalk with irregular to ringed granules present. None of these species are eaten.

Trichoglossum hirsutum
(Fries) Boudier

VELVETY EARTH TONGUE

FAMILY Geoglossaceae

Club-shaped structure, 4–8 cm tall, upper fertile portion (head) 10–15 mm long, 4–5 mm wide at the top, and 1.5–3 mm wide near the base, elliptical to elongated oval, often somewhat compressed, hollow, dark brown to black; surface dry and minutely velvety; lower sterile portion (stalk) 3–6 cm long and 2–3 mm wide, densely velvety; spores brown in mass, 100–150 × 6–7 µm, cylindrical or thread-like, smooth.

Habitat/Biological Role: Occurring on well-decomposed wood or on the ground, often among mosses, fruiting bodies solitary or in small groups; fruiting in summer and fall. Decomposer of wood and other types of plant debris.

Distribution: Widely distributed throughout North America.

Comments: Members of the genus *Geoglossum* (e.g., *G. difforme*) are morphologically very similar, but the surface of the fruiting bodies in these species is smooth, not velvety. *Trichoglossum hirsutum* is not the only *Trichoglossum* species found in the Southeast, but the other species can be separated only on the basis of subtle microscopic characters beyond the scope of this field guide.

Xylaria hypoxylon (Linnaeus) Greville

CANDLESNUFF FUNGUS, CARBON ANTLERS

FAMILY Xylariaceae

Slender, erect, more or less cylindrical structure arising from decomposing wood, lower portion more or less rounded and the upper portion often flattened and sometimes branched (antler-like), 3–10 cm long and 0.5–1 cm wide, at first white to gray with a powdery surface and then becoming black with age; stalk not clearly differentiated, but lower portion of the main axis black and hairy; texture of the fruiting body rubbery at first and brittle with age; spores black in mass, 11–14 × 5–6 μm, bean-shaped, smooth.

Habitat/Biological Role: Occurring on decomposing wood of broadleaf trees in broadleaf and mixed broadleaf-conifer forests, fruiting bodies scattered or in dense clusters; fruiting summer and fall, but fruiting bodies linger throughout the year. Decomposer of wood.

Distribution: Widely distributed throughout North America and often very common.

Comments: When immature, fruiting bodies of *Xylaria hypoxylon* are easily spotted because of their white color and a tendency to occur on the upper surface of decomposing logs and branches. The brittle texture and white interior distinguish this fungus from anything else likely to occur in the same ecological situations. Some members of this genus are morphologically similar, but they generally fruit from very specific substrates. Edibility not known.

Xylaria liquidambaris J. D. Rogers, Y. M. Ju & F. San Martín

LIQUIDAMBAR XYLARIA

FAMILY Xylariaceae

Slender, more or less cylindrical but somewhat irregular structure, 3–6 cm tall and 1–3 mm wide, typically unbranched; surface smooth or roughened, at first pale yellow to white but becoming brown to black with age, revealing a white interior when broken; stalk indistinct; spores brown in mass, 10–15 × 4–6.5 µm, elliptical to somewhat crescent-shaped, smooth.

Habitat/Biological Role: Occurring on old, decomposing fruits of sweetgum that have fallen to the forest floor, fruiting bodies solitary or more commonly in groups on a particular fruit; fruiting during spring to fall and sometimes in early winter. Decomposer of sweetgum fruits.

Distribution: Found throughout the Southeast wherever sweetgum occurs.

Comments: The substrate specificity of *Xylaria liquidambaris* makes this fungus exceedingly easy to identify. It can be very common in localities where there are numerous fruits on the forest floor. The mycelia of the fungus often turns the sweet gum fruits blackish in color. Other *Xylaria* species are rather similar but also very host-specific; for example, *X. magnoliae* occurs only on magnolia cones. Edibility not known.

Xylaria magnoliae J. D. Rogers

MAGNOLIA CONE XYLARIA

FAMILY Xylariaceae

Slender, more or less cylindrical but somewhat irregular structure arising from magnolia seed pods, 5–11 cm tall and 2–5 mm wide, occasionally branched; surface smooth or roughened, at first white and then becoming brown to black with age, if broken revealing a white interior; stalk indistinct; spores pale yellow in mass, 11–15 × 3–5 μm, elliptical to somewhat crescent-shaped, smooth.

Habitat/Biological Role: Occurring on old, decomposing magnolia seed pods/ aggregate fruit, especially those from Fraser magnolia, which have fallen to the forest floor, fruiting bodies solitary or more commonly in groups on a particular infructescence; fruiting from late summer to early winter. Decomposer of magnolia cones.

Distribution: Found throughout the Southeast wherever magnolia occurs.

Comments: The substrate specificity of *Xylaria magnoliae* makes this fungus exceedingly easy to identify. It can be abundant in localities where magnolias are common forest trees. *Strobilurus conigenoides* also fruits from magnolia cones, but it is a small basidiomycete mushroom with a white stalk and cap and thus looks nothing like this fungus. Edibility not known.

Xylaria polymorpha (Persoon)
Greville

DEAD MAN'S FINGERS

FAMILY Xylariaceae

Club-like structure, cylindrical to somewhat irregular in shape, 2–10 cm tall and 1–2.5 cm thick, powdery white to dirty white and gray when young but becoming black with age; surface crust-like and often cracked; stalk short, stout, cylindrical; spores dark brown to black in mass, 20–31 × 5–10 μm, widely fusiform, smooth.

Habitat/Biological Role: Occurring on decomposing logs and stumps of broadleaf trees, usually found in clusters, sometimes from roots; fruiting from spring to fall but sometimes persisting into winter. Decomposer of wood.

Distribution: Widely distributed throughout North America.

Comments: *Xylaria polymorpha* is variable in shape and not all fruiting bodies have the finger-like appearance that is the basis of the common name. The epithet *polymorpha* (having many forms) reflects this morphological variability. Many mycologists believe that this species is actually a group or complex of several similar species. When a fruiting body is broken apart, the pure white interior is revealed—a useful identification character. *Xylaria cubensis* and its anamorph, *Xylocoremium flabelliforme*, are very similar, but the latter has much smaller spores (7–13 × 3.5–6 μm). Medicinal compounds found in *Xylaria* have shown promise in clinical trials with insomnia patients.

Xylaria tentaculata Berkeley & Broome

FAIRY SPARKLERS

FAMILY Xylariaceae

Series of radiating (essentially stellate), elongated rod- or filament-like elements arising from an erect stalk; the latter 1.6–2.5 cm long and 1.5–3 mm wide, nearly equal to sometimes irregular and twisted, black at base; surface of radiating portion scurfy, gray to blackish; radiating elements often about eight but sometimes more, 1.3–4 cm long and up to 0.75 mm wide, more or less cylindrical but narrowing toward the tip and sometimes branching, pale gray to pinkish gray; surface becoming powdery with age; spores dark brown in mass, 19–22 × 7.5–9 μm, usually somewhat crescent-shaped, smooth, containing two prominent oil droplets.

Habitat/Biological Role: Occurring on the forest floor, where the fruiting bodies are associated with humus and decomposing woody plant debris in broadleaf and mixed broadleaf-conifer forests, fruiting bodies solitary to scattered or in small groups; fruiting summer and fall but sometimes persisting until winter. Decomposer of humus and wood.

Distribution: Most common in the Southeast but widely distributed in eastern North America.

Comments: The fruiting body of *Xylaria tentaculata* is tentacle-like, as the epithet suggests. The biology of the fruiting body of *X. tentaculata* is unusual; asexual spores (conidia) are produced on the radiating "tentacles," and then these structures fall off and sexual spores (ascospores) are produced inside of a "head" at the stalk apex. This fungus is very common in our region, but it is often missed because of its small size. Its edibility is not known.

Xylocoremium flabelliforme
(Schweinitz) J. D. Rogers

POWDERY XYLARIA

FAMILY Xylariaceae

Dendroid to somewhat brain-shaped structure arising from a narrow black stalk, up to 4 cm high, the upper portion whitish to pinkish, generally covered in powdery spores that disperse into the air if brushed; conidia white to pale pinkish in mass, 3–7 × 1.5–4 µm, obovate to elliptical, smooth; the preceding represents the asexual (anamorphic) stage of this fungus; the sexual (teleomorphic) stage, *Xylaria cubensis*, is club-like in shape, 2–8 cm long and 2–20 mm thick, with a surface roughened from the presence of numerous flask-shaped perithecia; generally smooth at the base where a stalk is sometimes present, overall brownish in color when young but becoming black with age; ascospores brownish in mass, 7–13 × 3.5–6 µm, elliptical to somewhat irregular, smooth.

Habitat/Biological Role: Occurring in clusters on decomposing logs, stumps, and branches of broadleaf trees; fruiting spring to fall but sometimes persisting into winter. Decomposer of wood.

Distribution: Particularly common in the Southeast and East and widely distributed east of the Rocky Mountains.

Comments: In our region, almost nothing else that occurs on wood is similar in appearance to the asexual stage of this fungus. *Xylaria cubensis* resembles many other species in the genus, particularly those in the *X. polymorpha* complex. These species are not known to be edible.

Plant Pathogens

Most species within the great diversity of ascomycete plant pathogens are very small and have little culinary value; however, many cause substantial economic damage to agricultural crops. This field guide covers three likely encountered species. Some Cup Fungi (page 50) are also plant pathogens, as are some rusts and smuts (page 328).

Apiosporina morbosa
(Schweinitz) van Arx

BLACK KNOT, BLACK KNOT OF CHERRY

SYNONYM *Dibotryon morbosum*

FAMILY Venturaceae

Irregular to spindle-shaped structure, 2.5–30 cm across, at first olive-green and corky but soon becoming black with age; surface rough, texture hard and brittle; spores pale yellowish brown in mass, 16–22 × 5–6.5 µm, elliptical, smooth.
    Habitat/Biological Role: Occurring on twigs, branches, and occasionally the trunk of cherry, plum, and apricot trees;

fruiting during summer and fall but can be found throughout the year. This fungus is a pathogen of some trees and shrubs in the family Rosaceae, but it is rarely fatal to the plant.
    Distribution: Widely distributed throughout North America but only where host trees occur.
    Comments: The knot-like infections of this fungus are especially apparent during the winter months, when the host trees are leafless. Black cherry is by far the most common host tree, and it is possible to identify the tree from a considerable distance when this distinctive fungus is present. This fungus is too hard to be of use as a food.

Rhytisma punctatum
(Persoon) Fries

PUNCTATE MAPLE TAR SPOT

FAMILY Rhytismataceae

Appearing as yellow spots up to 3 cm across on the leaves of maple; as the entire leaf yellows and falls from the tree, a circular green zone is retained, with a mass of black dots less than 1 mm broad at the center; spores hyaline in mass, 30–40 × 1.5–2 µm, slender to thread-like, smooth.

Habitat/Biological Role: Occurring as one or more clusters of spots on maple leaves; fruiting bodies becoming readily apparent in the fall. An endophyte of maple.

Distribution: Most frequently encountered in the Appalachian Mountains and widely distributed in North America but only where certain maple species occur.

Comments: This fungus is one member of a large group of black leaf spot fungi. Some mycologists report this species to be primarily associated with big leaf maple, which is restricted to the Pacific Northwest; however, we frequently find what we believe is the same species associated with striped maple in our region. This fungus seems to survive within the leaf for much of the growing season without causing harm and forms fruiting structures only after the leaf becomes senescent, possibly indicating that there may be some type of mutualism or symbiosis involved; and the portion of the leaf where the fruiting structures occur stays green, continuing to photosynthesize for a time after the leaf has fallen. *Rhytisma americanum*, found in the more northern portion of our region, is similar but produces only a single larger (5–12 mm) black spot and has longer spores (50–88 × 1.5–2.5 µm), and the similar *R. salicinum* occurs only on willow leaves. The edibility of all these species is not known, but they are too small to be of interest.

Taphrina robinsoniana
Giesenhagen

EASTERN ALDER TONGUE

FAMILY Taphrinaceae

Tongue-like structures up to 10 mm long and 5 mm wide, arising from the female catkins ("cones") of alder, generally flat and often twisting, typically with a blunt pointed end, at first reddish pink to greenish but eventually becoming brownish black; spores hyaline in mass, 2–6 × 1.5–4 μm, elliptical, smooth.

Habitat/Biological Role: Occurring on the female catkins of species of alder; appearing from summer to fall and sometimes persisting throughout the year. Parasite of alder.

Distribution: Widely distributed in eastern North America.

Comments: In some of the literature, *Taphrina alni* is reported from our region, but this is now believed to be a European name. Several *Taphrina* species are found in North America, and their respective distributions may be based on the distributions of different host species of alder. Some evidence suggests that *T. robinsoniana* is actually a species complex, and multiple species may occur in our region. The edibility of this fungus is not known.

Truffles

This unusual group of globular fungi are typically hypogeous (they fruit below the ground) or sometimes partially emergent. When mature, most species release aromas that are appealing to animals who dig them up, consume them, and then disperse the spores. Many small mammals depend on fungi and particularly the hypogeous species as a major food source. Large animals also opportunistically feed on them. Almost all truffles, both false truffles and true truffles, form important mycorrhizal affiliations with trees. At first these fungi can look like small dull-colored clods of dirt, but when cleaned off or cut open, many of the species are like little geodes, with unique patterns inside. In our region *Elaphomyces* is the most common and diverse genus, with likely more than thirty species in eastern North America. It is common to find piles of powdery *Elaphomyces* spores on stumps or logs where a small rodent ate the outer layer and left the spores behind, like a discarded hickory nut or acorn shell.

The European truffles (*Tuber* spp.), which are found using dogs or pigs, are among the most valuable legal culinary items in the world. Some farms in the Southeast have cultivated these well-known European species, but financially it is one of the highest-risk agricultural businesses. Most species native to the Southeast lack the pungent aromas that make the European species so valuable; however, several native species of *Tuber* may prove to be worthwhile for culinary purposes. The best way to find these fungi is to look for places where small animals have dug; pull back the leaf litter, and often you will find additional fruiting bodies left behind, in close proximity to the original dig. Also see Puffballs, False Truffles, Earthstars, Stinkhorns, and Bird's Nest Fungi (page 337).

Elaphomyces cibulae
Castellano, Trappe & D. Mitchell nom. prov.

CIBULA'S DEER TRUFFLE

FAMILY Elaphomycetaceae

Irregularly globose to oblong or irregularly flattened fruiting body, 0.4–2 cm broad, more or less enclosed in a mass of intermixed off-white hyphae, soil, and roots, hyphae often staining darker in color if bruised or dried and easily removed, revealing a smooth to finely pitted black surface; outer surface up to 2 mm thick, pale bluish to bluish gray if sectioned, sometimes briefly flushing pink and then fading to gray-green to blue; interior at first cottony and white but becoming filled with gray-blue to nearly black, powdery spores with age; spores dark grayish blue to nearly black in mass, 15–17 µm, globose, ornamentation up to 2 µm high, irregularly ridged and composed of patches of rods.

Habitat/Biological Role: Typically hypogeous or partially emergent and reported from a variety of habitats, fruiting bodies typically embedded in a large mass of off-white hyphae; usually fruiting from late spring to late fall. Forms mycorrhizal associations with trees.

Distribution: Apparently found primarily in the Southeast, from North Carolina south to Mississippi, but the exact distribution has yet to be determined.

Comments: This *Elaphomyces* species is unlike the others covered in this field guide because its black outer surface is embedded in a mass of off-white hyphae. *Elaphomyces loebiae* nom. prov. is black, but the surface is nearly smooth, the outer surface is off-white in section, and the spores are larger (21–22 µm). *Elaphomyces mitchelliae* nom. prov. is black but is typically embedded in a sparse mass of yellowish hyphae; it has large irregular warts on the fruiting body surface, and the spores are larger (24–27 µm). *Elaphomyces oreoides* (syn. *E. fallax*) is black, but the surface is completely smooth, there are four distinct surface layers, and the spores are larger (28–30 µm). Most previous publications that included black species of *Elaphomyces* from North America misapplied the European name *E. anthracinus*. These species are too leathery to be of any culinary interest, but they are an important food source for many mammals.

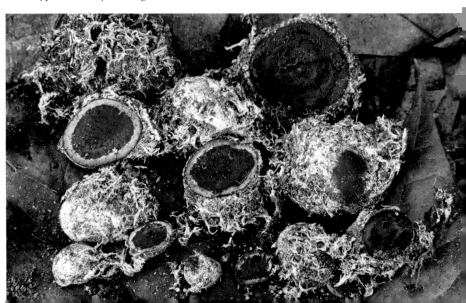

Elaphomyces macrosporus
Castellano & T. F. Elliott

BIG SPORED DEER TRUFFLE

FAMILY Elaphomycetaceae

Irregular to globose fruiting body, 0.5–2 cm broad, outer surface covered by fine irregular warts, warts covered with black hyphae and the yellowish warts beneath are revealed by rubbing the surface (if not rubbed it can falsely appear that the surface is black and rough, not warty); outer layer up to 1 mm thick, pale grayish to nearly white when sectioned, not marbled; interior at first cottony and white and with age becoming filled with black powdery spores; spores dark brown to nearly black in mass, 46–51 µm, globose, ornamentation up to 3 µm tall and composed of cones and ridges.

Habitat/Biological Role: Typically hypogeous or partially emergent and reported only from localities with Canadian hemlock present; usually fruiting from spring to late fall. Forms mycorrhizal associations with trees.

Distribution: In our region, this species seems to be restricted to the Appalachian Mountains; its range may follow that of Canadian hemlock.

Comments: Two morphologically distinct groups of brown *Elaphomyces* species occur in our region: those that in cross section have a marbled peridium, and those, like *E. macrosporus*, with a solid-colored peridium. *Elaphomyces verruculosus* with a solid-colored peridium is common in our region, but it differs from *E. macrosporus* in being paler in color and having smaller spores (36–45 µm). *Elaphomyces spinoreticulatus* could resemble this species, but it is found north of our region and has smaller spores (29–36 µm). There is a group of at least three brown species of *Elaphomyces* found in our region that most distinctly differ in having outer layers that are marbled in section. The most commonly encountered member of this group is *E. americanus*; aside from an outer layer that is marbled in section, it differs in having more prominent warts on its surface and smaller spores (28–34 µm).

Elaphomyces verruculosus
Castellano

LOW WARTED DEER TRUFFLE

FAMILY Elaphomycetaceae

Irregularly globose to irregularly flattened fruiting bodies, 0.5–2.7 cm broad, the outer surface covered by fine, irregular warts, warts sometimes partially obscured by fine hyphae and soil, overall surface pale yellow-brown when young and darkening slightly with age, in section the outer layer up to 2 mm thick, pale grayish to nearly white, not marbled, often grading from off-white to pale brown at the inner margin; interior at first cottony and white but with age filling with black powdery spores, often with well-developed, irregular, brown veins throughout the interior; spores dark brown to nearly black in mass, 36–45 µm, globose, ornamentation up to 3 µm tall, appearing fuzzy or coarse, composed of dense patches of rods.

Habitat/Biological Role: Typically hypogeous or partially emergent and reported from a variety of habitats; usually fruiting from late spring to late fall. Forms mycorrhizal associations with trees.

Distribution: Likely the most widely distributed and most common member of the genus *Elaphomyces* in our region, reported from Canada south to Florida and west to northeastern Mexico.

Comments: *Elaphomyces macrosporus* is similar but seems to be restricted to the Appalachian Mountains northward, and it is easily differentiated by its darker color and larger spores (46–51 µm). *Elaphomyces americanus*, aside from an outer layer that is marbled in section, differs in having more prominent warts on its surface and spores that are smaller (28–34 µm). Most previous publications called all the brown species of *Elaphomyces* from our region by the European names *E. granulatus* or *E. muricatus*, but we now know that these species do not occur in North America. These species are too leathery to be of any culinary interest, but they are an important food source for many mammals.

Imaia gigantea (S. Imai) Trappe & Kovács

APPALACHIAN TRUFFLE

SYNONYM *Terfezia gigantea*

FAMILY Morchellaceae

Irregularly globose structure, 3.5–15 cm broad, outer layer thin (less than 1 mm); surface at first finely warted but the warts becoming more prominent and polygonal with age; surface of some specimens lacking warts and finely scaly to scurfy with age, sometimes the outer surface with deep white polygonal cracks; outer surface layer thin, pale brown to dark brown, subpellis white to off-white; interior white when immature, sometimes slightly gelatinous, interior divided into irregular dark brown sections with age and maturation, these sections separated by an irregular system of white veins and pockets; stalk absent; spores brownish yellow in mass, 32–40 µm, globose or subglobose (37–47 × 30–36 µm), with a thick smooth outer layer around the spore.

Habitat/Biological Role: Hypogeous to partially emergent from soil, fruiting bodies scattered to gregarious in mixed broadleaf-conifer forests, with immature fruiting bodies first appearing in summer and then becoming mature in late fall and into winter. The ecology of this fungus is not known; it is possibly mycorrhizal or saprotrophic.

Distribution: Known only from the Appalachian Mountains from Pennsylvania to North Carolina and Tennessee, and also reported from Japan.

Comments: *Imaia gigantea* is the largest species of truffle we have encountered in our region. In some localities, this fungus can be common; however, its hypogeous to partially emergent fruiting habit causes it to be overlooked in most instances. It can be somewhat similar in appearance to some *Tuber* species, but members of the latter genus found in our region are generally smaller and have spores ornamented with a reticulum or prominent hairs. This fungus is one of the best-tasting of all species of truffles, with a rich earthy flavor that is reminiscent of morels.

Pachyphlodes carneus
(Harkness) Doweld

ORANGE PACHYPHLODES

SYNONYM *Pachyphloeus carneus*

FAMILY Pezizaceae

Irregularly globose to oblong structure up to 2.5 cm broad; surface ornamented with complex polygonal warts, overall surface bright orange-yellow to orangish red, sometimes with bright yellow apparent in pockets on the surface or at the apex of warts; interior firm, at first white but becoming grayish with maturation, irregular white veins frequently scattered throughout the interior; mature spores pale brown in mass, averaging 13–15 µm, globose, ornamented with spines that have an additional outer layer connecting the tips of the spines, sometimes creating a wrinkled surface view.

Habitat/Biological Role: Occurring below the layer of leaf litter on the forest floor or sometimes in the soil, often in small groups or as solitary fruiting bodies; fruiting summer to fall. Thought to be mycorrhizal with trees.

Distribution: Widely distributed in North America.

Comments: The members of the *Pachyphlodes carneus* clade are relatively common in our region although not often collected because of their hypogeous fruiting habit. The concept used herein likely lumps several undescribed species into what is referred to as *P. carneus.* Many species in this genus are found in North America, and only recently has the use of genetic tools made it possible to determine their ranges and identities. Members of the *P. citrinus* group are similar, but their fruiting bodies are typically more greenish to brownish in color. The edibility of these species is not known, but they are too small and lack sufficient fragrance to be of much culinary interest.

Tuber canaliculatum Gilkey

FRAGRANT EASTERN TRUFFLE

FAMILY Tuberaceae

Irregularly globular structure, 2–7 cm wide; surface covered by irregular polygonal to scale-like warts, brown to cinnamon or sometimes more yellowish orange, usually with irregular but prominent cracks or grooves in the outer surface that are paler orange; outer surface thin (less than 1 mm); interior marbled, at first off-white but becoming gray and then dark brown to nearly black with age, filled with irregular white veins; spores dark brown in mass, 48–72 × 40–52 μm, globose to ellipsoid, ornamentation honeycomb-like, with ridges 4–6 μm tall.

Habitat/Biological Role: Occurring under pines or broadleaf trees; usually collected from late summer to late fall, but fruiting bodies can be found at other times of the year. Forms mycorrhizal associations with trees.

Distribution: We frequently encounter it in western North Carolina. Widely distributed in eastern North America from Canada to the Carolinas.

Comments: Most mycologists report this species to be associated with white pine, but we have collected it in predominantly broadleaf forests where white pine was totally absent, and the identity of the truffles in question were verified as *Tuber canaliculatum* by DNA testing. This fungus belongs to the same genus as the famous gourmet truffles native to Europe. Its hypogeous habit makes it difficult to find, and it is likely to be more common than the small number of collections would seem to indicate. The orange cracks in the surface are a relatively reliable way to macroscopically separate this species from other members of the genus in our region. Some esteemed chefs consider this one of the best-tasting native North American truffles; however, in our experience its flavor and aroma are not as potent as those of European *Tuber* species. If you are using this species for food, place thin slices on a hot meal just as it is served, since by fully cooking the fruiting body, most of the flavor is lost.

Tuber lyonii Butters

PECAN TRUFFLE

SYNONYMS *Tuber lyoniae, T. texense*

FAMILY Tuberaceae

Irregularly rounded structure, 1–5 cm wide, unevenly lobed; surface smooth with roughened furrows, dull orangish brown to reddish brown; outer surface thin (less than 1 mm); interior marbled, at first white but becoming brown with age, filled with dense irregular white veins; spores brownish in mass, 30–37 × 22–24 µm, ellipsoid, ornamented with long spines at maturity.

Habitat/Biological Role: Occurring under oaks and pecan trees; usually collected from late summer to late fall, but fruiting bodies can be found at other times of the year. Forms mycorrhizal associations with trees.

Distribution: Most common in the Southeast but widely distributed in eastern North America from Ontario south to northeastern Mexico.

Comments: Although not the only tasty native truffle in the Southeast, this is the only species that has been extensively explored commercially. The market has been established in part because it sometimes fruits very prolifically in pecan orchards. As is the case with all truffles, this fungus has almost no flavor until it is fully mature. At maturity, it has a complex and very pleasing aroma.

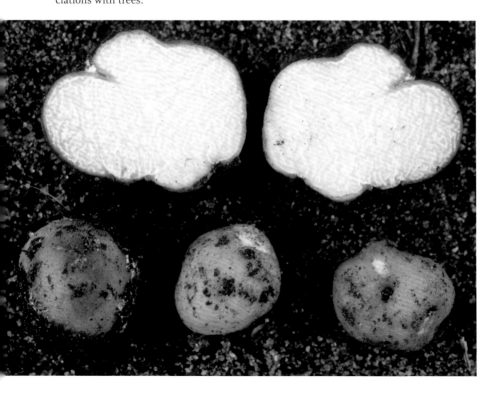

Tuber shearii Harkness

SHEAR'S TRUFFLE

FAMILY Tuberaceae

Irregularly globular structure, 5–20 mm wide; surface smooth to finely roughened, white to pale yellowish, becoming dark brown at maturity; outer layer thin (less than 1.5 mm); interior marbled, at first pale yellowish white but becoming dark brown with age, with a series of irregular white veins winding inward from the outer surface; spores brown in mass, 32–56 × 28–42 µm, broadly elliptical to subglobose, ornamentation honeycomb-like with ridges 3–4 µm tall.

Habitat/Biological Role: Occurring under broadleaf trees or conifers; usually collected from late summer to late fall, but fruiting bodies can be found at other times of the year. Forms mycorrhizal associations with trees.

Distribution: Widely distributed throughout North America.

Comments: Although some authors report it as rare, this is one of the more common *Tuber* species in our region; however, because of the lack of awareness and absence of studies of hypogeous fungi in the Southeast, it is seldom collected, and its below-ground habit makes it difficult to find. The range of the similar *T. mexiusanum* is still being determined, but it has been reported in the Midwest and Mexico and will likely eventually be found in our region; this species is challenging to separate from *T. shearii* but differs in staining olive-green on the outer surface and having slightly smaller spores (20–50 × 16–36 µm). *Tuber shearii* is edible, but as it lacks the strong flavor and aroma of the European truffle, it is of little culinary interest.

Mycoparasites

Members of this group of ascomycetes occur on other fungi, as parasites; this canni-
bal-like behavior, involving two types of fungi, is a fascinating demonstration of the
diversity of ways in which fungi have evolved to survive. Mycoparasites display a wide
diversity of morphologies and colors. The most common genus of mycoparasites in the
Southeast is *Hypomyces*; one of the best edible mushrooms covered in this field guide,
the lobster mushroom (*H. lactifluorum*), contorts the fruiting body of a gilled white
mushroom and turns it lobster red. A couple of small fungi are also featured in this
section, one of which occurs on slime molds, which are not true fungi. Some of the
genera (e.g., *Hypocrea*) include species that are not found on other fungi; these have
been placed in the Wood Mounds section (page 108). To see basidiomycete fungi that
occur on other mushrooms, visit *Asterophora* and *Entoloma* in the Gilled Mushrooms
section (page 114), some of the jelly fungi (page 359), and *Byssomerulius* in the Polypore
and Relatives section (page 289).

Hypocrea latizonata Peck

BIRD'S NEST MOLD

FAMILY Hypocreaceae

Flat cottony band on the outer surface of *Cyathus striatus* (a common bird's nest fungus in our region), 5–8 mm wide, white, often with numerous dark-colored dots (perithecia) present; spores hyaline in mass, 3–4 × 3–3.5 μm, elliptical to subglobose or occasionally cubical, smooth.

Habitat/Biological Role: Occurring in scattered groups on the fruiting bodies of *Cyathus striatus*; fruiting summer to fall. Parasite of at least this one species of bird's nest fungus.

Distribution: Common in eastern North America, wherever *Cyathus striatus* is found, frequently overlooked because of its fruiting habit. The total range has yet to be determined.

Comments: *Hypocrea* is a large and taxonomically complex genus, but thanks to its host specificity, *H. latizonata* is easy to identify. *Hypocrea americana* (syn. *Trichoderma americanum*) and *H. pulvinata* (syn. *T. pulvinatum*) are two others in the genus that are parasitic on other fungi; both are yellowish white and occur on the lower surfaces of polypores. *Hypocrea sulphurea* forms similar crusts but is found only on wood, is yellowish white to bright yellow, and primarily occurs in the northern portion of our region. Many field guides report *H. gelatinosa* as a small yellowish green to olive-green species that occurs on wood in our region, but this is now believed to be a European species. *Hypocrea chromosperma*, *H. chlorospora*, and *H. strictipilosa* are more accurate names to apply to the small yellowish green to olive-green species in our region; they can be reliably separated only with culturing studies, and some mycologist believe all three species should be placed in the genus *Trichoderma*. None of these species are eaten.

Hypomyces chrysospermus
Tulasne

BOLETE MOLD, GOLDEN HYPOMYCES

FAMILY Hypocreaceae

Thin layer of fungal mycelium covering the entire surface of the fruiting body of certain species of boletes and agarics; surface at first appearing moldy and white to yellow in color then darkening to dark reddish brown and developing a finely roughened surface enveloped by small bumps; presence of the fungus distorting the host mushroom; producing three different types of spores: conidia (produced when the mycelium is white) hyaline in mass, 10–30 × 5–12 µm, elliptical, smooth; aleuriospores (produced when mycelium is yellow), yellow to yellow-brown in mass, 10–25 µm, globose, with small rounded vein-like warts; ascospores (produced when the surface becomes roughened with small bumps) hyaline in mass, 22–25

× 4–5 µm, spindle-shaped to unequally septate with the upper cell larger, smooth.

Habitat/Biological Role: Occurring only on the fruiting bodies of certain mushrooms, most often boletes; fruiting from early summer to fall. Parasite of other fungi.

Distribution: Widely distributed throughout North America.

Comments: The yellow to golden yellow color of the mycelium covering the fruiting body of the host mushroom is distinctive. When white or brown it is less frequently noticed. The anamorphic (asexual) stage of this fungus is *Sepedonium chrysospermum*. *Hypomyces chlorinigenus* is one of several similar *Hypomyces* species that parasitize boletes in the Southeast, but it differs in having smaller ascospores (7.5–12 × 2.5–5 µm) and aleuriospores that are pale yellow, longitudinally ridged, and larger (35–45 × 15–18 µm). None of these species that parasitize boletes are considered edible.

Hypomyces hyalinus
(Schweinitz) Tulasne & C. Tulasne

AMANITA MOLD

FAMILY Hypocreaceae

Relatively thick layer of fungal mycelium covering and distorting the fruiting body of certain *Amanita* species, especially *A. rubescens*, surface roughened with a series of small bumps, chalky white to pink-tinged; highly parasitized fruiting body of the host mushroom typically taking the form of a thick, club-shaped structure; spores hyaline in mass, 13–22 × 4.5–6.5 µm, spindle-shaped, two-celled, strongly warted.

Habitat/Biological Role: Occurring only on the fruiting bodies of certain *Amanita* species; fruiting in summer and fall. Parasite of other fungi.

Distribution: Restricted largely to the Appalachian Mountains in our region but found elsewhere if suitable hosts occur; widely distributed in eastern North America.

Comments: *Hypomyces hyalinus* distorts the fruiting body of the host mushroom to such an extent that it is often no longer recognizable as *Amanita*. Since *Amanita* is one of the most toxic mushroom genera, fruiting bodies parasitized by *H. hyalinus* should not be collected for human consumption.

Hypomyces lactifluorum
(Schweinitz) Tulasne

LOBSTER MUSHROOM

FAMILY Hypocreaceae

Thin layer of fungal mycelium covering the entire surface of the fruiting body of certain *Russula* and *Lactarius* species; surface roughened with a series of small bumps, bright orange to orange-red; presence of the fungus distorting the gills of the host mushroom; spores hyaline in mass, 35–50 × 4.5–8 μm, spindle-shaped, with central crosswall, strongly warted.

Habitat/Biological Role: Occurring only on the fruiting bodies of certain mushrooms; we generally encounter this species in pine or hemlock forests; fruiting in summer and fall. Parasite of other fungi.

Distribution: Widely distributed throughout North America.

Comments: Because *Hypomyces lactifluorum* distorts the fruiting body of the host mushroom, it is often not possible to identify the latter; nevertheless, the parasitized mushroom is considered to be a choice edible, and it is also used as a textile dye. Typically, we have observed the host to be various white species of *Russula*. *Hypomyces aurantius* can be similar in color, but it is much rarer and occurs only on polypores and wood-decomposing agarics.

Hypomyces lateritius (Fries)
Tulasne & C. Tulasne

LACTARIUS MOLD

FAMILY Hypocreaceae

Layer of fungal mycelium covering and distorting only the gills of the host *Lactarius* species, the gills essentially are replaced by a firm mass of fungal tissue, at first white to lemon yellow and then becoming yellowish orange or tawny and finally brick red to brown or reddish black; surface roughened with a series of small bumps; spores hyaline in mass, 15–21 × 3.5–5 µm, spindle-shaped, not divided by crosswalls, two-celled, strongly warted.

Habitat/Biological Role: Occurring only on the fruiting bodies of certain *Lactarius* species; fruiting in summer and fall. Parasite of other fungi.

Distribution: Widely distributed throughout North America, wherever suitable hosts occur.

Comments: Unlike some *Hypomyces* species, *H. lateritius* tends to parasitize and distort only the gills of the host mushroom, but the presence of the fungus also affects the rest of the fruiting body. If the pimple-like surface caused by the parasite is not noticed, it can appear as if the mushroom is an agaric without gills or a bolete without pores. *Hypomyces lateritius* is known to exhibit considerable variation in color; this could be due to the wide variety of potential hosts and/or possibly because it is a species complex. The edibility of this fungus is not known. Many other *Hypomyces* species not included in this field guide parasitize mushrooms in our region, but they can be difficult to identify even on the basis of microscopic features.

Hypomyces luteovirens (Fries)
Tulasne & C. Tulasne

GREEN LOBSTER MUSHROOM, RUSSULA MOLD

FAMILY Hypocreaceae

Thin layer of fungal mycelium almost always covering just the gills and upper portion of the stalk of the fruiting body of *Russula* and *Lactarius* species; surface roughened with a series of small bumps, at first yellowish to bright yellow but then becoming yellowish green to dark green and finally blackish green and powdery with age; presence of the fungus somewhat distorting the gills of the host mushroom; spores hyaline in mass, 32–35 × 4.5–5.5 µm, spindle-shaped, not divided by crosswalls, finely warted.

Habitat/Biological Role: Occurring only on the fruiting bodies of certain *Russula* and *Lactarius* species; fruiting in summer and fall. Parasite of other fungi.

Distribution: Widely distributed throughout North America.

Comments: *Hypomyces luteovirens* can be recognized by its yellow-green color and the fact that the portion of the host mushroom affected is limited to the gills and upper portion of the stalk. We most often find it on the gills of *Russula* species that have bright red caps, which often creates a pretty red and green color combination. Mushrooms parasitized by this fungus are not considered to be edible.

Phaeocalicium polyporaeum (Nylander) Tibell

FAIRY PIN, POLYPORE CLUB LICHEN

FAMILY Mycocaliciaceae

Erect to curved structures, 1–5 mm tall and 1 mm or less wide, with a capitate head and arising from the upper surface of small polypores; surface smooth, black; spores pale brown in mass, 11–14 × 3–4 µm, broadly to narrowly ellipsoid, smooth.

Habitat/Biological Role: Occurring in a row on the upper surface of fruiting bodies of the polypore *Trichaptum biforme* or a similar turkey tail fungus; present throughout the year. Ecology not fully understood, but this species may not be a parasite.

Distribution: Widely distributed in eastern North America.

Comments: This fungus is very common but generally overlooked. Most logs that have older fruitings of *Trichaptum biforme* on them will also have this fungus present. *Phaeocalicium polyporaeum* may have a mutualistic association with the algae that grow on the upper surface of *T. biforme*. The habit of occurring on the upper surface of another fungus and the spore size make this species distinctive from other related fungi. *Mycocalicium subtile* is morphologically similar but does not occur on the upper surface of small polypores; instead, it decomposes wood and it has dark brown spores that are smaller (7–8 × 3.5–4 µm). *Chaenotheca brunneola* is also similar but differs in occurring on wood, sometimes with a layer of algae present, and in having smaller spherical spores (3.3–4.6 µm). The edibility of these fungi is not known.

Polycephalomyces tomentosus (Schrader) Seifert

SLIME MOLD PARASITE

FAMILY Clavicipitaceae

Cylindrical, rod-like structure with a rounded head, 0.2–0.3 mm long, white, arising from a white mycelium that covers at least the upper surface of the fruiting body of certain slime molds (myxomycetes); spores (conidia) hyaline in mass, shape either globose (1–2.5 µm) or ellipsoid (1–6 × 1.5–2 µm), smooth.

Habitat/Biological Role: Colonizing the fruiting bodies of slime molds; multiple rod-like structures arising from a single fruiting body; usually fruiting in late summer and fall, but colonized fruiting bodies can persist into winter. Parasite of the fruiting bodies of members of one taxonomic order (the Trichiales) of slime molds.

Distribution: Found throughout the world and present wherever appropriate slime mold hosts occur.

Comments: This fungus is sometimes very common, and large numbers of *Polycephalomyces tomentosus* fruiting bodies can be found if there are prolific fruitings of the host slime mold; however, its small size (the photo includes a pencil eraser for scale) means this species is frequently overlooked. To find it requires careful examination of decomposing logs, stumps, and other substrates suitable for the slime mold host. A few other species in this genus parasitize true fungi, but they are very rare in our region. This fungus is too small to be eaten.

Tolypocladium ophioglossoides (J. F. Gmelin) Quandt, Kepler & Spatafora

ADDER'S TONGUE, GOLDEN-THREAD ELAPHOCORDYCEPS

SYNONYMS *Cordyceps ophioglossoides*, *Elaphocordyceps ophioglossoides*

FAMILY Ophiocordycipitaceae

Club-shaped structure up to 10 cm tall, upper portion (head) 2–3 cm long and 5–15 mm wide, expanded, bumpy, yellowish brown to orange-brown when young but eventually becoming dark brownish black; stalk 2.5–14 cm long and 1.5–10 mm wide, nearly equal, smooth, color varying greatly depending on development, at first bright yellow but darkening to greenish brown and eventually nearly black in age, having bright yellow cords attached at the base of the stalk, these cords varying in length, sometimes up to 8 cm long, cords attached to the *Elaphomyces* host; spores hyaline in mass, partial spores 2–5 × 1.5–2 µm, elliptical, smooth.

Habitat/Biological Role: Occurring as solitary fruiting bodies or more commonly in groups in conifer or broadleaf forests, arising from the fruiting bodies of the hypogeous deer truffle *Elaphomyces*; fruiting from summer to late fall. Parasite of *Elaphomyces*.

Distribution: Widely distributed in North America and common in our region.

Comments: *Tolypocladium capitatum* (syn. *Cordyceps capitata*, *Elaphocordyceps capitata*) is also frequently found in our region, but it differs in having a more pronounced capitate head and a stalk that attaches directly to the *Elaphomyces* host instead of by several cords, the fruiting body is typically paler in color, and the partial spores much larger (8–27 × 1.5–3 µm). *Tolypocladium longisegmentum* (syn. *C. longisegmentis*, *Elaphocordyceps longisegmentis*) is macroscopically identical

to *T. capitatum* but has even larger partial spores (40–65 × 4–5 µm). Some club fungi are similar, but none are associated with truffle hosts. *Tolypocladium ophioglossoides* is not used for food, but it has some promising medicinal properties.

Wood Mounds

This group of fungi is based on a common shape and fruiting habit, and the various species included in this section are not necessarily taxonomically closely related. The species covered are not of any culinary interest, but some have medicinal applications, and all play important roles in the environment.

Camarops petersii (Berkeley & M. A. Curtis) Nannfeldt

DOG'S NOSE FUNGUS

SYNONYMS *Hypoxylon petersii, Peridozylon petersii*

FAMILY Bolinaceae

Broadly turbinate to shallow cup-shaped structure, fleshy to coriaceous, 1–5 cm wide and up to 2 cm thick, at first covered by a membranous layer, the latter varying in color from grayish white to brown to yellowish brown or pinkish, rupturing to expose a shiny black surface covered with pimple-like dots, these representing the openings to the tiny spaces in which the spores are produced; stalk usually absent; spores dark in mass, 6–8 × 3–5 µm, broadly elliptical at one end and broadly fusiform at the other, smooth.

Habitat/Biological Role: Occurring as solitary fruiting bodies or in small clusters on decorticated logs of broadleaf trees, usually oaks; typically fruiting in late summer and fall. Decomposer of wood.

Distribution: Widely distributed throughout North America.

Comments: This is an unusual-looking fungus, and typical fruiting bodies are not likely to be misidentified. Some *Daldinia* species can appear superficially similar, but they differ in being woodier and generally having concentric rings inside.

Daldinia concentrica (Bolton) Cesati & De Notaris

CARBON BALLS, CRAMP BALLS, KING ALFRED'S CAKES

SYNONYM *Hemisphaeria concentrica*

FAMILY Xylariaceae

Globose to somewhat pear-shaped structure, 2–5 cm in diameter, at first grayish white but becoming reddish brown or sometimes dark pink and then black, hard and brittle; surface rough, dotted with minute openings through which the spores are released; interior of the fruiting body with conspicuous concentric bands, purplish black and carbon-like (hence one of the common names); spores black or very dark brown in mass, 12–17 × 6–9 µm, elliptical to fusiform, smooth.

Habitat/Biological Role: Occurring on decomposing wood of dead branches and fallen logs of broadleaf trees, usually found in clusters; fruiting in late summer and early fall. Decomposer of wood.

Distribution: Found throughout North America.

Comments: The concentric rings on the inside of the fruiting body are a valuable diagnostic tool (and the basis of the epithet). Another of the common names, cramp balls, refers to the traditional medicinal use of powder derived from the fungus to alleviate cramps. The fungus can also be used as tinder for flint and steel or as a coal extender. *Daldinia childiae* is similar but typically has a smoother outer surface, is usually smaller in diameter, and has brownish pigments in KOH (*D. concentrica* has purple pigmentation in KOH). Some mycologists believe that *D. concentrica* is a European species, and we have a different species in North America, but this has not been fully resolved.

Hypocrea peltata Berkeley

PINK HYPOCREA

SYNONYM *Trichoderma peltatum*

FAMILY Hypocreaceae

Brain-like structure (or sometimes resembling a wad of used chewing gum), 1–8 × 1–3 cm in total extent, leathery texture; surface smooth, perithecia immersed and densely packed, surface often broadly convoluted, pale tan to whitish or pale pinkish; lower surface smooth to finely wrinkled, often with ridges radiating from the center, similar in general appearance to a gilled mushroom, sometimes having cottony white hyphae present, paler than the upper surface, white to off-white; stalk-like structure sometimes present, up to 5 mm long; spores hyaline in mass, 2–4.5 × 2–5 μm, subglobose, surface with fine spines.

Habitat/Biological Role: Occurring in scattered groups on decomposing stumps and logs of broadleaf trees or occasionally conifers; fruiting summer to fall. Decomposer of organic material or possibly having more complex ecological associations with other species of fungi living in wood.

Distribution: Frequently reported from the southern portion of our region; but we have collected it in northern Georgia and North Carolina, but it is generally reported from farther south. Found primarily in the tropics.

Comments: This unusual fungus, one of the largest *Hypocrea* species in our region, has highly antibiotic and antifungal properties that may have medical applications; it is also sometimes reported to be a problem in the shiitake (*Lentinula edodes*) industry in Japan. The edibility of *Hypocrea peltata* is not known, but as it has reportedly been isolated from a human lung, we advise against consumption. For more about this large and diverse genus, see comments under *H. latizonata* (page 99).

Kretzschmaria deusta
(Hoffmann) P. M. D. Martin

CARBON CUSHION

SYNONYM *Ustulina deusta*

FAMILY Xylariaceae

Irregularly rounded or appressed crust-like structure, 4.5–9 cm wide and 0.8–4 mm thick, sometimes forming an extensive sheet 50 cm or more across, asexual (anamorphic) stage appearing first, powdery mold-like texture, grayish at the center with a white margin; sexual (teleomorphic) stage appearing later, at first soft and white and then becoming brittle and charcoal black; surface sometimes slightly bumpy from the embedded perithecia just under the surface; spores dark brown in mass, 30–35 × 7–11 µm, elliptical to irregular elliptic, often having a flattened side, smooth.

Habitat/Biological Role: Occurring in scattered groups on stumps, roots, or logs of broadleaf trees, sometimes on wood with bark still present and sometimes on decorticated wood; fruiting summer to fall. Decomposer of wood.

Distribution: Widely distributed in North America and very common; we have collected it as far south as southern Florida.

Comments: This strange fungus is very common but often overlooked, thanks to its unusual fruiting habit. Members of the genus *Xylaria* are some of its closest relatives. The edibility of this fungus is not known.

Basidiomycetes

The gilled fungi are the most commonly recognized basidiomycetes, but the group also contains many other forms, each characterized by certain structural features and modes of spore dispersal. Some of the most common non-gilled basidiomycetes are the boletes, puffballs, chanterelles, coral fungi, stinkhorns, polypores, thelephores, and bird's nest fungi. The wide array of fungal shapes and sizes shows the numerous ways in which basidiomycetes have evolved to increase the reproductive surface area of the fruiting body.

The spores of basidiomycetes (basidiospores) develop on the tip of club-shaped cells called basidia. Each basidium typically produces two to four spores, and there are a multitude of basidia in each fruiting body. Even small fungi can produce millions of microscopic spores. Some estimates for spore numbers in large puffballs have been in the trillions! If you take a deep breath, you are almost guaranteed to inhale some fungal spores; but except in rare situations, basidiomycete spores are not harmful to humans. Since spores are typically several micrometers long, identifying some species will require examining the spores under a microscope at a magnification of 1,000×.

In most basidiomycetes an amazing phenomenon, ballistospore discharge, occurs. To understand this unusual dispersal adaptation, imagine the blade-shaped gill of a typical mushroom, its surface covered in the club-like basidia, which themselves are covered in spores. When those spores mature, a microscopic explosion occurs on the surface of the gill; the spores are shot out into the airspace between the gills and ideally are picked up by air currents and dispersed. That microscopic explosion has a gravitational force (G-force) of approximately 10,000—greater than any other known G-force in biology! The G-forces reached by fighter pilots and astronauts wearing G-suits are typically below 10.

The color and shape of individual basidiomycete spores cannot be determined without a microscope. Thankfully, it is easy to see spore color in mass by making a spore print (see page 25), and this is often an important identification character; mushrooms have a diversity of spore colors, including shades of white, yellow, brown, green, pinkish, and black. Making a spore print is not only useful for taxonomic purposes; it is also easy and can be a great art project to do with children and other nature enthusiasts.

KEY TO THE BASIDIOMYCETES

1. Lower surface of the fruiting body composed of gills, folds, ridges, or pores 2
1. Lower surface of the fruiting body smooth, toothed, labyrinth-like or the entire fruiting body amorphous, branching, ball-shaped, club-shaped, bird's-nest-like, star-shaped, jelly-like, or crust-like (not having gills or pores). 4

2. Lower surface composed of gills, folds, or ridges. . . . . ■ **Gilled Mushrooms** (page 114)
2. Lower surface composed of pores 3

3. Fruiting body "mushroom-shaped" with central stalk, fleshy in texture, not occurring on wood. . . . . ■ **Boletes and Relatives** (page 248)
3. Fruiting body occasionally with a central stalk but rubbery, woody, or leathery in texture, typically attached to wood or arising from roots . . . ■ **Polypores and Relatives** (page 289)

4. Fruiting body typically amorphous in form and jelly-like in texture
. . . . **Jelly Fungi** (page 359)
4. Fruiting body with a clearly defined form; lower surface smooth, toothed, labyrinth-like or the entire structure branching, ball-shaped, club-shaped, bird's-nest-like, star-shaped, or crust-like. 5

5. Lower surface of the fruiting body with tooth-like structures present. . . . .
. . . . **Tooth Fungi** (page 366)
5. Lower surface of the fruiting body smooth, labyrinth-like or the entire structure branching, ball-shaped, club-shaped, bird's-nest-like, star-shaped, or crust-like 6

6. Fruiting body ball-shaped, club-shaped, bird's-nest-like, or star-shaped and occurring above or below the ground . . . .
. . . . . **Puffballs, False Truffles, Earthstars, Stinkhorns, and Bird's Nest Fungi** (page 337)
6. Fruiting body branching, crust-like or amorphous; lower surface smooth, labyrinth-like . . . 7

7. Fruiting body branching or coral-like . . . . **Coral Fungi and Relatives** (page 273)
7. Fruiting body crust-like, amorphous, or with a lower fertile surface that is smooth or labyrinth-like, sometimes with a stalk arising from the soil . . . .
. . . . **Crust Fungi, Rusts, and Smuts** (page 328)

Gilled Mushrooms

Typical gilled mushrooms have rounded to flattened caps located at the apex of a stalk, although some species lack stalks or have very short stalks. Most species have stalks that attach at the cap center, but in some species the stalk is eccentric (coming from the side of the cap). The underside of the cap has thin, blade-like gills that typically radiate out from the stalk. Depending on the genus or species, the gills may be attached directly to the top of the stalk, be free from the stalk, or extend some distance down the stalk. Some genera (e.g., *Phylloporus*) are more closely related to the boletes than to other gilled mushrooms, but they have evolved gills and thus are placed in this section based on the fruiting structures and not necessarily their genetic affiliations. The gourmet group of mushrooms known as chanterelles (and their relatives) have also been included in this section even though they have folds or ridges, or are nearly smooth, and do not have true gills.

Some agarics develop fruiting bodies enclosed in universal veils that protect the developing fruiting body. When the cap expands and the stalk elongates, this causes the universal veil to rupture. It often remains as a volva (a cup-like structure at the base of the stalk) and/or as irregular scales on the upper surface of the cap. The presence or absence of a volva and/or scales can be an important character in identification of some agarics. Some gilled mushrooms have partial veils that extend from the margin of the cap to the top of the stalk. As the cap expands, the partial veil separates from the cap margin or stalk in a variety of ways, and the structures left behind are found on the stalk as a cobweb or ring (annulus) or sometimes adhering along the margin of the cap. These different features are important for identification. Gilled mushrooms fulfill a wide variety of ecological roles in forests and other ecosystems, including serving as decomposers, forming mycorrhizal associations with trees, and affecting other organisms as parasites or pathogens. Many agarics are choice edible species, while others are highly toxic.

KEY TO GILLED MUSHROOMS

1. Fruiting body arising from the mineral soil or highly decomposed soil-like organic matter 2
1. Fruiting body arising from leaf litter, twigs, wood, other mushrooms, dung, buried roots, or other non-soil substrates 23

2. Fruiting body fleshy, usually having a fruity aroma, lower surface composed of dull-edged folds or ridges (not true gills) but sometimes nearly smooth, often brightly colored or dark black or brown in color . . . . *Cantharellus, Craterellus, Gloeocantharellus, Gomphus*
2. Fruiting body not as above 3

3. Fruiting body brittle and chalk-like, audibly cracking when broken; either dry or producing latex where damaged. 4
3. Fruiting body not as above 5

4. Fruiting body brittle and audibly cracking when broken; not producing latex where damaged; gills always pale in color . . . . *Russula*

4. Fruiting body brittle and audibly cracking when broken; producing latex where damaged; gills pale or dark in color. . . . . *Lactarius*

5. Fruiting body classic mushroom-shaped, pale-colored gills, broad cap often (but not always) with scales or powder on the upper surface (when scales or powder are present, they are easily removed); often with a cup or bulb at the base of the stalk; an annulus, when present, is single-layered; spores pale-colored in mass . . . .*Amanita*

5. Fruiting body not as above 6

6. Fruiting body with a ring-like or web-like structure near the apex of the stalk (this structure becoming faint with age) 7

6. Fruiting body lacking a ring-like or web-like structure near the apex of the stalk. 13

7. Gills pink when young but becoming brown to black with age (never whitish, rusty brown, reddish, or purplish); stalk always with a prominent cottony ring near the apex; spores black in mass. . . . . *Agaricus*

7. Gills not as above (either whitish, yellowish rusty brown, reddish, or purplish) or if black then there is a frail web-like annulus between the cap margin and the stalk 8

8. Young gills covered from cap margin to near the apex of the stalk by a frail curtain-like structure, gills typically brown or rusty brown with age, in some species at first purplish or reddish in color, but with maturation rusty brown spores are apparent on the gill surface . . . .*Cortinarius*

8. Young gills with no evidence of a frail curtain-like structure present; gills either whitish or blackish 9

9. Gills blackish; fruiting body usually arising from compacted soil; with a fine, veil-like structure extending between the cap margin and the stalk . . . . *Lacrymaria lacrymabunda*

9. Gills not blackish or rusty brown; fruiting body with distinctive ring near the apex of the stalk 10

10. Fruiting body ephemeral, powdery yellow to translucent; a delicate ring present midway up stalk . . . . *Leucocoprinus fragilissimus*

10. Fruiting body fleshy; with two-layered ring present and usually occurring on mulched areas or in grassy habitats 11

11. Fruiting body white to off-white, with a prominent ring present, scaly patches present on the cap surface; spores green in mass. . . . .*Chlorophyllum molybdites*

11. Fruiting body of various colors; spores not green in mass. 12

12. Fruiting body typically occurring in mulched or humus-rich habitats; cap surface with reddish brown scales and a stalk 5–14 cm long; stalk reddish brown in color. . . . .*Leucoagaricus americanus*

12. Fruiting body typically occurring in grassy areas, stalk 15–30 cm long; stalk and cap surface lack any evidence of reddish colorations . . . .*Macrolepiota procera*

13. Fruiting body pale to gray-brown in color and with gray to black gills; some species translucent and ephemeral, turning inky with maturation. 14

13. Fruiting body not as above 15

14. Fruiting body occurring in grassy or disturbed areas, frail, translucent, cap plicate . . . .*Parasola plicatilis*

14. Fruiting body white, brown, or gray on upper surface, sometimes having scales on the cap; gills grayish white when young but becoming black with maturation; entire fruiting body becoming black and slimy at maturity . . . . *Coprinellus, Coprinopsis, Coprinus*

15. Fruiting body waxy in texture; gills broad, often (but not always) brightly colored (not purple or lilac), and spores pale in mass . . . .
. . . . *Cuphophyllus, Hygrocybe, Hymenopellis, Inocephalus, Megacollybia, Neohygrocybe*
15. Fruiting body not as above 16

16. Fruiting body with a fleshy cap, the latter with a reddish surface and broad bright yellow gills . . . . *Phylloporus rhodoxanthus*
16. Fruiting body not as above 17

17. Spores some shade of brown in mass and a cap surface that is radially fibrillose and lacks a web-like curtain near the apex of the stalk . . . . *Inocybe*
17. Spores pale-colored in mass 18

18. Spores white to buff in mass 19
18. Spores pale-colored but more peach to pinkish 22

19. Fruiting body occurring predominantly in the southernmost portion of our region or along the Gulf Coast; white, solid to nearly leathery, with cap 8–100 cm in diameter . . . .
. . . . *Macrocybe titans*
19. Fruiting body not as above 20

20. Gills or the entire fruiting body purplish to lilac . . . . *Laccaria*
20. Gills of the fruiting body white, with a wide range of colors possible for the cap surface . . . .
. . . . 21

21. Base of the stalk bulbous and club-like . . . . *Ampulloclitocybe clavipes*
21. Base of the stalk not as above; gills white or off-white; cap gelatinous or dry, sometimes with radiating fibrils. . . . . *Tricholoma*

22. Fruiting body robust with pale or purplish lilac tones and close gills . . . . *Lepista nuda*
22. Fruiting body often slender, variable in color and sometimes with dark-colored gill edges; in one species the fruiting body can arise from an amorphous off-white structure. . . *Entoloma*

23. Fruiting body arising from another mushroom. . . . . *Asterophora*
23. Fruiting body arising from leaf litter, twigs, wood, dung, buried roots, or other non-soil substrates. 24

24. Fruiting body arising from dung. . . . . *Panaeolus antillarum, Psilocybe cubensis*
24. Fruiting body arising from leaf litter, twigs, wood, buried roots, or other non-soil substrates. 25

25. Fruiting body usually lacking a stalk or the stalk present as a small stub/button and usually emerging from the side of the cap and not at the center; often occurring in clusters 26
25. Fruiting body with a distinct stalk 33

26. Fruiting body woody (similar to that of a polypore) 27
26. Fruiting body fleshy or rubbery. 28

27. Fruiting body pale-colored with distinct zones on the surface of the cap and whitish colored "gills" . . . . *Lenzites betulina* (page 310)
27. Fruiting body with yellowish to dark brown zones on the surface of the cap; gill-like pores pale brown . . . . *Gloeophyllum sepiarium* (page 302)

28. Spores pale, faintly yellowish or white in mass 29
28. Spores brown or reddish in mass. 32

29. Fruiting body fleshy, often occurring in clusters, when stalk is present the gills extend to the base; individual caps 5–20 cm across, with broad white gills on the lower surface and the upper surface of the cap white to off-white . . . . *Pleurotus*

29. Fruiting body not as above 30

30. Stalk short, button-like; gills never becoming decurrent and the stalk never with a veil . . . . *Panellus stipticus, Sarcomyxa serotina*

30. Stalk not as above 31

31. Upper surface of the fruiting body smooth and brownish; gills brownish and covered by a fine veil when young; the latter rupturing when the cap expands, with fragments adhering to the margin . . . . *Tectella patellaris*

31. Upper surface of the fruiting body white with erect or curving fibers, lacking a veil . . . . *Schizophyllum commune*

32. Fruiting body dull yellowish to orange; spores reddish in mass . . . . *Phyllotopsis nidulans*

32. Fruiting body white to off-white . . . . *Crepidotus malachius*

33. Fruiting body with a central stalk and spores that are white in mass 34

33. Fruiting body with central stalk and spores that are pinkish, yellowish, brownish, or blackish in mass 46

34. Fruiting body bright orange and typically occurring in clusters from buried roots or at the base of trees . . . . *Omphalotus illudens*

34. Fruiting body not as above 35

35. Fruiting body brownish to yellowish in color, occurring in clusters either from wood or at the base of trees; usually with a thin curtain-like veil covering the gills when young and then forming ring-like structure in older specimens . . . . *Armillaria*

35. Fruiting body not as above 36

36. Cap translucent striate; fruiting body relatively small, arising from leaf litter, shells of nuts, or wood; cap surface smooth or sometimes viscid but not radially grooved and not having ridges between the gills 37

36. Cap not as above 39

37. Fruiting body of various colors; stalk frail, translucent, and not rubbery . . . . *Mycena*

37. Fruiting body rusty brown to yellowish brown; stalk with fibers present and as dark or darker than the cap, not translucent 38

38. Fruiting body with a cap 1–3 cm broad; occurring in gregarious clusters or troops during the warm months of the year . . . . *Xeromphalina kauffmanii*

38. Fruiting body with a cap that is 2–5 cm broad; sometimes occurring in clusters, fruiting during the cold months of the year . . . . *Flammulina velutipes*

39. Fruiting body relatively small, cap often with radially oriented folds or ridges, usually with a wire-like stalk that is often dark in color . . . . *Marasmius, Marasmiellus*

39. Fruiting body not as above 40

40. Cap of fruiting body covered by layer of erect or curving tufts or scales 41

40. Cap surface smooth and not covered with tufts or scales 43

41. Fruiting body a vibrant yellow to orange . . . . *Cyptotrama asprata*

41. Fruiting body white or brown to yellowish brown, not vibrant in color 42

42. Fruiting body slender, leathery, base of the stalk becoming black (2–10 mm thick), most often found in the southernmost portion of our region. . . . .*Lentinus crinitus*

42. Fruiting body solid, fleshy, and occasionally fruiting from pressure-treated wood or cross-ties, stalk white throughout (10–20 mm thick) . . . . *Neolentinus lepideus*

43. Fruiting body with a brownish cap and broad white gills, often appearing to be arising from soil but in fact having a long radicating root-like structure attached to wood . . . .
. . . .*Hymenopellis*

43. Fruiting body not as above 44

44. Fruiting body arising from large pieces of decomposing wood; white and fleshy with broad gills that are attached and extend a short distance down the stalk. 45

44. Fruiting body arising from leaf litter or small branches less than 5 cm in diameter; gills not attached or if appear to be attached they do not extend down the stalk . . . . *Gymnopus*

45. Fruiting body pale yellow to white; funnel-shaped but margin not inrolled and lacking a veil or veil remnants on the stalk or cap margin, stalk slender. . . . .*Gerronema strombodes*

45. Fruiting body white; stalk dense, prominent; veil or veil remnants present either covering the gills when young or adhering to the margin and stalk with age. . . . .*Pleurotus dryinus*

46. Spores pinkish in mass 47

46. Spores brownish to blackish purple in mass 48

47. Fruiting body with a cap surface which is grayish, pale brownish, brownish yellow, or off-white; gills white to pinkish and the stalk with no cup or ring present . . . . . .*Pluteus cervinus*

47. Fruiting body often arising from a knot or hollow in a tree (or more rarely from woody debris); gills pink at maturity; a large and distinct cup present at the base of the stalk . . . . .
. . . .*Volvariella bombycina*

48. Stalk dark brown, fleshy, and covered by a velvety fuzz . . . . *Tapinella atrotomentosa*

48. Stalk not as above 49

49. Spores purplish brown to blackish brown in mass 50

49. Spores brownish to rusty/yellowish brown in mass 52

50. Fruiting body relatively small, fragile, cap nearly translucent and grayish to grayish brown, typically occurring in large groups . . . . *Coprinellus disseminatus*

50. Fruiting body not as above 51

51. Fruiting body yellowish or pale reddish brown, with gray to smoke-colored gills (white when young), fruiting body typically bitter in taste. . . . . *Hypholoma*

51. Fruiting body typically darker brownish in color, sometimes having radial wrinkles, spores dark. . . . . *Psathyrella delineata*

52. Spores smooth (visible only under a microscope); some species with distinct scaly cap surface. . . . . *Galerina, Pholiota*

52. Spores warted (visible only under microscope) . . . . *Gymnopilus*

Agaricus campestris Linnaeus: Fries

MEADOW MUSHROOM, PINK BOTTOM

FAMILY Agaricaceae

Cap 2.5–10 cm wide, at first white but then becoming light brown, upper surface smooth; gills closely spaced, bright pink when young but becoming chocolate brown with age; stalk white, 25–50 mm long and 10–15 mm thick; annulus white, membranous but often indistinct near stalk apex; spores chocolate brown in mass, 5.5–8 × 4–5 μm, elliptical, smooth.

Habitat/Biological Role: Occurring on the ground in old fields, lawns, and other grassy areas, usually in groups and sometimes forming rings; fruiting in late summer and fall. Decomposer of litter and humus.

Distribution: Found throughout North America.

Comments: This fungus is very similar in appearance to *Agaricus bisporus*, the commercial button mushroom sold in most supermarkets. It is considered a choice edible and widely collected for human consumption. Care should be taken not to confuse *A. campestris* with some poisonous species of *Amanita*, which have light-colored gills and sometimes a volva at the base of the stalk. *Agaricus xanthodermus* and related species can appear similar and are poisonous, but they quickly stain yellow and have unusual chemical-like odors. Since this species commonly fruits in lawns, golf courses, and other grassy areas, care should be taken to ensure the area hasn't been sprayed with lawn care chemicals before specimens are harvested for food.

Agaricus placomyces Peck

WOODLAND PLACOMYCES

FAMILY Agaricaceae

Cap 2.5–9 cm wide, at first narrowly conic but becoming flat with age; surface dry, covered by small to prominent appressed scales, scales gray to brown, generally most dense at the center of the cap and becoming more sparse to absent at the margin; surface of the cap between and under the scales white; gills free, close to crowded, at first white, then pink, and finally dark brown in age; stalk 3.5–10 cm long and 5–10 mm wide, equal to gradually enlarged toward the base, smooth, white, sometimes pale gray above the annulus, base of the stalk sometimes staining yellowish if broken or rubbed; partial veil membranous, cottony, white, sometimes an unbroken veil will have brown droplets or brown stains present; spores dark brown in mass, 4.5–7 × 3.5–5 μm, broadly elliptical to nearly oval, smooth.

Habitat/Biological Role: Occurring on the ground, usually in forested areas and often found in groups; fruiting in late summer and fall. Decomposer of litter and humus.

Distribution: Found throughout eastern North America north of Florida.

Comments: Most woodland species of *Agaricus* are very challenging to identify and mildly poisonous (or their edibility is not known). What is usually referred to as *A. placomyces* likely represents a species complex, the members of which are subtly different and difficult to differentiate even with the use of microscopic characters. *Agaricus pocillator* is very similar and differs primarily in having an abrupt bulb at the base of the stalk, smaller scales on the surface of the cap, and an unpleasant phenol-like odor. *Agaricus subrutilescens* is also very similar, but this species is primarily found in the southernmost portion of our region; its most distinctive character is a green staining reaction on the surface of the cap with the application of KOH.

Amanita bisporigera
G. F. Atkinson

DESTROYING ANGEL

FAMILY Amanitaceae

Cap 5–12.5 cm wide, dull to shiny white, smooth upper surface; gills free, closely spaced, white; stalk 6.5–19 cm long and 5–20 mm thick, enlarged toward the base; annulus present near the top of the stalk, white; volva present at base of the stalk, sac-like, white; spores white in mass, 7–10 × 6–9 μm, globose to subglobose, smooth, amyloid.

Habitat/Biological Role: Occurring on the ground under oaks and other broadleaf trees; usually solitary but sometimes occurring in scattered groups; fruiting primarily in summer. Forms mycorrhizal associations with trees.

Distribution: Found throughout eastern North America.

Comments: This striking fungus, one of about five pure white species of *Amanita* found in our region, is deadly if consumed. These species can be difficult to separate, but none of them should ever be eaten. In general, *A. bisporigera* is found in the summer months and is less robust than the other species. The very similar *A. suballiacea* is primarily found in the southern portion of our region; it differs in having a garlicky odor, a more robust fruiting body, slightly narrower spores, and four sterigmata per basidia (instead of two). *Amanita alliacea* is another white species that smells garlicky, but it has larger spores (13–14.5 × 4–4.5 μm) than either *A. bisporigera* or *A. suballiacea*. *Amanita amerivirosa* is the provisional name for one of two unpublished species in eastern North America that are very similar; however, the distinguishing characters are still being determined and are primarily based on genetic evidence. *Amanita virosa* and *A. verna* are two very similar species included in many American

mushroom books, but recent studies have shown that these species likely do not occur in North America. *Amanita cokeri* and other white warty species of *Amanita* will sometimes lose their warts in wet weather and can be confused with this species; however, the presence or absence of a volva and microscopic characters can help separate these taxa.

Amanita brunnescens
G. F. Atkinson

BROWN AMERICAN STAR-FOOTED AMANITA, BROWN BLUSHER, CLEFT-FOOTED AMANITA

FAMILY Amanitaceae

Cap 6–11 cm wide, at first convex but becoming flat with age, gray-brown to dark brown but sometimes pale yellowish white or with olivaceous or reddish tints, fruiting bodies generally darkest at the center of the cap, sometimes with radial streaks present; surface dull when moist and shiny if dry, sometimes with scattered cottony patches and in other instances patches are absent due to weathering; gills free to nearly free, white, close; stalk 4–15 cm long and 8–20 mm wide, equal to tapering slightly toward the apex, white but sometimes slowly developing brownish to reddish stains near the base; annulus present near the apex of the stalk, skirt-like, thin, frail, sometimes breaking irregularly or sometimes breaking off; stalk smooth above the annulus and finely hairy below, stalk with an abruptly enlarged basal bulb, the latter up to 3 cm broad, with several vertical splits or clefts; flesh reported to smell like potatoes; spores white in mass, 7–9.5 × 7–9 μm, globose to subglobose, smooth, amyloid.

Habitat/Biological Role: Occurring on the ground under oaks and other broadleaf trees or in mixed broadleaf-conifer forests; solitary or in scattered groups; fruiting summer to fall. Forms mycorrhizal associations with trees.

Distribution: Widespread in eastern North America.

Comments: Fruiting bodies of *Amanita brunnescens* are very variable in color, and individuals occurring in close proximity to one another can range from pale yellowish white to brown. There is some skepticism over the validity of the name *A. aestivalis* (sometimes applied to a similar species) because it is remarkably similar to the light-colored *A. brunnescens* var. *pallida*, which itself is recognized by only some mycologists; genetic data is needed to resolve these issues. *Amanita porphyria* is one of the most similar species (currently, this name is applied in both North America and Europe); it differs in having fine, dark-colored longitudinal fibers on the stalk, not having a split/cleft basal bulb, and if remnants of the universal veil are left on cap surface, they exist as broader plaque-like sections. *Amanita submaculata* can appear similar, but it lacks the prominent basal bulb and has an odor that is fruity to anise-like (sometimes with a hint of chlorine), a universal veil that sometimes leaves grayish to brownish remnants on the cap or the margin of veil, and faint floccose remnants of the volva at the base of the stalk. Members of the *A. rubescens* group of species also can appear similar. Because of its olivaceous colors and bulbous base, *A. brunnescens* is sometimes misidentified as the deadly poisonous *A. phalloides*. Its own edibility is controversial, and considering that it belongs to one of the most poisonous groups of mushrooms, we discourage readers from experimenting with it.

Amanita daucipes (Saccardo) Lloyd

CARROT-FOOTED LEPIDELLA

FAMILY Amanitaceae

Cap 6–30 cm wide, at first convex but becoming flat with age, white to dirty beige and often darker toward the center of the cap; surface covered by powdery granules that range from dirty white to reddish brown, portions of the universal veil frequently hang from the margin of freshly expanded caps; gills free, crowded, creamy whitish to faintly yellowish; stalk 8–21 cm long and 8–25 mm wide, equal to slightly tapered toward the apex and with a prominent rooting basal bulb, stalk surface covered with a white to pale pinkish granular powder that is easily removed with handling, occasionally in young specimens there is a very frail, skirt-like ring present near the apex of the stalk but this usually falls to the ground soon after the cap expands, the basal bulb suddenly flaring out and then tapering toward the base, often irregularly radish-shaped, up to 15 cm wide, sometimes with vertical clefts, bulb surface often stains/bruises pale reddish at maturity; odor sweetish, reminiscent of soap, or meat-like; spores white in mass, 8–12 × 5–7 µm, ellipsoid to elongate, smooth, amyloid.

Habitat/Biological Role: Occurring as solitary fruiting bodies or in scattered groups on the ground under oaks and other broadleaf trees or in mixed broadleaf-conifer forests; fruiting summer to fall. Forms mycorrhizal associations with trees.

Distribution: Widespread in eastern North America.

Comments: It can be challenging to distinguish among the several large powdery white species of *Amanita* in our region. *Amanita daucipes* is best differentiated by its distinctive basal bulb, mild odor (not like bleach or chlorine), and the darker coloration of the cap surface and around the basal bulb. *Amanita rhopalopus*, one of the most morphologically

similar species, differs in having a very long rooting or a turnip-shaped base, and the entire mushroom has a pungent chlorine-like odor. *Amanita abrupta* is a mild-smelling white powdery species that is somewhat similar but differs in being smaller in stature and having an abruptly bulbous non-radicating base, a purer white color, a typically thicker skirt-like annulus, and slightly shorter spores (7–9.5 × 5–8.5 μm). *Amanita longipes* can appear similar; however, it is typically much smaller (cap less than 10 cm wide) and has a purer white coloration, much finer granules covering the surface, and larger spores (9–19 × 4–9 μm). *Amanita atkinsoniana* is a very similar species but differs in usually having a very faint chlorine smell and the basal portion of the stalk and upper portion of the bulb have reddish brown rings or scales. *Amanita polypyramis* and *A. chlorinosma* are similar

but differ in being purer white and in having smaller basal bulbs and usually the distinct odor of bleach or chlorine. *Amanita onusta* is superficially similar but has larger gray-colored granules covering the cap surface, similarly colored volval warts densely packed at the apex of the basal bulb, and a chloride-like smell. *Amanita cokeri* is a mild-smelling species that is similar but differs in having more pyramidal warts on the cap surface, more prominent scales that are typically recurved and form rows at the apex of the bulb, and generally a prominent sticky ring. A provisional name, *A. subcokeri*, is applied to what appear to be representatives of a second species formerly lumped with *A. cokeri*; this *A. subcokeri* shares many characters in common with *A. daucipes* but stains pinkish on the upper surface of the bulb. All these large white powdery amanitas are believed to be poisonous.

Amanita flavoconia
G. F. Atkinson

YELLOW PATCHES

FAMILY Amanitaceae

Cap 3–7.5 cm wide, bright yellow to orange and with small bright yellow "patches" (hence the common name) on upper surface; gills free, closely spaced, white or tinged yellow on edges; stalk 4–10 cm long and 5–15 mm wide, noticeably expanded at the base, white to pale yellow; annulus present near top of the stalk, white; powdery volva remnants present at the base of stalk, fragile, yellow; spores white in mass, 7–8 × 4.5–5 µm, ovate to elliptical, smooth, amyloid.

Habitat/Biological Role: Occurring on the ground under hemlocks and in mixed broadleaf forests, particularly those containing oaks; fruiting from midsummer until early fall. Forms mycorrhizal associations with trees.

Distribution: Particularly common in forests of the Appalachian Mountains but found throughout eastern North America.

Comments: Because of its bright color, this fungus is usually easy to spot on the forest floor. The much less common *Amanita frostiana* is very similar in appearance but has a cap with a striate margin. *Amanita flavoconia* is poisonous and should never be collected for human consumption.

Amanita jacksonii Pomerleau

AMERICAN CAESAR'S MUSHROOM

FAMILY Amanitaceae

Cap 5–15 cm wide, convex at first and becoming flat with age, bright red to orange-red at center and becoming yellow at the margin, smooth upper surface, margin striate; gills closely spaced, pale yellow; stalk 6.5–19 cm long and 0.3–2 cm wide, tapering upward, yellow with orange-yellow scale-like patches present; annulus present near stalk apex, yellowish orange; volva present at base of the stalk, sac-like, white; spores white in mass, 7.5–10 × 5.5–7.5 µm, ellipsoid, smooth, nonamyloid.

Habitat/Biological Role: Occurring on the ground in mixed oak or pine forests, often solitary but sometimes very prolific in large scattered groups; fruiting from midsummer to fall. Forms mycorrhizal associations with trees.

Distribution: Widely distributed throughout eastern North America.

Comments: This fungus was once considered to be the same as the European *Amanita caesarea* and is still listed under that name in many field guides. Unlike many other members of the genus, *A. jacksonii* is not poisonous; however, since some similar-looking species are poisonous, it is not recommended for beginning mushroom foragers. Two somewhat similar-looking species, *A. arkansana* and *A. cahokiana*, occur in the western portion of the Southeast. Since *A. cahokiana* is a provisional name, the differentiating characters are still being determined, but *A. arkansana* differs from *A. jacksonii* in having white gills, a pale stalk, and orange-brown cap. *Amanita jacksonii* could also be confused with *A. flavoconia*, *A. parcivolvata*, or some color forms or varieties of *A. muscaria*. A pale specimen of *A. fulva* could appear similar, but this species generally has a duller-colored cap that is grayish orange to brownish orange, lacks a ring, and has slightly larger spores (9–13 × 8.5–12 µm). Some taxonomists who study this genus believe that the *A. jacksonii* found in the Southeast is actually a species complex of multiple very similar taxa; however, this may be sorted out at least to some extent by further study of *A. arkansana* and *A. cahokiana*.

Amanita lavendula (Coker)
Tulloss, K. W. Hughes, Rodríguez Caycedo & Kudzma

COKER'S LAVENDER STAINING AMANITA, CITRON AMANITA

SYNONYM *Amanita citrina* var. *lavendula*

FAMILY Amanitaceae

Cap 5–10 cm wide, lemon yellow to pale yellowish green, upper surface usually with scattered irregular white patches; gills closely spaced, white; stalk 7–12 cm long and 1–1.5 cm thick, enlarged toward the base, white; annulus present near top of the stalk, yellowish white, darkening with age or handling; volva present at the stalk base, usually present only as fragments clinging to base, white to dingy buff; spores white in mass, 6–8 × 5–7 μm, globose, smooth, amyloid.

Habitat/Biological Role: Occurring on the ground in broadleaf or conifer (especially pine) forests, usually solitary but sometimes in scattered groups; fruiting during late summer. Forms mycorrhizal associations with trees.

Distribution: Quite common in some oak or pine forests and found throughout North America.

Comments: Some individuals are light-colored, occasionally nearly white. It is possible that *Amanita lavendula* could be confused with a faded specimen of *A. jacksonii* (not poisonous) or *A. flavoconia* (poisonous). Two other species similar in appearance to *A. lavendula* have yet to be published; they differ slightly from *A. lavendula* in average spore size and other subtle microscopic characters. *Amanita lavendula* is considered poisonous, and the related species are likely also toxic.

Amanita muscaria var. guessowii Veselý

FLY AGARIC

SYNONYM Amanita muscaria var. formosa

FAMILY Amanitaceae

Cap 4.5–20 cm wide, at first conic to convex but becoming flat with age; surface dry to subviscid when moist, pale yellow to orange-yellow, becoming lighter toward the margin, white wart-like patches present on the cap; stalk 7.5–15 cm long and 13–30 mm wide, with an enlarged to roundish base and tapering slightly toward the apex, usually with two or three rings of tissue encircling the top of the base, annulus present near apex of stalk, white, often falling away with age; gills free, crowded, white to pale cream; spores white in mass, 8–12 × 6–8 μm, broadly ellipsoid, nonamyloid.

Habitat/Biological Role: Occurring as solitary fruiting bodies or sometimes in clusters on the ground in conifer forests; fruiting from early summer to early fall. Forms mycorrhizal associations with trees.

Distribution: Widely distributed throughout North America.

Comments: The common name refers to the belief that the caps of this mushroom, when placed in a dish of milk, will attract and stupefy flies. Amanita muscaria is one of the most widely recognized mushrooms, but confusion surrounds just what species are actually present in North America, and nomenclatural changes are, as always, forthcoming. Variety guessowii is only one of several currently recognized color variations. A distinctly red-capped form found in more western regions of North America is generally referred to as A. muscaria var. muscaria; however, this North American taxon is not yet described. The "true" A. muscaria is not likely in North America. In our region A. persicina (syn. A. muscaria var. persicina) is nearly identical, but it has slightly larger spores, more of a peach coloration, and generally fewer ring-like structures on the bulbous base. Amanita muscaria was traditionally used as a psychedelic in some regions of Europe—a very risky practice as the genus Amanita contains deadly toxins. Some mushroom hunters in the United States cook out the toxins and regularly ingest species in the A. muscaria group, avoiding both the toxins and the psychedelic effects. This is a risky practice, particularly for beginning mushroom hunters, and we do not encourage it.

Amanita parcivolvata (Peck)
J. E. Gilbert

FALSE CAESAR'S MUSHROOM

FAMILY Amanitaceae

Cap 3–7 cm wide, at first bell-shaped to convex but becoming flat with age, red to orange-red, sometimes covered with yellow to cream warts and at other times these are completely lacking, margin striate; gills free or nearly free, pale yellow; stalk 4–12 cm long and 3–15 mm thick, tapering slightly upward from a small subglobose basal bulb, typically pale yellow but sometimes nearly white; annulus absent; spores white in mass, 8–10 × 6–8 μm, ellipsoid, nonamyloid.

Habitat/Biological Role: Occurring on the ground under oaks and other broadleaf trees and also in mixed broadleaf-conifer forests; solitary or in scattered groups; fruiting summer to fall. Forms mycorrhizal associations with trees.

Distribution: Especially common in the Southeast and widespread in eastern North America.

Comments: This is one of the more colorful species of *Amanita* commonly encountered in the Southeast. It is suspected to be poisonous. Some red-capped forms of *A. muscaria* are similar, but they have white gills and an annulus. *Amanita jacksonii* is similar; however, it has an annulus and a volva at the base of the stalk.

Amanita polypyramis
(Berkeley & M. A. Curtis) Saccardo

PYRAMIDAL WART CAP

FAMILY Amanitaceae

Cap 7–20 cm wide (but sometimes substantially larger), at first convex but becoming flat with age; surface dry to slightly viscid, in dry weather the cap of mature specimens is covered by powdery conical warts, these easily rubbed off or washed off from rain, chalky white in color, sometimes with veil remnants hanging from the margin; gills free to partially attached, close, cream to white; stalk 10–21 cm long and 1–4 cm wide, more or less equal but tapering slightly upward, dry; surface pulverulent, with scattered to abundant fibrils, white, prominent partial veil usually covering the gills at first and then with an annulus located near the apex of the stalk or breaking into pieces that are scattered on ground at the base of the stalk, base of the stalk ovoid to bulbous, not rooting; often smelling like bleach or chlorine; spores yellowish white in mass, 9–14 × 5.5–8 μm, ellipsoid to elongate, smooth, amyloid.

Habitat/Biological Role: Occurring in scattered groups in broadleaf and mixed broadleaf-conifer forests; fruiting summer to fall. Forms mycorrhizal associations with trees.

Distribution: Widely distributed in eastern North America, particularly in the Southeast.

Comments: *Amanita polypyramis* belongs to a taxonomically challenging group of large powdery white species of *Amanita* that are very common in our region. *Amanita chlorinosma* is very similar and often misidentified; however, it has a less pronounced basal bulb and smaller spores (8–11 × 5.5–6.5 μm). *Amanita abrupta* is similar but has a much smaller cap (5–10 cm) and smaller spores (7–9.5 × 5–8.5 μm). *Amanita ravenelii* could be mistaken for this species; however, it has prominent warts on its cap surface that are usually arranged in concentric zones, it typically develops a pale brownish orange hue, the stalk has a rooting bulb at base, the fruiting body smells like chloride, and the spores are generally smaller (8–11 × 5.5–7.5 μm). *Amanita cokeri* is also very similar but differs primarily in the occurrence of recurved scales along the apex of the rooting bulb and in having a partial veil that usually clings to the stalk near the apex and does not disintegrate like those of similar species; *A. subcokeri* shares many characters in common but stains pinkish on the upper surface of the bulb. *Amanita rhopalopus* is similar but differs in having a very long rooting bulb. *Amanita longipes* can appear similar; however, it is typically much smaller (cap less than 10 cm wide), lacks the bleach or chlorine odor, and has larger spores (9–19 × 4–9 μm). *Amanita daucipes* should be compared but differs in having a larger basal bulb that roots, a darker color, a mild indistinct odor (not like bleach or chlorine), and spores that are white in mass and slightly smaller (8–12 × 5–7 μm). These powdery white species of *Amanita* should not be experimented with for edibility; they are believed to be poisonous.

Amanita rubescens (Persoon ex Fries) S. F. Gray

THE BLUSHER

FAMILY Amanitaceae

Cap 4–20 cm wide, convex to flat, dull reddish brown to bronze-brown, often shaded with buff or gray tones, covered with olive-gray to pink irregular warts, margin faintly striate; gills nearly free, white but developing pink to red stains with age; stalk 8–20 cm long and 5–20 mm wide, tapering upward from an enlarged basal bulb, annulus present near apex of the stalk, white, membranous, fragile, skirt-like; spores white in mass, 7.5–9.5 × 6–7 µm, elliptical, smooth, amyloid.

Habitat/Biological Role: Occurring on the ground under oaks and other broadleaf trees; solitary or in scattered groups; fruiting summer to fall. Forms mycorrhizal associations with trees.

Distribution: Widespread in eastern North America.

Comments: The flesh of this fungus slowly stains red to reddish brown when cut or bruised (hence the common name). This feature, in combination with the cap color, is usually enough to make a correct identification; the discoloration often occurs where invertebrates have damaged the flesh near the base. *Amanita rubescens* var. *alba* is lighter in color. *Amanita flavorubens* (syn. *A. flavorubescens*), one of the most similar species in our region, also stains reddish, but it is has a more yellowish brown coloration, typically stains more slowly, and has slightly longer spores (8–11.5 × 5–8 µm). Comparisons should also be made with *A. brunnescens*, which can appear similar. In North America *Amanita rubescens* has historically been considered edible and relatively distinctive; however, since it is related to some of the most toxic mushrooms, we cannot recommend eating it. What's more, controversy relating to the taxonomy of this species could further impact our understanding of its toxicity. It is now thought unlikely that we have *A. rubescens* in our region or anywhere else in North America. Moreover, genetic evidence shows that this "species" is a complex of approximately six very similar species that have yet to be described. Given the current confusion in this species concept and lack of validly published names, we chose to continue to apply the traditional name *A. rubescens* rather than the provisional name *A. amerirubescens*.

Amanita spreta (Peck) Saccardo

HATED CAESAR, HATED AMANITA

FAMILY Amanitaceae

Cap 5–13 cm wide, at first convex but becoming almost flat with age, margin finely striate, grayish brown and darkest at center; surface smooth, often shiny, sometimes with a few off-white fragments of the universal veil present on surface, slightly sticky when wet; gills free but sometimes almost reaching the stalk, crowded to very crowded, white; stalk 6–18 cm long and 1–2 cm wide, tapering slightly toward the apex, white, smooth to minutely hairy on upper portion and hairs becoming more prominent toward base, hairs sometimes appressed, membranous white to off-white ring near stalk apex, lacking basal bulb but having cup-like volva present, small, white, membranous, persistent, usually closely appressed to the stalk; spores white in mass, 9–14 × 6–8 μm, elongated to cylindrical, nonamyloid.

Habitat/Biological Role: Occurring as solitary fruiting bodies or in small groups on the ground in broadleaf forests (usually with oaks present) or mixed broadleaf-conifer forests; fruiting from mid- to late summer. Forms mycorrhizal associations with trees.

Distribution: Most common in the Southeast but widespread in eastern North America.

Comments: *Amanita spreta* is most similar to *A. phalloides*, one of the most toxic *Amanita* species, which was introduced from Europe and is very infrequent in our region. *Amanita phalloides* differs in having pale greenish colorations on the cap surface, no striations on the cap margin, a more bulbous base, and amyloid spores. The edibility of this species is not known and given its similarity to *A. phalloides*, a mistake could be fatal.

Amanita volvata (Peck) Lloyd

VOLVATE AMANITA, AMERICAN AMIDELLA

FAMILY Amanitaceae

Cap 2–10 cm wide, convex at first and becoming flat with age, margin usually has short striations, surface white to cream-colored, often darkest at center, and bruising reddish brown to brown, occasionally slightly pinkish; surface typically covered by a mat of appressed universal veil fragments that often turn reddish brown quicker than other portions of the fruiting body, surface layer often forms a radial pattern; gills free, crowded, white; stalk 3–10 cm tall and 3–9 mm wide, tapering slightly toward apex, surface floccose-shaggy to powdery, white to cream, bruising reddish brown, no ring present and stalk base is not bulbous; volva present at base of the stalk, thick, membranous, fleshy, cup-like; spores white in mass, 8–13 × 5–8 µm, elliptical, smooth, amyloid.

Habitat/Biological Role: Occurring as solitary fruiting bodies or in small groups on the ground in broadleaf forests (usually with oaks present) or mixed broadleaf-conifer forests; fruiting from midsummer to fall. Forms mycorrhizal associations with trees.

Distribution: Widespread in eastern North America.

Comments: *Amanita volvata* is a distinctive species. It is possible to confuse it with *A. rubescens* and members of its group because both species stain a similar reddish brown, but *A. rubescens* differs in having a ring, lacking a volva, and in having a smooth cap and stalk surface. *Amanita peckiana* is generally similar in appearance but differs in having a pinkish volva, a basal bulb, and longer spores (11–16 × 5–7 µm). *Amanita volvata* is suspected to be poisonous and is similar to species that are highly toxic, so it should not be eaten. There is little doubt that what has been traditionally recognized as *A. volvata* actually consists of a complex of similar species. For the specimens matching this description and found in our region, it may be better to apply the provisional name *A. pseudovolvata*.

Ampulloclitocybe clavipes
(Persoon) Redhead, Lutzoni, Moncalvo & Vilgalys

CLUB-FOOTED CLITOCYBE

SYNONYM *Clitocybe clavipes*

FAMILY Hygrophoraceae

Cap 2–9 cm wide, at first convex to flat but becoming upturned with age, sometimes with a broad central umbo; surface moist, smooth, occasionally with appressed fibrils, olive-brown to grayish brown but sometimes fading to pale grayish, usually paler toward the margin; gills attached and decurrent, close, often forking, at first white but becoming yellowish with age; stalk 2–6 cm long and 4–12 mm thick, usually with a very bulbous to club-shaped base and tapering toward the apex, streaked longitudinally with appressed pale grayish brown fibrils; spores white in mass, 6–10 × 3.5–5 μm, broadly elliptical to oval, smooth, nonamyloid.

Habitat/Biological Role: Usually occurring in abundant clusters in conifer forests but also sometimes associated with broadleaf forests; fruiting summer to fall. Decomposer of organic material.

Distribution: Frequently encountered in the Southeast and widely distributed in North America.

Comments: The thick, meaty cap and the club-like base of the stalk make this species very distinctive. *Clitocybe gibba* is somewhat similar but has more of a vase-like shape, the cap is paler in color, and the stalk is equal instead of club-like. *Clitocybe odora* is similar in stature but has an equal stalk, bluish gray cap, and smells like anise. *Ampulloclitocybe clavipes* is edible; however, there are reports of gastrointestinal issues if it is consumed along with alcohol.

Armillaria gallica Marxmüller & Romagnesi

HONEY MUSHROOM

FAMILY Physalacriaceae

Cap 2–6 cm wide, at first convex to broadly convex but becoming flat with age, dry or sticky, tan to pinkish brown or tawny brown, usually with fine yellowish hairs, often with fragments of the white partial veil attached to the margin; gills extending down the stalk, nearly distant, whitish but sometimes bruising pinkish to brownish; stalk 5–11 cm long and 10–30 mm thick at the apex, whitish, arising from a swollen base that often stains yellow, with a yellow annulus that is web-like; attached at the base to black rhizomorphs; spores white in mass, 7–9.5 × 4.5–6 μm, more or less elliptical, smooth, nonamyloid.

Habitat/Biological Role: Occurring as solitary or more commonly scattered to clustered fruiting bodies on the ground near a tree or stump, sometimes fruiting directly on decomposing wood, usually in broadleaf forests; fruiting late summer to fall and sometimes into winter. Decomposer of wood but also a weak parasite if associated with trees that are still alive.

Distribution: Widely distributed throughout eastern North America.

Comments: All the several species of honey mushrooms were once grouped under a single species, *Armillaria mellea*. Fruiting bodies of *A. gallica* are brown and usually smaller than those of *A. mellea*, and the former seems to be much more common in the Southeast. *Armillaria tabescens*, another similar species, most obviously differs in lacking a ring. All these species are good edibles if thoroughly cooked.

Armillaria mellea (Vahl) P. Kummer

HONEY MUSHROOM, SHOESTRING FUNGUS

SYNONYM *Armillariella mellea*

FAMILY Physalacriaceae

Cap 4–10 cm wide, with a distinct umbo, yellow to honey yellow; upper surface with small, hair-like scales; gills closely spaced, white; stalk 4–14 cm long, 5–20 mm thick, at first white but becoming rusty brown to cinnamon-pink; annulus present near top of the stalk, cottony, white but often with a yellow margin; spores white in mass, 7–9 × 6–7 μm, elliptical, smooth.

Habitat/Biological Role: Commonly occurring in large clusters around the base of living or dead trees and stumps or on the ground arising from roots; fruiting from late summer to fall. Both a decomposer of wood and a pathogen that can kill trees.

Distribution: Found throughout eastern North America.

Comments: *Armillaria mellea* is actually a complex of several southeastern species. This mushroom is considered edible only if it has been very well cooked. One common name refers to the dark, shoestring-like rhizomorphs that can be found beneath the bark of trees or logs upon which it occurs. The mycelium of *A. mellea* is bioluminescent and glows in the dark when moist; other bioluminescent mushrooms found in the Southeast are *Omphalotus illudens* and *Panellus stipticus*. A western North American species of *Armillaria* has been shown to be the largest organism on the planet.

Asterophora lycoperdoides
(Bulliard) Ditmar: Gray

POWDER CAP

SYNONYM *Nyctalis asterophora*

FAMILY Lyophyllaceae

Cap 1–2 cm wide, nearly globose, at first powdery white but becoming brown with age; surface dry, pale buff, sometimes becoming powdery; gills rather poorly developed, adnate, well separated, narrow, at first white but becoming brown-stained with age; stalk 2–3 cm long and 3–8 mm wide, equal throughout, at first white but becoming brown with age; spores white in mass, 5–6 × 3.5–4 µm, oval, smooth, nonamyloid.

Habitat/Biological Role: Occurring on the old, decomposing caps of other mushrooms, usually species of *Lactarius* or *Russula*; typically fruiting during summer and fall when conditions are favorable for mushrooms that serve as its hosts. Parasite of other fungi.

Distribution: Widely distributed in North America but most common in the East.

Comments: Since this unusual fungus is an agaric that parasitizes other fungi, it is unlikely to be misidentified. *Squamanita umbonata* and *S. odorata* are agarics that also grow on other mushrooms, but these are very rare, tend to be very smelly, and have less apparent attachments to the host. *Asterophora parasitica* is somewhat similar, but it is generally much smaller and paler in color. The powdery cap surface of *A. lycoperdoides* is the result of the production of asexual spores (chlamydospores), a most unusual reproductive strategy among agarics; these spores are globose, spiny, and 12–18 µm. The edibility of *A. lycoperdoides* is unknown.

Asterophora parasitica
(Bulliard ex Fries) Singer

SILKY PIGGYBACK

SYNONYM *Nyctalis parasitica*

FAMILY Lyophyllaceae

Cap 5–15 mm wide, at first convex to bell-shaped and then expanding to become flat, at first inrolled, white with grayish lilac tints; surface smooth but covered by smooth fibrils; gills thick, widely spaced, attached to somewhat decurrent; stalk 10–30 mm long and 1–10 mm wide, becoming hollow with age; spores white in mass, 5–5.5 × 3–4 µm, broadly ovate, smooth.

Habitat/Biological Role: Occurring in clusters on the old, decomposing caps of other mushrooms, usually species of *Lactarius* or *Russula*; typically fruiting when conditions are favorable for the hosts. Parasite of other fungi.

Distribution: Widely distributed in North America but never abundant.

Comments: The photo shows this fungus fruiting out of a lobster mushroom (*Hypomyces lactifluorum*). *Asterophora parasitica* has the same reproductive strategy as *A. lycoperdoides*, producing chlamydospores. In this species, these asexual spores are produced on the gills, not on the surface of the cap; they are spindle-shaped, smooth, and 12–16 × 9–11 µm. The two species occur in similar situations, but the fruiting bodies of *A. parasitica* are smaller and lack the powdery surface of the cap found in *A. lycoperdoides*. *Entoloma parasiticum* and *E. pseudoparasiticum* (spores pinkish in mass) are two rare, much smaller fungi that are reported to grow on species of *Cantharellus*, *Coltricia*, *Craterellus*, and *Trametes* in our region. *Squamanita umbonata* and *S. odorata* are agarics that also grow on other mushrooms, but these are very rare, tend to be very smelly, and have less apparent attachments to the host.

Cantharellus appalachiensis
R. H. Petersen

APPALACHIAN CHANTERELLE
FAMILY Cantharellaceae

Cap 1.3–4 cm wide, convex at first and then becoming flat with a central depression or somewhat funnel-shaped, incurved, wavy margin, yellow-brown to yellowish orange, center of cap having a pale to dark brown patch; spore-bearing surface gill-like, with ridged veins, crossveins, or blunt ribs, cream, pale yellow or pale tan; stalk 2–5 cm long and 5–25 mm wide, flaring toward the apex, becoming hollow with age, color similar to that of the cap, base white, smooth; spores white to pale ochraceous salmon in mass, 6–10 × 4–6 μm, elliptical, smooth, nonamyloid.

Habitat/Biological Role: Solitary, scattered, or in clusters of fruiting bodies on the ground under broadleaf trees; typically fruiting during the summer. Forms mycorrhizal associations with trees.

Distribution: Frequently found across the Southeast and widely distributed throughout eastern North America; not restricted to the Appalachian Mountains, as the common name might suggest.

Comments: Having a brown center on the upper surface of the cap makes *Cantharellus appalachiensis* particularly distinctive in its genus. It is a choice edible.

Cantharellus cibarius Fries

GOLDEN CHANTERELLE

FAMILY Cantharellaceae

Cap 2.5–10 cm wide, bright yellow to orange at first, becoming paler with age, upper surface smooth, noticeably depressed in the center; margin recurved at first and then becoming wavy; spore-bearing surface pale orange, consisting of a series of thick ribs or folds with blunt edges, these extending down the stalk; stalk 2–6.5 cm long and 0.3–2.5 cm wide, tapering downward, light to dark orange; spores pale yellow in mass, 8–10 × 4.5–5.5 μm, elliptical, smooth.

Habitat/Biological Role: Occurring on the ground in both broadleaf and conifer forests but especially common under oaks; solitary or in scattered groups; fruiting throughout the summer and into fall. Forms mycorrhizal associations with trees.

Distribution: Widely distributed throughout North America.

Comments: *Cantharellus cibarius* is one of the best-known wild edible mushrooms. The fruiting bodies vary considerably in size, color, and shape. It can be confused with other edible species in the genus such as *C. appalachiensis*, which is smaller and not as brightly colored. Care should be taken to avoid confusing it with *Omphalotus illudens*, a poisonous agaric that occurs on decomposing stumps or roots.

Cantharellus cinnabarinus
(Schweinitz) Schweinitz

CINNABAR-RED CHANTERELLE

FAMILY Cantharellaceae

Cap 1.3–4 cm wide, convex at first but becoming flat to upturned with central depression, bright red to reddish orange, upper surface smooth, margin incurved at first, wavy; spore-bearing surface colored like the cap or paler, consisting of a series of thick ribs or folds with blunt edges, these forked and with crossveins present, extending down the stalk; stalk 1.5–4 cm long and 3–10 mm wide, tapering downward, sometimes curved, dull red; spores pinkish cream in mass, 6–8 × 3.5–5 μm, ellipsoid, smooth.

Habitat/Biological Role: Occurring on the ground in broadleaf and mixed broadleaf-conifer forests; usually scattered or in groups; fruiting throughout the summer and into the fall. Forms mycorrhizal associations with trees.

Distribution: Widely distributed throughout eastern North America.

Comments: Although the fruiting bodies of *Cantharellus cinnabarinus* are relatively small, their color renders them rather conspicuous in nature. As with other chanterelles, appearances can be deceiving unless one takes a closer look: what might seem to be gills beneath the cap are blunt ridges, not true sharp-edged gills. *Cantharellus texensis*, a very similar species described from Texas, has spores that are shorter (8–9 × 3–4 μm). Both are edible and frequently collected by foragers. *Cantharellus coccolobae* is a newly described species from south Florida and the Keys that looks similar but is more pink in color and grows in association with sea grapes (*Coccoloba* spp.). Some species in the genera *Hygrocybe* and *Hygrophorus* can appear somewhat similar, but they all have true gills and a waxy tissue.

Cantharellus ignicolor
R. H. Petersen

FLAME-COLORED CHANTERELLE

FAMILY Cantharellaceae

Cap 1–6 cm wide, convex with a shallow central depression and incurved margin at first but becoming flat with a central perforation and an uplifted, wavy margin with age; surface scurfy with tiny erect fibrous scales when young but becoming almost smooth with age, orange to yellow-orange when young but becoming pale yellow-orange to brownish orange or pale yellow-brown with age; spore-bearing surface slightly decurrent, with blunt gill-like ridges that fork and sometimes form crossveins, orange-yellow but developing a pinkish tinge with maturity; stalk 2–6 cm long and 3–15 mm wide, nearly equal, smooth, orange to yellow-orange or yellow, becoming hollow with age; spores pale ochraceous salmon in mass, 9–13 × 6–9 µm, elliptical, smooth.

Habitat/Biological Role: Occurring on the ground in broadleaf or conifer forests, typically found as scattered or clustered fruiting bodies and often associated with mosses; fruiting from midsummer to fall. Forms mycorrhizal associations with trees.

Distribution: Widely distributed throughout eastern North America.

Comments: Fruiting bodies of *Cantharellus ignicolor* are distinguished by their relatively small size, the fairly well-developed false gills, the bright yellow-orange cap with a central perforation, and the pinkish color of the fertile surface. This species is edible, but it is rarely found in large quantities. *Cantharellus tubaeformis* is most similar, but it is not as bright.

Cantharellus lateritius
(Berkeley) Singer

SMOOTH CHANTERELLE

SYNONYM *Craterellus cantharellus*

FAMILY Cantharellaceae

Cap 2.5–10 cm wide, smooth, funnel-shaped at first and then becoming flattened with a central depression with age, margin inrolled when young, becoming wavy with age, bright orange to yellowish, darkening to blackish with age; spore-bearing surface smooth to finely wrinkled, rarely with veins or crossveins, these extending down the stalk, color similar to the cap or paler; stalk 2.5–10 cm long and 5–25 mm wide, tapering downward, sometimes curving or off-center, color similar to the cap or paler; spores pale pinkish yellow in mass, 7.5–12.5 × 4.5–6.5 μm, elliptical, smooth, nonamyloid.

Habitat/Biological Role: Solitary or in scattered fruitings on the ground, usually under oaks and not uncommon along trails and in parks in urban areas; typically fruiting from midsummer to early fall. Forms mycorrhizal associations with trees.

Distribution: Particularly common in the Southeast and widely distributed in eastern North America.

Comments: *Cantharellus lateritius* usually can be recognized from the smooth to shallowly wrinkled spore-bearing surface. Other species of chanterelles tend to have more clearly formed gill-like ridges. This fungus is regarded as a choice edible. The very similar *C. confluens*, also edible, differs only in forming confluent clusters.

Cantharellus minor Peck

SMALL CHANTERELLE

FAMILY Cantharellaceae

Cap 5–30 mm wide, at first conic to convex with an inrolled margin but becoming flat and deeply depressed with age, margin finally wavy, bright yellow-orange to orange, smooth; spore-bearing surface decurrent, with blunt ridges and veins, orange; stalk 15–40 mm long and 3–7 mm wide, equal, furrowed and often curved, dry, bright yellow similar to cap; spores light yellow in mass, 6–19 × 3–7 μm, elliptical, smooth, nonamyloid.

Habitat/Biological Role: Occurring on the ground in broadleaf or mixed broadleaf-conifer forests; solitary or scattered fruiting bodies that are often associated with mosses; fruiting from midsummer to fall. Forms mycorrhizal associations with trees.

Distribution: Found throughout eastern North America.

Comments: The distinguishing features of *Cantharellus minor* are the relatively small overall size of the fruiting body and the fact that the stalk is much longer than the width of the cap. In fact, until one examines the spore-bearing surface, the general appearance of the fruiting body is that of an agaric, not a chanterelle. This species is considered edible, but its small size is a constraint on collecting enough for a meal. It is possible to confuse this with some of the waxy cap mushrooms. *Hygrocybe chlorophana* is similar but differs in having a sticky stalk, a very viscid cap surface, and whitish yellow gills. *Hygrocybe nitida* is another similar species; however, it has true sharp-edged gills and a waxy texture.

Cantharellus persicinus
R. H. Petersen

PEACH CHANTERELLE, PINK CHANTERELLE

FAMILY Cantharellaceae

Cap 1–4.5 cm wide, at first hemispherical and then becoming convex and finally nearly flat with age, margin inrolled when young and becoming wavy or irregular with age; surface smooth, moist or dry, salmon-orange to pinkish orange, the margin bruising yellowish; spore-bearing surface decurrent, with distant, well-developed gill-like ridges and crossveins, colored like the cap or somewhat paler; stalk 2–5 cm long and 5–15 mm wide, tapering downward to the base, colored like the cap but with a whitish base, bruising yellowish to brownish yellow; spores whitish to pinkish in mass, 7–10 × 4–5 μm, ellipsoid, smooth.

Habitat/Biological Role: Occurring on the ground in broadleaf or mixed broadleaf-conifer forests but usually those with oak or hemlock present, fruiting bodies scattered or occurring in groups; fruiting from early summer to early fall. Forms mycorrhizal associations with trees.

Distribution: Apparently restricted to the northern portion of our region and the Appalachian Mountains, where it is most common at higher elevations, but we have also collected it in the foothills of the Appalachians and in the Piedmont.

Comments: The single most important distinguishing feature of *Cantharellus persicinus* is the peach-like pinkish color of the fruiting body. *Cantharellus cinnabarinus* is morphologically similar but is more reddish orange and smaller/slender. *Cantharellus persicinus* is a choice edible.

Cantharellus tubaeformis
Fries

TRUMPET CHANTERELLE

SYNONYM *Craterellus tubaeformis*

FAMILY Cantharellaceae

Cap 1.5–7 cm wide, convex to flat or depressed, eventually becoming perforated in the center, margin wavy, dark brown to yellow-brown; surface dry, smooth or roughened with small fibrous scales; spore-bearing surface decurrent, with widely spaced and often forked blunt ridges with veins between them, orange-gray to light gray; stalk 15–50 mm long and 3–12 mm wide, equal or somewhat fluted at the apex, yellow-gray to orange-gray or gray, smooth; spores white to buff in mass, 8–12 × 6–8 µm, elliptical, smooth, nonamyloid.

Habitat/Biological Role: Occurring as solitary or scattered fruiting bodies on the ground in conifer forests, usually associated with mosses and sometimes fruiting on well-decomposed, usually moss-covered wood; fruiting from mid-summer until late fall. Forms mycorrhizal associations with trees.

Distribution: More common in the more northern portion of our region and at higher elevations but found throughout eastern North America.

Comments: *Cantharellus tubaeformis* tends to fruit later in the year than most chanterelles. The dark brown to yellow-brown cap and well-developed false gills are major distinguishing features of this species. There has been recent indication that this species in eastern North America might be a complex. *Cantharellus sphaerosporus* is almost identical but has nearly perfectly round spores. *Craterellus pallidipes* has a stalk that is paler and longer; *C. flavobrunneus* has a cap that is yellowish when young but becomes darker brown in age. These species' ranges and differences are poorly understood; however, from a culinary standpoint, these taxonomic subtleties are of little concern. They are all good edibles!

Chlorophyllum molybdites
Massee

GREEN-SPORED LEPIOTA

FAMILY Agaricaceae

Cap 7–30 cm wide, at first rounded but becoming convex to nearly flat with age; surface dry, white, covered with numerous slightly raised scales, the latter buff to cinnamon; gills free, close, broad, at first white but becoming green with age, bruising yellow to brownish; stalk 10–25 cm long and 10–25 mm wide, enlarging toward the base, smooth, white with brownish stains at the base; partial veil thick, white, leaving an annulus with a fringed edge; mature spores green in mass, 8–13 × 6.5–8 μm, elliptical, smooth.

Habitat/Biological Role: Usually in grassy areas on the ground, but sometimes at the forest edge or in mulch piles, solitary or scattered and sometimes forming partial to complete fairy rings or clusters; usually fruiting from midsummer to late fall but occasionally appearing in spring. Decomposer of litter and humus.

Distribution: Found throughout North America.

Comments: In theory, mature fruiting bodies of *Chlorophyllum molybdites* should be easy to identify from the green spores, a most unusual spore color in the agarics. However, this toxic fungus has been involved in numerous poison cases as a result of having been confused with edible species, such as the morphologically similar *C. rachodes*, which has white spores. It is sometimes challenging to obtain a spore print from a young specimen. Also see *Macrolepiota procera*, which shares some similar characters.

Coprinellus disseminatus
(Persoon) J. E. Lange

NON-INKY COPRINUS, LITTLE HELMETS

SYNONYM *Coprinus disseminatus*

FAMILY Psathyrellaceae

Cap 5–20 mm, at first oval but expanding to become broadly convex or bell-shaped with age, deeply pleated, almost white when young and darkening to grayish or grayish brown with age, usually pale brown patch at cap center, paler toward the margin, smooth to minutely hairy when young; gills attached or free, close to almost distant, at first white but then becoming gray and finally blackish but not deliquescing; stalk 15–40 mm long and 1–2 mm wide, equal but often curved, smooth, hollow, white; texture of the fruiting body exceedingly fragile; spores black to blackish brown in mass, 6.5–10 × 4–6 µm, elliptical, smooth.

Habitat/Biological Role: Occurring on various types of woody debris from broadleaf trees, in both forests and in urban areas, fruiting bodies almost always occurring in dense masses; fruiting from late spring until fall. Decomposer of wood.

Distribution: Widely distributed throughout North America.

Comments: *Coprinellus disseminatus* is a fairly distinctive species because it occurs in dense masses on decomposing wood, is very small in size, and does not deliquesce. Though edible, it is so small that it is hardly worth the effort of cooking. *Coprinus floridanus* (known only from Florida) is so similar (aside from its much more restricted range) that it is nearly impossible to differentiate.

Coprinellus micaceus (Bulliard) Vilgalys, Hopple & Jacques Johnson

MICA CAP MUSHROOM

SYNONYM *Coprinus micaceus*

FAMILY Psathyrellaceae

Cap 2–5 cm, reddish brown, oval to bell-shaped; surface covered with fine glistening white particles that disappear with age, margin striate; gills closely spaced, at first white but becoming black and then inky; stalk 2.5–5 mm long and 3–5 mm wide, hollow, fragile, white; spores blackish brown in mass, 7–10 × 3.5–5 µm, elliptical, smooth.

Habitat/Biological Role: Occurring in dense clusters on various types of woody debris, but most commonly found on or around decomposing stumps or standing dead or dying trees; fruiting summer to fall. Decomposer of wood.

Distribution: Widely distributed throughout North America.

Comments: The fruiting bodies of *Coprinellus micaceus* typically occur in dense clusters that are relatively conspicuous. When they are young (and still have white gills) the fruiting bodies of this fungus are edible. *Coprinellus disseminatus* is similar but much smaller, more delicate in stature, and has a cap that is strongly striate to almost translucent.

Coprinopsis atramentaria
(Bulliard) Redhead, Vilgalys & Moncalvo

ALCOHOL INKY

SYNONYM *Coprinus atramentarius*

FAMILY Psathyrellaceae

Cap 3–7 cm wide, at first oval and then becoming bell-shaped to convex, margin pleated; surface dry, smooth, gray to gray-brown; stalk 7.5–15 cm long and 1–2 cm wide, dry, silky to fibrous, white, hollow; gills free, crowded, at first white but becoming black and inky with age; partial veil present, membranous, leaving behind a small fibrous annulus; spores black in mass, 7–11 × 4–6 μm, elliptical, smooth.

Habitat/Biological Role: Often occurring in dense clusters on decomposing wood, sometimes buried in the ground; not uncommon in lawns and urban parks; fruiting summer to late fall. Decomposer of wood.

Distribution: Widely distributed throughout North America.

Comments: This fungus is considered edible by most authors only if not consumed along with alcohol, in order to prevent coprine poisoning, and since this is one of the inky cap mushrooms, it should be collected for the table only when the fruiting bodies are still relatively immature and the gills have not started to deliquesce. We advise against eating this species until more is known about the toxin coprine (see page 22).

Coprinus comatus (O. F. Müller) Persoon

SHAGGY MANE, SHAGGY INKY CAP

FAMILY Agaricaceae

Cap 5–15 cm wide, at first cylindrical but gradually expanding to become conic with a flared margin but almost never becoming flat; surface white with brownish cap center, coated with curled white to pale brownish scales; gills attached when young but becoming free with maturity, crowded, at first white, then pale pink, and eventually slimy black; stalk 7–30 cm long and 1–2.5 cm wide, brittle, enlarged toward the base, base often bulbous; surface smooth, white, sometimes with a frail white partial veil present, the latter leaving a thin annulus on the stalk; spores black in mass, 10–14 × 6–8.5 µm, ellipsoid with a truncate end and an apical pore, smooth.

Habitat/Biological Role: Occurring in scattered groups, generally in piles of wood chips, in gravel parking lots, trail edges or other disturbed habitats; fruiting spring to late fall. Decomposer of organic material.

Distribution: Common in the Southeast and widely distributed worldwide.

Comments: This is a well-known edible species and regarded by many as one of the best. Be sure to collect this species only in areas free of heavy metal toxins: it and several other related species are recognized bioaccumulators. Collect *Coprinus comatus* when it is young if intended for cooking; otherwise, specimens begin to deliquesce. The caps of older specimens begin deliquescing into a slimy black liquid, so ink-like that it can be used for writing and detailed line drawings. *Coprinopsis variegata* (syn. *Coprinus quadrifidus*) is similar but has smaller spores (7.5–10 × 4–5 µm), typically fruits in clusters from decomposing logs or stumps (or sometimes buried wood), and usually has larger, more appressed scales on its cap surface; it is not poisonous but is generally reported to have a poor taste. *Coprinus sterquilinus* is morphologically similar, but fruiting bodies occur on dung or soil with manure mixed in and its spores are larger (16–22 × 10–13 µm). *Coprinus americanus* is a similar fungus found in our region; however, the name has not yet been validly published.

Cortinarius armillatus (Fries)
Fries

BRACELET CORTINARIUS, RED-BANDED CORTINARIUS

FAMILY Cortinariaceae

Cap 5–12 cm wide, at first convex and becoming flat with broad central umbo with age; surface dry, covered by radially appressed hairs, pale yellow-brown to burnt orange to reddish brown, rust-colored veil remnants frequently cling to the cap margin; gills attached, moderately well spaced, at first pale brown but becoming rusty brown with age; stalk 7–15 cm long and 1–3 cm wide, enlarging toward a bulbous base, dull brownish overall, frequently encircled by several appressed zones of reddish cottony tissue, thin rusty brown veil remnants present near the apex of the stalk; spores rusty brown in mass, 7–12 × 5–6.5 µm, elliptical, surface covered by warts, nonamyloid.

Habitat/Biological Role: Usually occurring in groups on the ground in broadleaf and mixed broadleaf-conifer forests; fruiting summer to fall. Forms mycorrhizal associations with trees, particularly birch.

Distribution: In our region found mostly in the Appalachian Mountains but widely distributed in North America, primarily in the eastern portion of the continent.

Comments: The pattern of reddish zones on the stalk is the easiest character to separate this species from others in this large and taxonomically challenging genus; the epithet *armillatus* ("banded") refers to this character. This species is edible but not considered very tasty, and since it belongs to a genus that contains some very toxic species great care should be taken before it is consumed. *Armillaria* can look somewhat similar, but it has white spore prints.

Cortinarius caperatus
(Persoon) Fries

GYPSY

SYNONYM *Rozites caperatus*

FAMILY Cortinariaceae

Cap 5–10 cm wide, at first globose but becoming convex to flat with age; surface covered by fine whitish hair-like fibrils when young, these remaining at the center of the cap into maturity, surface becoming radially wrinkled with age, pale yellowish brown to orange-brown but generally paler toward the margin; gills attached to partially free with age, close, at first dull white but becoming rusty with age; stalk 6–12 cm long and 1–2 cm wide, gradually enlarged toward the base, smooth, off-white, usually with a membranous annulus (unusual for this genus) adhering to the upper portion of the stalk; spores rusty brown to yellowish brown in mass, 11–14 × 7–9 μm, elliptical, surface covered by fine warts, nonamyloid.

Habitat/Biological Role: Occurring as solitary to scattered fruiting bodies on the ground in broadleaf and mixed broadleaf-conifer forests; fruiting summer to fall. Forms mycorrhizal associations with trees.

Distribution: Widely distributed throughout North America.

Comments: The prominent annulus on the stalk of this fungus is not typical for species of *Cortinarius*, which usually have a thin cobweb-like annulus. This feature has in part caused it to be placed in other genera; however, other characters have shown that it belongs in this genus. *Cortinarius caperatus* is a favorite edible of many mushroom hunters.

Cortinarius corrugatus Peck

WRINKLED CORTINARIUS

FAMILY Cortinariaceae

Cap 4–20 cm wide, campanulate to convex when young but becoming broadly convex to almost flat with a low, broad umbo with age, margin uplifted with age; surface viscid when wet, conspicuously wrinkled, tawny ochre to orange-brown or reddish brown; gills adnate to adnexed, close, at first violet but becoming cinnamon-brown; stalk 5–10 cm long and 5–20 mm wide, somewhat enlarged toward the base and terminating in a basal bulb; surface tawny ochre with some brown tints; partial veil web-like, sometimes leaving a thin, viscid annulus; spores rusty brown in mass, 10–13 × 7–9 μm, elliptical, minutely roughened, nonamyloid.

Habitat/Biological Role: Solitary or scattered under broadleaf trees; typically fruiting from early summer to mid-fall. Forms mycorrhizal associations with trees.

Distribution: Widely distributed in eastern North America.

Comments: The prominently wrinkled "corrugated" cap is the main distinguishing feature of this fungus. The dried fruiting bodies of *Cortinarius corrugatus* can produce a beige natural dye. This is a potentially poisonous genus, whose members are notoriously difficult to identify, and we do not recommend eating this species. *Cortinarius olearioides* can appear similar in color but differs in lacking wrinkles and having a much thicker stalk. Also see *Psathyrella delineata*.

Cortinarius iodes Berkeley & M. A. Curtis

VISCID VIOLET CORTINARIUS, SPOTTED CORTINARIUS

FAMILY Cortinariaceae

Cap 2.5–5.5 cm wide, convex to broadly convex with a low umbo; surface viscid to slimy when moist, purple but often with mottled pale yellow to off-white oval spots; gills adnate, close, pale violet; stalk 3.5–8 cm long and 5–20 mm wide, enlarging somewhat toward the base, pale violet to nearly white with age, partial veil web-like, leaving scattered fibrils over the surface of the stalk; spores rust-colored in mass, 8–12 × 5–6.5 μm, elliptical, minutely roughened.

Habitat/Biological Role: Usually occurring in small to sometimes large clusters under broadleaf trees; typically fruiting during late summer to fall. Forms mycorrhizal associations with trees.

Distribution: Most common in the northern portion of our region but widely distributed throughout eastern North America.

Comments: The distinguishing feature of this fungus is the viscid purple cap with the creamy yellow spots. This species is reported by some to be edible, but as a member of this genus, we do not recommend eating it. *Cortinarius iodeoides* is morphologically similar but has slightly smaller fruiting bodies and spores. Interestingly, the slime present on the cap of *C. iodeoides* is said to have a bitter taste, while the slime of *C. iodes* has a mild taste. *Cortinarius collinitus* is likely a species complex, but some members the group are purplish and can appear similar; however, they differ in having a very gelatinous cap surface and a stalk that is covered in slime.

Cortinarius marylandensis
(Ammirati) Ammirati, Niskanen & Liimatainen

RED CORT

FAMILY Cortinariaceae

Cap 1–6 cm wide, at first convex or bell-shaped but becoming broadly bell-shaped to nearly flat with age, dry, finely hairy, bright brick red to brownish red, often fading to pale reddish brown with age; gills attached, close, colored like the cap when young and becoming cinnamon to rusty red with age, in young specimens covered by a partial veil, the latter web-like, pinkish to red; stalk 2–7 cm long and 10–15 mm wide, equal, dry, finely hairy, the upper portion pale reddish and the lower portion colored like the cap, often darker reddish brown at the base or having pinkish mycelium; spores rusty brown in mass, 6.5–9 × 4–5 µm, broadly ellipsoid, slightly roughened.

Habitat/Biological Role: Occurring on the ground in broadleaf forests; fruiting bodies solitary or scattered; fruiting from late summer to fall. Forms mycorrhizal associations with trees, especially oaks and beech.

Distribution: Found in eastern North America and most common in the Southeast.

Comments: *Cortinarius* is an exceedingly large and diverse genus, but the red cap and gills of *C. marylandensis* are distinct. *Cortinarius hesleri* is nearly identical but is usually bright orange (not reddish) and has more prominently ornamented spores. *Cortinarius harrisonii* is similar, but it has yellowish mycelium at the stalk base. The edibility of these species is unknown, and since this genus has some very poisonous members, we discourage readers from eating this species.

Cortinarius violaceus (Fries)
S. F. Gray

VIOLET CORT

FAMILY Cortinariaceae

Cap 4–12 cm wide, convex but becoming broadly convex to nearly flat with age and generally retaining a central umbo; surface dry, covered by a layer of dense hairs, becoming fuzzy or scaly, at first deep purple but becoming brownish purple and eventually dark brown; gills adnate, fairly well separated, at first dark purple but becoming grayish to blackish and then rusty brown with age, covered by a purple web-like partial veil when young, the latter leaving a web-like annulus on the stalk; stalk 6–16 cm long and 1–2 cm wide, enlarging downward to a swollen or club-shaped base, dry, purple and finely hairy when young and then becoming purplish gray to nearly black or brown with age, becoming hollow; spores rusty brown in mass, 12–17 × 8–10 μm, ellipsoid to almond-shaped, finely roughened, nonamyloid.

Habitat/Biological Role: Occurring on the ground as solitary to clustered fruiting bodies in broadleaf or conifer forests; fruiting in the fall. Forms mycorrhizal associations with trees.

Distribution: Widely distributed in North America.

Comments: This species usually can be identified from the uniform dark violet color of the fruiting body; however, recent molecular evidence has shown that this is a complex of several closely related species that can be challenging to separate. For the purposes of this field guide, we are forced to lump them under this name. Other violet-colored species of *Cortinarius* that are not a part of this complex can be distinguished on the basis of macroscopic morphological features; for example, *C. iodes* has a viscid cap, while the cap of *C. violaceus* is dry. *Cortinarius alboviolaceus* is similar, but it has a cap that is silvery lilac instead of dark violet. Some consider *C. violaceus* to be edible, but edibility data concerning all the similar species are insufficient; we therefore advise against eating this species.

Craterellus cinereus Persoon: Fries

BLACK CHANTERELLE

SYNONYM *Cantharellus cinereus*

FAMILY Cantharellaceae

Cap 3–5 cm wide, usually deeply depressed or funnel-shaped but sometimes shallowly depressed, margin wavy; surface smooth or minutely scaly, dry, at first black and then becoming dark grayish brown with age; spore-bearing surface with thick, widely spaced blunt gill-like ridges, these forked near the margin, at first bluish black but becoming bluish gray or dark gray with age; stalk 3–5 cm long and 5–15 mm wide, continuous with the cap but tapering downward, hollow except at the very base, dry, color similar to that of the cap surface; spores white in mass, 8–11 × 5–6 µm, elliptical, smooth.

Habitat/Biological Role: Occurring as scattered fruiting bodies or in small clusters on the ground in broadleaf or mixed broadleaf-conifer forests; fruiting from early summer until fall. Forms mycorrhizal associations with trees.

Distribution: Widely distributed throughout North America.

Comments: The bluish gray color of the spore-bearing surface and well-developed gill-like ridges are the distinguishing features of *Craterellus cinereus*. *Craterellus fallax* is morphologically similar, but the spore-bearing surface is either smooth or the gill-like ridges are poorly developed. The former tends to be the more common of the two species. Both are considered choice edibles.

Craterellus fallax A. H. Smith

BLACK TRUMPET

FAMILY Cantharellaceae

Cap 2–8 cm wide, funnel-shaped and hollow, entire structure 3–14 cm tall, inner surface of the fruiting body pale to dark gray, minutely scaly with blackish-tipped scales over a paler, grayish or grayish brown background color, the margin often black; the outer surface of the fruiting body smooth or very shallowly wrinkled, at first dark gray to black but becoming dull gray with some orange or yellow tints with age, darker toward the base; lacking a distinct stalk but the lowest portion of the fruiting body often hollow and dark brown to black; spores ochraceous orange to ochraceous buff in mass, 10–20 × 7–11 µm, broadly elliptical, smooth, nonamyloid.

Habitat/Biological Role: Occurring as scattered fruiting bodies or often in tightly packed clusters on the ground in broadleaf or conifer forests, commonly associated with mosses; fruiting from midsummer to fall. Forms mycorrhizal associations with trees.

Distribution: Widely distributed throughout North America.

Comments: The shape and color of fruiting bodies of *Craterellus fallax* are distinctive. *Pseudocraterellus calyculus* (syn. *C. calyculus*) is similar but much less common, far smaller (cap up to 1 cm wide), stalk shorter (up to 3 cm long) and solid, and spores are smaller (10–11.5 × 7–8 µm). Although the overall appearance of this fungus might not seem particularly appealing, it is a choice edible. See comments under *C. cinereus* and *C. foetidus*.

Craterellus foetidus
A. H. Smith

FRAGRANT BLACK TRUMPET
FAMILY Cantharellaceae

Cap 3.5–10 cm wide, funnel-shaped, grayish brown with darker fibrous scales present, margin wavy; spore-bearing surface with low ridges and crossveins, the latter decurrent, grayish brown; stalk 28–75 mm long and 10–28 mm wide, thick at the apex and tapering downward, sometimes hollow, fibrous to smooth, grayish buff to grayish brown; spores ochraceous orange to ochraceous buff in mass, 8.5–12 × 5–7 μm, oblong, smooth.

Habitat/Biological Role: Occurring as scattered groups of fruiting bodies on the ground, usually under oaks; typically fruiting from late spring to early fall. Forms mycorrhizal associations with trees.

Distribution: Widely distributed in eastern North America.

Comments: *Pseudocraterellus calyculus* (syn. *Craterellus calyculus*) is similar to this and other species of black trumpets, but it is smaller (caps generally under 1 cm wide), lacks a hole in cap center, and has a lower surface that is smooth to slightly wrinkled. *Craterellus fallax* is very similar, but it has a spore-bearing surface that is nearly smooth and the fruiting body is darker in color. One character that makes *C. foetidus* distinctive from other black trumpets is its tendency to occur in almost cespitose clusters. It is a choice edible.

Craterellus odoratus
(Schweinitz) Fries

FRAGRANT CHANTERELLE

FAMILY Cantharellaceae

Cap 7.5–15 cm wide, funnel-shaped, several fruiting structures attached at base; surface moist or dry, smooth, bright orange at the center and paler toward the margin, margin wavy and lobed; spore-bearing surface smooth or slightly wrinkled, pale orange-yellow to creamy yellow; stalk short but not clearly distinct from the fertile portion of the fruiting body, smooth, hollow; spores pale apricot in mass, 8–12 × 4–6.5 μm, elliptical to narrowly oval, smooth.

Habitat/Biological Role: Occurring as solitary fruiting bodies or in scattered clusters on the ground in broadleaf or conifer forests; fruiting from late spring until mid-fall. Forms mycorrhizal associations with trees.

Distribution: Found throughout eastern North America.

Comments: As its common name suggests, *Craterellus odoratus* is characterized by a strongly fragrant odor. The composite nature of the fruiting body is somewhat reminiscent of a bouquet of flowers, and the bright orange color and cespitose fruiting habit make this an easy fungus to identify. It is edible, although rarely found in sufficient quantities to make a meal.

Crepidotus malachius
(Berkeley & M. A. Curtis) Saccardo

SOFT-SKINNED CREPIDOTUS

FAMILY Inocybaceae

Cap 1–6.5 cm wide, usually more or less kidney-shaped to somewhat petal-shaped, at first convex but becoming nearly flat with age, somewhat depressed where it is attached to the substrate, the base often slightly hairy, white, watery white or grayish white when young and becoming pale buff with age; gills radiating from a basal lateral point, crowded or close, broad, at first white and then becoming rusty brown or brownish ferruginous; stalk lacking but cap sometimes narrowed where it is attached to the substrate to form a stalk-like structure; spores brown in mass, 5–7.5 × 5–7.5 µm, globose or sometimes subovoid, minutely warted.

Habitat/Biological Role: Occurring on broadleaf logs and stumps as solitary fruiting bodies or more often in small clusters and sometimes overlapping; fruiting from late spring to mid-fall. Decomposer of wood.

Distribution: Widely distributed in eastern North America.

Comments: *Crepidotus malachius* is one of several species in the genus found in the Southeast. The fruiting bodies of these fungi are generally small and always occur on decomposing wood. Because the gills are white when young, this species might be confused with some other fungi (e.g., *Pleurotus ostreatus*). Older fruiting bodies, in which the gills have turned brown, are relatively distinctive. *Crepidotus mollis* has fine brown hairs covering the upper surface of the cap.

Cuphophyllus pratensis (Fries) Bon

MEADOW WAXY CAP, SALMON WAXY CAP

SYNONYMS *Camarophyllus pratensis, Hygrocybe pratensis, Hygrophorus pratensis*

FAMILY Hygrophoraceae

Cap 2.5–7.5 cm wide, bell-shaped to broadly convex and becoming flat to slightly upturned with age, usually retaining broad central umbo, cap surface dry, smooth, sometimes cracking in center, pale brownish orange or salmon-orange to tawny but fading to ochre-buff with age; gills shortly decurrent, nearly distant, often having crossveins between gills, similar to or paler than cap surface in color; stalk 2.5–7.5 cm long and 0.5–2 cm wide, tapering downward or equal; surface smooth, similar to gills in color and having white at the base; spores white in mass, 5–8 × 4–5 μm, broadly elliptical to almost round, smooth, nonamyloid.

Habitat/Biological Role: Occurring in clusters on the ground; fruiting spring to fall. Historically thought to be a decomposer of organic material; however, some evidence suggests that the ecology of this fungus may be more complex.

Distribution: Common in the East and Southeast (although not typically encountered in the southern portion of our region), and widely distributed in North America.

Comments: This distinctive fungus is unlikely to be confused with many fungi in our region. A large specimen could possibly resemble a pale chanterelle. *Cuphophyllus borealis* (syn. *Camarophyllus borealis, Hygrocybe borealis, Hygrophorus borealis*) is also found in our region; however, it is bright white. *Cuphophyllus pratensis* is edible.

Cyptotrama asprata (Berkeley) Redhead & Ginns

GOLDEN SCRUFFY COLLYBIA

SYNONYMS *Cyptotrama chrysopepla, Collybia lacunosa*

FAMILY Physalacriaceae

Cap 0.5–2 cm wide, at first convex but becoming broadly convex to nearly flat with age; surface finely granular to covered with tufts and sometimes becoming wrinkled or furrowed with age, dry, at first golden yellow to bright or dull yellow but darkening to brownish yellow with age; gills attached, broad, distant, slightly decurrent, white; stalk 2.5–5 cm long and 1.5–3 mm wide, more or less equal but often with a slight basal swelling, finely granular; color similar to that of the cap or paler; spores white in mass, 7–11 × 6–7 μm, lemon-shaped to broadly oval, smooth, nonamyloid.

Habitat/Biological Role: Occurring on twigs and other types of woody debris in broadleaf or conifer forests, fruiting bodies scattered or in small groups; fruiting in summer. Decomposer of wood.

Distribution: Widely distributed in eastern North America.

Comments: *Cyptotrama asprata* can be recognized on the basis of the yellow color of the fruiting bodies, their occurrence on decomposing wood, and the widely spaced and slightly decurrent gills. The edibility of this species is not known.

Entoloma abortivum (Berkeley & M. A. Curtis) Donk

ABORTED ENTOLOMA, SHRIMP OF THE WOODS

FAMILY Entolomataceae

Cap 5–9 cm wide, at first convex with an inrolled margin and then becoming broadly convex to flat, sometimes with a central umbo; surface fibrous to scaly, gray or grayish brown; gills attached or descending the stalk a short distance, close to crowded, at first pale grayish and then becoming pink as the spores mature; stalk 2–8 cm long and 5–15 mm wide, usually with an enlarged base, solid, smooth or finely hairy, white mycelium often evident at the base; usually numerous convoluted to round white structures scattered on the ground close to fruiting bodies, these structures sterile and 2–10 cm across; spores pink in mass, 8–10 × 4–6 µm, elliptical-angular and usually six-sided.

Habitat/Biological Role: Occurring on the ground in broadleaf forests, usually found near decomposing woody debris associated with species of *Armillaria*; fruiting bodies scattered to clustered; fruiting in late summer to mid-winter. This fungus is believed to be a decomposer of organic matter and is also known to parasitize *Armillaria* species.

Distribution: Widely distributed in eastern North America.

Comments: If the aborted structures of fungal tissue found near the fruiting bodies are sectioned from top to bottom, the outline of a compressed and contorted armillaria can sometimes be seen. This fungus is easy to identify if the aborted structures are present, but it can resemble several other fungi without the presence of these structures. Both forms are edible, but the aborted structures are a favorite edible of many foragers if cooked thoroughly. They can be collected in substantial quantities. The rare and much smaller *Entoloma parasiticum* is reported to grow on species of *Cantharellus, Coltricia, Craterellus,* and *Trametes* in our region.

Entoloma serrulatum (Fries) Hesler

BLUE-TOOTH ENTOLOMA, SAW-GILLED LEPTONIA

SYNONYM *Leptonia serrulata*

FAMILY Entolomataceae

Cap 1–4 cm wide, at first convex but becoming flat to upturned and wavy with age; surface smooth or finely scaly at the center in older specimens, bluish to gray-black or sometimes bluish gray-brown; gills attached to shortly decurrent, close, somewhat broad, at first off-white and then becoming grayish to pinkish, gill edges finely serrated and bluish gray; stalk 3–8 cm long and 1.5–3 mm wide, equal to tapering slightly toward the base, smooth to slightly roughened toward the apex, color similar to the cap surface, usually with a prominent tuft of hyphae at the base; spores salmon-pink in mass, 7–11 × 5–9 µm, broadly elliptical to oval, angular, nonamyloid.

Habitat/Biological Role: Fruiting bodies solitary or occurring in small groups on the ground, in forests or sometimes in grassy areas; fruiting summer to fall. Decomposer of organic material.

Distribution: Most common from the Carolinas northward in our region and widely distributed in North America.

Comments: Some species of *Psilocybe* are similar in appearance, but they have dark spores. The edibility of this fungus is not known.

Flammulina velutipes (Fries) Karsten

WINTER MUSHROOM, VELVET FOOT, ENOKI

SYNONYM *Collybia velutipes*

FAMILY Physalacriaceae

Cap 2–5 cm wide, at first convex but becoming nearly flat with age, orange-brown to reddish yellow, darker at the center; surface slimy to tacky, smooth, margin incurved at first and ultimately becoming striate; gills attached, close, becoming subdecurrent, white to more often yellowish; stalk 2.5–7.5 cm long and 3–7 mm wide, upper portion smooth and yellowish but becoming dark reddish brown and velvety at the base; spores white in mass, 7–9 × 3–6 μm, elliptical, smooth, nonamyloid.

Habitat/Biological Role: Occurring in clusters on logs and stumps of broadleaf trees; typically fruiting during early spring or late fall and sometimes appearing in winter, even in the snow, but rarely in warm weather. Decomposer of wood.

Distribution: Widely distributed in North America.

Comments: This widely known edible is sold in Asian markets as the enoki mushrom. It is grown commercially without light, which is why the cultivated forms of *Flammulina velutipes* are white and look very different from what is found in nature. The fact that fruiting bodies often appear during the winter months is an unusual feature of agarics, making it unlikely this species would be confused with anything else. Care should be taken not to mistake it for the deadly *Galerina marginata*, which can also fruit in the winter. Some promising medicinal compounds have been found in *F. velutipes*.

Galerina marginata (Batsch) Kühner

DEADLY GALERINA

FAMILY Cortinariaceae

Cap 2.5–7 cm wide, at first convex but becoming nearly flat with age, sometimes with a broad umbo; surface smooth and sometimes slightly viscid, dark brown or sometimes dark reddish brown, in dry weather or with age fading to pale brown or yellowish; gills attached to shortly decurrent, close, pale brown to rusty brown; stalk 3–9 cm long and 3–8 mm wide, equal except for a slightly enlarged base, smooth; surface covered by a thin layer of finely appressed fibrils, similar in color to the cap or much darker, sometimes nearly black at the base, typically with an annulus formed from the partial veil near the apex of the stalk; spores rusty brown in mass, 8.5–10.5 × 5–6.5 μm, elliptical, smooth to roughened.

Habitat/Biological Role: Occurring in clusters or larger groups on broadleaf logs and stumps or occasionally from buried wood; fruiting year-round. Decomposer of wood.

Distribution: Common in our region and widely distributed in North America.

Comments: This small unassuming brown mushroom is one of the most poisonous species in our region. It has toxins similar to those found in the genus *Amanita* and can cause severe liver and kidney damage. There is a chance that foragers gathering *Armillaria* species for food could mistake this species as edible; however, members of the genus *Armillaria* have a white spore print. Some species of *Gymnopilus* can be morphologically similar; for example, *G. bellulus* can appear similar but lacks the annulus near the apex of the stalk and the spores are warted and smaller (3.5–5.5 × 2.8–3.5 μm). The edible fungus *Kuehneromyces mutabilis* (syn. *Pholiota mutabilis*) is very similar but differs in being paler in color, often has white fibrils on the margin, and the spores are smaller (5.5–7.5 ×3.5–5 μm). *Flammulina velutipes* should also be compared to this species. In our region, *Galerina marginata* has been incorrectly called *G. autumnalis*.

Gerronema strombodes
(Berkeley & Montagne) Singer

GRAY GERRONEMA
FAMILY Marasmiaceae

Cap 2.5–8 cm wide, at first convex but becoming centrally depressed or saucer-shaped to shallowly vase-shaped with age, gray to gray-brown, sometimes pale yellow; surface smooth but uniformly covered with appressed brown to grayish brown fibers, margin becoming wavy with age; gills decurrent, broad, noticeably distant, yellowish white to pale yellow, some gills not extending all the way to the stalk; stalk 3–6 cm long and 3–10 mm wide, more or less equal, dry, minutely hairy, whitish, yellowish or pale grayish; spores white in mass, 7.5–9 × 3–5 μm, elliptical, smooth, nonamyloid.

Habitat/Biological Role: Occurring on decomposing wood in broadleaf or conifer forests; fruiting bodies solitary or more commonly occurring in clusters; fruiting from late summer to fall. Decomposer of wood.

Distribution: Thought to be restricted to the Southeast.

Comments: Fruiting bodies of *Gerronema strombodes* are somewhat chanterelle-like in overall aspect, but *G. strombodes* has true gills and occurs on wood, which is never the case for chanterelles. Its edibility is not known.

Gloeocantharellus purpurascens (Hesler) Singer

VIOLET-STAINING CHANTERELLE

SYNONYM *Cantharellus purpurascens*

FAMILY Gomphaceae

Cap 6–12 cm wide, flat to concave, dry, yellow-orange to orange-pink, margin thin and at first inrolled, bruising violet to nearly black; spore-bearing surface with gill-like ridges up to 3 mm tall, narrow, decurrent, forking one to three times toward margin; stalk 4–10 cm long and 0.8–2 cm wide, tapering downward and rounded at the base, at first creamy yellow but the color becoming similar to that of the cap with age; spores white in mass, 8–11 × 3.5–5.5 μm, ellipsoid to obovoid, warted.

Habitat/Biological Role: Occurring as solitary fruiting bodies or scattered on the ground in broadleaf or mixed broadleaf-conifer forests; fruiting from early summer to early fall. Forms mycorrhizal associations with trees.

Distribution: Known to occur only in the Southeast; rare to regionally common, apparently limited to the Appalachian Mountains and foothills.

Comments: This fungus could be confused with some species of *Cantharellus* or more likely *Gomphus*; however, members of these genera do not bruise or stain violet to blackish. The edibility of this fungus is not known.

Gomphus floccosus
(Schweinitz) Singer

SCALY VASE CHANTERELLE

FAMILY Gomphaceae

Cap 5–15 cm wide, depressed to funnel- or vase-shaped when mature; surface dry, covered with coarse orange to reddish orange scales, these at first flattened and then becoming erect to even recurved, remainder of cap paler orange; spore-bearing surface decurrent, with narrow, low, blunt ridges that form irregular veins and crossveins, buff to yellow; stalk not clearly distinct from the spore-bearing surface, up to 10 cm long and up to 6 cm wide at the apex, tapering downward to a narrowed base, buff-colored, becoming hollow with age; spores ochraceous in mass, 11.5–17 × 6–8 μm, elliptical, minutely warted, nonamyloid.

Habitat/Biological Role: Occurring on the ground in conifer or mixed broadleaf-conifer forests, sometimes solitary but usually occurring in clusters; fruiting from early summer to fall. Forms mycorrhizal associations with trees.

Distribution: In our region particularly common in the Appalachian Mountains but found throughout North America.

Comments: *Gomphus floccosus* can be recognized from the vase-shaped fruiting body that has a cap with a deep central depression and coarse orange to reddish orange scales. This fungus is eaten by some people, but others have had gastrointestinal issues with it. As such, this species is not recommended for consumption.

Gymnopilus junonius (Fries) P. D. Orton

LAUGHING GYM, LAUGHING CAP, SPECTACULAR RUSTGILL

SYNONYM *Gymnopilus spectabilis*

FAMILY Strophariaceae

Cap 5–18 cm wide, at first convex but becoming nearly flat with age; surface smooth, dry, sometimes superficially cracking and becoming scaly with age, pale orangish yellow to dull yellow in color; gills attached and shortly decurrent, close, dingy yellow to orangish yellow and becoming rusty with age; stalk 3–19 cm long and 1–3 cm wide, equal to enlarged toward the base, the very bottom of the stalk tapered, smooth, similar in color to the surface of the cap, sometimes with whitish streaks extending longitudinally, yellow membranous partial veil near the apex of the stalk; spores orange to rusty orangish brown, 7–10 × 4.5–6 µm, elliptical to broadly elliptical, roughened/warted, nonamyloid.

Habitat/Biological Role: Occurring on decomposing wood or sometimes from buried wood of both conifers and broadleaf trees; fruiting summer to early winter. Decomposer of wood.

Distribution: Widely distributed in North America and particularly common in the East.

Comments: *Gymnopilus junonius* is hallucinogenic to varying degrees, from very potent to producing no effects; this could be explained by misidentifications, since some related species have no detectable hallucinogenic properties. *Gymnopilus luteus* (poisonous to hallucinogenic) is similar and difficult to separate, but this species is generally more slender, paler in color, and its distribution is restricted to decomposing wood from broadleaf trees in eastern North America. *Gymnopilus luteofolius* (poisonous to mildly hallucinogenic) has a similar growth habit but smaller spores (5.5–8.5 × 3.5–4.5 µm) and reddish to purplish appressed scales when young that disappear with age, revealing a pinkish red to yellowish red cap surface. *Gymnopilus junonius* is reported to be extremely bitter and among the connoisseurs of magic mushrooms is generally not eaten by itself. This genus of mushrooms contains compounds that are similar to those found in members of the genus *Psilocybe*. These species are currently illegal in the United States and other parts of the world, so we discourage their use.

Gymnopilus liquiritiae
(Persoon) P. Karsten

REDDISH BROWN GYMNOPILUS

FAMILY Strophariaceae

Cap 2–8 cm wide, at first convex but becoming nearly flat with age; surface dry to moist, smooth, reddish brown to orangish brown; gills attached to notched, close, reddish orange; stalk 3–7.5 cm long and 3–11 mm wide, nearly equal to tapering in both directions, nearly smooth to finely longitudinally fibrillose, rusty brown; spores rusty brown in mass, 6–10 × 4–6 µm, ellipsoid, finely warted.

Habitat/Biological Role: Occurring on decomposing wood, typically wood from conifers but occasionally on wood from broadleaf trees; fruiting summer to winter. Decomposer of wood.

Distribution: Found throughout eastern North America as well as along the Gulf Coast.

Comments: *Flammulina velutipes* is somewhat similar but differs in having dark hairs at the base of the stalk and a white spore print. *Gymnopilus bellulus* can appear similar in color but is not typically found south of Tennessee; it is also much smaller (caps usually less than 2.5 cm wide) and has spores that are smaller (3.5–5.5 × 2.8–3.5 µm) and more distinctly warted. *Gymnopilus sapineus* is morphologically similar; however, it differs in being much paler in color and in having scattered patches of fine scales or hairs on the surface of the cap and a frail yellowish partial veil or annulus near the apex of the stalk. *Gymnopilus penetrans* is very similar to *G. sapineus* and *G. liquiritiae* but differs from both species in having a frail white veil. *Gymnopilus palmicola* is also similar, but this species is found only in the southernmost portion of our region; it occurs primarily on decomposing palms and has a floccose cap and coarsely warted spores. *Gymnopilus liquiritiae* contains hallucinogenic compounds and is therefore not recommended as food.

Gymnopus biformis (Peck) Halling

VARIABLE COLLYBIA

SYNONYMS *Collybia biformis, Marasmius biformis*

FAMILY Omphalotaceae

Cap 1–2.5 cm wide, at first convex with an incurved and entire margin, becoming depressed to flat or umbilicate with age; surface dry, at first reddish brown and then fading to brown and finally to tan with age; gills adnate, close, thin to moderately broad, white to cinereous; stalk 1.5–6 cm long and 1–5 mm wide, equal, terete or occasionally somewhat flattened, upper portion white and the lower portion tawny or brown, densely and minutely hairy, hollow; spores white to cream in mass, 6.5–8.5 × 3.5–4.5 µm, more or less ellipsoid, smooth, nonamyloid.

Habitat/Biological Role: Occurring on litter and twigs on forest floor in broadleaf or mixed broadleaf-conifer forests, commonly in somewhat disturbed areas along roads and trails; fruiting from midsummer to fall. Decomposer of litter and humus.

Distribution: Widely distributed throughout eastern North America.

Comments: Distinguishing features of *Gymnopus biformis* include its smaller stature, crowded gills, brown coloration, and occurrence on forest litter. It may sometimes seem to occur on bare soil. The similar-looking *G. subnudus* is larger and has less-crowded gills, usually occurs on decomposing branches and pieces of wood, usually has a darker and thicker stalk, and the spores are larger (8–11 × 3–4.5 µm). Edibility of these species is not known.

Gymnopus dryophilus
(Bulliard) Murrill

OAK-LOVING GYMNOPUS, OAK-LOVING COLLYBIA

SYNONYM *Collybia dryophila*

FAMILY Omphalotaceae

Cap 1–7 cm wide, at first convex but becoming flat with age; surface moist, smooth, dark reddish brown to dark grayish brown and often fading to yellowish tan, sometimes darker in the center of the cap in older specimens; gills attached to free, close, white to pale whitish pink; stalk 3–10 cm long and 2–7 mm wide, equal to enlarged toward the base, stalk flexible, surface smooth, sometimes developing fine striations with age, white mycelium sometimes abundant at the base, stalk nearly white at the apex and becoming darker toward base, lower half of the stalk similar in color to the surface of the cap; spores whitish cream in mass, 5–7 × 2.5–3.5 µm, elliptical, smooth, nonamyloid.

Habitat/Biological Role: Occurring in scattered groups on the ground, with fruiting bodies arising from dead leaves, humus, or decaying organic material; fruiting summer to fall. Decomposer of organic material.

Distribution: Very common in the Southeast and widely distributed in North America.

Comments: This is one of the most common *Gymnopus* species in our region. It is edible but not widely eaten. The stalks of *G. dryophilus* are often the host for the parasitic jelly fungus *Syzygospora mycetophila*. *Gymnopus subsulphureus* (edibility unknown) is similar but most obviously differs in having pinkish yellow rhizomorphs at the base of the stalk. *Rhodocollybia butyracea* (edible) is somewhat similar; however, it has a thicker stalk and pinkish spores. *Marasmius strictipes* is similar but has a pure white stalk and larger, more elongated spores (6–10.5 × 3–4.5 µm).

Gymnopus iocephalus
(Berkeley & M. A. Curtis) Halling

VIOLET COLLYBIA

SYNONYM *Collybia iocephala*

FAMILY Omphalotaceae

Cap 1–2 cm wide, at first convex with an incurved margin and then becoming broadly convex to flat with an uplifted and wavy margin with age, wrinkled or lined, moist or dry, at first purple and then fading to lilac or grayish lilac with age; gills narrowly attached or nearly free, close or approaching distant, reddish purple or similar to cap surface; stalk 2–5 cm long and 1–5 mm wide, more or less equal or tapering slightly to the apex, dry, minutely hairy, hairs white, upper portion purplish and lower portion drab grayish or yellowish lilac; the odor is distinctly garlicky; spores white in mass, 6.5–8.5 × 3–4.5 μm, more or less ovoid, smooth, nonamyloid.

Habitat/Biological Role: Occurring on the ground and associated with forest floor litter in broadleaf or conifer forests; fruiting bodies solitary, scattered, or found in clusters; fruiting summer to fall. Decomposer of litter.

Distribution: Scattered throughout the Southeast, in certain localities very common, and widely distributed throughout eastern North America.

Comments: The distinguishing features of *Gymnopus iocephalus* are the purple fruiting bodies, garlicky odor, and growth in forest litter. Not much is known about the edibility of this fungus, but it is generally too small and infrequent to be of culinary value.

Gymnopus spongiosus
(Berkeley & M. A. Curtis) Halling

HAIRY-STALKED COLLYBIA

SYNONYMS *Collybia spongiosa, Marasmius spongiosus*

FAMILY Omphalotaceae

Cap 1–3.5 cm wide, at first convex with a central umbo and incurved margin and then becoming broadly convex to flat with age, at first smooth but sometimes becoming slightly wrinkled, dry or sticky, at first reddish brown but fading to pinkish tan or pinkish buff, becoming nearly white at margin; gills attached or nearly free, close, cream-colored; stalk 2–6 cm long and 2–5 mm wide, more or less equal, pale above and reddish brown below, lower portion expanded, spongy, dry, densely hairy from the base to near the apex, hairs reddish brown; spores white in mass, 6–8.5 × 3.5–4 µm, more or less elliptical, smooth, nonamyloid.

Habitat/Biological Role: Occurring on decomposing wood or leaf litter in broadleaf or conifer forests, fruiting bodies solitary, scattered, or in clusters; fruiting in summer and fall. Decomposer of litter.

Distribution: Widely distributed throughout eastern North America.

Comments: The finely hairy reddish brown stalk and the expanded spongy base are key distinguishing features of *Gymnopus spongiosus*. Another closely related species, *G. semihirtipes*, is usually smaller and has reddish hairs over only the lower half of the stalk. Not very much is known about the edibility of this species.

Gymnopus subnudus (Ellis ex Peck) Halling

BROWN-CAP COLLYBIA

SYNONYM *Collybia subnuda*

FAMILY Omphalotaceae

Cap 1–5 cm wide, at first convex with an incurved margin and then becoming broadly convex, flat or shallowly depressed with age, dry, at first cinnamon-brown to dark brown or reddish brown but fading to pinkish tan with age, also becoming somewhat wrinkled and developing a broadly lined margin with age; gills attached or nearly free, distant or nearly so, whitish when young but darkening to pinkish buff; stalk 2–7 cm long and 2–3 mm wide, usually expanding somewhat at the apex, dry, upper portion smooth and lower portion finely hairy, brownish, reddish brown or nearly black near the base; spores white in mass, 8–11 × 3–4.5 μm, smooth, more or less elliptical, nonamyloid.

Habitat/Biological Role: Occurring on wood and leaf litter in broadleaf forests, either scattered or in loose clusters; fruiting from late spring to fall. Decomposer of litter and wood.

Distribution: This is one of the most common species of *Gymnopus* in the forests of eastern North America.

Comments: *Gymnopus subnudus* may be counted among the LBMs ("little brown mushrooms"), so called because an absence of readily apparent morphological features makes it difficult to identify members of this group of fungi to species. However, it is usually possible to distinguish *G. subnudus* on the basis of the brown cap, a stalk that is hairy toward the base, and the association of fruiting bodies with woody litter. *Gymnopus biformis* is similar but is usually smaller and typically occurs on leaf litter, the stalk is usually thinner and lighter in color, and the spores are smaller (6.5–8.5 × 3.5–4.5 μm). Edibility is not known.

Gymnopus subsulphureus
(Peck) Murrill

YELLOW-CAP COLLYBIA

SYNONYM *Collybia subsulphurea*

FAMILY Omphalotaceae

Cap 1–4 cm wide, at first convex but becoming almost flat with age, smooth, moist, at first pale to bright yellow but fading to buff or yellowish with age; gills attached, very crowded, yellowish; stalk 2–10 cm long and 5–7 mm wide, more or less equal but with a small basal bulb, dry to slightly slimy, hollow, smooth except for a slightly hairy base, pinkish to yellowish rhizomorphs attached to the base often apparent; spores white in mass, 5–6.5 × 2.5–3.5 µm, elliptical, smooth, nonamyloid.

Habitat/Biological Role: Occurring on the ground and associated with leaf litter in broadleaf forests; fruiting bodies scattered or occurring in loose clusters; fruiting in late spring and summer. Decomposer of litter.

Distribution: Widely distributed in eastern North America.

Comments: *Gymnopus subsulphureus* can resemble many little brown mushrooms, which makes it challenging to identify. It is most similar to *G. dryophilus*, which lacks pinkish to yellowish rhizomorphs at the base of the stalk. Nothing is known of its edibility.

Hygrocybe conica (Schaeffer) P. Kummer

WITCHES' HAT

SYNONYM *Hygrophorus conicus*

FAMILY Hygrophoraceae

Cap 2–6.5 cm wide, cone-shaped, pointed conic to bell-shaped but sometimes becoming flattened with age, almost always with a prominent umbo throughout development; surface smooth to scurfy, sometimes sticky, blood red to bright red or orange-red but often pale orange toward the margin, cap quickly staining black; gills usually free, close, waxy, pale yellowish to greenish orange, becoming black if bruised or with age; stalk 2–10 cm long and 3–10 mm wide, equal, surface smooth or sometimes with fine hair-like fibrils present, longitudinally striate or occasionally the striations appearing twisted, yellowish orange becoming paler toward the base, bruising black quickly; spores white in mass, 8–11 × 5–6.5 μm, elliptical, smooth, nonamyloid.

Habitat/Biological Role: Occurring in clusters on the ground; fruiting spring to fall. Historically thought to be a decomposer of organic material; however, some evidence indicates the ecology of this fungus may be more complex.

Distribution: Common in the Southeast and East and widely distributed in North America.

Comments: This poisonous fungus is one of the best-known members of a group of red *Hygrocybe* species with cone-shaped caps. *Hygrocybe conicoides* (probably poisonous) is very similar but generally occurs in sandy dune habitats, has a more orange gill color, stains black more slowly, and has slightly longer spores (9–14 × 4.5–7 μm). There is a question as to whether or not *H. cuspidata* (darker red) and *H. acutoconica* (paler orange) are distinct species, since the primary difference relates to shades of red to orange color; however, these species are easily separated from *H. conica* because their tissues do not stain black. *Hygrocybe coccinea* (syn. *Hygrophorus coccineus*) is somewhat similar and reported to be edible by some, but this fungus is usually brighter red, has a more broadly conic cap that is not cone-shaped, and its stalk is similar in color to the cap and has white basal mycelia.

Hygrocybe flavescens
(Kauffman) Singer

GOLDEN WAXY CAP

FAMILY Hygrophoraceae

Cap 2–6.5 cm wide, at first convex but becoming flat to upturned with age, sometimes with a broad umbo at the center of the cap; surface smooth, viscid to waxy, yellowish with a faint orange color when young or at the center of the cap, becoming bright yellow toward margin; gills narrowly attached to notched, spacing average, pale whitish orange to pale yellowish white; stalk 3–6.5 cm long and 0.5–1 cm wide, equal, smooth, sticky, brittle and splitting into strips, similar in color to the surface of the cap, sometimes with a white base; spores 7–9.5 × 4.5–6 μm, elliptical, smooth, nonamyloid.

Habitat/Biological Role: Occurring in groups on the ground; fruiting spring to fall. Historically thought to be a decomposer of organic material; however, some evidence indicates the ecology of this fungus may be more complex.

Distribution: Common in the Southeast and East and widely distributed in North America.

Comments: *Hygrocybe marginata* is somewhat similar but generally has a prominent umbo and bright orange gills. *Hygrocybe flavescens* is edible but not widely eaten.

Hymenopellis furfuracea
(Peck) R. H. Petersen

ROOTED AGARIC, ROOTING COLLYBIA, ROOTING OUDEMANSIELLA

SYNONYMS *Oudemansiella furfuracea, O. radicata, Xerula furfuracea*

FAMILY Physalacriaceae

Cap 3–15 cm wide, at first convex but becoming flat with age, often with an umbo in the center; surface rubbery, finely velvety to smooth, often prominently wrinkled around the umbo, dark grayish brown when young to pale brown with age; at first gills attached but then becoming free with age, nearly distant, white; stalk (aboveground portion) 7–20 cm long and 3–20 mm thick, enlarged slightly downward, smooth to finely scaled, gray to brownish on the surface and with a white interior, stalk usually with a white rooting base that sometimes extends as much as 15 cm below the surface of the ground; spores white in mass, 13–18 × 9–12 µm, broadly oval to elliptical, smooth, nonamyloid.

Habitat/Biological Role: Occurring as solitary fruiting bodies or in small groups on the ground or on very decomposed logs, also sometimes arising from the ground at the base of stumps; fruiting spring to summer. Decomposer of wood.

Distribution: In our region most common in the Appalachian Mountains and widely distributed in eastern North America.

Comments: The long rooting stalk is a distinctive character of this genus. *Hymenopellis megalospora* (syn. *Collybia radicata* var. *pusilla, Xerula megalospora*) is very similar but differs in being smaller, paler in color, and having larger spores (18–23 × 11–14 µm). *Hymenopellis incognita* (syn. *X. incognita*) is another species from our region that is morphologically similar and has almost identical spores (12–18 × 9–13 µm) that are nearly lemon-shaped;

the main way to distinguish these species from *H. furfuracea* without mating or genetic studies is on the basis of the size and shape of the microscopic pleurocystidia. The pleurocystidia of *H. furfuracea* are typically widely cylindrical and 125 × 40 µm, while those of *H. incognita* are widely cylindrical to very broadly fusiform or subfusiform and 75 × 25 µm. Some older books list *H. radicata* (syn. *X. radicata*) as occurring in our region, but this species is now believed to be found only in Europe. Regardless of these taxonomic challenges, members of this genus are edible but not commonly eaten.

Hypholoma sublateritium
(Fries) Quélet

BRICK CAP, BRICK TOPS

SYNONYM *Naematoloma sublateritium*

FAMILY Strophariaceae

Cap 4–8 cm wide, at first convex but becoming broadly convex to nearly flat with age; surface smooth, moist or dry, with scattered fibrils, brick red but with a paler margin, margin inrolled and frequently retaining veil remnants; gills attached, close, narrow, at first whitish to pale greenish yellow but becoming smoky purplish gray to purplish brown with age; stalk 5–10 cm long and 5–15 mm wide, more or less equal, upper portion whitish and lower portion dull brown or grayish, covered with reddish brown fibrils, partial veil fine to web-like and leaving an annular zone; spores purple-brown in mass, 6–7 × 3.5–4.5 μm, elliptical, smooth.

Habitat/Biological Role: Occurring on fallen logs and stumps of broadleaf trees, fruiting bodies frequently form dense clusters; fruiting from midsummer to late fall. Decomposer of wood.

Distribution: Found throughout eastern North America.

Comments: The cap's brick red color (hence the common names), the occurrence of fruiting bodies in clusters on decomposing wood of broadleaf trees, and the purple-brown spores are the distinguishing features of this relatively common mushroom. *Hypholoma capnoides* is similar in stature and spore color, but it is generally paler in color and occurs on the wood of conifers. Both species are edible.

Hypholoma subviride
(Berkeley & M. A. Curtis) Dennis

SULFUR TUFT

FAMILY Strophariaceae

Cap 2–8 cm wide, at first convex but becoming broadly convex to almost flat with age, often with an umbo, smooth, moist or dry, at first sometimes tawny reddish brown or orange but becoming bright yellow to greenish yellow or golden yellow with age, even in pale young specimens individuals usually retaining brownish orange cap center, the margin often retaining small fragments of the partial veil; gills attached, crowded, at first sulfur yellow to greenish yellow and then becoming grayish and finally purple-brown; stalk 5–12 cm tall and 2–10 mm wide, nearly equal or narrowing at the base, pale yellow to yellow, partial veil whitish, typically leaving a relatively faint annular zone; spores purple-brown in mass, 6.5–8 × 3.5–4 μm, elliptical, smooth.

Habitat/Biological Role: Occurring on fallen logs and stumps of conifers or less commonly broadleaf trees, often forming dense clusters of sometimes hundreds of fruiting bodies; fruiting in fall and early winter and sometimes also in spring. Decomposer of wood.

Distribution: Particularly common in our region but widely distributed throughout North America.

Comments: The distinguishing features of *Hypholoma subviride* are the occurrence of fruiting bodies in dense clusters, a fruiting season that is typically late in the year, and the purple-brown spores. This is also one of the smallest species in this genus found in our region. The edibility of this fungus is not known. Some field guides misapply to *H. subviride* the name *H. fasciculare* (syn. *Naematoloma fasciculare*), which is in fact a larger species sometimes encountered in our region.

Inocephalus murrayi (Berkeley & M. A. Curtis) Rutter & Watling

YELLOW UNICORN ENTOLOMA

SYNONYMS *Entoloma murrayi, Nolanea murrayi, N. murraii*

FAMILY Entolomataceae

Cap 1–4 cm wide, at first conic to bell-shaped but often becoming nearly convex with age, retaining a pointed nipple-like apex throughout development; surface usually dry, smooth, bright yellow to mustard yellow or sometimes becoming pale orange-yellow; gills attached to nearly free, close, pale yellow to pale pinkish with age; stalk 4.5–12 cm long and 2–4 mm wide, equal to slightly enlarged at the base, smooth, dry, similar to the color of the cap but paler, usually a patch of white hair-like mycelium at the base; spores pinkish salmon to cinnamon in mass, 9–12 × 8–10 µm, angular, usually four-sided, smooth, nonamyloid.

Habitat/Biological Role: Occurring on the ground, usually in moist to nearly swampy or marshy areas but sometimes fruiting in more typical drier woodland habitats, fruiting bodies generally found in scattered groups; fruiting early summer to fall. Believed to be a decomposer of litter, but some related groups are mycorrhizal.

Distribution: Particularly common in the Southeast and widely distributed in eastern North America.

Comments: This showy fungus is unlikely to be misidentified in our region. *Entoloma quadratum* (syn. *E. salmoneum, Nolanea quadrata*) is most similar, but the fruiting body is generally more salmon to orange in color, has less of a prominent apical point, and has a more slender frail stalk. *Entoloma luteum* (syn. *Inocephalus luteus*) is somewhat similar but is dull brownish to slightly yellow with light-colored gills. Some *Hygrocybe* species are somewhat similar in color, but they lack the pointed apex, have a flesh with waxy texture, and their spores are not angular. The edibility of this fungus is not known.

Inocybe calamistrata (Fries)
Gillet

SCALY-CAP INOCYBE

SYNONYM *Inocybe hirsuta*

FAMILY Inocybaceae

Cap 1–3 cm wide, at first conic with inflexed margin but becoming convex with age; surface dry, finely scaly, scales curling in age, brown to dark brown; gills attached, close, off-white when young but becoming brown with age; stalk 2–7 cm long and 2–6 mm wide, equal, partially to totally covered by scattered scales, light brown near the apex and darkening toward the base, with dark bluish green coloration at the very base; sometimes very faint curtain-like veil remnants present near the apex of the stalk; odor generally and distinctively fishy; spores yellow-brown in mass, 9.5–13.5 × 5–6.5 µm, elliptical, smooth, nonamyloid.

Habitat/Biological Role: Usually occurring in scattered clusters in mixed broadleaf and conifer forests; fruiting summer to fall. Forms mycorrhizal associations with trees.

Distribution: Frequently encountered in the Southeast and widely distributed in North America.

Comments: Members of the genus *Inocybe* can be challenging to identify to species and are regarded as poisonous. *Inocybe calamistrata* is similar to some of the other brown scaly species in the genus; however, the following morphologically similar species all lack the bluish green coloration at the base of the stalk. *Inocybe fraudans* (possibly a species complex) is paler with a smoother cap and stalk that can have greenish tints; it has a spicy-pungent odor. *Inocybe lacera*, a scaly species, differs in being shorter and having longer spores (11–15 × 4.8–6 µm). *Inocybe lanuginosa* has smaller spores (6.5–10 × 4.5–7 µm) and is one of the few species in the genus associated with wood. *Inocybe tenebrosa* is more yellow-brown in color, with a dark stalk base. *Inocybe tahquamenonensis* differs in being much darker, often almost black, and having smaller (6–8.5 × 5–6 µm), angular-nodulose spores.

Inocybe geophylla var. *geophylla* (Bulliard) P. Kummer

EARTHY INOCYBE, COMMON WHITE INOCYBE, WHITE FIBERCAP

FAMILY Inocybaceae

Cap 1–3 cm wide, at first conic but becoming flat with age, usually with a small umbo at the apex; surface silky and sparsely covered by appressed hairs, at first white but darkening slightly in age; gills attached to shallowly notched, averagely spaced to somewhat distant, white when young and becoming off-white to pale brown with age; stalk 2–6 cm long and 2–4 mm wide, equal, sometimes slightly enlarged at the base, white to off-white, covered by fine appressed hairs, delicate curtain-like partial veil sometimes present near the apex; odor considered by some to be unpleasant or similar to that of green corn; spores brownish in mass, 7–10 × 4.5–6 µm, elliptical, smooth, nonamyloid.

Habitat/Biological Role: Usually occurring in scattered clusters in mixed broadleaf and conifer forests; fruiting summer to fall. Forms mycorrhizal associations with trees.

Distribution: Frequently encountered in the Southeast and widely distributed in North America.

Comments: Members of the genus *Inocybe* can be challenging to identify to species and are regarded as poisonous. *Inocybe geophylla* var. *lilacina* is essentially identical in stature but is lilac in color. The two color varieties can be found fruiting together.

Inocybe geophylla var. *lilacina* (Peck) Gillet

LILAC FIBER HEAD

FAMILY Inocybaceae

Cap 1.5–4 cm wide, at first conic but becoming flat with age, small umbo present at the apex of the cap; surface silky and covered by appressed radially arranged fibrils, central umbo dark lilac and the cap becoming paler lilac toward the margin or with age; gills attached to shallowly notched, averagely spaced to somewhat distant, whitish to faintly lilac when young and becoming off-white to pale gray-brown with age; stalk 2–7 cm long and 2–7 mm wide, equal, sometimes slightly enlarged at the base, lilac to grayish white, covered by fine appressed hairs or fibrils, delicate curtain-like partial veil sometimes near the apex; odor unpleasant; spores brownish in mass, 7–9.5 × 4.5–6 μm, elliptical, smooth, nonamyloid.

Habitat/Biological Role: Usually occurring in scattered clusters in mixed broadleaf and conifer forests; fruiting summer to fall. Forms mycorrhizal associations with trees.

Distribution: Frequently encountered in the Southeast and widely distributed in North America.

Comments: Although the genus *Inocybe* can be challenging to identify to species, the distinctive lilac color and unpleasant odor of this fungus make it relatively easy to identify. *Inocybe geophylla* var. *geophylla* is essentially identical in stature but pure white in color. The two varieties sometimes occur together, and both are considered poisonous. It is possible that *I. geophylla* var. *lilacina* will soon be elevated to species status (as *I. lilacina*).

Inocybe nemorosa (R. Heim) Grund & D. E. Stuntz

SMALL BROWN FIBER CAP

FAMILY Inocybaceae

Cap 1–3.5 cm wide, at first bell-shaped but becoming flat with age; surface dry, covered by appressed fibrils, upper grayish brown layer often splitting radially to reveal a paler-colored lower layer; gills attached to shallowly notched, close, white to off-white when young, becoming pale gray to pale grayish brown with age; stalk 2–5 cm long and 2–5 mm wide, equal to slightly enlarged at the base, surface in lower half covered by minute fibrils, color of the stalk paler than that of the cap surface, pale gray-brown; spores brownish in mass, 8–12 × 5.5–6.5 µm, almond-shaped, smooth, probably nonamyloid.

Habitat/Biological Role: Usually occurring in scattered clusters in mixed broadleaf and conifer forests; fruiting summer to fall. Forms mycorrhizal associations with trees.

Distribution: Most common in the mountainous or northern portion of our region and widely distributed in North America.

Comments: Members of the genus *Inocybe* can be challenging to identify to species and are regarded as poisonous. This small brown mushroom resembles a number of other species in the genus, but careful examination of macroscopic and microscopic characters makes identification possible. Moreover, it often has an unpleasant sour odor. In some publications, *I. nemorosa* is considered to represent a color form of *I. nitidiuscula* (syn. *I. friesii*) that has a dark brown cap and pale orange stalk, but to our knowledge the latter species has not been reported from the Southeast.

Inocybe sororia Kauffman

CORN SILK INOCYBE, PUNGENT FIBER HEAD

FAMILY Inocybaceae

Cap 2–8 cm wide, conic to nearly flat with age, usually retaining an umbo through-out development, margin splitting with age; surface dry, glossy, radially fibrillose, yellowish brown to pale brown; gills attached to free, close, off-white when young but becoming yellowish to brownish with age; stalk 2–10 cm long and 2–6 mm wide, equal with a slightly enlarged base, smooth to finely fibrillose often nearly scurfy near the apex of the stalk; odor sometimes reported to be reminiscent of green corn; spores brown in mass, 9–17 × 5–8 µm, elliptical, smooth.

Habitat/Biological Role: Usually occurring in scattered clusters in mixed broadleaf and conifer forests; fruiting summer to fall. Forms mycorrhizal associations with trees.

Distribution: Encountered in the Appalachian Mountains but most common in the western United States and widely distributed in North America.

Comments: Members of the genus *Inocybe* can be challenging to identify to species and are regarded as poisonous. *Inocybe sororia* is distinctive in part because it is larger than many of the other species in the genus. *Inocybe armoricana* (syn. *I. lanatodisca* var. *phaeoderma*) is very similar but has a darker cap and smaller spores (9–11 × 5–6 µm).

Laccaria ochropurpurea
(Berkeley) Peck

PURPLE GILLED LACCARIA

FAMILY Hydnangiaceae

Cap 4–15 cm wide, at first convex but becoming flat to uplifted with age; surface dry, smooth to finely fibrillose, pale purple to lilac when young and usually fading early in development to pale grayish brown or sometimes almost white; gills attached and shortly decurrent, close to distant, dark purple to violet, typically retaining a vivid color long after the color of the cap has faded; stalk 5–15 cm long and 2–4 cm wide, frequently bulbous at the base and tapering toward the apex, surface sparsely covered by erect to recurved fibrils, longitudinal striations frequently present, usually pale brownish violet and fading with age, color similar to that of the cap; spores white in mass, 6.5–11 × 6.5–9.5 µm, globose to subglobose, very spiny (spines up to 1.5 µm long), nonamyloid.

Habitat/Biological Role: Usually occurring in scattered clusters in mixed broadleaf (particularly oak) and conifer forests or at the forest edge; fruiting summer to fall. Forms mycorrhizal associations with trees.

Distribution: Frequently encountered in our region and widely distributed in eastern North America.

Comments: Many of the *Laccaria* species in our region are small and rather similar in appearance; for example, *L. bicolor*, with a cinnamon cap and pale lilac gills, is very similar to *L. laccata* except that the former has lilac hyphae at the base of the stalk. *Laccaria ochropurpurea* is one of the largest and most distinctive members of this somewhat taxonomically challenging genus. *Laccaria trullisata* is nearly identical; however, it occurs in coastal regions in very sandy soil or dune habitats and has spores that are nearly smooth and substantially larger (14–21 × 5.5–8 µm). The *Cortinarius violaceus* species complex and some other members of the genus *Cortinarius* are morphologically similar, but they all have a rusty brown spore print and a curtain-like annulus near the apex of the stalk. *Laccaria ochropurpurea* is edible but generally considered to be of poor quality and occasionally reported to cause gastrointestinal issues.

Lacrymaria lacrymabunda
(Bulliard) Patouillard

WEEPING WIDOW MUSHROOM, VELVETY PSATHYRELLA

SYNONYM *Psathyrella velutina*

FAMILY Psathyrellaceae

Cap 2–5 cm wide, bell-shaped at first but becoming more broadly bell-shaped with a central umbo with age, margins often retaining fringe-like veil remnants; surface dry, brown, covered by mat of fine dark brown hairs, often lighter toward the margin; gills closely spaced, nearly free to partially attached to the top of the stalk, dark brown, in young specimens the gills are obscured by a partial veil; veil thin and web-like, white to off-white, in age sometimes leaving a faint annulus near apex of the stalk; stalk 3–9 cm long and 0.3–2 cm wide, equal or sometimes slightly enlarged at base, stalk surface finely hairy, color the same to slightly lighter than cap surface, spores sometimes adhering to veil remnants near the apex, creating a dark zone; spores blackish brown in mass, 8.5–12 × 5.5–7 µm, elliptical, warted to roughened, with a prominent apical pore.

Habitat/Biological Role: Occurring on the ground, usually fruiting in groups or clusters, often on compacted soil, edges of dirt roads, fields, trails, and mulched beds; fruiting spring to fall. Decomposer of organic matter.

Distribution: Particularly common in the Southeast and East but widely distributed in North America.

Comments: *Lacrymaria lacrymabunda* is considered edible, but it often fruits in potentially polluted locations and can resemble members of several toxic groups of mushrooms. Species in *Inocybe* are similar, but they have rusty brown spores and do not have a thin veil. Some *Cortinarius* species are similar, but their spore prints are rusty brown. The genera *Panaeolus* and *Psilocybe* can appear similar; however, they do not have the frail partial veil.

Lactarius atroviridis Peck

EASTERN TOADSKIN LACTARIUS

FAMILY Russulaceae

Cap 6–15 cm wide, at first convex to flat but becoming uplifted with age; surface dry, rough to finely scaly, usually with irregular oval-shaped pits scattered across the surface, surface varying from shades of dark green to pale greenish gray, pits usually dark olive-green; gills attached to shortly decurrent, close, white to off-white, often appearing dirty gray-white with age, staining greenish gray, gill edges often similar in color to the surface of the cap; latex scant to nearly copious, white and very slowly turning greenish, very acrid in taste; stalk 2–8 cm long and 1–3 cm wide, equal to irregular, dry, surface often rough, colored like the cap and also with pits present; spores cream to buff in mass, 7–10 × 6–9 µm, elliptical to subglobose, ornamented with a reticulum composed of irregular ridges and warts, amyloid.

Habitat/Biological Role: Occurring in scattered groups, primarily under broadleaf trees but also in mixed forests; fruiting summer to fall. Forms mycorrhizal associations with trees.

Distribution: Infrequently encountered or regionally common and widely distributed in eastern North America from Canada to Florida west to Texas, occasionally collected as far west as California.

Comments: The unusual color and pattern of pits on the surface of *Lactarius atroviridis* often cause it to blend in with the leaf litter on the forest floor, but its green color makes it unlikely to be confused with any other fungus in our region, once spotted. *Lactarius sordidus* is a morphologically similar species in our region; however, it is primarily associated with conifers. Some mycologists treat it as a synonym of *L. turpis*. *Lactarius turpis* is also associated with conifers (especially spruce and balsam fir), which restricts it primarily to high elevations in the Appalachian Mountains. *Lactarius turpis* differs from *L. atroviridis* in having slightly smaller spores (6.3–8.8 × 4.8–6.5 µm) and more of a yellow tint, lacking much of the dark green coloration. None of these species are edible.

Lactarius corrugis Peck

CORRUGATED-CAP MILKY

SYNONYM *Lactifluus corrugis*

FAMILY Russulaceae

Cap 5–20 cm wide, at first convex but becoming flat to centrally depressed or uplifted with age; surface finely pubescent to velvety, dry, wrinkled to corrugated (generally most prominent in older specimens), dark brown or sometimes fading to pale brown or orange-brown, often with a faint white to silvery bloom on the surface, particularly in young specimens; gills attached, close, sometimes forking, pale brown to golden brown, staining dark brown if bruised; as it ages sometimes smelling fishy; latex copious, white, mild to slightly astringent; stalk 5–12 cm long and 2–4 cm wide, equal, smooth to velvety, pale brown to yellowish brown, sometimes with a faint white to silvery bloom on the surface; spores white in mass, 9–12 × 8.5–12 μm, subglobose, ornamented with a partial reticulum composed of warts and ridges, amyloid.

Habitat/Biological Role: Occurring in scattered groups, generally in broadleaf and mixed broadleaf-conifer forests; fruiting summer to fall. Forms mycorrhizal associations with trees.

Distribution: Particularly common in the Southeast and widely distributed in eastern North America.

Comments: This is typically the largest brown-capped *Lactarius* species found in our region. The thick stalk and cap, overall darker color, prominent wrinkles on the cap surface, and slightly larger spores make this species easy to separate from *L. volemus* and *L. hygrophoroides*. All three species are choice edibles, but *L. corrugis* is generally the largest, meatiest, and best suited to gathering in large quantities.

Lactarius hygrophoroides
Berkeley & M. A. Curtis

HYGROPHORUS MILKY

SYNONYM *Lactifluus hygrophoroides*

FAMILY Russulaceae

Cap 3–10 cm wide, at first convex to flat but often becoming upturned with age; surface smooth, dry, sometimes broadly or irregularly scalloped along the margin, dull orange to pale brown, occasionally pale yellow-brown, usually paler toward margin; gills attached and often shortly decurrent, distant at maturity, sometimes with crossveins, white to pale yellowish cream; latex often copious, white, unchanging, not staining flesh, taste mild; stalk 3–5 cm long and 5–15 cm wide, equal, sometimes tapering toward the base, smooth, dry, often paler than or similar to the cap in color; spores white in mass, 7.5–10.5 × 6–7.5 µm, elliptical, ornamentation a combination of warts and ridges, amyloid.

Habitat/Biological Role: Occurring in scattered groups, primarily in broadleaf forests; fruiting summer to fall. Forms mycorrhizal associations with trees.

Distribution: Widely distributed in eastern North America, Canada to Florida and west to Texas.

Comments: *Lactarius rugatus* (syn. *Lactifluus rugatus*) is morphologically similar but differs in having obvious concentric wrinkles along the margin of the cap. There is indication that *L. rugatus* is European and may not actually be in North America. *Lactarius hygrophoroides* and related species (e.g., *L. volemus* and *L. corrugis*) are considered choice edibles.

Lactarius indigo (Schweinitz) Fries

INDIGO MILKY, INDIGO LACTARIUS

FAMILY Russulaceae

Cap 5–16 cm wide, at first convex to flat but becoming upturned with age; surface dry to lightly viscid, frequently zonate but sometimes lacking any zonation, dark vivid blue when fresh or young and fading to grayish or pale greenish blue with age, if bruised generally dark greenish gray; gills attached, close, occasionally forking, dark vivid blue when young but becoming paler with maturation and age, staining greenish if bruised; latex scant to copious, at first dark blue but then turning dark green, taste mild; stalk 2–8 cm long and 1–3 cm wide, equal or sometimes tapering slightly toward the base, viscid when young but becoming dry, sometimes pitted, at first dark blue but fading with age; spores creamy to white in mass, 7–9 × 5.5–7.5 µm, ellipsoid to nearly globose, surface with reticulations composed of ridges, amyloid.

Habitat/Biological Role: Occurring in scattered groups, generally in broadleaf forests or under conifers; fruiting summer to late fall. Forms mycorrhizal associations with trees.

Distribution: Most common in the Southeast but widely distributed in North America and south to Central America.

Comments: *Lactarius indigo* is not only one of the most distinctive and charismatic mushrooms in our region, it is also edible. In our experience, it can be quite flavorful when young; however, once specimens age and begin to stain green they can develop a bitter flavor. Some mycologists recognize an additional variety in our region that is morphologically very similar and found only along the Gulf Coast from Florida to Texas; this *L. indigo* var. *diminutivus* primarily differs in being smaller in stature and producing copious amounts of latex. *Lactarius paradoxus* (also edible) is somewhat similar but more purplish in color and has brownish latex.

Lactarius maculatipes
Burlingham

YELLOW MILKING ZONATE LACTARIUS

FAMILY Russulaceae

Cap 5–9 cm wide, at first convex but becoming flat to upturned with age; surface smooth, usually sticky to viscid (unless fruiting during very dry weather), off-white to cream-colored or sometimes pale yellowish, faintly zoned; gills decurrent, close, sometime forking, at first off-white and darkening to a color similar to that of the cap surface, quickly staining pale yellowish; latex white but generally causing a yellow staining reaction that makes the latex appear yellowish, slowly acrid in taste; stalk 3–8 cm long and 1–3 cm thick, tapering toward the base, smooth, often slimy in wet weather, similar in color to the surface of the cap, often becoming irregularly spotted with spherical darker-colored spots, sometimes streaked, also staining yellow like the gills; spores pale pinkish to yellowish in mass, 6.5–8 × 6–7.5 µm, nearly globose to ellipsoid, ornamentation reticulum-like, amyloid.

Habitat/Biological Role: Occurring in scattered groups, generally in broadleaf forests, particularly under oaks; fruiting summer to late fall. Forms mycorrhizal associations with trees.

Distribution: Most common from West Virginia south to Florida and west to Texas but widely distributed in eastern North America.

Comments: The yellow staining reaction that makes the latex appear yellow is one of the best diagnostic characters to separate this species from others in the genus with zonate caps. *Lactarius chrysorrheus* has latex that is white at first and then quickly changes to yellow, but this species differs in having a cap that is generally darker and lacks the circular spots on the stalk. *Lactarius yazooensis* (found in Florida and along the Gulf Coast) is similar but has much darker zonation, does not stain, and has copious white latex that is very acrid. *Lactarius psammicola* is also similar in having a pale zonation; however, its latex slowly stains the tissues dingy. The very rare *L. dunfordii*, known only from Tennessee, appears to be associated with pines and has a latex that does not stain the flesh. *Lactarius carolinensis* is infrequently encountered and is reported to be morphologically similar but differs in having darker zonations and a white spore print. The edibility of all these species is unknown.

Lactarius marylandicus
A. H. Smith & Hesler

SCALLOPED MARGIN LACTARIUS

SYNONYMS *Lactarius subplinthogalus,*
Lactifluus subplinthogalus

FAMILY Russulaceae

Cap 3–7.5 cm wide, at first flat but becoming funnel-shaped with age; surface smooth to finely wrinkled, margin plicate to scalloped, at first whitish to pale yellowish brown and then becoming darker brownish with age; gills attached and sometimes shortly decurrent, distant, broad, similar in color to the cap surface, staining rosy; latex white, unchanging, acrid in taste; stalk 3–8 cm long and 7–15 mm wide, equal or tapering slightly downward, smooth, color similar to the cap surface or lighter, sometimes pale reddish stains present with age; spores pinkish to pale brownish buff in mass, 8–9.5 × 7–8 µm, subglobose to elliptical, spore surface covered by irregular warts and ridges, amyloid.

Habitat/Biological Role: Fruiting bodies solitary or occurring in groups on the ground, usually under oaks; fruiting summer to fall. Forms mycorrhizal associations with trees.

Distribution: Found primarily in the Southeast.

Comments: *Lactarius sumstinei* can appear somewhat similar but has latex that does not stain the gills or other tissues. *Lactarius fumosus* is similar in color but has a cap margin that is not plicate, the gills are close, and the spores are slightly smaller (6–8 µm). *Lactarius subvernalis* differs in having a cap margin that is not plicate, and the gills are close and often forked. The edibility of all these species is not known.

Lactarius paradoxus Beardslee & Burlingham

SILVER-BLUE MILKY

FAMILY Russulaceae

Cap 5–8 cm wide, at first broadly convex but becoming upturned with age; surface smooth, viscid to sticky when wet, sometimes zoned or frequently the zonation is poorly defined, surface purplish gray to bluish silver, staining greenish; gills attached and shortly decurrent, close, sometimes forking near the stalk, pale purplish pink to pinkish orange, staining blue-green; latex scant, dark reddish brown, mild to subtly acrid in taste; stalk 2–3 cm long and 1–2 cm wide, equal to slightly tapered toward the base, surface smooth, color similar to the gills or sometimes similar to that of the surface of the cap; spores creamy to yellowish in mass, 7–9 × 5.5–6.5 µm, broadly elliptical, ornamented with a partial reticulum composed of warts and ridges, amyloid.

Habitat/Biological Role: Occurring in scattered groups, particularly in grassy areas under broadleaf trees and conifers; in warm portions of its range fruiting bodies can be found nearly year-round. Forms mycorrhizal associations with trees.

Distribution: Most common in the Southeast, especially in the eastern foothills of the Appalachians and along the Gulf Coast, but widely distributed in eastern North America.

Comments: Fruiting bodies of this unusually colored fungus are frequently encountered in grassy areas at the edges of fields under pines or oaks. This species is edible. Faded individuals of *Lactarius indigo* can appear similar, but they are typically much bluer in color. *Lactarius chelidonium* (edibility unknown) is somewhat similar and has a grayish greenish cap color, but this species is found in the more northern portion of our region and has yellowish latex and a pale yellow-orange flesh color. *Lactarius subpurpureus* (edibility unknown) can be similar in color but is generally more pinkish to pinkish gray or occasionally purplish, more distinctly zoned, and has pits on the stalk and larger spores (8–11 × 6.5–8 µm). *Lactarius incarnatozonatus*, a rarely collected species, is somewhat similar but differs most notably in having prominent zonations and white latex that changes to yellow.

Lactarius peckii Burlingham

PECK'S MILK CAP

FAMILY Russulaceae

Cap 4–16 cm wide, at first convex with a central depression but becoming flat to upturned with age; surface dry, smooth to finely scurfy, usually distinctly zonate, zones brownish red and pale brownish orange, margin inrolled when young and expanding with age; gills decurrent, close, narrow, pale brownish orange when young, darkening with age, staining varying tones of brown; latex plentiful, white, tasting very peppery; stalk 2–6 cm long and 1–2.5 cm wide, equal, smooth, surface with a whitish dusting present when young, stalk similar but paler in color when compared to the cap, sometimes becoming spotty with age; spores white in mass, 6–7 μm, round, prominently ornamented with partial to complete reticulum, amyloid.

Habitat/Biological Role: Occurring in scattered groups, generally under broadleaf trees, particularly oaks; fruiting summer into late fall. Forms mycorrhizal associations with trees.

Distribution: Particularly common in the Southeast and widely distributed in eastern North America.

Comments: *Lactarius peckii* has darker-colored gills than many species in the genus. Other brown or yellow-brown zonate species produce white latex, but most of these are paler in color and the latex is less peppery. Some mycologists recognize two varieties of this species in our region, which are most easily identified by the dried latex; the latex of *L. peckii* var. *glaucescens* dries pale bluish green and the latex of *L. peckii* var. *lactolutescens* turns yellow on exposure to air and dries yellowish green. The edibility of all these taxa is not known; however, they are likely too peppery to be of much culinary interest.

Lactarius piperatus (Linnaeus) Persoon

PEPPERY MILKY, PEPPERY WHITE MILK CAP

FAMILY Russulaceae

Cap 3–16 cm wide, at first convex but becoming flat or upturned with age; surface dry, smooth or sometimes finely wrinkled, white to off-white in age, sometimes developing dingy pale brown stains on the cap surface with age; gills attached and shortly decurrent, very crowded, usually forking multiple times, white when young and sometimes becoming pale creamy with age, occasionally staining yellowish if bruised; latex copious, white on exposure and often drying yellowish, suddenly and intensely spicy or peppery in taste; stalk 2–8 cm long and 1–2.5 cm wide, equal or tapering slightly toward the base, dry, sometimes with very fine powdery dusting on the surface; spores white in mass, 4.5–7 × 5–5.5 µm, ellipsoid, ornamentation consisting of fine lines and occasional warts (not forming a reticulum), amyloid.

Habitat/Biological Role: Occurring in scattered groups under broadleaf trees or conifers; fruiting summer to fall. Forms mycorrhizal associations with trees.

Distribution: Widely distributed in eastern North America and also reported from California.

Comments: The pure white cap without zonation and very close gills make this mushroom a rather distinctive species of *Lactarius* in our region. Only one similar species is reported from the Southeast. *Lactifluus glaucescens* (syn. *Lactarius glaucescens*, *L. piperatus* var. *glaucescens*) is essentially identical to *L. piperatus* macroscopically but differs in having latex that dries pale bluish green and slightly larger spores (6.5–9 × 5–7 µm). Reports on the edibility of both species are mixed, but there has been at least one report of a poisoning by *Lactifluus glaucescens*, so we advise against consuming these or similar species.

Lactarius psammicola
A. H. Smith

WHITE MILKING ZONATE LACTARIUS

FAMILY Russulaceae

Cap 4–15 cm wide, at first convex but becoming flat to uplifted in age; surface smooth to somewhat hairy, viscid, distinctly zonate, with alternating zones of pale yellowish white and orangish brown; gills attached, close, sometimes forked, at first whitish but becoming pale yellowish brown with age; latex copious to scant, at first white but drying darker, very acrid in taste; stalk 2–5 cm long and 1–2 cm wide, tapering toward the base, surface whitish, sometimes roughened, with smooth spots; spores pinkish to yellowish in mass, 7.5–9 × 6–7.5 μm, ellipsoid, ornamentation reticulum-like and composed of ridges and warts, amyloid.

Habitat/Biological Role: Occurring in scattered groups, generally under broadleaf trees but sometimes in mixed forests; fruiting summer to late fall. Forms mycorrhizal associations with trees.

Distribution: Particularly common in the Southeast and widely distributed in eastern North America.

Comments: *Lactarius psammicola* is sometimes split by taxonomists into two forms, f. *psammicola*, which has a particularly hairy or fibrillose cap, and f. *glaber*, which has a smooth viscid cap. Nothing is known regarding the edibility of either form. To learn more about similar zonate species in our region, see comments under *L. maculatipes*.

Lactarius salmoneus Peck

SOUTHEASTERN SAFFRON MILKY

SYNONYM *Lactarius curtisii*

FAMILY Russulaceae

Cap 2.5–8 cm wide, at first convex to flat but becoming centrally depressed with age, entire fruiting body staining orange if bruised; surface dry and finely pubescent, usually not zoned, surface color varying from nearly white when young to vibrant pale orange in age, margin usually inrolled; gills attached to sometimes slightly decurrent, subdistant to distant, narrow, bright orange to pale orange depending on age, staining greenish with age; latex bright orange, mild to peppery in taste; stalk 12–30 mm long and 6–13 mm thick, equal and tapering slightly toward the base, smooth, similar in color to the cap surface; spores creamy white in mass, 7.5–9 × 5–6 μm, ellipsoid to round, ornamentation partially to irregularly reticulate, amyloid.

Habitat/Biological Role: Occurring as solitary fruiting bodies or in groups, generally under pines, sometimes in mixed oak/pine forests; fruiting summer to fall. Forms mycorrhizal associations with trees.

Distribution: Found primarily in the Southeast and usually not reported north of the Carolinas.

Comments: *Lactarius pseudodeliciosus* is similar, but it reportedly occurs only under oaks in the southernmost portion of our region. *Lactarius thyinos* is similar but has concentric zones on the cap surface, the tissue does not stain green, and fruiting bodies occur in boggy areas in the northern or mountainous parts of our region. The similar *L. deliciosus*, a European species, has been introduced in pine plantations worldwide; some authors report it as occurring in North America, but its distribution in our region is unclear. *Lactarius salmoneus* is considered edible, as are most other similar species.

Lactarius volemus (Fries) Fries

LEATHER BACK LACTARIUS, BRADLEY

SYNONYM *Lactifluus volemus*

FAMILY Russulaceae

Cap 5–10 cm wide, at first convex but becoming flat to upturned with age; surface dry, pruinose, occasionally very shallowly wrinkled at the margin, dark orange-brown to pale brown at the center and becoming paler toward margin, sometimes fading to dull yellow in age; gills attached, close, frequently forking, whitish to pale yellowish, slowly staining dark brown when broken or bruised; latex copious, white, astringent in taste; stalk 5–12 cm long and 5–20 mm wide, equal or sometimes tapering slightly toward the base, smooth, almost always lighter in color than the cap, generally pale brown to nearly yellowish orange; spores white in mass, 7.5–10 × 7.5–9 µm, globose to subglobose, ornamented with a reticulum composed of warts and ridges, amyloid.

Habitat/Biological Role: Occurring in scattered groups, generally under broad-leaf trees and in mixed forests; fruiting summer to fall. Forms mycorrhizal associations with trees.

Distribution: Particularly common in the Southeast and East and widely distributed in North America.

Comments: These average-sized, brown-capped, and brown-staining *Lactarius* species that produce copious astringent-tasting latex likely represent a species complex. *Lactarius volemus* and related species generally develop a fishy odor with age or a few hours after being picked. Some mycologists recognize two varieties, *L. volemus* var. *volemus* and *L. volemus* var. *flavus*; the two are essentially identical, but the latter is paler in color. In the Southeast, *L. volemus* and relatives are popular edibles. *Lactarius hygrophoroides* (also a choice edible) is morphologically similar but generally smaller in stature, with a shorter stalk and much more widely spaced gills. *Lactarius corrugis* (another choice edible) is similar but usually much larger, darker throughout, and has a much more wrinkled cap. The rarely collected *L. subvelutinus* (edibility unknown) is reported to be similar but differs in not staining when bruised or broken, not having the distinctive fishy odor, and producing a latex with a mild (not astringent) taste. Most other species with a similar color either have zonation on the cap and/or have peppery-tasting latex.

Lentinus crinitus (Linnaeus) Fries

HAIRY CAPPED LENTINUS

FAMILY Polyporaceae

Cap 2–9 cm wide, at first convex with a shallow central depression but becoming more funnel-shaped with age, margin generally downturned, in older specimens the outer one-third of the margin is sometimes broadly folded or wavy; surface covered by dense radiating hairs, these often sticking together and appressed to the surface as scales at the center of the cap and erect toward the margin, hairs grade from dark brown to reddish brown at the center to pale yellowish brown to white at the margin, cap surface below the hairs whitish when young to pale yellowish brown with age; gills attached and decurrent, close to crowded, narrow, edges finely serrated, white when young and becoming yellowish with age; stalk 2–5 cm long and 2–10 mm thick, equal or sometimes tapering or enlarging in either direction, often having a small bulb at the base, not hollow, leathery in texture, surface slightly roughened, similar in color to the surface of the cap but generally paler near the apex and often gray to nearly black at the base; spores white in mass, $5.5–8 \times 1.8–3$ µm, rounded, smooth, nonamyloid.

Habitat/Biological Role: Occurring on dead logs and stumps of broadleaf trees, and often found in gregarious clusters; since this fungus is primarily a tropical species, it fruits throughout much of the year in the regions where it is most common. Decomposer of wood.

Distribution: This fungus is restricted to the southernmost portion of our region and is very common in Florida and along the Gulf Coast, southward into Central America.

Comments: In the southern portion of our region, *Lentinus crinitus* can be exceedingly common, often fruiting in large clusters along fallen logs. We have observed that the mycelium of this fungus sometimes produces a hard, smooth outer layer on wood that is typically dark in color, and when specimens grow on small pieces of wood, it can appear that they are fruiting from a dark-colored tuber. *Lentinus tigrinus* has a more northern range but can appear morphologically similar; it differs in having a thicker fruiting body and stalk, larger spores ($6–10 \times 2.5–3.5$ µm), and less-erect hairs on cap surface. *Lentinus suavissimus*, a somewhat similar but uncommon species, has a smooth cap that lacks any hairs or scales. *Lentinus tephroleucus* is another southern species that is somewhat similar; it is darker in color on the cap surface and stalk, generally has shorter hairs, and often arises from a sclerotium in the ground or sometimes decaying wood. *Crinipellis zonata* and other members of that genus can appear similar, but they are less commonly encountered and generally more slender, with distinct zonations composed of dense appressed hairs on the cap surface, a cap margin that often splits radially at maturity, and a more slender stalk that is hollow and darker in color. *Neolentinus lepideus* should also be compared; however, its larger size and more robust fruiting habit make it unlikely to be confused with *L. crinitus*. *Lentinus crinitus* is edible but rather leathery in texture.

Lepista nuda (Bulliard) Cooke

BLEWIT

SYNONYM *Clitocybe nuda*

FAMILY Tricholomataceae

Cap 5–12.5 cm wide, convex at first but becoming flattened with age, often developing a sunken center, violet to grayish violet when young but fading to tan or pinkish buff; surface of cap smooth, margin incurved at first but expanding and becoming wavy; gills close, purple to pale violet but fading to tan or light brown; stalk 3–7.5 cm long and 1–2.5 cm wide, somewhat enlarged at the base, the same color as the cap or paler; spores pinkish buff in mass, 5.5–8 × 3.5–5 µm, ellipsoid, minutely roughened to smooth.

Habitat/Biological Role: Occurring on the ground in broadleaf or conifer forests; occasionally solitary but usually occurring in small groups; time of fruiting variable and depending largely upon climate. Decomposer of litter and humus.

Distribution: Found throughout North America.

Comments: Its distinctive violet color is usually enough to identify *Lepista nuda* but it often fades substantially. It tends to fruit late in the season but can be relatively abundant. This species is a choice edible and is sometimes cultivated. *Laccaria ochropurpurea* is one of the most similar fungi, but it is mycorrhizal and typically has a pale lilac cap, dark lilac gills, a white spore print, and spiny spores.

Leucoagaricus americanus
(Peck) Vellinga

REDDENING LEPIOTA

SYNONYMS *Lepiota americana*, *L. bresadolae*

FAMILY Agaricaceae

Cap 3–15 cm broad, at first pointed bell-shaped to convex but eventually becoming flat with age; surface dry, smooth, reddish brown when young, as cap expands the reddish brown surface layer breaks into regular concentric rings of scales revealing the white color of the lower surface, reddish brown upper layer frequently intact at the center of the cap and the scales becoming more sparse toward the margin of the cap, lower surface white but bruising yellowish and then to darkening reddish brown; gills free, close, white, also bruising in a manner similar to the cap; stalk 5–14 cm long and 6–23 mm wide, tapering toward the apex and base, often with a bulbous middle portion, dry, smooth, white when young but with age or bruising becoming dull reddish, partial veil white and present as membranous annulus near the apex of the stalk, generally with two distinct edges; spores white in mass, 8–13 × 5–9 µm, elliptical, smooth.

Habitat/Biological Role: Occurring as solitary fruiting bodies or in groups, on wood chips or near other types of decomposing wood; fruiting summer to late fall. Decomposer of wood.

Distribution: Most common in the Southeast and East but found throughout North America.

Comments: *Lepiota besseyi* (edibility unknown) is morphologically similar but has smaller scales on the cap and also has scales on the lower portion of the stalk. *Leucoagaricus rubrotinctus* (syn. *Lepiota rubrotincta*) is similar in color, but besides being smaller (cap up to 6 cm broad), it differs in having tissue that does not stain or bruise and a cap surface that usually cracks radially or has densely packed small scales. *Lepiota clypeolaria* (poisonous) is similar but differs in having brown scales on the cap and a covering of cottony fibers on the stalk. *Lepiota cristata* is another similar species, but it has brownish scales, a smooth stalk that is not reported to stain or bruise, a chemical odor similar to that of tire rubber, and smaller spores (6–8 × 3–4.5 µm). *Leucoagaricus americanus* is not recommended for consumption since there are many similar species, some of which are poisonous.

Leucocoprinus fragilissimus
(Ravenel ex Berkeley & M. A. Curtis)
Patouillard

FRAGILE LEUCOCOPRINUS

SYNONYM *Lepiota fragilissima*

FAMILY Agaricaceae

Cap 1–4.5 cm wide, at first thimble-shaped but expanding to become convex and then eventually becoming flat with a central umbo and downturned or upturned margin; surface translucent striate and grooved, pale yellowish green, covered by fine granules that become more sparse with age; gills attached to free, narrow, white to off-white; stalk 4–16 cm long and 1–3 mm wide, equal to slightly enlarged toward the base, very frail, usually covered by fine granules like the cap surface, similar in color to the cap surface or slightly darker, very thin annulus present near the apex of the stalk; spores white in mass, 9–13 × 7–8 μm, elliptical, smooth, dextrinoid.

Habitat/Biological Role: Occurring as solitary fruiting bodies but usually with others found in the general vicinity, usually arising from the litter layer; fruiting after summer or fall rains. Decomposer of leaf litter.

Distribution: Particularly common throughout our region and widely distributed in eastern North America, south to Central America.

Comments: The fruiting bodies of this beautiful but delicate fungus are so frail that it is nearly impossible to harvest one without having the stalk crumble in your hands. The fruiting bodies rarely last more than a day or two. *Leucocoprinus birnbaumii* (syn. *L. luteus*, *Lepiota lutea*) is morphologically similar but is a more vivid yellow, not as frail or translucent, and generally occurs on wood chips or in flower pots. *Leucocoprinus flavescens* is similar in color and frailness but is generally smaller and shorter in stature and the spores are smaller (4–6.5 × 3.5–4.5 μm). The rarely observed *L. magnicystidiosus* has been reported from Texas and is so similar in appearance to *L. fragilissimus* that the two species are impossible to distinguish without using microscopic characters (it has very large pleurocystidia and cheilocystidia). *Leucocoprinus cepaestipes* (syn. *Lepiota cepistipes*) and *Leucocoprinus ianthinus* (syn. *L. lilacinogranulosus*) are also similar, but the fruiting bodies of both are more robust in stature and white to brownish instead of yellow. The edibility of these species is not known.

Macrocybe titans (H. E. Bigelow & Kimbrough) Pegler, Lodge & Nakasone

GIANT MACROCYBE

SYNONYM *Tricholoma titans*

FAMILY Tricholomataceae

Cap 8–100 cm, at first convex but becoming flat with age; surface dry to moist and rather variable, sometimes with smooth or moist spots or fine scales, with older specimens often developing large irregular cracks, surface itself whitish to pale creamy brown, often darkest toward the center of the cap, margin often steeply upturned and undulate in mature specimens; gills attached to notched, crowded, pale grayish to grayish yellow; stalk 7–45 cm long and 1.5–15 cm wide, overall whitish to dingy off-white with age, equal to bulbous at the base, base often club-shaped or when fruiting bodies occur in a cluster usually with a pointed base, dry, firm, frequently with fine tufts or recurved scales that are darker than the stalk; spores whitish to cream in mass, 5.5–8 × 4–5.5 μm, broadly ellipsoid, smooth, nonamyloid.

Habitat/Biological Role: Occurring as solitary fruiting bodies or in groups, sometimes in dense clusters, on the ground in open or forested areas; fruiting summer to fall. Decomposer of organic matter or possibly having a complex biological association with ants.

Distribution: It is most common from north Florida south to Central and South America and seems to be moving northward. There are a few recent records from central Georgia and possibly one or two from the Piedmont of the Carolinas.

Comments: This fungus, which can produce one of the largest non-perennial fruiting bodies of any fungus found in North America, is unlikely to be confused with any other fungus in our region. Its biology and ecology are still unclear. Some reports of *Macrocybe titans* in Central America indicate that the fruiting bodies occur on the mounds of living colonies of ants known to cultivate fungi, which hints at a possible symbiosis or mutualism; however, this is yet to be determined. The edibility of the fungus is likewise unclear; most American references advise caution or list its edibility as unknown, although indigenous people in northern South America do consume what is believed to be the same species.

Macrolepiota procera
(Scopoli) Singer

PARASOL MUSHROOM

SYNONYM *Lepiota procera*

FAMILY Agaricaceae

Cap 7–25 cm wide, at first oval to bell-shaped but eventually expanding to become almost flat; surface dry, at first brownish gray and then breaking into scaly patches revealing the off-white color of the lower surface, scales often arranged in zones, margin inrolled, sometimes the scales on the cap are lost with age; gills free, close, broad, usually white when young and darkening slightly with age; stalk 15–30 cm long and 1–1.5 cm wide, equal but with an enlarged base, dry, generally similar in color to the cap surface; prominent annulus present near the apex of the stalk, membranous and composed of several layers, movable (up and down the stalk); spores white in mass, 15–20 × 10–13 µm, broadly elliptical, smooth, dextrinoid, with a prominent apical pore.

Habitat/Biological Role: Fruiting bodies solitary or sometimes occurring in large clusters on the ground in mixed forests or cleared areas; fruiting from early summer into winter. Decomposer of organic material.

Distribution: Depending on the species concept being used (see comments), this fungus is widely distributed in North America but most common east of the Rocky Mountains.

Comments: The taxonomy of this species is undergoing more careful evaluation. It appears this may be a species complex, with the name *Macrolepiota procera* referring only to a European species; however, this is currently the best name we know for this species or group of species found in the Southeast. The edible look-alike *Chlorophyllum rachodes* (syn. *Lepiota rachodes*, *Macrolepiota rachodes*) has smaller spores (6–10 × 6–7 µm) and

differs in having flesh that stains vividly (white flesh of the cap stains orange to reddish brown and the stalk stains yellowish orange) as well. The edible *M. gracilenta* (syn. *L. gracilenta*) is also morphologically similar but is smaller in stature and has smaller spores (10–13 × 7–8 µm). *Macrolepiota procera*, *M. gracilenta*, and *Chlorophyllum rachodes* are edible, but great care should be taken to avoid confusing any of these with the similar but toxic *C. molybdites*.

Marasmiellus candidus (Fries) Singer

WHITE MARASMIELLUS

SYNONYM *Marasmiellus albocorticis*

FAMILY Omphalotaceae

Cap 1–3.5 cm wide, at first convex but becoming flat to upturned with age; surface finely hairy, dry, striate to plicate depending on age, over all white; gills attached, sometimes shortly decurrent, widely spaced, cross-veined, white to off-white; stalk 1–2 cm long and 1–1.5 mm wide, equal, often curved, stiff to rubbery, at first white but becoming shiny brownish black from the base upward with age; spores white in mass, 10–15 × 3.5–6 μm, spindle-shaped, smooth.

Habitat/Biological Role: Usually occurring in large groups on decomposing twigs and branches; fruiting spring to late fall. Decomposer of wood.

Distribution: Very common throughout our region and widely distributed in North America.

Comments: *Marasmiellus praeacutus,* one of several morphologically similar fungi in our region, differs in having a lighter-colored (reddish brown) stalk with a white and tapered base and smaller spores (5.5–8.5 × 2.5–3.5 μm). *Mycetinis opacus* (syn. *Marasmiellus opacus*) is superficially similar but differs in having a much longer stalk (up to 6 cm long); moreover, its stalk never gets darker than pale brown and its spores are smaller (6–11 × 3–4.5 μm). *Tetrapyrgos nigripes* (syn. *M. nigripes*) is a very similar species but has a stalk that is black and coated with fine white hairs and spores that are pyramid/triangle-shaped and smaller (8–9 μm). All these fungi are too small to be of any culinary value.

Marasmius siccus (Schweinitz) Fries

ORANGE PINWHEEL MARASMIUS

FAMILY Marasmiaceae

Cap 3–25 mm wide, bell-shaped to convex; surface appearing plicate to broadly folded, finely roughened, pale orange-brown, pale reddish brown, or pale yellowish brown; gills notched to free, distant, white to pale yellowish; stalk 1–7 cm long and 0.2–1 mm wide, equal, smooth, wire-like, at first whitish to pale yellowish and then becoming brown to blackish brown with age or near the base; spores white in mass, 15–22 × 3–5 µm, curved to club-shaped, smooth.

Habitat/Biological Role: Occurring in clusters on fallen leaves, needles, and twigs; fruiting spring to fall. Decomposer of organic material.

Distribution: Most common in the East and widely distributed in North America.

Comments: This small fungus is commonly found on the forest floor during periods of wet weather. *Marasmius fulvoferrugineus*, found throughout southern and southeastern North America, is very similar; however, it is generally larger, darker in color, and has slightly smaller spores (15–18 × 3–4.5 µm). *Marasmius pulcherripes* is similar with respect to the appearance of the cap but is generally pinkish to purplish in color and often smaller.

Marasmius sullivantii
Montagne

SMALL ORANGE MARASMIUS

FAMILY Marasmiaceae

Cap 8–25 mm wide, at first convex but becoming flat with age; surface smooth, not striate, sometimes finely pubescent, dark reddish brown to yellowish orange overall but often with a paler-colored margin with age; gills free to attached, close, white; stalk 10–35 mm long and 1–1.5 mm wide, equal but sometimes slightly enlarged at both the apex and base, rubbery, hollow, usually with fine white hairs at the base of the stalk, lower portion of the stalk generally dark reddish brown to orange-brown, very finely hairy, upper portion white to buff but in some very young specimens the entire stalk is white; spores white in mass, 6.5–9 × 3–4.5 µm, elliptical, smooth, nonamyloid.

Habitat/Biological Role: Occurring as solitary fruiting bodies or in scattered groups on broadleaf leaf litter and sometimes woody branches; fruiting summer to fall. Decomposer of leaf litter.

Distribution: Common east of the Rocky Mountains from New England south to Alabama and Texas.

Comments: *Marasmius cohaerens* is similar but paler in color, has a smooth stalk, usually occurs in nearly cespitose clusters, and has larger spores (7–10 × 3–5.5 µm). *Marasmius floridanus* is morphologically similar but differs in having a completely smooth stalk and slightly longer spores (7–11 × 3–4 µm). Both *M. siccus* and *M. fulvoferrugineus* are similar in color, but the former has a plicate to broadly striate cap, the latter has a prominently plicate cap, and both have larger spores and wire-like stalks. *Rhizomarasmius pyrrhocephalus* (syn. *M. pyrrhocephalus*) can also appear similar but has a stalk that is nearly black, densely hairy, and much longer (3–10 cm). All these species are too small and leathery to be of any culinary value.

Megacollybia platyphylla
(Persoon) Kotlaba & Pouzar

BROAD GILL

SYNONYM *Tricholomopsis platyphylla*

FAMILY Marasmiaceae

Cap 5–15 cm wide, at first broadly convex and becoming flat to upturned with age; surface smooth, dark gray to gray-brown, with fine radially arranged fibrils; gills attached, close to well spaced, broad, white to pale whitish gray; stalk 4–15 cm long and 1–2 cm wide, tapering slightly toward the apex, white to pale grayish, usually with several prominent white rhizomorphs at the base; spores white in mass, 7–10 × 5–7 μm, oval, smooth, nonamyloid.

Habitat/Biological Role: Occurring as solitary fruiting bodies or in scattered groups on or near well-decomposed stumps and logs of broadleaf trees; fruiting from spring to fall. Decomposer of wood.

Distribution: Most frequently encountered in the Appalachian Mountains, but the distribution of this fungus depends upon the species concept being used (see comments); members of this complex are most common in eastern North America.

Comments: The taxonomy of the group to which *Megacollybia platyphylla* belongs has undergone major changes, and the distribution patterns of certain species are just now being determined. Genetic work has shown that "true" *M. platyphylla* (which until 2007 was the only species recognized in the genus) occurs only in Europe. At least four other nearly identical species (morphologically) occur in North America, and they are very challenging to separate without genetics and a careful examination of subtle microscopic characters. Our understanding is that *M. texensis* is generally found in eastern Texas (and likely in other areas of the Gulf Coast), *M. subfurfuracea* is reported from the southern Appalachians west to Arkansas, and two forms of *M. rodmanii* (likely the species illustrated) are generally reported from eastern North America south to Costa Rica. It may be possible to distinguish *M. subfurfuracea* from other species on the basis of having dark-colored gill edges. Members of the North American *M. platyphylla* complex are generally considered edible if cooked thoroughly, although there are occasional reports of gastrointestinal issues.

Mycena acicula (Schaeffer) P. Kummer

CORAL SPRING MYCENA

FAMILY Mycenaceae

Cap 3–10 mm wide, at first conic to bell-shaped and flattening to become convex with age, sometimes with an upturned margin; surface smooth, bright orange to reddish but becoming yellowish toward the margin; gills attached, close, somewhat broad, pale yellowish orange to off-white; stalk 1–7.5 cm long and usually less than 1 mm wide, equal, delicate, smooth, translucent, orange-yellow to pale yellow; spores white in mass, 9–11 × 3.5–4.5 μm, oblong to spindle-shaped, smooth, nonamyloid.

Habitat/Biological Role: Usually occurring as solitary fruiting bodies or in sparse groups on wet leaves, twigs, pieces of wood, and other organic debris; most commonly encountered in the early spring in our region but can also be found through the summer and into the early fall. Decomposer of organic material.

Distribution: In eastern North America typically reported from North Carolina north to Canada but known from widely scattered localities throughout the continent, including California.

Comments: This is a rather distinctive species of *Mycena* in the Southeast. The most similar species generally occur on conifer needles and are found north or west of our region. *Mycena crocea* is quite similar but occurs only on the nuts of walnut and hickory. This fungus is too small to be of culinary value and some members of its genus contain toxins, so it is not recommended for the table.

Mycena crocea Maas Geesteranus

WALNUT MYCENA, NUT MYCENA

SYNONYM *Mycena luteopallens*

FAMILY Mycenaceae

Cap 8–15 mm wide, at first broadly conic and becoming convex to flat with age, surface smooth, at first bright orange to reddish but becoming pale yellow to white with age, margin becoming translucent striate with age; gills attached, close, somewhat broad, off-white to pale yellow, sometimes very pale pinkish; stalk 5–10 cm long and 1–2 mm wide, hollow, frail, translucent, smooth with a small tuft of mycelia at the base, the same color as the cap; spores white in mass, 7–9 × 4–5.5 µm, oval, faintly roughened, slightly amyloid.

Habitat/Biological Role: Occurring only on nuts, usually on buried walnut or hickory nuts; fruiting bodies solitary or sometimes found in clusters arising from the same nut; often fruiting in sparse clusters under the host nut-producing trees from summer to late fall. Decomposer of nuts.

Distribution: Particularly common in the Southeast and generally restricted to eastern North America.

Comments: If the nut substrate upon which this fungus occurs is excavated from the soil, it is easy to identify this species. Many members of this genus can be challenging to identify. *Mycena acicula* is quite similar but does not occur on nuts. The edibility of this fungus is not known, but some members of the genus contain dangerous toxins. In any case, this species is too small to be of much culinary interest. *Strobilurus conigenoides* is similar in stature but is whitish to pale yellowish and fruits on magnolia seed pods. *Baeospora myosura* is similar in stature but is white in color and fruits from pine cones.

Mycena leaiana (Berkeley) Saccardo

ORANGE MYCENA

FAMILY Mycenaceae

Cap 1–4 cm wide, bell-shaped at first but becoming convex with age; upper surface viscid and shiny, reddish orange fading to orange-yellow; margin striate; gills moderately close, pinkish orange to pinkish yellow, bruising yellow-orange, edges of gills deep reddish orange; stalk 2.5–5 cm long and 2–4 mm wide, smooth, viscid, orange to yellow with dense orange hairs at the base; spores white in mass, 7–10 × 5–6 µm, elliptical, smooth, amyloid.

Habitat/Biological Role: Occurring on decomposing wood of broadleaf trees; especially common on beech, usually occurring in clusters; fruiting summer and fall. Decomposer of wood.

Distribution: Found throughout eastern North America.

Comments: Its bright orange color makes *Mycena leaiana* one of the most noticeable and distinctive members of a very large and taxonomically challenging genus. During the summer months, it can be very common on decomposing beech logs and stumps. This fungus produces a watery latex that will stain fingers orange when the fruiting body is handled. Edibility is unknown.

Neohygrocybe subovina
(Hesler & A. H. Smith) Lodge & Padamsee

BROWN SUGAR WAXY CAP

SYNONYM *Hygrophorus subovinus*

FAMILY Hygrophoraceae

Cap 1.5–5 cm wide, at first hemispherical to convex but becoming broadly convex with age, often with a broad low umbo, margin even to wavy, inrolled at first and then becoming upturned with age; surface dry, smooth, dark grayish brown to grayish black but sometimes with reddish brown to olivaceous tints; gills adnexed, subdistant, broad, thick, edges finely serrated, at first light gray to cream but developing grayish or brownish tints with age, bruising reddish or slowly becoming blackish; stalk 4–9 cm long and 4–15 mm wide, nearly equal or expanding downward, often furrowed, dry, smooth, color the same as the cap surface or pale brown with a whitish base; spores white in mass, 5–7 × 5–6 μm, ellipsoid to subovoid, smooth, nonamyloid.

Habitat/Biological Role: Occurring on the ground in broadleaf forests, often on bare soil or in grassy areas; fruiting bodies solitary or more often in small groups; fruiting from summer through the fall. Decomposer of humus and litter.

Distribution: Widely distributed in eastern North America.

Comments: *Neohygrocybe subovina*, the most commonly encountered dull-colored waxy cap mushroom in the Southeast, is fairly distinctive. It sometimes has the odor of brown sugar. *Hygrocybe ovina* (syn. *Hygrophorus ovinus*) is the most similar species, but it has larger spores (6–10 × 4.5–7 μm), lacks cystidia on the gills, and has a more ammonia-like odor. The edibility of both species is unknown.

Neolentinus lepideus (Fries)
Redhead & Ginns

TRAIN WRECKER, SCALY LENTINUS

SYNONYM *Lentinus lepideus*

FAMILY Polyporaceae

Cap 4–25 cm wide, at first convex but becoming flat with age; surface sometimes viscid when young and then becoming dry, at first white and then developing coarse raised brown scales, margin incurved to upturned; gills attached and shortly decurrent, close, broad, edges finely serrated, white to off-white, sometimes reported to stain when bruised; stalk 3–10 cm long and 1–2 cm thick, equal or slightly tapered toward the base, when associated with a buried substrate sometimes having a radicating base, central to nearly lateral, at first off-white and smooth and then becoming pale brown to reddish brown and scaly, sometimes having a membranous partial veil when young that leaves a frail, easily lost annulus near the apex of the stalk; spores white in mass, 8–15 × 4–6 μm, nearly cylindrical, smooth, nonamyloid.

Habitat/Biological Role: Occurring as solitary fruiting bodies or in nearly cespitose clusters on conifers or broadleaf trees and commonly found on creosote-treated railroad ties; usually fruiting in spring and fall between periods of cool wet weather. Decomposer of wood.

Distribution: Most common in the Southeast and East but widely distributed in North America.

Comments: One common name is based on its unusual ability to grow on creosote-treated railroad ties, which could possibly lead to a train wreck. This fungus was previously placed in *Lentinus*, which then included the shiitake; this led the USDA to ban shiitake mushrooms from entering the United States until the early 1970s, under the erroneous assumption that they could cause the same economic damage as *Neolentinus lepideus*. In our region, *N. lepideus* is relatively distinctive; older fruiting bodies of *Lentinus crinitus* can be somewhat similar in appearance, but the caps are very thin, densely hairy, and they have a much thinner stalk. *Neolentinus lepideus* is considered to be a good edible mushroom when young and not fruiting from creosote-treated wood; it has also been shown to contain some medicinal properties.

Omphalotus illudens
(Schweinitz) Bresinsky & Besl

JACK-O-LANTERN MUSHROOM

FAMILY Omphalotaceae

Cap 5–15 cm wide, at first convex but becoming flat to upturned with age, often with a small central raised area, bright orange to yellow-orange but becoming brownish orange in age; upper surface smooth; gills closely spaced, decurrent, color the same as the cap; stalk 4–19 cm long and 1–1.5 cm wide, narrowed at the base, color same as cap or paler; spores white to pale yellow in mass, 3.5–4.5 µm, subglobose, smooth.

Habitat/Biological Role: Occurring on decomposing wood of broadleaf trees, often found at the base of dead or dying trees, sometimes occurring in dense clusters seemingly arising from the ground but actually attached to dead buried roots; fruiting from midsummer to fall. Decomposer of wood.

Distribution: Widely distributed throughout eastern North America.

Comments: The most unusual feature of *Omphalotus illudens* can be observed only in the dark. If a fresh moist specimen is in complete darkness, the gills have an eerie green glow. Some individuals glow so dimly that it takes several minutes for the eyes to adjust, but other, more moist specimens are incredibly bright (see photo on page 16). Other bioluminescent fungi found in the Southeast are *Armillaria mellea* and *Panellus stipticus*. Some people confuse the poisonous *O. illudens* with edible chanterelles of the genus *Cantharellus*; however, chanterelles are found on the ground, lack true gills, and never occur in dense clusters.

Panaeolus antillarum (Fries) Dennis

WHITE DUNG PANAEOLUS

SYNONYMS *Panaeolus phalaenarum*, *P. solidipes*

FAMILY Psathyrellaceae

Cap 3–10 cm broad, at first bell-shaped but becoming broadly convex with age; surface smooth to finely radially wrinkled, white, sometimes developing a yellowish color at the center of the cap; gills attached to notched, close, off-white to pale grayish when young and then becoming nearly black with age; stalk 3–20 cm long and 4–15 mm wide, equal to enlarged at the base, smooth, sometimes with faint striations near the apex, whitish to grayish; spores black in mass, 16–21 × 10–12.5 µm, ellipsoid, smooth.

Habitat/Biological Role: Occurring as solitary fruiting bodies or often in small clusters on herbivore dung; fruiting summer to winter (depending on the region). Decomposer of dung.

Distribution: Found throughout North America, particularly in the Southeast and on the East Coast. We have collected this species in central Mexico, and it is also reported from South America.

Comments: This fungus is found primarily on horse or cow dung, and its large stature and bright white cap make it easy to spot in pastures. *Panaeolus semiovatus* (syn. *P. phalenarum*, *P. separatus*, *Anellaria separata*) is very similar (and nonpoisonous); however, it differs in having a partial veil that leaves a membranous annulus near the apex of the stalk. *Panaeolus cyanescens* (known only from the southernmost portion of our region) is somewhat similar but much more delicate, and the flesh bruises bluish. *Panaeolus antillarum* is edible but not held in high regard; unlike many other dung fungi, it is not reported to be hallucinogenic.

Panellus stipticus (Bulliard)
P. Karsten

LUMINESCENT PANELLUS

SYNONYM *Panus stipticus*

FAMILY Mycenaceae

Cap 1–3 cm across and 1.5–3 mm thick, semicircular, shell- to kidney-shaped structure, brown to buff or tan; surface hairy to scruffy-scaly; gills moderately close, pale to salmon to orange-buff; stalk short, off-center, 3–5 mm long and 3–10 mm wide, dirty white to yellowish brown, densely hairy; spores white in mass, 3–5 × 1–3 µm, elliptical, smooth.

Habitat/Biological Role: Occurring on decomposing wood, solitary or in small clusters, typically found in groups of overlapping fruiting bodies; fruiting summer to fall. Decomposer of wood.

Distribution: Widely distributed throughout North America.

Comments: As indicated by its common name, *Panellus stipticus* is one of the bioluminescent fungi included in this field guide (the others are *Armillaria mellea* and *Omphalotus illudens*). The gills give off a green glow in complete darkness. This fungus is not edible and might actually be poisonous, but the fruiting bodies have been used in traditional medicine to stop bleeding. This species should be compared with *Schizophyllum commune*.

Parasola plicatilis (Curtis)
Redhead, Vilgalys & Hopple

JAPANESE UMBRELLA INKY

SYNONYMS *Coprinus plicatilis,*
Pseudocoprinus plicatilis

FAMILY Psathyrellaceae

Cap 0.5–2 cm wide, very thin and frail,
at first narrowly bell-shaped to conic
but becoming flat to shallowly upturned
with age; surface at first pale brownish
and then becoming gray with age, center
and apex of the ridges usually remaining reddish brown, dry, deeply folded
to striate, margin usually downturned;
gills distantly spaced, usually free or with
a ring-like attachment, at first gray but
becoming nearly black and then deliquescing; stalk 4–7 cm long, and 1–2 mm wide,
equal with small bulb at the base, brittle,
same color as the cap to nearly transparent
with age; spores black in mass, 10–12 ×
7.5–9.5 µm, broadly elliptical, smooth,
nonamyloid.

Habitat/Biological Role: Occurring
on the ground in yards and fields during
periods of wet weather, often in scattered
groups and primarily appearing during
the early part of the day; fruiting from
summer into fall. Decomposer of humus
and litter.

Distribution: Frequently encountered
in the Southeast and widely distributed in
North America.

Comments: This fungus is so small
that not much is known about its edibility.
Several small inky caps, many of them
in the genera *Coprinus, Coprinopsis,* and
Coprinellus, have a similar appearance.
Two features that make *Parasola plicatilis*
distinctive: it does not have a dusting of
fine granules on the cap and it does not
occur on dung. *Conocybe lactea* occurs in
similar habitats but has a cap that is generally white, more conic, and lacks the prominent striations. *Coprinellus disseminatus*
and *Coprinus floridanus* (known only from

Florida) are similar, but their fruiting bodies are much smaller and usually occur in
large clusters on wood.

Pholiota flammans (Batsch)
P. Kummer

FLAMING PHOLIOTA, FLAME SCALECAP, YELLOW PHOLIOTA

FAMILY Strophariaceae

Cap 4–8 cm wide, at first broadly conic, frequently with an umbo, but often becoming flat with age; surface viscid, covered by recurved scales, sometimes with age the scales are lost, cap margin sometimes retaining veil remnants, overall color brilliant yellow to orangish, sometimes a brilliant lemon yellow, usually darkening or fading with age; gills notched to attached, close to crowded, bright yellow, staining pale yellow-brown, particularly along the edges; stalk 4–11 cm long and 4–10 mm wide, equal to slightly enlarged at the base, covered by a dense layer of recurved scales, typically with an irregular annulus near the apex and with a smoother paler-colored portion above the annulus, stalk similar in color to the surface of the cap but sometimes darker, particularly toward base; spores brown in mass, 4–5 × 2.5–3 µm, oblong to ellipsoid, smooth, nonamyloid.

Habitat/Biological Role: Occurring as a single cespitose cluster or sometimes in a series of large clusters on decomposing logs, generally reported to be on conifers; fruiting summer to fall. Decomposer of wood.

Distribution: Widely distributed in North America.

Comments: This species is one of the more colorful members of what is a large genus; however, fruiting bodies are often faded by the time they are found and thus can be dull in color, making it much more challenging to separate this species from others in the genus. Most of the several similar species are duller in color and require a consideration of microscopic features for identification. *Pholiota aurivella* is a name widely applied to a similar-looking species complex in our region, but its members are generally more tawny orange in color and have larger spores (7–10 × 4.5–6 µm). *Pholiota limonella* is another similar fungus with yellowish orange fruiting bodies, but the latter are dull in color; this species is encountered primarily in the northern portion of our region and the fruiting bodies differ from faded specimens of *P. flammans* most distinctly in having larger spores (6–7.5 × 4–5 µm). *Pholiota polychroa* is somewhat similar in shape, but the fruiting bodies lack the numerous scales and have very little yellow or orange color. *Pholiota flammans* is not recommended for food.

Pholiota polychroa (Berkeley)
A. H. Smith & H. J. Brodie

VARIABLE PHOLIOTA

FAMILY Strophariaceae

Cap 1.5–10 cm wide, at first convex but becoming nearly flat with age, typically having a broad umbo at the center of the cap; surface viscid with scattered to sparse reddish brown scales, scales most common at the cap center and toward the margin, scales often frail and becoming nearly absent with age, surface color very variable, frequently some shade of greenish gray with purplish tones or sometimes bluish green or becoming dark olive-green, with some specimens being pale olive-gray with yellowish hues; gills attached to shortly decurrent, close, edges whitish, entire gill variable in color, cream to faintly purple when young and becoming grayish brown to greenish brown with age, sometimes retaining purplish hues; stalk 2–7.5 cm long and 3–7 mm wide, equal or tapering toward the base, surface finely scaly except for near the apex, sometimes the entire stalk becoming smooth with age, frail annulus often present near the apex of the stalk, above this structure the stalk is smooth, stalk yellowish to grayish green near the apex and becoming reddish to pale brown toward the base, base sometimes covered by mass of fine hairs; spores brownish in mass and if moist sometimes having a purplish tint, 6–7.5 × 3.5–4.5 µm, oblong to elliptical, smooth, nonamyloid.

Habitat/Biological Role: Occurring as a single cespitose cluster or sometimes in larger clusters on logs, stumps, or at the base of living broadleaf trees, occasionally found on conifers; fruiting summer to fall. Decomposer of wood and in some situations possibly parasitic.

Distribution: Primarily reported in the Southeast but widely distributed in North America.

Comments: The variability in the color of this fungus can be confusing, but this character can also help with identification. *Pholiota polychroa* typically has green or purplish tints on the cap when young, which is unusual for this genus. *Pholiota lenta*, reported from South Carolina northward, is morphologically similar but occurs on humus-rich soil or soil with a lot of woody debris present; it generally has white scales on the cap surface. The edibility of these species is not well established, but most members of this genus are either mildly poisonous or inferior in taste.

Pholiota squarrosoides (Peck) Saccardo

SHAGGY SCALYCAP, SHAGGY PHOLIOTA, SCALY PHOLIOTA

FAMILY Strophariaceae

Cap 3–12 cm wide, broadly conic when young, frequently with an umbo, and often becoming flattened with age, margin inrolled; surface dry, covered by closely spaced recurved scales near the center of the cap but scales becoming more widely spaced toward the margin, scales pale brown to pale reddish brown, color between the scales usually a shade of pale yellow; gills attached to the stalk and shortly decurrent, close, at first whitish and then becoming rusty brown with age; stalk 4–13 cm long and 1–2.5 cm wide, equal to tapering downward, surface covered by closely spaced recurved scales similar to cap, with a scale-free zone near the apex of the stalk, partial veil sometimes present as an annulus near the apex of the stalk or occurring as remnants along the margin of the cap; spores brown in mass, 4–6 × 2.5–3.5 µm, elliptical to ovate, smooth, nonamyloid.

Habitat/Biological Role: Occurring as a single cespitose cluster or sometimes in a series of clusters on logs, stumps, or at the base of living broadleaf trees; fruiting summer to fall. Decomposer of wood and in some situations possibly parasitic.

Distribution: Most common in the northern portion of our region but widely distributed in North America.

Comments: Scalycaps are distinctive, but there are some similar species. *Leucopholiota decorosa* can appear similar, but it has a white spore print and generally darker and denser scales on the cap surface. *Pholiota aurivella* is somewhat similar but has larger, sparser scales on the cap surface and larger spores (7–10 × 4.5–6 µm). As its epithet suggests, *P. squarrosa* is very similar, but it often has a garlic-like odor, gills that become greenish as it matures, and larger spores (6–7.5 × 3.5–4.5 µm) with apical pores. Some authors consider these species edible; however, there have been reports of poisonings, primarily gastrointestinal issues. Most people who report eating this fungus found the texture and flavor not very appealing; as such, we encourage foragers to seek other, safer, more desirable edible mushrooms.

Phylloporus rhodoxanthus
(Schweinitz) Bresadola

GILLED BOLETE

FAMILY Boletaceae

Cap 2–10 cm broad, convex but becoming nearly flat to centrally depressed with age, upper surface brown to dull reddish brown, dry, finely velvety when young, cracking in age to reveal the bright yellow flesh; gills decurrent, subdistant, sometimes with crossveins to almost poroid, bright yellow when young and darkening with age; stalk 2–7.5 cm long and 0.5–2 cm wide, becoming thicker toward the apex, buff to yellowish or sometimes colored like the cap surface, staining dingy red with age or handling, evidence of yellow mycelium present at the base; spores orange-brown to olivaceous yellowish brown in mass, 9–14 × 3.5–6 μm, narrowly elliptical, smooth, nonamyloid.

Habitat/Biological Role: Occurring on the ground as scattered fruiting bodies or in groups, under broadleaf trees and conifers; fruiting throughout summer and early fall. Forms mycorrhizal associations with trees.

Distribution: Particularly common in the Southeast and widely distributed in North America.

Comments: Although this fungus has gills, not pores, it is closely related to the boletes, and collectors often take it for a bolete when observing it only from the top. It is edible and tasty but rarely prolific enough to be widely eaten. *Phylloporus leucomycelinus* (edible) is nearly identical, but the mycelium at the base of the stalk is white, not yellow. *Phylloporus boletinoides* (edibility unknown) is similar in stature; however, the cap surface is a darker grayish brown and its "gills," which are much more poroid, are grayish with many ridges and veins between them. *Boletinellus merulioides* is somewhat similar in general appearance but does not have a gill-like lower surface.

Phyllotopsis nidulans
(Persoon) Singer

ORANGE MOCK OYSTER MUSHROOM

SYNONYMS *Crepidotus nidulans, Panus nidulans, Pleurotus nidulans*

FAMILY Tricholomataceae

Cap 3–8 cm across, fan-shaped, semicircular, margin usually inrolled, upper surface bright orange to pale yellowish orange, often one paler zone near the margin; surface covered by short dense hairs; gills close, generally the same color as the surface of the cap; stalk usually absent; spores pale pink to reddish in mass, 5–8 × 2–4 µm, elliptical to sausage-shaped, smooth, nonamyloid.

Habitat/Biological Role: Commonly occurring in overlapping clusters on broadleaf and conifer logs and stumps; fruiting from early spring to fall, often during cold weather. Decomposer of wood.

Distribution: Widely distributed throughout North America but more common east of the Rocky Mountains.

Comments: The color of this fungus makes it rather distinctive; it is not considered to be edible. *Tapinella panuoides* is the most similar species in the Southeast, but this species occurs only on the wood of conifers, its color is not as bright, the cap surface lacks the dense covering of hairs, the gills are regularly forking, and it yields a yellowish spore print. *Sarcomyxa serotina* is somewhat similar but is greenish gray in color, lacks the surface hairs, and has smaller spores (4–6 × 1–2 µm).

Pleurotus dryinus (Persoon)
P. Kummer

VEILED OYSTER MUSHROOM

SYNONYMS *Pleurotus corticatus, Armillaria dryina*

FAMILY Pleurotaceae

Cap 4–13 cm broad, semicircular to broadly fan-shaped, upper surface white to pale yellowish with age; surface usually sparsely covered by appressed tufts of hairs, margin inrolled when young and often with striation-like tufts forming ridges along the margin; gills subdistant and decurrent, white when young but sometimes becoming pale yellow with age, covered by a thin partial veil when young; stalk 4–10 cm long and 1–3 cm wide, usually centered to slightly off-center, more or less equal in thickness, white, firm, smooth, sometimes with the veil forming fragile annulus near the apex; spores white in mass, 9–14 × 3.5–5 µm, elliptical, smooth.

Habitat/Biological Role: Occurring on decomposing wood of broadleaf trees, usually found in small groups but sometimes as solitary fruiting bodies; fruiting early summer to fall. Decomposer of wood.

Distribution: Frequently encountered in the Southeast but widely distributed in North America.

Comments: This is believed to be the only member of the genus *Pleurotus* that has a partial veil, and the stalk is unusually prominent for this group, making the fungus relatively distinctive. This species is edible but is tougher than the related and commonly eaten *P. ostreatus*. The most similar-looking fungus is *Lentinus levis* (syn. *P. levis*), which differs in having a very hairy stalk, no partial veil, and often a pale yellow coloration overall. *Hypsizygus tessulatus* (syn. *H. elongatipes, H. marmoreus, H. ulmarius*) is similar, but it grows mostly on live broadleaf trees (particularly elm and sometimes box elder), gills are not as decurrent, it lacks a veil, and it has round spores that are smaller (5–7 µm); this species is also edible.

Pleurotus ostreatus (Jacquin)
P. Kummer

OYSTER MUSHROOM

FAMILY Pleurotaceae

Cap 5–20 cm across and 0.3–2 cm thick, fan-shaped, semicircular or oyster shell–shaped (hence the common name), upper surface white to dull grayish brown, smooth; margin often shallowly lobed or wavy; gills subdistant and attached to the base of the stalk, white at first but becoming pale yellow in age; stalk often absent but when present off-center and rudimentary; spores white to buff to pale lilac-gray in mass, 8–10.5 × 3–3.5 µm, cylindrical to narrowly kidney-shaped, smooth.

Habitat/Biological Role: Occurring as overlapping clusters on logs and stumps of broadleaf trees and occasionally conifers, found on a wide diversity of different hosts including tulip poplar, hickories, willows, maples, and magnolias; fruiting throughout the year—we have even collected this fungus frozen in snow. Decomposer of wood.

Distribution: More common in the East but widely distributed throughout North America.

Comments: The fungus recognized in most field guides as *Pleurotus ostreatus* is a species complex consisting of two similar forms. Both are considered choice edibles and among the easiest and safest edible mushrooms to learn. *Pleurotus pulmonarius* (summer oyster) is similar to *P. ostreatus* except that it is more delicate and lighter in color, sometimes nearly transparent. Several species of *Crepidotus* are somewhat similar in appearance, but these are poisonous. One of the major differences between the two genera is spore color: *Pleurotus* has a light to white spore print, while *Crepidotus* has a spore print that is some shade of brown. *Pleurocybella porrigens* can appear similar; however, it lacks any stalk-like structure, is smaller and thinner, and has smaller spores (5–7 × 4.5–6.5 µm).

Pluteus cervinus (Schaeffer) P. Kummer

FAWN MUSHROOM, DEER MUSHROOM

SYNONYM *Pluteus atricapillus*

FAMILY Pluteaceae

Cap 3–12 cm wide, at first convex but becoming flat with age; surface smooth, occasionally having streaks of fine fibrils, surface sometimes with wrinkles when young and sometimes retaining wrinkles at the center of the cap with age, brownish to grayish in color; gills free, close, at first white but becoming pinkish to salmon in color with age; stalk 5–11 cm long and 0.6–2 cm wide, equal to slightly enlarged at the base, surface smooth or finely fibrillose; spores pinkish to brownish pink in mass, 6–7 × 4–6 µm, ellipsoid, smooth.

Habitat/Biological Role: Occurring as solitary fruiting bodies or in small groups on the decomposing wood of broadleaf trees or conifers, fruiting from spring to early winter. Decomposer of wood.

Distribution: Widely distributed in North America.

Comments: *Pluteus cervinus* is edible, but it is likely a species complex, so there is no easy way to determine which species have been eaten. Several other *Pluteus* species in North America are similar. *Pluteus petasatus* is morphologically similar but occurs more frequently on piles of wood chips, has gills that are usually paler in color for a longer period of time, and typically has a whiter cap, slightly smaller spores (5–7 × 3.5–5 µm), and fewer cheilocystidia. *Pluteus thomsonii* differs in being smaller (cap up to 7 cm) and having prominent wrinkles and/or veins on the cap surface. *Pluteus longistriatus* differs in being smaller (cap up to 5 cm), with prominent striations that reach nearly to the center of the cap and slightly larger spores (6–7.5 × 5–5.5 µm). *Pluteus flavofuligineus* is sometimes encountered in our region, but it is much smaller and has a yellowish cap. Any specimen tentatively identified as *Pluteus cervinus* should also be compared with species of *Volvariella* and *Megacollybia*.

Psathyrella delineata (Peck)
A. H. Smith

WRINKLED-CAP PSATHYRELLA

SYNONYMS *Drosophila delineata,*
Hypholoma delineatum

FAMILY Psathyrellaceae

Cap 3–10 cm wide, broadly bell-shaped, sometimes becoming nearly flat to upturned with a central umbo with age, margins in some young specimens retaining veil remnants; surface dry, reddish brown to dark brown often paler in color toward margin, surface radially wrinkled; gills closely spaced, attached to stalk, grayish brown darkening with age, in young specimens gills obscured by partial veil; veil off-white thin and cottony to web-like, primarily remaining on cap margin and not forming ring on stalk; stalk 5–10 cm long and 5–15 mm wide, equal to enlarged toward the base, surface silky to scurfy, off-white to pale yellowish brown, veil remnants rarely present near apex; spores purple-brown to nearly black in mass, 6.5–9 × 4.5–5.5 µm, ellipsoid to oval, smooth.

Habitat/Biological Role: Usually occurring in small groups (but occasionally as solitary fruiting bodies) on larger pieces of decomposing wood; fruiting from spring to fall. Decomposer of wood.

Distribution: Found primarily in southeastern and eastern North America.

Comments: The combination of a wrinkled cap, dark spores, and fruiting on wood generally makes this a distinctive species with one exception. *Psathyrella rugocephala* is essentially identical but has substantially larger spores (9–11 × 6–8 µm) and is considered edible. Information about the edibility of *P. delineata* is limited, but since this species is so similar to the known edible *P. rugocephala*, it has likely been misidentified and eaten without any problems. Based on this logic, some would consider *P. delineata* to be edible. Also see *Cortinarius corrugatus*.

Psilocybe cubensis (Earle) Singer

GIGGLE MUSHROOM, MAGIC MUSHROOM

SYNONYMS *Stropharia cubensis, S. cyanescens*

FAMILY Strophariaceae

Cap 2–9 cm wide, bell-shaped to conic when young and becoming nearly flat with age; surface smooth, viscid when moist, whitish yellow to pale yellowish brown, darkest at the center and becoming paler toward the margin, often staining bluish near the margin or with age; gills attached to notched, close, at first whitish gray and then becoming faintly purplish gray to dark gray with age; stalk 4–16 cm long and 4–13 mm wide, typically enlarged toward the base, sometimes with a bulbous base, surface typically smooth or finely grooved near the apex, white and bruising bluish, partial veil usually present as a frail annulus near the apex of the stalk or adhering irregularly to the margin of the cap; spores purple-brown in mass, 11–17 × 7–12 µm, broadly elliptical to oval, smooth, nonamyloid.

Habitat/Biological Role: Occurring as solitary fruiting bodies or in small groups on the dung of herbivores; restricted to the warmer months of the year but in the southern portion of our region fruiting throughout the year. Decomposer of dung.

Distribution: In the United States, rare outside of the Southeast; most commonly encountered from South Carolina south to Florida and west along the Gulf Coast south into Mexico.

Comments: The unusual association of this fungus with dung is a character shared by a number of related species. *Psilocybe coprophila* is another dung inhabitant in our region, but it is much smaller, dark brownish orange to reddish brown or grayish brown, and lacks an annulus on the stalk. *Psilocybe merdaria* is nearly

identical to *P. coprophila* except that it (like *P. cubensis*) has a very faint annulus near the apex of the stalk. *Panaeolus sepulchralis* (syn. *Anellaria sepulchralis*) also occurs on dung but is white, lacks an annulus, and has truncated spores. *Psilocybe cubensis* is illegal in the United States; it contains psilocybin and psilocin, highly hallucinogenic compounds, and there is a significant illegal market for it and other psychedelic species of fungi. This market has driven it to be widely cultivated. Among indigenous cultures in Mexico, *P. cubensis* and related fungi have been used for thousands of years as tools in shamanic healing. Recent research shows that the compounds in *P. cubensis* and related species may have important applications in modern medicine, particularly for treatment of certain psychological conditions including PTSD, and the legalization of these species for medical use is now being considered.

Russula brevipes Peck

SHORT-STEMMED RUSSULA

FAMILY Russulaceae

Cap 9–20 cm wide, at first convex but becoming uplifted to funnel-shaped with age; surface dry, covered by fine appressed fibrils, white to off-white or cream, staining dull yellowish to nearly brown with age; gills attached and not all reaching to the cap margin, close, white to cream, occasionally with a bluish hue, often staining brown to reddish brown; stalk 2.5–8 cm long and 2.5–4 cm wide, equal or tapering slightly toward the base, dry, smooth, white to off-white, staining in the same manner as the cap; taste mild, slowly becoming slightly spicy; odor faintly of chlorine; spores white to cream in mass, 8–11 × 6–8 µm, shortly elliptical, ornamented with a reticulum composed of warts and ridges, amyloid.

Habitat/Biological Role: Occurring as solitary fruiting bodies or in groups on the ground, sometimes hardly breaking through the leaves, only forming "mushrumps" in mixed broadleaf-conifer forests; fruiting summer to fall. Forms mycorrhizal associations, primarily with conifers.

Distribution: Frequently encountered in our region and widely distributed in eastern North America.

Comments: This fungus is edible but not as flavorful as it will be if parasitized by the lobster mushroom *Hypomyces lactifluorum*. The white color, short stalk, and mild to strongly acrid taste are characters that make *Russula brevipes* distinctive within what is a taxonomically challenging genus. It is more likely to be mistaken for a *Lactarius* species with scant milk than another *Russula* species. *Russula perlactea* is also white, but it generally fruits from sandy soils and has a far longer stalk in proportion to the cap and broadly elliptical spores.

Russula compacta Frost

FIRM RUSSULA

FAMILY Russulaceae

Cap 6.5–15 cm wide, convex at first but becoming nearly flat to upturned with age; surface tacky to dry, sometimes in young specimens off-white to pale buff, becoming pale brown to reddish brown with age, frequently developing central cracks; gills closely spaced, attached to partly attached to the stalk, off-white to buff in color, generally staining darker with handling; stalk 4–8 cm long and 1–2.5 cm wide, equal, smooth, white or similar in color to the cap, bruising brownish; taste mild to nutty; odor sometimes reported to be similar to fresh trout; spores white in mass, 7–10 × 6–8 μm, elliptical, with irregular warts and ridges, amyloid.

Habitat/Biological Role: Occurring on the ground, sometimes in groups; fruiting summer into fall. Forms mycorrhizal associations with conifers.

Distribution: Frequently encountered in the Southeast and apparently restricted to eastern North America, with reports from Quebec south to central Florida.

Comments: This is one of the more distinctive *Russula* species found in the Southeast. *Russula ballouii* is somewhat similar but can be differentiated on the basis of having gills that do not bruise and a cap and stalk surface that break up into small scale-like spots. *Russula barlae* looks similar and shares a similar bruising reaction and an odor reminiscent of fish or shrimp, but it can be differentiated by spores that are yellow in mass. *Russula compacta* is considered edible but is not widely eaten.

Russula flavida Frost

YELLOW RUSSULA

FAMILY Russulaceae

Cap 3–10 cm wide, at first convex but becoming nearly flat to upturned with age; surface dry, bright yellow to orange but becoming paler toward the margin and/or with age; gills closely spaced, attached to the stalk, bright white; stalk 4–8 cm long and 1–2 cm wide, clavate to sometimes tapering toward the base, smooth, same bright cap surface color at base, grading to white at apex of the stalk; taste mild; odor indistinct; spores white in mass, 5–8 × 5.5–8.5 μm, subglobose, ornamented with a reticulum composed of irregular warts, weakly amyloid.

Habitat/Biological Role: Occurring on the ground, sometimes in groups and frequently under oaks; fruiting from summer into fall. Forms mycorrhizal associations with trees.

Distribution: Most commonly encountered in the Southeast but widely distributed in eastern North America.

Comments: This is one of the most brightly colored members of the genus. *Russula claroflava* is similar but generally found in the more northern portion of our region; it differs in having a paler cap and a stalk that is solid white and bruises gray. *Russula lutea*, also found on the northern edge of our region, is most easily separated from these two species by its yellow spores that turn the gills pale yellow. *Russula flavida* is generally considered edible but is not widely eaten; it is rare to find enough fruiting bodies at once to collect for the table.

Russula flavisiccans Bills

YELLOWING ROSY RUSSULA

FAMILY Russulaceae

Cap up to 11 cm wide, bell-shaped to convex; surface dry, velvety, very firm, skin not separating, frequently cracking into scales that turn yellow-brown at maturity, mostly pink and red mottled with cream patches, occasionally completely cream; gills closely spaced, attached or extending shortly down stalk, cream, often discoloring brown along the edges; stalk 3.5–6 cm long and 1–2.5 cm wide, expanded toward base, smooth, white, covered in a fine powder, bruising yellow-brown when damaged; taste extremely bitter; odor indistinct; spores cream in mass, 7–9 × 6.5–8 µm, subglobose, ornamentation loosely reticulate, very low, amyloid.

Habitat/Biological Role: Occurring on the ground, sometimes in groups; fruiting from summer into fall. Forms mycorrhizal associations with broadleaf trees.

Distribution: Frequently encountered in our region and widely distributed in eastern North America.

Comments: *Russula flavisiccans* is one of the few red russulas with enough distinctive features to be readily identified in the field. The epithet refers to the characteristic yellowing of the exposed inner flesh as it dries. This is evident in the fresh condition from the yellow-brown stains that develop where the fruiting body is damaged. *Russula pulchra* shares the red, velvety cap and cream-colored spores but can be separated based on a completely mild taste and flesh that stays white. A much rarer look-alike is *R. hixsoni*, which is similar but much larger and has scales that turn gray instead of yellow-brown. There are likely dozens of russulas in our region with red or reddish cap surfaces, and they represent one of the most confusing species complexes in any fungal genus; learning to identify them is beyond the scope of this field guide. *Russula flavisiccans* is not toxic but is not regarded as a good edible, and considering the taxonomic complexities of the red-capped group, it is hard to know what species have actually been eaten.

Russula parvovirescens Buyck, D. Mitchell & Parrent

QUILTED GREEN RUSSULA

FAMILY Russulaceae

Cap 4–8 cm wide, convex at first but becoming nearly flat with age, developing a shallow central depression, nearly perfectly round, surface sometimes faintly striate toward the margin, overall greenish to nearly brown to dark olive-green, cracking into patchwork-like scales that expose paler tissue; gills closely spaced, partially attached at the stalk to nearly free, bright white, occasionally forking; stalk 3–6 cm long and 8–15 mm wide, more or less equal, smooth, white, rounded at the base; taste mild; odor indistinct; spores white in mass, 6.5–9 × 5.5–7 µm, subglobose, ornamentation an incomplete to interconnected mass of warts, amyloid.

Habitat/Biological Role: Occurring on the ground, sometimes in groups; fruiting from summer into fall. Forms mycorrhizal associations with trees.

Distribution: Particularly common in the Southeast and widely distributed in eastern North America from Maine to Mississippi and west to Texas.

Comments: *Russula parvovirescens* was "discovered" in 2006, and most images labeled *R. virescens* or *R. crustosa* in field guides for our region prior to this date are likely to be this species. *Russula crustosa* and *R. virescens* are similar, but the most reliable way to separate these three species is by microscopic comparison of the shape of terminal cells in the outer surface of the cap; in *R. crustosa* and *R. virescens* these cells typically taper to a point or are somewhat awl-shaped. As with many *Russula* species from the Southeast, several different species are likely lumped under the names *R. crustosa* and *R. virescens*. Some taxonomists suspect that each of these names actually encompasses more than a dozen species. At least five green-capped species of *Russula* are known to occur in the Southeast, but these species do not develop the patchwork-like scales on the cap; the most commonly found of these are *R. variata*, *R. aeruginea*, *R. cyanoxantha*, and *R. subgraminicolor*. Given the taxonomic confusion, it is impossible to know just which species have actually been eaten, but the quilted-capped species of *Russula* are generally regarded as edible.

Sarcomyxa serotina (Persoon) P. Karsten

LATE FALL OYSTER

SYNONYMS *Panellus serotinus, Pleurotus serotinus*

FAMILY Mycenaceae

Cap 2.5–10 cm wide, broadly convex, semi-circular, shell- to kidney-shaped, solitary or occurring in clusters; upper surface varying in color from olive-buff to greenish buff or tan but sometimes yellowish green, smooth, sometimes viscid, margin downturned; gills subdistant, sometimes shortly decurrent, off-white to pale orange-buff to yellowish tan; stalk a lateral basal stub or often lacking, usually similar in color to the gills, sometimes densely hairy or scaly; spores yellow in mass, 4–6 × 1–2 µm, sausage-shaped, smooth, amyloid.

Habitat/Biological Role: Occurring on decomposing wood, typically in groups of overlapping fruiting bodies; usually fruiting from mid-fall to mid-winter. Decomposer of wood.

Distribution: Within our region most common in the Appalachian Mountains but widely distributed throughout North America.

Comments: The fruiting phenology of this species is useful in identification because in late fall and early winter, very few gilled fleshy fungi produce fruiting bodies. This species is regarded as edible although not widely eaten. Some *Pleurotus* species (also edible) can fruit at the same time of the year and are similar in general appearance, but they have white spores and are thinner and usually more white or gray. Some members of the genus *Crepidotus* are morphologically similar, but their fruiting bodies are very thin in comparison and usually have brown spores.

Schizophyllum commune
Fries

COMMON SPLIT-GILL

FAMILY Schizophyllaceae

Fan- to shell-shaped, 1–4 cm across and up to 3 mm thick, concave to almost flat, tough and leathery; upper surface densely hairy, light grayish brown when moist, ashy gray to white when dry; margin lobed, wavy, densely hairy; spore-bearing surface consisting of well-spaced, longitudinally split gill-like structures, light gray; stalk lacking or rudimentary; spores white in mass, 3–4 × 1–1.5 µm, cylindrical to elliptical, smooth.

Habitat/Biological Role: Occurring as solitary fruiting bodies or in small groups (the individual fruiting bodies sometimes fused and often overlapping) on fallen branches and woody debris of broadleaf trees; fruiting throughout the year. Decomposer of wood.

Distribution: More common in the East within North America but found worldwide.

Comments: *Schizophyllum commune* is an unusual fungus that appears to have gills but is not closely related to the agarics. Fungal mating studies have shown that this fungus has more than 28,000 different mating types! (And you thought that finding a suitable partner was confusing!) Some mycologists argue that this diversity has led to its being one of the most common macrofungi worldwide. This fungus occurs on a large diversity of different substrates; there are even a handful of cases where people with immune issues had strange growths that were discovered to be caused by *S. commune*! There are different traditional ways to eat this fungus in many parts of the world, including India, Mexico, Southeast Asia, and Zaire, but we cannot recommend it as a food without a cultural context and/or extensive cooking. *Schizophyllum commune* also displays some of the most promising antitumor activities known for any fungus. Few fungi resemble this fungus. The uncommon *Plicaturopsis crispa* is somewhat similar on the lower surface but generally has a zoned upper surface that is some shade of yellowish to pale brown. Also see *Panellus stipticus*.

Tapinella atrotomentosa
(Batsch) Šutara

VELVET FOOT, VELVET PAXILLUS

SYNONYM *Paxillus atrotomentosus*

FAMILY Tapinellaceae

Cap 5–22 cm across, convex with an inrolled margin when young but becoming flat with a central depression with age, upper surface yellowish brown to dark brown, dry, velvety; lower surface pale yellowish tan when young, darkening with age, composed of closely spaced gills that sometime extend partially down the stalk, gills sometimes forking; stalk 3–12.5 cm long and 0.8–4 cm wide, robust, equal, often lateral (attached to cap at an angle), surface covered by a thick mat of dark brown to black hairs; spores yellowish to brown, 4.5–7 × 3–5 μm, elliptical, smooth, yellowish to dextrinoid in Melzer's reagent.

Habitat/Biological Role: Occurring as solitary fruiting bodies or in small groups on well-decomposed stumps; fruiting throughout the summer and fall. Decomposer of wood.

Distribution: Particularly common in the Appalachian Mountains but scattered throughout North America.

Comments: This fungus was previously placed in *Paxillus*; however, members of that genus have been shown to be mycorrhizal, and this species is generally believed to be a decomposer, which in part is why taxonomists moved it to *Tapinella*. The dark velvety stalk makes it difficult to confuse this species with any other fungus known from the Southeast. *Tapinella panuoides* (syn. *P. panuoides*) is somewhat similar in the color of the cap and gills but lacks a stalk. *Paxillus involutus* is similar but more slender, lacks the hairy stalk, has gills that stain brown, and typically fruits from soil.

Tectella patellaris (Fries) Murrill

VEILED PANUS

SYNONYMS *Panellus patellaris, Panus operculatus*

FAMILY Mycenaceae

Typically a shell-shaped structure, 0.7–3 cm across, convex to drooping; upper surface viscid when young and becoming dry with age; margin inrolled, frequently retaining remnants of veil tissue; lower surface brownish, composed of close to subdistantly spaced gills, generally radiating from a central point, when young the gills are covered by a veil; stalk lacking or rudimentary; spores white in mass, 3–5 × 1–1.5 µm, cylindrical, smooth, weakly amyloid.

Habitat/Biological Role: Occurring in small groups on fallen branches and woody debris of broadleaf trees; fruiting summer to fall. Decomposer of wood.

Distribution: Most common in the Appalachian Mountains in our region and generally found in eastern North America.

Comments: *Tectella* is a small genus, and not many fungi are similar to this species. *Schizophyllum commune* is somewhat similar; however, it lacks the veil, has a lobed margin at maturity, and is lighter in color.

Tricholoma aurantium
(Schaeffer) Ricken

GOLDEN ORANGE TRICHOLOMA

FAMILY Tricholomataceae

Cap 4–12.5 cm wide, bell-shaped at first but becoming nearly flat with age, margins inrolled when young, low central umbo often present in older specimens; surface very viscid when wet and developing small scales when dry, bright yellow-orange to orange-brown depending on age and moisture; gills closely spaced, sometimes crowded, partially attached to the stalk, bright white; stalk 3–10 cm long and 1–3.5 cm wide, typically equal but occasionally swollen in the middle, the same color as the cap surface from the base until near the apex where it is often white, stalk surface breaking up into fine scales or patches; spores white in mass, 4–6 × 3–4 μm, subglobose to nearly elliptical, smooth.

Habitat/Biological Role: Occurring on the ground, usually in groups and sometimes forming rings; fruiting from summer into fall. Forms mycorrhizal associations with trees.

Distribution: Most often found in the Appalachian Mountains in our region but widely distributed in North America.

Comments: This is one of the showiest mushrooms in our region and certainly one of the most distinctive *Tricholoma* species. It superficially resembles *T. pessundatum*, which has a smooth reddish brown cap and a stalk that is not as brightly colored. Neither species is edible. It is possible that *T. aurantium* could be confused with some of the colorful species of *Hygrocybe* or *Hygrophorus*; however, fruiting bodies of species in these two genera have a very waxy texture and differ microscopically.

Tricholoma equestre (Linnaeus) P. Kummer

CANARY TRICHOLOMA, MAN ON HORSEBACK

SYNONYM *Tricholoma flavovirens*

FAMILY Tricholomataceae

Cap 5–10 cm wide, bell-shaped at first but becoming nearly flat with age; surface viscid when wet, brown to reddish brown but becoming bright yellow toward the margin; gills closely spaced, partially attached to the stalk, bright to dull yellow; stalk 3–8 cm long and 1–2 cm wide, equal to enlarged at the base, faintly yellowish white to buff; spores white in mass, 6–7 × 4–5 μm, elliptical, smooth.

Habitat/Biological Role: Occurring on the ground, often in scattered groups, and primarily under conifers; fruiting from summer into fall and in the extreme south fruiting into late winter. Forms mycorrhizal associations with trees.

Distribution: Particularly common in the Southeast and widely distributed in North America.

Comments: *Tricholoma equestre* has a long history of being eaten in Europe and was generally considered edible if correctly identified, but in the last 15 years there have been reports of hospitalization and death from the consumption of this fungus. It is likely that a species complex is involved with the North American *T. equestre*, and until further research has been carried out, we advise against eating it. *Tricholoma sejunctum* is similar but has radial streaks on the cap surface and white to light yellowish gills. *Tricholoma intermedium* is also similar; however, its gills and stalk do not have the yellow coloration.

Tricholoma sejunctum
(Sowerby) Quélet

SEPARATED TRICHOLOMA

FAMILY Tricholomataceae

Cap 4–9 cm wide, conical to bell-shaped at first and then becoming nearly flat with a central umbo, smooth, somewhat slimy or sticky when wet; greenish gray at the center and becoming yellow to yellowish green outward, sometimes white at margin, usually streaked radially; gills closely spaced, partially attached to the stalk, white or sometimes yellowish; stalk 5–9 cm long and 1–2.5 cm wide, equal, faintly yellow; spores white in mass, 6–7 × 3.5–5.5 µm, subglobose, smooth.

Habitat/Biological Role: Occurring on the ground in scattered groups or as solitary fruiting bodies under broadleaf trees and conifers; fruiting from summer into fall. Forms mycorrhizal associations with trees.

Distribution: Particularly common in the Southeast and widely distributed in North America.

Comments: *Tricholoma* is a large and diverse genus in our region, with several similar species. *Tricholoma intermedium* and some yellow color phases of *T. saponaceum* and the *T. equestre* complex can appear similar; however, they lack the radially streaked fibrils on the cap. *Tricholoma sejunctum* is not edible and may actually be poisonous.

Volvariella bombycina
(Schaeffer) Singer

TREE VOLVARIELLA

FAMILY Pluteaceae

Cap 5–20 cm wide, convex to flat, white to faintly yellow; gills free from the stalk, close, white when young but darkening to brownish pink with age; stalk up to 20 cm long and 2 cm wide, becoming larger toward the base; prominent white to light brown volva at the base; spores pink to brownish pink in mass, 6.5–10.5 × 4.5–6.5 µm, elliptical, smooth, hyaline.

Habitat/Biological Role: Often associated with cavities in trees or occasionally occurring on stumps; fruiting from early summer into fall. Decomposer of wood.

Distribution: Most common in the Southeast and East but found throughout North America.

Comments: *Volvariella bombycina* is a striking but uncommon to rare mushroom. It is edible and one of the safer species in the genus to eat because it occurs on wood, which helps prevent confusion with some of the deadly white species of *Amanita*. The species diversity of the genus *Volvariella* increases as one moves southward; most species are rare in our region and some of the southern taxa are known from only one or two collections. *Volvariella volvacea* is somewhat similar but has a brownish cap that is often streaked. Another southeastern species, *V. gloiocephala*, is easily differentiated, as it is found on dung-enriched soil, not decomposing wood.

Xeromphalina kauffmanii
A. H. Smith

GOLDEN TRUMPET, CROSS-VEINED TROOP MUSHROOM

FAMILY Mycenaceae

Cap 1–3 cm broad, orange-yellow overall but darker at the center and paler toward margin; bell-shaped at first and eventually becoming upturned with age; radially arranged striations extending to the margin; gills yellowish at first and then darkening with age, decurrent, subdistant to distant, with crossveins; stalk tough, up to 4 cm long and up to 5 mm thick at the apex and tapering toward the base, varying in color from yellowish at the apex to dark brown at base, sometimes a bulbous tuft of orange hairs present at the base; spores white in mass, 4.5–6.5 × 2–3 µm, elliptical, smooth, amyloid.

Habitat/Biological Role: Occurring in large clusters on the decomposing logs of broadleaf trees; fruiting during summer and fall. Decomposer of wood.

Distribution: Most common in the Appalachian Mountains in our region but reported from much of eastern North America.

Comments: *Xeromphalina kauffmanii* is a beautiful, tiny fungus that can form impressive clusters of hundreds of fruiting bodies that cover decomposing stumps or logs. This fungus is not considered to be edible. *Xeromphalina campanella* is nearly identical and is found in our region, but it is reported to occur only on conifers and has minor microscopic differences. *Flammulina velutipes* and *X. tenuipes* are only marginally similar, being much larger in stature. It is possible that some species of *Marasmius* and *Mycena* could be mistaken for *X. kauffmanii*, but members of these genera do not fruit in such extensive clusters.

Boletes and Relatives

The boletes can superficially resemble gilled mushrooms in the overall shape of the fruiting bodies, but they have tube-like pores on the undersides of their fleshy caps instead of gills. Ours is one of the most diverse regions in the world for boletes, and similarities among species found in the Southeast make members of this group very challenging to identify. We show only a small selection of the diversity of this group that the Southeast is home to, so if you become particularly interested in boletes, there are a number of texts that focus just on this group of mushrooms in North America. Boletes often have distinctive bruising reactions that result in certain portions of the fruiting body turning blue or reddish. Boletes primarily form mycorrhizal associations with trees.

Boletes have recently undergone major taxonomic revisions, based primarily on genetic evidence; many of the previously used generic concepts have been destroyed—and the changes are ongoing. This field guide attempts to apply names that will likely be used long-term, even though some of them may not be the currently applied name. Because the names are changing so rapidly, we do not include a key to the genera.

Very few species in this group of mushrooms contain toxins. Many species are edible, although some are too slimy in texture to be of interest and others have not been well studied. It is possible to mistake some members of this group for species covered in Polypores and Relatives (page 289).

Baorangia bicolor (Kuntze)
G. Wu, Halling & Zhu L. Yang

TWO-COLORED BOLETE, RED AND YELLOW BOLETE

SYNONYM *Boletus bicolor*

FAMILY Boletaceae

Cap 5–12.5 cm wide, convex with a strongly incurved margin at first and then becoming broadly convex to nearly flat or depressed with age; surface dry, dull, glabrous to somewhat velvety when young, smooth but often developing cracks in dry weather, color varying from dark red to purple-red, rose-red, or rose-pink but fading to ochraceous or tan with age; flesh unchanging or slowly and weakly staining blue when cut; pore-bearing surface bright yellow, becoming olive-yellow with age, quickly bruising blue, pores one or two per mm; stalk 4–10 cm long and 10–28 mm wide, nearly equal to slightly enlarged toward the base, mostly colored like the cap but often yellow at the apex and occasionally nearly yellow throughout, smooth or with a slight reticulation near the apex; spores olive-brown in mass, 9–15 × 4–5 µm, oblong to spindle-shaped, smooth.

Habitat/Biological Role: Occurring as solitary or scattered fruiting bodies on the ground in broadleaf and mixed broadleaf-conifer forests; typically fruiting during summer and fall. Forms mycorrhizal associations with trees, particularly various species of oak.

Distribution: Found from Florida to New England and widely distributed throughout eastern North America, depending on your concept of the species or species complex.

Comments: This is likely to be a complex of very similar species, and some may be less desirable for eating. *Baorangia bicolor* is considered edible, but some individuals have experienced gastrointestinal upset after consuming it. Various varieties have been recognized in an effort to understand the taxonomy of this species, and there are approximately ten very similar species with which this fungus could be confused. One such is *Boletus pallidoroseus*, but it has shorter tubes, a flesh that smells like beef or chicken bouillon, and a stalk that is more pinkish in color. *Boletus sensibilis* is similar in stature but differs in having a yellow stalk with a pinkish blush toward the base.

Boletellus ananas (M. A. Curtis) Murrill

PINEAPPLE BOLETE

SYNONYMS *Boletus ananus, B. coccineus*

FAMILY Boletaceae

Cap 3–10 cm wide, obtuse at first but becoming convex to broadly convex with age; surface dry, covered with coarse and overlapping scales, these purplish red to dark red at first but becoming dull pinkish tan to dingy yellow with age, some scales extending beyond the margin of the cap; pore-bearing surface yellow when young but becoming deep olive-brown with age, bruising blue, pores irregular to angular, 1–2 mm wide; stalk 6–15 cm long and 7–20 mm wide, nearly equal or enlarging downward, white to pale tan, sometimes yellowish to reddish near apex, smooth to finely roughened; partial veil whitish, often leaving remnants on the margin of the cap but not forming a distinct annulus; spores dark rusty brown to dark brown in mass, 15–25 × 7–11 µm, fusoid, with conspicuous longitudinal ridges, nonamyloid.

Habitat/Biological Role: Occurring on the ground as solitary or scattered fruiting bodies in broadleaf or conifer forests, usually associated with oak or pine; fruiting from early summer until fall. Forms mycorrhizal associations with trees.

Distribution: Apparently restricted to the Southeast in North America but reported from other regions of the world, including New Zealand and South America. We have collected this species as far south as northeastern South America.

Comments: The coarse and overlapping scales on the cap are distinctive, making this an easy species to identify. The very rare Florida species *Boletellus pictiformis* (syn. *Suillellus pictformis*) is somewhat similar but has brown scales on the cap surface and stalk surface. Although its common name might suggest otherwise, *B. ananas* is inedible. Also see *Suillus spraguei.*

Boletinellus merulioides
(Schweinitz) Murrill

ASH TREE BOLETE

SYNONYM *Gyrodon merulioides*

FAMILY Boletinellaceae

Cap 4–12.5 cm wide, somewhat irregular to distinctly kidney-shaped in outline, yellow-brown to red-brown, upper surface smooth, viscid when moist, margin incurved; spore-bearing surface bright yellow to dingy yellow with age, bruising slightly blue-green, consisting of numerous shallow irregular to elongated pores that are radially arranged and extend a short distance down the top of the stalk; stalk 2–4 cm long and 0.5–2.5 cm wide, expanding upward, off-center and sometimes almost lateral; spores olive-brown in mass, 7–10 × 6–7.5 µm, ovate, smooth.

Habitat/Biological Role: Occurring on the ground near ash trees, usually in small groups; fruiting summer and fall. This fungus forms a symbiotic relationship with an insect, the woolly ash aphid (*Prociphilus fraxinifolii*), which feeds on the roots of ash trees.

Distribution: Widely distributed throughout eastern North America wherever ash is found.

Comments: The fact that *Boletinellus merulioides* is invariably associated with ash makes it easy to identify. In the aforementioned symbiotic relationship, the vegetative body of the fungus (or mycelium) forms little knots of tissue (sclerotia) that surround and protect the aphid; in return, the aphid produces a sugary "honeydew" that is utilized by the fungus. These sclerotia can sometimes be found if the base of fruiting bodies are carefully excavated from the soil. This species is considered edible.

Boletus auriflammeus
Berkeley & M. A. Curtis

FLAMING GOLD BOLETE

SYNONYM *Pulveroboletus auriflammeus*

FAMILY Boletaceae

Cap 2.5–9 cm wide, hemispherical to convex at first and then becoming broadly convex to nearly flat with age; surface dry to subviscid when moist, sometimes finely cracked with age, velvety to powdery, brilliant golden orange to brownish orange, golden yellow or chrome yellow; pore-bearing surface yellow to orange-yellow, unchanging when bruised, pores one or two per mm; stalk 5–9 cm long and 5–15 mm wide, nearly equal to enlarged in either direction, surface somewhat powdery at first, deeply wrinkled or more often coarsely reticulate, colored like the cap; spores olive-brown to ochre-brown in mass, 8–12 × 3–5 µm, oblong ellipsoid to spindle-shaped, smooth.

Habitat/Biological Role: Occurring as solitary or scattered fruiting bodies in broadleaf forests, particularly those containing oaks; typically fruiting from midsummer until fall. Forms mycorrhizal associations with trees.

Distribution: Widely distributed in eastern North America.

Comments: *Boletus auriflammeus* is easily recognized by the golden orange color of the fruiting bodies and the coarsely reticulate stalk. Handling this fungus will stain fingers and hands yellow. Although considered edible, the flesh of *B. auriflammeus* is slightly acidic and can leave an unpleasant aftertaste when consumed. The uncommon southeastern species *B. aurantiosplendens* is similar in color but more robust in stature and does not stain the fingers when handled. *Retiboletus ornatipes* can appear similar at first, but it too is generally more robust in stature and has a grayish yellow cap surface and entirely yellow reticulate stalk. It is rare to find more than one or two fruiting bodes of *B. auriflammeus* in one location; in our experience this is generally a very solitary species.

Boletus auripes Peck

BUTTER-FOOT BOLETE

FAMILY Boletaceae

Cap 5–15 cm wide, convex at first but becoming broadly convex and then somewhat flattened with age, dry, finely velvety or nearly smooth, yellow-brown to chestnut brown or grayish brown when young but the color fading with age; pore-bearing surface at first pale yellow to nearly white becoming bright yellow and then becoming brownish yellow or olive, not bruising blue; pores round to angular, less than 1 mm wide; stalk 5–12 cm long and 15–30 mm wide, more or less equal above but with an expanded lower portion, finely reticulate over the upper portion, bright yellow at first and then becoming brownish yellow; spores yellow-brown in mass, 9.5–15 × 3.5–5.5 µm, subfusiform, smooth.

Habitat/Biological Role: Occurring as solitary or scattered fruiting bodies on the ground in broadleaf forests, usually those containing oaks; fruiting during summer and fall. Forms mycorrhizal associations with trees.

Distribution: Widely distributed in eastern North America.

Comments: *Boletus auripes* can be identified from a combination of features: the yellow stalk, the brown cap, the fine reticulation on the upper portion of the stalk, and the fact that it does not bruise blue, as is the case for a number of other morphologically similar species in the genus. *Boletus aureissimus* is similar but generally has a yellow cap surface and is believed to be restricted to the Gulf Coast. *Aureoboletus auriporus* (syn. *Boletus auriporus*) is also somewhat similar but is generally more slender, the stalk is usually more brown to faintly yellow, and the spores are olive-brown in mass.

Boletus frostii J. L. Russell

FROST'S BOLETE

FAMILY Boletaceae

Cap 4–12.5 cm wide, hemispherical to convex at first and then becoming broadly convex to flat or shallowly depressed in age, surface smooth, shiny, tacky to somewhat viscid when fresh, blood red or candy apple red, often with a paler, yellow margin, fading and developing yellow areas with age; stalk 5–12.5 cm long and 1–2.5 cm wide, nearly equal throughout or tapering upward from an enlarged base, surface coarsely and deeply reticulate over the entire length, dark red to pink with evidence of white or yellow mycelium at the base; pore-bearing surface dark red to dark orange-red or pinkish red, becoming paler with age, instantly staining blackish blue when cut, often exuding golden moisture droplets when young, pores small, two or three per mm; spores olive-brown in mass, 11–17 × 4–5 µm, ellipsoid, smooth.

Habitat/Biological Role: Occurring on the ground in broadleaf forests containing oaks, solitary to scattered; fruiting from late summer into fall. Forms mycorrhizal associations with trees.

Distribution: Widely distributed throughout eastern North America.

Comments: The shiny, candy apple–red cap and coarsely reticulate stalk are the distinctive features of what some believe is the most striking mushroom species in the Southeast. This is one of the few edible bolete species with a red pore surface. The edible *Heimioporus betula* has a similar type of reticulation on the stalk but is much taller and generally more yellow to orange in color. The edible *Boletellus russellii* also has a similarly shaggy reticulation on the stalk, but it is more drab in color overall (yellow-brown to reddish brown or cinnamon-brown), taller and slender in stature, and has a yellow to greenish yellow pore surface that does not bruise blue.

Boletus separans Peck

EASTERN KING

SYNONYM *Xanthoconium separans*

FAMILY Boletaceae

Cap 5–20 cm wide, broadly umbonate to convex; surface dry, wrinkled and pitted, sometimes corrugated, variable in color but often having faint lilac colorations, cap is liver red in color when young but eventually becomes brownish purple to dirty brownish yellow; pore-bearing surface white when young and then becoming yellowish to ochre-brown with age, unchanging when bruised; stalk 6–15 cm long and 1–3 cm wide, equal to slightly enlarged at the base, surface finely reticulate over the upper half, color similar to that of the cap, whitish when young and often with reddish or purplish tones in age; spores brown to reddish brown in mass, 12–16 × 3.5–4.5 µm, ellipsoid to spindle-shaped, smooth.

Habitat/Biological Role: Occurring as solitary fruiting bodies or scattered in broadleaf and mixed broadleaf-conifer forests; typically fruiting from early summer until fall. Forms mycorrhizal associations with trees.

Distribution: Widely distributed in eastern North America from Canada to Florida and as far west as Texas.

Comments: *Boletus hortonii* (syn. *Xerocomus hortonii*) is the most similar species; it too has a wrinkled cap and similar coloration except for a yellow pore surface (even when young) that sometimes bruises slightly blue, a yellowish stalk, and a cap that is usually browner in color. Both species are edible, and we rank them among the better-tasting southeastern boletes. *Hemileccinum subglabripes* (syn. *B. subglabripes*) is similar and also edible, but it has a smooth nonwrinkled cap and a stalk that has little granular dots.

Caloboletus firmus (Frost)
Vizzini

PIEDMONT BOLETE, RED-MOUTH BOLETE

SYNONYMS *Boletus firmus,
B. piedmontensis*

FAMILY Boletaceae

Cap 5–15 cm wide, convex with a strongly incurved margin at first and then becoming broadly convex to nearly flat with age; surface dry, dull, glabrous to minutely velvety, white to gray, grayish brown, pinkish tan, or pale grayish olive and flesh staining blue; pore-bearing surface red to reddish orange, sometimes pink to yellowish pink when young, bluing when bruised, pores one or two per mm; stalk 5–12.5 cm long and 1–2.8 cm wide, nearly equal or tapering in either direction, surface smooth, colored more or less like the cap but often with red tints, usually with a fine red reticulation near the apex of the stalk, but this is sometimes lacking; spores olive-brown in mass, 9–15 × 3.5–5 µm, ellipsoid, smooth.

Habitat/Biological Role: Occurring as solitary or scattered fruiting bodies on the ground in broadleaf and mixed broadleaf-conifer forests; typically fruiting from midsummer until fall. Forms mycorrhizal associations with trees.

Distribution: Frequently found as far south as Georgia and Mississippi and widely distributed throughout eastern North America.

Comments: *Caloboletus firmus* has been confused with several other species, including the poisonous *Boletus satanas*, which appears to be restricted to western North America. The edibility of *C. firmus* is not well known, but it is generally considered too bitter to eat.

Gyroporus castaneus (Bulliard) Quélet

CHESTNUT BOLETE

FAMILY Gyroporaceae

Cap 3–10 cm wide, at first rounded to broadly convex and then becoming nearly flat with age, sometimes slightly depressed, orange-gray to rusty red or chestnut brown; surface minutely hairy, dry, margin often splitting and flaring outward with age; pore-bearing surface whitish to buff or yellowish, pores round, one to three per mm; stalk 3–9 cm long and 6–22 mm wide, enlarging slightly toward the base, colored like the cap or slightly paler, hollow or filled with a cottony mass of hyphae; spores pale yellow to buff in mass, 8–13 × 5–6 µm, elliptical to ovoid, smooth, nonamyloid.

Habitat/Biological Role: Occurring on the ground in broadleaf forests, particularly those with oak present; solitary or scattered fruiting bodies; fruiting in summer and fall. Forms mycorrhizal associations with trees.

Distribution: Most common in the Southeast and East but widely distributed throughout North America.

Comments: The distinguishing features of *Gyroporus castaneus* are the chestnut-brown cap, hollow stalk, and spores that are pale yellow in mass. This species is a choice edible. *Gyroporus cyanescens* is uncommon and can look superficially similar, but it is generally larger, more yellowish throughout, and the tissue stains a vivid blue.

Heimioporus betula
(Schweinitz) E. Horak

SHAGGY-STALKED BOLETE

SYNONYMS *Austroboletus betula*, *Boletellus betula*

FAMILY Boletaceae

Cap 3–9 cm wide, at first convex and becoming broadly convex with age, surface smooth, in wet weather slimy and in dry weather slightly sticky, yellow when young, becoming reddish orange to reddish yellow with age, margin usually yellow; pore-bearing surface at first yellow and then becoming greenish yellow with age, sunken around the stalk and with a thin sterile strip around the margin, pores round to angular, one or two per mm; stalk 10–30 cm tall and 10–30 mm wide, tapered slightly toward the apex, more or less equal, deeply and coarsely reticulate, upper portion red or yellow and lower portion reddish, typically a mass of white hyphae at base of stalk; spores olive to olive-brown in mass, 13–22 × 6–10 μm, narrowly ellipsoid, finely pitted.

Habitat/Biological Role: Occurring on the ground as solitary to scattered fruiting bodies in broadleaf or mixed broadleaf-conifer forests; fruiting from late summer to mid-fall. Forms mycorrhizal associations with trees.

Distribution: Most common in the Appalachian Mountains and Piedmont but found throughout eastern North America.

Comments: The relatively long, deeply and coarsely reticulate stalk makes *Heimioporus betula* easy to identify. It is one of the more distinctive species found in the entire Southeast. This species is edible; the stalks are particularly flavorful and have a firm texture, unlike most species of boletes found in our region. Compare with *Boletellus russellii* (see comments under *Boletus frostii*).

Leccinellum albellum (Peck) Bresinsky & Manfred Binder

SLENDER SCABER STALK

SYNONYMS *Boletus albellus, Leccinum albellum*

FAMILY Boletaceae

Cap 2–6.5 cm wide, convex to nearly flat; surface dry, usually irregularly pitted and sometimes cracking with age, whitish to gray to grayish brown; pore-bearing surface at first whitish but becoming yellowish to pale yellowish brown with age, unchanging when bruised, pores broadly angular, small, less than 1 mm wide; stalk 5–10 cm long and 6–10 mm wide, equal but with a slightly enlarged base, generally similar but paler in color than the cap surface, stalk surface covered by fine off-white to grayish brown scabers, scabers usually arranged longitudinally; spores brownish olive in mass, 14–22 × 4–6 μm, oblong to cylindrical, smooth.

Habitat/Biological Role: Occurring on the ground as solitary fruiting bodies or in groups in broadleaf forests, often under white oaks; fruiting in summer to fall. Forms mycorrhizal associations with trees.

Distribution: Frequent in our region and widely distributed in eastern North America.

Comments: *Leccinellum albellum* resembles some members of the genus *Leccinum* in both coloration and the presence of scabers on the stalk; however, the latter fungi differ macroscopically in generally having much thicker stalks. *Leccinum scabrum* is infrequent in our region but differs in having a thicker stalk that usually has blue-green stains at base. *Leccinum snellii*, found in the more northern portion of our region, differs in having a dark, nearly black cap and usually more prominent black scabers on the stalk. All these species are considered edible. Some *Tylopilus* species are somewhat similar in appearance; however, members of this genus generally lack the scabers on the stalk.

Leccinum snellii A. H. Smith, Thiers & Watling

SNELL'S LECCINUM

FAMILY Boletaceae

Cap 3–9 cm wide, rounded to convex and sometimes becoming nearly flat with age; surface dry and covered by fine brown to black fibrils when young, these fading to yellowish brown with age; flesh whitish when first exposed and generally slowly staining pinkish to reddish, the staining usually most obvious where the stalk and cap meet, with time the stain turns grayish to blackish; pore-bearing surface whitish when young and discoloring to pale grayish to brownish with age, pore surface unchanging or sometimes subtly bruising to yellowish or brownish, pores two or three per mm; stalk 4–11 cm long and 1–2 cm wide, nearly equal to slightly enlarged toward the base, surface covered by blackish to grayish granules but white below these granules, sometimes staining slightly blue-green near the base and faintly reddish near the apex; spores brown in mass, 16–22 × 5–7.5 µm, oblong to spindle-shaped, smooth.

Habitat/Biological Role: Occurring as solitary to scattered fruiting bodies on the ground in broadleaf and mixed broadleaf-conifer forests, often found under yellow birch; typically found from early summer into fall. Forms mycorrhizal associations with trees.

Distribution: Reported from east of Minnesota north into eastern Canada and south into the Appalachians.

Comments: *Leccinum* is primarily a northern and subarctic genus; however, a few species make it south into our region. The other commonly encountered species in our region is *L. nigrescens* (syn. *L. crocipodium*, *Leccinellum crocipodium*), which differs in having a cap that usually cracks in age, paler granules on the stalk, a pore surface that is pale yellowish, and spores that are honey yellow in mass. Both species are edible.

Pseudoboletus parasiticus
(Bulliard) Šutara

EARTHBALL BOLETE, PARASITIC BOLETE

SYNONYM *Boletus parasiticus*

FAMILY Boletaceae

Cap 2.5–6.5 cm wide, hemispherical to convex, margin strongly incurved when young; surface dry, viscid when wet, smooth to minutely velvety at first but becoming glabrous and shiny with age, sometimes cracking, ochre-brown to tawny olive or having the appearance of tarnished brass; stalk 2.5–6.5 cm long and 1–1.5 cm wide, nearly equal throughout but often curved, solid, surface smooth to somewhat scurfy, colored like the cap but with evidence of white mycelium at the base; pore-bearing surface yellow at first but becoming olivaceous with age, sometimes with reddish or rust-colored tints, pores one or two per mm; spores dark olive-brown in mass, 12–18 × 3.5–5 μm, ellipsoid to spindle-shaped, smooth.

Habitat/Biological Role: Attached at the base to the earthball *Scleroderma citrinum* in various forests where the host fungus occurs, solitary or commonly occurring in clusters; fruiting from midsummer to fall. Generally regarded as a parasitic fungus, but the relationship involved may not be quite this simple.

Distribution: Most common in forests of the Appalachians but widely distributed throughout eastern North America.

Comments: As long as the direct association with earthballs is observed, *Pseudoboletus parasiticus* is impossible to confuse with any other fungus. This fungus is reported to be edible, but the earthball host should not be consumed.

Pulveroboletus ravenelii
(Berkeley & M. A. Curtis) Murrill

RAVENEL'S BOLETE, POWDERY SULPHUR BOLETE

SYNONYM *Boletus ravenelii*

FAMILY Suillaceae

Cap 1–10 cm broad, at first rounded to convex and then becoming nearly flat, bright yellow when young, becoming pale with age, upper surface dry and sometimes powdery, velvet-like; margin incurved, typically retaining portions of the veil along the margin; pore surface covered by delicate yellow veil when young, pores bright yellow when young and darkening greenish olive with age, pores small, one to three per mm, bruising greenish blue; stalk 4–10 cm long and 6–16 mm wide, equal or slightly larger toward the base, color similar to the cap, covered by contiguous tufts of yellow hyphae, smooth above the annulus, remnant veil usually adhered to the margin but occasionally forming an annulus near the apex; spores olive-brown to olive-gray in mass, 8–10.5 × 4–5 μm, elliptical to oval, smooth.

Habitat/Biological Role: Occurring as solitary fruiting bodies or in small groups, believed to be associated primarily with pines and hemlocks; fruiting throughout the summer and fall. Forms mycorrhizal associations with trees.

Distribution: Often collected throughout our region, from the Appalachian Mountains to the Gulf Coast, and widely distributed in North America.

Comments: This unusual fungus is edible but usually not found in sufficient quantities to be widely eaten. It is rather distinctive, although it is possible that an older specimen might be mistaken for a species of *Suillus*. The uncommon *Boletus melleoluteus* could possibly be confused with *Pulveroboletus ravenelii*, but the former has a much smaller cap and lacks a veil or annulus.

Retiboletus griseus (Frost)
Manfred Binder & Bresinsky

GRAY BOLETE

SYNONYMS *Boletus griseus*, *Xerocomus griseus*

FAMILY Boletaceae

Cap 5–12.5 cm wide, convex at first but becoming broadly convex to nearly flat with age; surface dry, dull, slightly velvety at first, often cracking into small scales with age, pale gray to gray, grayish brown or charcoal gray, with or without yellow to ochre tints; pore-bearing surface white to pale gray, becoming darker with age, unchanging or brown when bruised, pores one or two per mm; stalk 4–11.5 cm long and 1–3 cm wide, nearly equal but often tapered at the base; surface white with a yellow base, at times with red stains, covered with a coarse white to yellowish reticulation that becomes brown with age; spores olive-brown in mass, 9–13 × 3–5 µm, oblong, smooth.

Habitat/Biological Role: Occurring as solitary fruiting bodies or more often in clusters on the ground in broadleaf and mixed broadleaf-conifer forests; usually fruiting from early summer until fall. Forms mycorrhizal associations with trees.

Distribution: Widely distributed in eastern North America.

Comments: This species is considered to be edible but is rarely abundant enough to be collected for the table. Grayish forms of *Retiboletus ornatipes* can be very similar in appearance, but the flesh of that fungus is bitter and it lacks the white stalk.

Retiboletus ornatipes (Peck) Manfred Binder & Bresinsky

GOLD-STALK BOLETE, ORNATE-STALKED BOLETE

SYNONYM *Boletus ornatipes*

FAMILY Boletaceae

Cap 4–20 cm wide, convex to broadly convex at first and then becoming nearly flat to depressed with age; surface dry to somewhat viscid when moist, dull, indistinctly powdery to slightly velvety, color varying from deep yellow to mustard yellow, olive-yellow, or gray; flesh unchanging when cut; pore-bearing surface lemon yellow to deep golden yellow, bruising yellow-orange to orange-brown, pores small, one or two per mm; stalk 6.5–15 cm long and 10–35 mm wide, nearly equal to slightly swollen in the middle, tapered toward the base, pale yellow to deep chrome yellow or somewhat brown; surface with a coarse yellow reticulation; spores olive-brown to dark yellow-brown in mass, 9–13 × 3–4 µm, ellipsoid, smooth.

Habitat/Biological Role: Occurring as solitary fruiting bodies or more often in groups on the ground in broadleaf forests, particularly those containing oaks; typically fruiting during the summer and early fall. Forms mycorrhizal associations with trees.

Distribution: Most common in the Southeast and East but found as far west as Minnesota.

Comments: *Retiboletus ornatipes* is easily recognized by the entirely yellow reticulate stalk. *Retiboletus retipes* (syn. *Boletus retipes*), supposedly found in the extreme Southeast, is reported to have a powdery cap. Both species are generally too bitter to be eaten. *Retiboletus griseus* is similar in stature and also has a reticulate stalk, but it is white to occasionally yellow at the base.

Strobilomyces strobilaceus
(Scopoli) Berkeley

OLD MAN OF THE WOODS
SYNONYM *Strobilomyces floccopus*
FAMILY Boletaceae

Cap 5–15 cm wide, hemispherical at first but becoming flattened with age; upper surface dry, densely covered with coarse, black, woolly scales; lower surface of cap white to grayish white, becoming darker with age, staining red when bruised, pores angular, large, one or two per mm; stalk 4–12 cm long and 1.3–2 cm wide, sometimes slightly enlarged at the base, woolly, scaly, dark gray; annulus sometimes present as a shaggy gray ring on the stalk; spores black in mass, 7–15 × 7–12 μm, globose to broadly ellipsoid, complete reticulum present.

Habitat/Biological Role: Occurring on the ground under oaks and other broadleaf trees or more rarely conifers, often solitary but also occurring in scattered groups; fruiting throughout the summer and into fall. Forms mycorrhizal associations with trees, especially oaks.

Distribution: Found throughout eastern North America.

Comments: In our region, all recognized species of *Strobilomyces* are edible, but their texture is not particularly appealing. The fruiting bodies of these fungi are somewhat resistant to decay and can persist as shriveled blackish remnants for several weeks. Three species are very similar and can reliably be distinguished only on the basis of microscopic features. The spores of *S. confusus* have an incomplete reticulation of irregular ridges, while the spores of *S. strobilaceus* and the slightly smaller spores of *S. dryophilus* have a complete reticulum. Continued genetic work will likely reveal additional species in our region.

Suillus granulatus (Linnaeus) Roussel

GRANULATED SLIPPERY JACK, DOTTED-STALK SUILLUS

FAMILY Suillaceae

Cap 5–15 cm broad, convex at first and then becoming broadly convex with age, upper surface usually viscid, variable and mottled in color ranging from pale pinkish gray to pale yellowish to pale tan, often streaked or checkered in pattern; pore surface nearly white to pale yellow when young and then darkening to yellowish, staining or with age becoming dull cinnamon, pores irregular, one per mm; stalk 3.5–8 cm long and 1–2.5 cm wide, equal, white when young and then becoming pale yellowish with age and toward stalk apex, covered by scattered red-brown grain-like dots; partial veil and annulus absent; spores brown in mass, 7–10 × 2.5–3.5 µm, elliptical to slightly tapered toward apex, smooth.

Habitat/Biological Role: Occurring as solitary fruiting bodies or in groups on the ground, associated with pines; fruiting throughout summer and fall. Forms mycorrhizal associations with trees.

Distribution: Found widely in North America.

Comments: The genus *Suillus* can be challenging to identify to species. *Suillus granulatus* is edible, although some people have experienced gastric upset after eating it, and in a few rare cases individuals developed contact dermatitis and an itchy rash from handling the fruiting bodies. In the Southeast, the most similar species is *S. brevipes* (edible), which differs in having a shorter stocky stalk that lacks the granular dots and a cap surface that is usually darker.

Suillus hirtellus (Peck) Snell

HAIRY SUILLUS

FAMILY Suillaceae

Cap 5–12 cm broad, convex at first but becoming nearly flat with age, upper surface viscid in moist weather, sparsely covered by reddish tufts that disappear with age, margin incurved when young; pore surface pale yellow when young and then darkening to olive-yellow, occasionally young specimens have whitish droplets on the pore surface, bruising reddish brown, pores one per mm; stalk 3–8 cm long and 1–2 cm wide, equal or slightly larger toward the base, color and tufts similar to those of the cap, becoming more yellow toward the apex of the stalk; partial veil and annulus absent; spores dull cinnamon to brownish in mass, 7–9 × 3–3.5 μm, somewhat oblong, smooth.

Habitat/Biological Role: Occurring as solitary fruiting bodies or in groups, associated with pines and other conifers; fruiting throughout summer and fall. Forms mycorrhizal associations with trees.

Distribution: Found throughout the Southeast and north to Canada.

Comments: This species is edible. *Suillus subaureus* (edible) is somewhat similar but is found in the northern part of our region; its tufts are not as prominent, and the cap is typically darker. *Suillus americanus* and *S. spraguei* (both edible) are also somewhat similar, but both these species have veils and are believed to be associated only with white pine. *Suillus americanus* is not generally found south of North Carolina, and it generally has a bright yellow cap color under the fibrils and larger spores (8–11 × 3–4 μm).

Suillus spraguei (Berkeley & M. A. Curtis) Kuntze

PAINTED BOLETE

SYNONYMS *Suillus pictus, Boletinus pictus*

FAMILY Suillaceae

Cap 3–13 cm broad, at first convex but becoming broadly convex to nearly flat with age, upper surface dry, covered by appressed reddish scales, velvet-like, scales sometimes becoming sparse with age; margin incurved, often retaining parts of the veil; pore surface covered by delicate veil when young, pores light yellow when young and darkening with age, arranged radially, bruising reddish brown, pores large, one or two per mm; stalk 4–9 cm long and 0.8–2 cm wide, equal or slightly larger toward the base, color similar to that of the cap, scales usually more dense on the stalk than on the cap, remnant veil usually present as irregular annulus near the apex, above the ring the stalk is yellowish; spores olive-brown in mass, 8–12 × 3.5–5 μm, elliptical, smooth.

Habitat/Biological Role: Occurring as solitary fruiting bodies or in large groups, believed to be associated almost exclusively with white pine; fruiting throughout summer and fall. Forms mycorrhizal associations with trees.

Distribution: Found throughout eastern North America wherever white pine occurs.

Comments: This is one of the most common and distinctive species in this challenging genus. *Suillus spraguei* is edible and can be found in great abundance. Despite its slimy texture, some mushroom hunters regard it as a choice edible. *Suillus americanus* and *S. hirtellus* are somewhat similar, but their scales and the veil in *S. americanus* are not as prominent and the fruiting body is more yellow overall (see comments under *S. hirtellus*).

Tylopilus alboater (Schweinitz) Murrill

BLACK VELVET BOLETE

FAMILY Boletaceae

Cap 2–15 cm broad, becoming convex to nearly flat to slightly upturned with age, margin often with a narrow sterile/pore-free band, upper surface dry, velvety, and sometimes cracking with age, blackish to brownish to grayish, sometimes having a whitish bloom when young; pore surface white to faintly gray when young, becoming dull pinkish tan to dirty gray-brown with age, staining reddish and eventually black when bruised, cap flesh white to grayish and staining reddish gray to pinkish and then eventually blackish when cut; stalk 4–11 cm long and 2–4 cm wide, equal to slightly thicker toward the base, similar in color to the cap surface or darker, and sometimes having a whitish bloom on the surface, occasionally slightly reticulate near the apex of the stalk; spores pinkish brown in mass, 7–11 × 3.5–5 µm, narrowly oval, smooth.

Habitat/Biological Role: Occurring as scattered fruiting bodies or in groups, usually on the ground under broadleaf trees, typically oaks; fruiting throughout summer and early fall. Forms mycorrhizal associations with trees.

Distribution: Found throughout eastern North America, from New England south to Florida and Mexico.

Comments: With its stately size and solemn black velvety color, this is one of the more striking *Tylopilus* species. Most members of the genus are incredibly bitter; however, this species is mild and when young is a favorite edible of some mushroom foragers. The dark color and the reddish to brownish staining reaction help distinguish this species from members of other genera in the Boletaceae. *Tylopilus griseocarneus*, found in sandy soils from Florida to New Jersey, is superficially similar but has a prominently reticulate stalk and a black pore surface when young which fades to gray with age. *Tylopilus nebulosus* is similar, but its cap surface is typically paler when young, it is not typically found south of North Carolina, and it has larger spores (11–20 × 5–8 µm). *Tylopilus atronicotianus* is similar but differs in having a cap that is smooth and olive-brown; the range of this species is not well documented, but it is primarily reported from West Virginia northward and also possibly occurs at high elevations in the southern Appalachians. Edibility for these three species is unknown.

Tylopilus balloui (Peck) Singer

BURNT-ORANGE BOLETE

SYNONYM *Rubinoboletus balloui*

FAMILY Boletaceae

Cap 5–12 cm broad, convex at first but becoming nearly flat with age; surface generally dry, bright orange to red when young, fading with age to tan or cinnamon; pores small, one or two per mm, white when young and darkening to tan or pinkish with age, but never yellow, staining brown when bruised; stalk variable 2–12 cm long and 0.6–3 cm wide, off-white to yellowish orange, smooth, slender, equal to swollen slightly at base; spores pale brown to reddish in mass, 5–11 × 3–5 µm, elliptical, smooth.

Habitat/Biological Role: Occurring as scattered fruiting bodies and in groups, on the ground under trees in lawns and in forests, especially near beech, oaks, and pines; fruiting throughout the summer and until late fall. Forms mycorrhizal associations with trees.

Distribution: Widely distributed in the Southeast, and we have collected this species as far south as northeastern South America.

Comments: The relatively small size of the fruiting body and the distinctive color combination make *Tylopilus balloui* one of the more easily identifiable boletes in our region. It can be bitter but is considered edible.

Tylopilus plumbeoviolaceus
(Snell & E. A. Dick) Snell & E. A. Dick

VIOLET-GRAY BOLETE

FAMILY Boletaceae

Cap 4–15 cm broad, becoming convex to nearly flat with age, upper surface dry, velvet-like when young but later becoming smooth, violet to purple when young, fading to pale purplish gray or purplish brown with age; pore surface white when young, becoming pinkish to pale tan, unchanging when bruised; stalk 8–12 cm long and 1–2 cm wide, proportionally stocky when young, with maturation becoming more equal to slightly thicker toward the base, mostly purple to violet with occasional white flecks, darkening to more grayish purple with age; spores pinkish brown in mass, 10–13 × 3–4 µm, elliptical, smooth.

Habitat/Biological Role: Occurring as scattered fruiting bodies or in groups, usually on the ground under broadleaf trees, typically oaks; fruiting throughout summer and early fall. Forms mycorrhizal associations with trees.

Distribution: Found throughout eastern North America, and there are some reports of a similar or possibly the same species occurring in oak forests all the way into Central America.

Comments: Many of the large gray to purple species in the genus *Tylopilus* have a very bitter taste; these so-called bitter boletes are generally considered to be inedible. It can be challenging to identify many of the *Tylopilus* found in the Southeast to species. *Tylopilus rubrobrunneus* is similar to *T. plumbeoviolaceus*, but the pore surface of the former stains brown when bruised and the overall color is not as bright. *Tylopilus violatinctus* is morphologically similar but paler in color, and this species also has slightly smaller spores (7–10 × 3–4 µm) that are reddish brown in mass.

Tylopilus rubrobrunneus
Mazzer & A. H. Smith

REDDISH BROWN BITTER BOLETE

FAMILY Boletaceae

Cap 8–30 cm broad, becoming flat to upturned with age, upper surface dry, smooth, sometimes cracking, dark purple when young, becoming purplish brown to dull reddish brown with age; pore surface white when young but later becoming pinkish to pale brown, staining brown when bruised; stalk white to brown, 6–20 cm long and 1–5 cm wide, equal in thickness, developing olive to brownish stains with age or handling; spores dull pinkish brown to dull reddish in mass, 10–13 × 3–4 μm, elliptical, smooth.

Habitat/Biological Role: Occurring as scattered fruiting bodies or in groups and sometimes forming clusters, usually on the ground; fruiting throughout the summer and early fall. Forms mycorrhizal associations with trees.

Distribution: Particularly common in the Southeast and found throughout eastern North America.

Comments: This is another of the many large gray to purple *Tylopilus* species known as bitter boletes, because their very bitter taste generally causes them to be considered inedible. It can be challenging to identify specimens of *Tylopilus* found in the Southeast to species. *Tylopilus plumbeoviolaceus* is similar to this species, but the pore surface does not stain brown when bruised and the overall color is usually more bright purple to violet. *Tylopilus violatinctus* is very similar but has slightly smaller spores (7–10 × 3–4 μm).

Coral Fungi and Relatives

Coral fungi are a diverse group, ranging from single club-shaped structures to fruiting bodies composed of a complex series of branches arising from a single stalk, which in some forms can resemble a cauliflower. The spores are produced on the smooth sides of the clubs or branches. The fungi in this section are decomposers, possibly parasites, or form mycorrhizal associations with trees. Most are not commonly eaten, although the genus *Sparassis* provides several favorite edible mushrooms in our region. *Thelephora*, which has more fan-like fruiting bodies, has also been included in this section; this genus is important from a mycorrhizal standpoint. Also see the jelly fungus *Calocera cornea* (page 361) and several ascomycetes that produce club-shaped fruiting bodies (Club Fungi page 71).

KEY TO CORAL FUNGI AND RELATIVES

1. Fruiting body occurring directly on wood 2
1. Fruiting body occurring on soil, leaf litter, or buried wood 3

2. Fruiting body large; a white coral-like structure . . . . *Artomyces pyxidatus*
2. Fruiting body a single white club arising from alga-covered logs . . . . . . *Multiclavula mucida*

3. Fruiting body whitish; a rosette or cauliflower-like structure . . . .
. . . . *Sparassis, Tremellodendron schweinitzii*
3. Fruiting body not as above 4

4. Fruiting body fleshy, branching and sharing a common base . . . . *Clavulina cinerea, Ramaria*
4. Fruiting body fan-like or appearing either as a single club or occurring in clusters but the latter rarely arising from common base. 5

5. Fruiting body fan-like. . . . .*Thelephora*
5. Fruiting body appearing either as a single club or occurring in clusters but the latter rarely arising from common base. . . . .*Clavaria, Clavariadelphus, Clavulinopsis*

Artomyces pyxidatus (Fries) Doty

CROWN-TIPPED CORAL

SYNONYM *Clavicorona pyxidata*

FAMILY Auriscalpiaceae

Repeatedly branched coral-like structure, 4–13 × 2–10 cm, solitary or sometimes occurring in small clusters, white at first but becoming yellowish to very pale brown, sometimes with a pinkish tinge; the tips of the ultimate branches shaped like tiny crowns (i.e., with a depressed center surrounded by a series of three to six points); spores white in mass, 4–5 × 2–3 μm, elliptical, smooth.

Habitat/Biological Role: Occurring on the decomposing wood of broadleaf trees; fruiting summer to fall. Decomposer of wood.

Distribution: Widely distributed in North America east of the Rocky Mountains.

Comments: The fruiting bodies of *Artomyces pyxidatus* are distinctive, with characteristic crown-like tips at the apex of the branches. Moreover, they are associated with decomposing wood, which is an uncommon substrate for coral fungi. This fungus is regarded as edible. Some species of *Ramaria* are similar; however, they are generally thicker, not white in color, and usually do not occur on wood.

Clavaria fragilis Holmskjold

WHITE WORM CORAL

SYNONYM *Clavaria vermicularis*

FAMILY Clavariaceae

Cylindrical to spindle-shaped structure, typically unbranched, occurring in small groups or clusters, 3–12 cm high and 1–5 cm wide, often curved and sometimes flattened or grooved, dry or moist, white or translucent, usually with a somewhat pointed tip that becomes yellowish or pale brownish with age; stalk indistinct; spores white in mass, 4–7 × 3–5 µm, elliptical, smooth.

Habitat/Biological Role: Occurring on the ground in broadleaf or mixed broadleaf-conifer forests as well as in non-forested situations, usually in low, moist areas and often associated with mosses; fruiting from summer through fall. Decomposer of litter and humus.

Distribution: Widely distributed throughout North America.

Comments: The white color and lack of branches separates this species from other similar fungi. It is reportedly edible but generally fruits in small numbers.

Clavaria zollingeri Léveillé

VIOLET CORAL

FAMILY Clavariaceae

Coral-shaped structure, with individual erect elements antler-like, cylindrical with rounded or irregular tips, 2–8 cm tall and 2–5 mm wide, rarely branched, deep violet to pinkish purple, fading slightly with age, smooth, sharing a common base, the base whitish; spores white in mass, 4–7 × 3–5.5 µm, ellipsoid, smooth, nonamyloid.

Habitat/Biological Role: Occurring on the ground in broadleaf and mixed broadleaf-conifer forests; fruiting in summer and fall. Decomposer of organic matter.

Distribution: Found throughout eastern North America.

Comments: The deep violet color of *Clavaria zollingeri* makes this fungus readily apparent in nature and rather easy to identify. It certainly qualifies as one of the more beautiful coral fungi found in the Southeast. This fungus is considered edible but is rarely found in sufficient quantities to be eaten. *Clavulina amethystina* (syn. *Clavaria amethystina*) is the most similar species (edible) and reliably differs only on microscopic characters, having two-spored basidia (*C. zollingeri* has four-spored basidia) and larger spores (7–12 × 6–8 µm). Some *Ramaria* species are similar, but they generally arise from a trunk-like base.

Clavariadelphus pistillaris var. *americanus* Corner

PESTLE-SHAPED CORAL

FAMILY Clavariadelphaceae

Club-shaped structure, 7–20 cm tall and 2–6 cm wide, unbranched or very rarely forked, tapering downward toward the base; surface smooth to longitudinally wrinkled, apex usually rounded and expanded, at first yellowish to orange-yellow and then becoming brownish orange to pale reddish brown with age; stalk indistinct, but the base white and sparsely covered with fine white hairs; spores white to pale brownish yellow in mass, 10–16 × 5–10 µm, elliptical, smooth, nonamyloid.

Habitat/Biological Role: Occurring as solitary or more likely scattered to clustered fruiting bodies on the ground in broadleaf forests; fruiting from midsummer through fall. Forms mycorrhizal associations with trees.

Distribution: Widely distributed throughout North America.

Comments: The relatively large size and distinctly club-shaped fruiting body make *Clavariadelphus pistillaris* var. *americanus* an easy fungus to identify; however, it should be noted that immature and still-developing fruiting bodies are cylindrical, not club-shaped. *Clavariadelphus truncatus* is similar in general aspect but has fruiting bodies that are usually somewhat smaller and have a broad, flattened apex; moreover, it is almost invariably found in conifer, not broadleaf, forests. *Clavariadelphus* is undergoing a major taxonomic revision that will likely split some of the existing species concepts based on genetics; most current species are considered edible but often too bitter to be eaten.

Clavulina cinerea (Bulliard) J. Schröter

GRAY CORAL

SYNONYM *Clavaria cinerea*

FAMILY Clavulinaceae

Coral-like structure with numerous individual branches more or less arising from a single base, branches tending to be sinuous, 6–10 mm wide, flattened and with rounded or pointed tips; surface smooth to slightly wrinkled; entire fruiting body 3–10 cm tall and as much as 10 cm across, ash gray or gray-brown, occasionally tinged with lilac; stalk lacking or small; spores white in mass, 6.5–11 × 6–10 μm, ellipsoid to subglobose, smooth, nonamyloid.

Habitat/Biological Role: Occurring on the ground as scattered fruiting bodies or in small groups in broadleaf or mixed broadleaf-conifer forests, apparently most common in pine-dominated forests;

fruiting from midsummer through fall. Thought to form mycorrhizal associations with trees, but some closely related species are decomposers of litter and humus.

Distribution: Widely distributed throughout North America.

Comments: *Clavulina cinerea* is subject to being parasitized by another fungus, the ascomycete *Helminthosphaeria clavariorum*. This parasite (visible on the base of the upturned specimens in the photo) is typically present at the base of the fruiting body and can cause the specimen to become purple-tinged to almost black at the base. *Clavulina coralloides* (syn. *C. cristata*) is similar to *C. cinerea* but is more sparely branched and white in color. Both species are edible.

Clavulinopsis laeticolor
(Berkeley & M. A. Curtis)
R. H. Petersen

GOLDEN FAIRY CLUB

FAMILY Clavariaceae

Cylindrical to somewhat flattened structure, unbranched and sometimes with a groove or slightly twisted, 1.5–6.5 cm tall and 1–5 mm wide, dry, at first bright orange to yellow-orange and then fading with age, tips pointed and discoloring to reddish or orange; stalk indistinct but white at the very base; spores white in mass, 4.5–7 × 3.5–5.5 μm, broadly ellipsoid to subglobose or somewhat irregularly shaped, smooth.

Habitat/Biological Role: Occurring as solitary to scattered fruiting bodies on the ground in broadleaf or conifer forests, commonly associated with mosses or found on bare soil; fruiting in summer and fall. Decomposer of litter and humus.

Distribution: Widely distributed in North America and also reported from Europe and Asia (genetics will likely show these to be different).

Comments: This rather small fungus would be easily overlooked if not for the bright color of its fruiting bodies. Its edibility is not known. The size and the white base of the stalk distinguish it from similar coral fungi. *Clavulinopsis aurantio-cinnabarina* (also bright orange) and *C. fusiformis* (yellow) generally occur in cespitose clusters. *Clavulinopsis helveola* (yellow) is typically taller, and its spores are 7–8 × 2–3 μm.

Multiclavula mucida (Persoon)
R. H. Petersen

WHITE GREEN-ALGAE CORAL

SYNONYMS *Clavaria mucida, Lentaria mucida, Stichoclavaria mucida*

FAMILY Clavulinaceae

Club-shaped structure, 3–15 mm high and 1–1.5 mm wide, very rarely forked, typically tapering slightly toward the base, white overall but sometimes with brown tips with age, arising from thin basal mat formed by *Coccomyxa*, a genus of green algae; spores white in mass, 4.5–7.5 × 2–3 μm, narrowly elliptical, smooth, nonamyloid.

Habitat/Biological Role: Usually fruiting in large clusters on decorticated logs that are covered by thin mats of a green alga; fruiting summer to late fall. This fungus forms a mycorrhizal-like symbiotic association with green algae.

Distribution: Widely distributed throughout North America and the rest of the world.

Comments: Most fungi that make up the larger component of the composite organisms known as lichens are members of the phylum Ascomycota; however, *Multiclavula mucida* is a member of an unusual group in the Basidiomycota commonly referred to as basidiolichens, because of the symbiotic relationship they form with algae. The genus *Multiclavula* is related to the chanterelles. None of the morphologically similar club-shaped coral fungi are associated with mats of green algae. The genus *Typhula* could be confused with *M. mucida*, since most *Typhula* species are solitary stalked club fungi, relatively small (less than 3 cm tall), and tend to be white, gray, or pale brown; these fungi usually have a clearly distinct stalk and generally occur on leaves or twigs in swampy areas. *Typhula ishikariensis* and *T. incarnata* cause gray snow mold, a phenomenon that has an economic impact on the turf grass industry and golf courses. *Multiclavula mucida* is too small to have any culinary value, and its edibility is not known.

Ramaria formosa (Persoon) Quélet

BEAUTIFUL CLAVARIA, YELLOW-TIPPED CORAL

FAMILY Gomphaceae

Coral-like structure up to 13 cm high and wide, pinkish orange or pale salmon when young but fading to pale orange-yellow, branch tips often lighter in color, branching from a central base, surface can bruise brownish; spores pale yellow-brown in mass, 10–15 × 4.5–6 μm, elliptical, with fine warts.

Habitat/Biological Role: Occurring as solitary fruiting bodies or sometimes in scattered clusters, on the ground in mixed forests; fruiting summer to fall. Possibly forms mycorrhizal associations with trees, but its ecology is not fully understood.

Distribution: Frequently found in the southern Appalachians and west to Arkansas, and also common throughout much of eastern North America.

Comments: *Ramaria formosa* is a distinctive fungus and one of the larger corals in our region. It is poisonous and can cause serious gastrointestinal issues. *Ramaria stricta* is a similar species found in the northern portion of our region; it occurs on wood, not soil, and further differs in having longer, straighter branches with yellow tips and smaller spores (7.5–10 × 4–5 μm). *Artomyces pyxidatus* is similar in form but also occurs on wood and is generally nearly white to off-white in color.

Ramaria fumigata (Peck) Corner

VIOLET CORAL MUSHROOM

FAMILY Gomphaceae

Coral-like structure, 5–14 × 8–12 cm, violet to lilac, fading to dingy purple and sometimes becoming almost brown, branch tips often lighter in color, branching from a central base; spores pale brown in mass, 8.5–11 × 3–4 μm, elliptical, surface rough.

Habitat/Biological Role: Occurring as solitary fruiting bodies or sometimes in scattered clusters on the ground in mixed forests; fruiting summer to fall. Believed to form mycorrhizal associations with trees.

Distribution: Frequently encountered in the southern Appalachians and known from scattered localities in eastern North America. Occasionally reported from western North America.

Comments: This species is part of the *Ramaria fennica* group. Some taxonomists consider the true *R. fennica* to be a European species; the North American *R. fennica* is generally not found in our region and does not have the same violet to purple colors. *Ramaria botrytis* is similar but is pale pink, generally paler in color, and has larger spores (11–16 × 3.5–5.5 μm). *Ramaria subbotrytis* is also similar in stature and spore size, but its fruiting bodies are pale salmon to rose-colored. Most other purple coral fungi in our region form less compact fruiting bodies or have white spores. *Clavaria zollingeri* and *Clavulina amethystina* are similar in color but are much less branched, typically more vibrant in color, and have white spores. *Ramaria fumigata* is likely to cause gastrointestinal issues if eaten.

Ramaria grandis (Peck) Corner

GRAND RAMARIA

SYNONYM *Clavaria grandis*

FAMILY Gomphaceae

Coral-like structure, 4–15 cm tall and up to 12 cm wide near the apex, branches smooth, brown to gray-brown, tips rounded and abruptly whitish, when young the branches are stocky but they become more slender and elongated with age, typically branching twice or more from a central base; base up to 6 cm long and up to 2 cm wide, sometimes bulbous or rooting into the soil; spores brownish in mass, 4–6 × 8–12 μm, narrowly elliptical, with prominent sharp spines (1.5 μm long).

Habitat/Biological Role: Typically occurring in scattered clusters on the ground in mixed forests; fruiting summer to fall. Possibly forms mycorrhizal associations with trees.

Distribution: Eastern and southeastern North America, particularly common in the mountains of North Carolina and Tennessee.

Comments: The drab color of *Ramaria grandis* makes it one of the most easily recognized species in the genus. *Ramaria murrillii* (syn. *Clavaria murrilli*) is sometimes confused with this species, but it is smaller and much more delicately branched. *Phaeoclavulina longicaulis* (syn. *C. longicaulis, R. longicaulis*) is somewhat similar in color but has prominent rhizomorphs at the base. The edibility of these species is not known, so collecting them for food is not recommended.

Sparassis americana
R. H. Petersen

CAULIFLOWER MUSHROOM

FAMILY Sparassidaceae

Cauliflower-like structure, 10–45 cm across, complex in shape and composed of convoluted off-white to cream-colored ribbon-like branches arising from a sterile root-like base; the branches thin and very brittle; entire structure becoming darker with age; spores white in mass, 5–6.5 × 3–3.5 μm, oval, smooth, hyaline.

Habitat/Biological Role: Occurring as a solitary fruiting body at the base of old or dead pine trees or pine stumps; fruiting in the late summer and early fall. Believed to be a root pathogen of members of the Pinaceae (pine tree family).

Distribution: Throughout the Southeast as well as in other parts of North America.

Comments: The genus *Sparassis* is undergoing a taxonomic revision; however, all species are choice edibles, particularly when young. There are reports of individuals weighing as much as 22 kg. *Sparassis spathulata* is morphologically similar and should be compared. *Tremellodendron schweinitzii* can appear vaguely similar but is smaller and not as convoluted in form.

Sparassis spathulata
(Schweinitz) Fries

CAULIFLOWER MUSHROOM

SYNONYMS *Sparassis caroliniense, S. herbstii*

FAMILY Sparassidaceae

Head-of-lettuce-like structure, up to 30 cm across, complex in shape and composed of wavy off-white to cream-colored erect ribbon-like branches arising from a sterile base, upper edges of ribbon-like structures often bright white and the older/lower portion off-white to cream, sometimes even pale brown with age; branches thin and somewhat flexible to rubbery; spores white in mass, 4–7 × 3–4 µm, oval, smooth.

Habitat/Biological Role: Occurring as a solitary fruiting body on the ground at the base of old broadleaf trees, particularly old oak stumps; fruiting in late summer and early fall. This fungus is believed to be a root pathogen and/or a decomposer of the roots of some broadleaf trees, particularly oaks, in our region.

Distribution: Particularly common in the Southeast but found throughout much of eastern North America.

Comments: All *Sparassis* species are choice edibles, particularly when young. *Sparassis americana* has much denser and more convoluted branches. *Tremellodendron schweinitzii* can appear similar, but it is generally smaller, whiter, and more rubbery, and its spores are substantially larger.

Thelephora palmata (Scopoli) Fries

SMALL THELEPHORA

FAMILY Thelephoraceae

Coral-shaped structure consisting of numerous narrow, flat leathery branches arising from single base, entire structure typically 2–7 cm wide, dingy white to grayish white when young or near the apex and becoming grayish brown with age; lower portion of the branches smooth, grayish purple; stalk absent or short, up to 3 cm long and 5 mm wide, off-white and rubbery; inner tissue stains a deep blue in KOH; spores brown in mass, 8–10 × 6–9 µm, elliptical and ornamented by fine spines or warts.

Habitat/Biological Role: Occurring as solitary fruiting bodies or in scattered clusters on the ground, usually in mixed forests; fruiting from late summer into fall. Forms mycorrhizal associations with trees.

Distribution: Occasionally found in the Southeast and widely distributed in North America.

Comments: This fungus is too small and rubbery to be of any culinary interest. One of the best diagnostic characters of this species is the fetid or disagreeable odor. Some authors report *Thelephora anthocephala*, which is very similar to *T. palmata*, as having the same type of disagreeable odor (others do not); in any case, its inner tissue does not stain deep blue in KOH. *Thelephora terrestris* is very variable in form and sometimes produces a structure that somewhat resembles a very dark version of *T. palmata*, but it does not have the pale upper surface.

Thelephora vialis Schweinitz

VASE THELEPHORA

FAMILY Thelephoraceae

Fan-shaped structure consisting of broad, leathery fused branches or sometimes more complex and then vase- or cup-shaped, 2.5–15 cm tall and 2.5–10 cm across, typically arising from single base, off-white to buff or sometimes nearly yellow toward the apex, lower portion smooth, grayish purple to almost black; stalk usually absent or consisting of a mass of fused fans up to 3 cm thick; spores brown in mass, 4.5–8 × 4.5–6.5 µm, angular and warted, minutely spiny.

Habitat/Biological Role: Occurring as solitary fruiting bodies or in scattered clusters on the ground, usually in mixed forests although some reports say this species prefers oaks; fruiting from late summer into fall. Forms mycorrhizal associations with trees.

Distribution: Very common in the Southeast and found throughout much of eastern North America.

Comments: This fungus is too rubbery to be of any culinary interest. *Tremellodendron schweinitzii* is somewhat similar with respect to the overall fruiting body structure but is usually bright white. The very variable *Thelephora terrestris* can produce a structure that somewhat resembles a very dark version of *T. vialis*, but it does not have the pale upper surface. *Thelephora palmata* is similar but is entirely brown and has a coral-like growth form.

Tremellodendron
schweinitzii (Peck) G. F. Atkinson

FALSE CORAL MUSHROOM

SYNONYM *Tremellodendron pallidum*

FAMILY Sebacinaceae

Coral-like structure, 5–15 × 2–10 cm, white to buff, composed of tough, broadly flattened branches, these fused at the base and arising from one or several stalks; spores white in mass, 7.5–11 × 4–6.5 μm, elliptical to sausage-shaped, smooth.

Habitat/Biological Role: Occurring as a solitary fruiting body but more often found in groups on the ground under broadleaf trees; fruiting bodies develop slowly and can be found in early spring but typically are not readily apparent until midsummer or fall. Reports relating to the biological role of this fungus are mixed, but it is now generally considered to form mycorrhizal associations with trees.

Distribution: Most common in the Southeast and East but found throughout North America.

Comments: *Tremellodendron schweinitzii* is generally considered nonpoisonous or edible, depending on the source; however, it is too rubbery and tough to be of much culinary interest. It is possible to mistake this fungus for some of the choice edibles in the wood-decomposing genus *Sparassis*. One difference between these two genera is that *Sparassis* always occurs close to the base of a tree, stump, or root, while *Tremellodendron* is mycorrhizal and typically arises from the mineral soil layer.

Polypores and Relatives

Most of the polypores and related fungi are woody or at least rubbery, and they typically fruit directly from wood. Most are either parasites or decomposers, but some have more complex relationships. There is a large diversity of fruiting structures, ranging from globular burl-like to shelf-shaped fruiting bodies.

Many species of polypores have been used by humans to transport fire. Some species work better than others, but if a small hollow is created in most of the woody species and a small ember from a fire is place inside of the hollow, a fire can smolder for days. In prehistoric times, starting fire while traveling or in wet conditions was challenging, so many different groups of people around the world used this group of fungi as a way to transport a campfire from one place to another.

Some of the best-known edible and medicinal mushrooms are members of this group. Clinical studies reveal that certain important traditional medicinal mushrooms, including reishi (*Ganoderma* spp.), maitake (*Grifola frondosa*), horse hoof fungus (*Fomes fomentarius*), and turkey tail (*Trametes versicolor*), have promising western medical applications. Fungi in Boletes and Relatives (page 248) and Crust Fungi, Rusts, and Smuts (page 328) should also be compared.

KEY TO POLYPORES AND RELATIVES

1. Fruiting body solitary or occurring in groups but not forming clusters or sharing a common base 7
1. Fruiting body occurring in dense clusters or rosettes with a common base 2

2. Fruiting body composed of clusters of numerous caps with an upper surface that is pale gray to grayish brown; overall up to 80 cm across, caps sharing a common base 3
2. Fruiting body not as above 4

3. Fruiting body staining black . . . . *Meripilus sumstinei*
3. Fruiting body not staining black. . . . . *Bondarzewia berkeleyi, Grifola frondosa*

4. Fruiting body woody, knot-like, and composed of many crowded drooping caps that are fused to each other . . . . *Globifomes graveolens*
4. Fruiting body not as above 5

5. Fruiting body bright orange with a yellow margin and yellow pore surface or pale pinkish with a white margin and a white pore surface, either occurring as a large clump at the base of a host tree or in dense fans along the sides of logs . . . . *Laetiporus*
5. Fruiting body not as above 6

6. Fruiting body occurring at the base of conifers or from conifer roots, usually with a central stalk, yellow to dark brownish red when young, becoming dark brown with age, upper surface fuzzy, pore surface usually dark in color . . . . *Phaeolus schweinitzii*
6. Fruiting body occurring on the ground, rubbery and with a smooth upper surface; pore surface usually pale-colored. . . . . *Laeticutis cristata*

7. Upper surface of the fruiting body glossy with a velvety sheen and zoned in different shades of brown or covered by a dense layer of coarse bristle-like hairs 8
7. Upper surface of the fruiting body not as above 9

8. Fruiting body shelf-like, upper surface covered by erect bristle-like hairs; found only in the southern portion of our region . . . . *Hexagonia hydnoides*
8. Fruiting body thin and plate-like, upper surface of cap and stalk some shade of brown; upper surface velvety and zoned but not hairy . . . . *Coltricia cinnamomea*

9. Upper surface of the fruiting body gelatinous, rubbery, and reddish in color; lower surface consisting of hanging tubes . . . . *Fistulina hepatica*
9. Fruiting body not as above 10

10. Fruiting body woody and rather hard when mature (even when wet) 11
10. Fruiting body rubbery, leathery, or bendable (except when dry) 12

11. Fruiting body shelf-like, bright red, orange, or pinkish . . . . *Fomitopsis cajanderi, Pycnoporus cinnabarinus*
11. Fruiting body not as above; usually hard and woody, shelf-like, typically perennial and sometimes reaching a large size . . . . *Fomes, Ganoderma, Inonotus, Phellinus*

12. Fruiting body often reddish brown, appearing varnished and when young with a white to yellowish outer margin; when fresh the texture is fleshy, soft to rubbery . . . . *Ganoderma*
12. Fruiting body not as above 13

13. Fruiting body generally occurring in groups along logs, stumps, or standing dead trees, with turkey-tail-like color zones on the upper surface and fine white pores on the lower surface . . . . *Trametes versicolor*
13. Fruiting body not as above 14

14. Fruiting body at first white and then yellowing with age; when young nearly translucent, with large angular pores and a lateral stalk; found in the southern portion of our region. . . . . *Favolus tenuiculus*
14. Fruiting body not as above . . . . *Inonotus, Lenzites, Neofavolus, Piptoporus, Polyporus*

Bondarzewia berkeleyi (Fries)
Bondartsev & Singer

BERKELEY'S POLYPORE

FAMILY Bondarzewiaceae

Compound rosette with multiple lobes, individual lobes 7.5–25 cm wide, overall specimens can reach more than 100 cm across, convex when young, becoming flat but with a depressed center with age; surface dry, hairy or glabrous, often rough or pitted, creamy white to yellow, often zonate; pore-bearing surface white, pores 0.5–2 mm wide, angular; stalk 5–10 cm long and 3–5 cm wide, short, stout, irregularly shaped, yellow to yellowish brown; spores white in mass, 6–8 μm round, strongly warted, amyloid.

Habitat/Biological Role: Occurring as solitary to clustered fruiting bodies at the base of living broadleaf trees and stumps; fruiting from early summer to early fall. Decomposer of wood.

Distribution: Widely distributed throughout the Southeast, less common in other parts of North America.

Comments: The fruiting bodies of *Bondarzewia berkeleyi* can become rather large, weighing as much as 15 kg. This fungus is edible when young but becomes bitter-tasting and fibrous with age. It is possible to confuse a young specimen of *B. berkeleyi* with the edible *Meripilus sumstinei*, but the latter stains black and has smaller individual lobes. *Grifola frondosa* is also similar and edible, but it has smaller individual lobes.

Byssomerulius incarnatus
(Schweinitz) Gilbertson

CORAL PINK POLYPORE

SYNONYMS *Merulius incarnatus, Phlebia incarnata*

FAMILY Phanerochaetaceae

Irregular to somewhat fan-shaped or crust-like structure, often projecting as shelf-like caps, up to 15 cm across, often occurring in overlapping clusters, spongy to waxy texture; upper surface at first pale pink to bright pink but becoming reddish with age, paler toward the margins; surface smooth or sometimes with a sparse covering of small white hairs; fertile surface pale cream in color, becoming darker upon drying, wrinkled, pores irregular, ridge-like, one or two per mm; stalk lacking; spores white in mass, 4–5.5 × 2–2.5 µm, narrowly ovoid, smooth, nonamyloid.

Habitat/Biological Role: Occurring on decomposing logs and stumps in broad-leaf forests; fruiting from late spring to fall. The ecology of this species is not fully understood—possibly a wood decomposer, but likely has a parasitic relationship with *Stereum* species and other mushrooms.

Distribution: Most common in the southern and western parts of our region but found throughout North America.

Comments: The coral pink color and unusual texture (for a polypore) of this fungus make it relatively easy to identify. Its edibility is not known. *Merulius tremellosus* is similar, but it is generally much thinner and paler in color. *Byssomerulius incarnatus* almost always fruits on logs that also have fruitings of *Stereum* species (see photo).

Coltricia cinnamomea
(Jacquin) Murrill

SHINY CINNAMON POLYPORE, TIGER'S EYE POLYPORE

FAMILY Hymenochaetaceae

Cap circular, 10–20 (–60) mm wide, flat to depressed, sometimes funnel-shaped, margin smooth to fibrillose, upper surface smooth and glossy to reflective, cinnamon-brown to sometimes almost black with age, margin similar in color or lighter; lower surface buff-brown to pale cinnamon-brown, pores usually angular, two to four per mm, slightly decurrent; stalk 5–20 (–40) mm long and 2–4 (–7) mm wide, centrally located, round to slightly compressed, solid, equal except for an expanded base, dingy brown to almost black; texture of entire fruiting body leathery when fresh and becoming rigid when dry; spores pale yellowish brown in mass, 6–10 × 4–7 µm, elliptical, smooth.

Habitat/Biological Role: Occurring as solitary fruiting bodies or sometimes in groups (in the latter situation, the caps of adjacent fruiting bodies are often partially fused) on the ground in mixed forests, often found along paths, roadways, and other disturbed areas; fruiting from early summer through the fall. Forms mycorrhizal associations with trees.

Distribution: Particularly common in the Southeast but widely distributed throughout North America.

Comments: Because of its leathery texture *Coltricia cinnamomea* is generally considered inedible. *Coltricia perennis* is similar but usually larger, the surface of the cap is velvety to woolly, and the pores are generally decurrent. *Coltricia montagnei* is related but very different, with a much larger stature, prominent irregular to concentrically zonate pores, and a very velvety surface. *Coltricia oblectabilis* (syn. *C. pseudocinnamomea*) is morphologically almost identical to *C. cinnamomea* except that the former has ornamented reddish brown spores.

Favolus tenuiculus P. Beauvois

HONEYCOMB FUNGUS

SYNONYMS *Favolus brasiliensis, Polyporus tenuiculus*

FAMILY Polyporaceae

Cap 4–8 cm wide, kidney-, fan-, or elongated petal-shaped; surface finely hairy at the base but otherwise usually smooth, at first white and then becoming cream-colored to pale tan with age; pore-bearing surface at first white to cream-colored but becoming pale yellow with age, the pores elongated-hexagonal, 1–3.5 × 0.5–2 mm; stalk ranging from distinct and central to indistinct and lateral, 1–3 cm long and 0.2–2 cm wide; spores hyaline in mass, 8–11 × 3–4 µm, short-cylindrical, smooth.

Habitat/Biological Role: Occurring on the dead wood of trees, fruiting bodies usually in clusters; fruiting throughout the year in our region. Decomposer of wood.

Distribution: Found in the southern portion of our region; we have frequently encountered it on logs in cypress swamps in Florida.

Comments: The white color of the fruiting bodies and the large, hexagonal pores make this an easy fungus to identify. Edibility is unknown.

Fistulina hepatica (Schaeffer) Withering

BEEFSTEAK POLYPORE, BEEFSTEAK FUNGUS

FAMILY Fistulinaceae

Fan- to spoon-shaped structure, cap 7.5–25 cm across (occasionally larger) and 2–5 cm thick; surface roughened to velvety, gelatinous when wet, dark red; flesh soft and exuding a dark red juice when cut; spore-bearing surface often paler in color than the upper surface, consisting of closely packed, discrete tubes (one to three per mm) that are 10–15 mm long; stalk dark red, lateral, short, thick, and sometimes absent; spores pinkish salmon in mass, 4–6 × 3–4 μm, elliptical, smooth.

Habitat/Biological Role: Occurring on stumps or logs or at the bases of living broadleaf trees, especially oaks; fruiting summer to fall. Decomposer of wood, or a pathogen if the tree is still living.

Distribution: Most common in the East but widely distributed throughout North America.

Comments: Although commonly called the beefsteak polypore, this distinctive fungus is not a true polypore. *Fistulina hepatica* differs from many polypores because it is very soft in texture and has pores that hang as independent tubes. The fruiting bodies are also frequently cooked and sometimes even eaten raw. When sliced open, the fruiting body has the general appearance of uncooked beef (hence the common names). Some foragers make a tasty vegan "beef" jerky from this fungus. *Pseudofistulina radicata* (syn. *F. radicata*) is somewhat similar morphologically and is also found in our region; however, it is quite rare, brown to yellowish white in color, and has a prominent radicating stalk.

Fomes fomentarius (Linnaeus) J. J. Kickz

TINDER POLYPORE, HORSE HOOF FUNGUS

FAMILY Polyporaceae

Shell-shaped or more commonly hoof-shaped structure, 5–20 cm wide, upper surface gray to gray-brown, with dark gray to brownish black zones; dry, velvety to smooth; pore-bearing surface slightly concave, tan to cream-colored at first and then becoming pale brown, pores three or four per mm, circular; spores gray to white in mass, 15–20 × 4.5–7 μm, cylindrical, smooth, nonamyloid.

Habitat/Biological Role: Occurring on living or dead broadleaf trees, logs, and stumps, especially those of birch and alder, persisting for several years and increasing in size each year; present throughout the year but releasing spores spring to fall. Decomposer of wood if associated with a dead tree or log but considered parasitic if the tree is still living.

Distribution: Common in the Appalachian Mountains and widely distributed throughout central and northern North America.

Comments: One common name originates with its use as a tinder for starting fires and carrying coals. This tradition dates back several thousand years: fragments of this fungus were found among the possessions of Ötzi the Iceman, the 5,000-year-old mummy discovered in the Italian Alps. A type of felt made from the mushrooms was used by musketeers to discharge early matchlock firearms and has been used to create hats in some regions of Europe. *Fomes fomentarius* is too hard to be eaten, but it has anticancer, antibacterial, and other medicinal properties. In the southern portion of our region, *F. fasciatus* is very similar macroscopically, but it has a flatter fruiting habit, smaller spores (10–14 × 4–5 μm), and a more southern distribution, extending into Central America.

Fomitopsis cajanderi (Karsten) Kotlaba & Pouzar

ROSY POLYPORE

FAMILY Fomitopsidaceae

Cap 2.5–10 cm wide, fan-shaped to semicircular or irregular, often fused laterally with other caps, convex to nearly flat, at first pinkish red to pinkish gray-brown but becoming brownish black with age; surface at first finely hairy and then becoming smooth with age; pore-bearing surface rosy pink to pinkish brown, pores round to angular, three to five per mm; stalk lacking; spores white in mass, 4–7 × 1.5–2 μm, sausage-shaped, smooth.

Habitat/Biological Role: Occurring on dead conifers or sometimes associated with living conifers as a heart rot, in our region particularly common on Virginia pine; fruiting bodies can be found throughout the entire year. Decomposer of wood but considered parasitic when found on a living tree.

Distribution: Not uncommon in the Appalachian Mountains and widely distributed throughout central and northern North America, although less common southward.

Comments: It is usually possible to recognize fruiting bodies of *Fomitopsis cajanderi* from the pink color of the pore-bearing surface and the fact that they occur on conifers. Fruiting bodies of this fungus sometimes grown in appressed forms on the sides or lower surfaces of logs. They are too tough to be eaten, and research concerning any medicinal properties is limited.

Ganoderma applanatum
(Persoon) Patouillard

ARTIST'S CONK

FAMILY Ganodermataceae

Fan-shaped, shelf-like, or (more rarely) hoof-shaped structure; cap 5–50 cm across (occasionally even larger) and 5–50 mm thick; upper surface dull grayish brown to pale brown, concentric darker lines delimiting areas with a lighter color, tough and leathery texture; margin of cap white; spore-bearing surface white, becoming darker with age and bruising brown when disrupted, pores very small and difficult to see; stalk usually lacking; spores brown in mass, 8–12 × 6.5–8 μm, elliptical with a truncated end, double-walled, with an ornamented inner wall and a smooth outer wall.

Habitat/Biological Role: Occurring on fallen logs and stumps of broadleaf trees or more rarely conifers; fruiting throughout the year and in some instances continuing to grow for decades. Decomposer of wood but considered pathogenic when present on living trees.

Distribution: Widely distributed throughout almost all North America.

Comments: *Ganoderma applanatum* is one of the better-known polypores. Because the white pore surface bruises easily and the color change is permanent (if harvested), it is possible to make drawings or sketches with a pointed object. Fruiting bodies used in such a manner often show up at craft fairs, and the drawings that have been done can be very detailed. *Fomes fasciatus* is very similar in appearance but generally has more gray colorations on the upper surface, a more southerly distribution, the spore-bearing surface is usually pale brown to dark grayish brown, and the spores are larger (10–14 × 4–5 μm). *Fomes fomentarius* is similar but more hoof-shaped and never gets as broad or as thin. With its antiviral, antitumor, antibacterial, anti-inflammatory, and antidiabetic properties, *G. applanatum* has significant medicinal potential, but it is too woody to cook for food.

Ganoderma curtisii (Berkeley) Murrill

AMERICAN REISHI, AMERICAN LINGZHI

FAMILY Ganodermataceae

Cap 5–15 cm wide, hemispherical to kidney-shaped, dry, shiny; surface covered with a thin crust that is varnish-like, at first white and then bright ochraceous to nearly yellow, sometimes becoming dark reddish brown with age, concentric color zones usually apparent; pore-bearing surface at first creamy white and then becoming brownish yellow with age, bruising dark brown to dark purple-brown when young, pores round to angular, four or five per mm; stalk 4–10 cm long and 6–40 mm wide or nearly absent, nearly equal or tapered in either direction, centrally located or lateral, upper portion ochraceous and lower portion red, sometimes developing purplish hues; texture of entire fruiting body tough to leathery; spores brown in mass, 9–11 × 5–7 μm, ovoid with a truncate apex, double-walled, with a spiny inner wall and a smooth outer wall.

Habitat/Biological Role: Occurring at the base of dead broadleaf trees or stumps but sometimes associated with a living tree; fruiting from late spring to late fall. Decomposer of wood but considered parasitic when found on a living tree.

Distribution: Found throughout southeastern North America.

Comments: Some mycologist call this species *Ganoderma lucidum* (the name most often applied to the famous Asian medicinal species), but recent genetic studies indicate that *G. lucidum* is not found in North America. Taxonomists now believe that the species most commonly encountered in our region is likely *G. curtisii*. Further north and more into the Midwest *G. sessile* is considered more common; however, the range of *G. sessile* is not well determined. Its epithet indicates that *G. sessile* (unlike *G. curtisii*) typically does not have a pronounced stalk, and it is also typically darker in color. *Ganoderma meredithae* is morphologically rather similar but occurs on pines. In the southern portion of our region *G. zonatum* is similar but fruits on palm trees and usually lacks a stalk. Regardless of the taxonomic confusion, it seems that many of these species share common medicinal features with their prized Asian counterparts, who have shown potency both in traditional medicine and in clinical trials; see comments under *G. tsugae*.

Ganoderma tsugae Murrill

HEMLOCK POLYPORE, HEMLOCK REISHI

FAMILY Ganodermataceae

Cap 7.5–30 cm across and 13–30 mm thick; paddle-, kidney-, or fan-shaped; upper surface smooth and shiny, appearing varnished, brownish orange to reddish brown; margin of cap white to pale yellow; stalk absent or present, same color as surface, short and eccentric; spore-bearing surface white when young but becoming dingy yellow to dull brown with age, pores very small, four to six per mm; spores brown in mass, 13–15 × 7.5–8.5 µm, elliptical, double-walled, with a smooth outer wall and a roughened inner wall.

Habitat/Biological Role: Occurring on dead hemlocks; fruiting in the spring and early summer. Decomposer of wood.

Distribution: Particularly common in the Appalachians but widely distributed throughout North America.

Comments: Since *Ganoderma tsugae* occurs primarily on hemlocks, it is easy to identify (see comments under *G. curtisii*). Our region has several similar species, including *G. meredithae* (on pines) and *G. zonatum* (on palm trees); the latter can cause issues for the landscaping industry. Many of these similar *Ganoderma* species display medicinal properties similar to those attributed for thousands of years to the famous Asian medicinal mushrooms reishi or lingzhi. Extensive medical studies show that this fungus has considerable potential for use in western medicine; on a smaller scale, it can be made into a tea or tincture. Some mushroom hunters trim away and cook the white outer edge of this species when it is young.

Globifomes graveolens
(Schweinitz) Murrill

SWEET KNOT

SYNONYM *Polyporus graveolens*

FAMILY Polyporaceae

Dense mass of densely overlapping shell-shaped or thin hoof-shaped structures, individual caps 2–3 cm wide and 2–4 cm deep, the total mass up to 15 cm wide, 15 cm thick, and 25 cm high, tightly appressed to the substrate; upper surface brown to gray with a tan margin, finely pubescent, rugose, becoming gray to nearly black with age; stalk lacking; pore-bearing surface at first grayish purple but then becoming dark brown, pores four to six per mm, circular; spores hyaline in mass, 10–14 × 3–4.5 µm, cylindrical, nonamyloid.

Habitat/Biological Role: Occurring on dead or sometimes still living broadleaf trees; typically fruiting from midsummer until fall. Decomposer of wood but a weak parasite when present on living trees.

Distribution: Widely distributed in eastern North America.

Comments: Some specimens have a pleasant sweet odor reminiscent of rotting apples, but other specimens are odorless. Although usually considered to be an annual fungus, the fruiting bodies often persist through the winter months and based on personal observations may grow more than one season. Fruiting bodies are too hard to be eaten, but there are reports of them being used as air fresheners by early Americans. This uncommon fungus has such unusual fruiting bodies, it is unlikely to be confused with any other mushroom in our region.

Gloeophyllum sepiarium
(Fries) Karsten

YELLOW-RED GILLED POLYPORE

FAMILY Gloeophyllaceae

Irregularly bracket-shaped to semicircular or kidney-shaped structure, 3–12 cm wide, flat to slightly convex; surface velvety to hairy, with concentric color zones, at first yellow to orange but becoming yellow-brown to dark brown with age, the outer margin remaining lighter in color; pore-bearing surface golden brown to rusty brown, pores gill- or slot-like and then forming a network; stalk lacking; spores white in mass, 9–13 × 3–5 μm, cylindrical, smooth, nonamyloid.

Habitat/Biological Role: Occurring on dead but still standing trees, fallen logs, and stumps of conifers, solitary to scattered or found in small groups consisting of fused fruiting bodies; fruiting during summer and fall, but fruiting bodies can be found throughout the entire year. Decomposer of wood.

Distribution: Widely distributed throughout North America and often very common.

Comments: *Gloeophyllum striatum* is similar but is generally restricted to the Gulf Coast, grows on broadleaf trees, and has smaller spores (6–10 × 2.5–3.5 μm). *Lenzites betulina* is a similar "gilled" polypore that occurs on the decomposing wood of broadleaf trees and has a white pore-bearing surface.

Grifola frondosa (Dickson) Gray

HEN OF THE WOODS, AMERICAN MAITAKE, SHEEP'S HEAD

SYNONYM *Polyporus frondosus*

FAMILY Meripilaceae

Dense cluster of numerous fan-shaped to spatulate lobes arising laterally from a thick-branched stalk, individual lobes 2–8 cm across and the entire structure 30 cm or more in total; upper surface of lobes fibrous, ochre-brown to grayish brown or blackish brown, color zonate; lower pore-bearing surface white to off-white, pores one to three per mm, round to angular; stalk 2–5 cm long and up to 10 cm thick, branched, white; spores white in mass, 5–7 × 3.5–5.5 µm, elliptical, smooth.

Habitat/Biological Role: Occurring in small to sometimes massive clusters on the ground near the bases of living trees or on standing dead trees and stumps, usually oaks; fruiting late summer to fall.

Considered to be a weak parasite on the root system of living trees but persists as a decomposer of wood after the tree has died.

Distribution: Widely distributed in eastern North America.

Comments: When fresh, *Grifola frondosa* is considered to be a choice edible and can be quite large. It has antitumor, antiviral, and antibacterial properties, and there is strong evidence that it helps the immune system and reduces stress. *Polyporus umbellatus* is a more northern and rarer species that looks somewhat similar, but its multiple thin umbrella-shaped caps are all joined in a common base. *Meripilus sumstinei* is very similar but has larger individual lobes; it also stains black and its pores are more cream-colored. *Bondarzewia berkeleyi* is somewhat similar in habit but has considerably larger individual fans and is much paler in color. All are edible, but *G. frondosa* is the most popular culinary species.

Hexagonia hydnoides (Swartz)
M. Fidalgo

BRISTLY CAPPED POLYPORE

SYNONYM *Polyporus hydnoides*

FAMILY Polyporaceae

Thin, semicircular to fan-shaped structure, 3–20 cm across, leathery to corky, sometimes fused with adjacent fruiting bodies, upper surface dark brown to nearly black, covered with erect stiff bristles (these sometimes more than 5 mm tall); lower surface pale brown to dark brown, pores round and small, three to five per mm; stalk absent; spores 11–14.5 × 3.5–5 µm, cylindrical, smooth.

Habitat/Biological Role: Occurring as solitary fruiting bodies or in groups on fallen logs, stumps, or standing dead trees, reported from broadleaf trees; persisting throughout the year but primarily releasing spores from late spring to fall. Thought to be a decomposer of wood.

Distribution: Very common in the southern portion of our region, Florida west to Texas, but rare or completely absent in other parts of North America.

Comments: The dark erect bristles on the cap make it nearly impossible to confuse this unusual fungus with anything else found in the Southeast. This species is considered inedible but may have medicinal properties.

Inonotus hispidus (Bulliard) P. Karsten

SHAGGY POLYPORE

FAMILY Hymenochaetaceae

Irregularly fan-shaped structure, up to 10 × 15 cm in total extent and up to 5 cm thick, sometimes thicker if fan-shaped structures fuse; surface at first reddish orange and then becoming reddish brown to nearly black, with coarse hairs; stalk lacking or rudimentary; pore-bearing surface yellowish brown but becoming dark brown with age, pores one to three per mm, angular, becoming eroded and uneven in older specimens; spores ochrebrown to chestnut brown in mass, 8–11 × 6–8 μm, broadly ovoid to subglobose, nonamyloid.

Habitat/Biological Role: Occurring on living broadleaf trees, usually oaks; often occurring as a solitary fruiting body but sometimes with two or more partially fused sections; typically fruiting during summer and fall. Decomposer of wood but considered parasitic if present on a living tree.

Distribution: Widely distributed throughout eastern North America and also known from Europe (further genetic studies may show the European species to be different from the American).

Comments: The fruiting bodies of this fungus are inedible, but they have been used as a source of natural dyes, producing colors ranging from golden to reddish brown. *Inonotus texanus* is similar but is found on the southwestern edge of our region and fruits on acacia and mesquite trees. *Inonotus quercustris* is very similar but typically more yellow in color when young, darkening to pale rusty brown with age. *Inonotus cuticularis* is also similar, but its microscopic setae are usually curved and it is generally paler in color. *Inonotus rickii* is similar, but it generally has a more rounded form and smaller spores (6–8.5 × 4.5–5.5 μm). *Ischnoderma resinosum* is similar but has a pale outer margin when young (often with liquid drops), an upper surface that is not coarsely hairy but smooth to wrinkled, and smaller spores (4.5–7 × 1.5–2.5 μm).

Inonotus obliquus (Fries) Pilat

BIRCH CONK, CLINKER POLYPORE, CHAGA

FAMILY Hymenochaetaceae

Amorphous to somewhat hoof-shaped mass, 25–40 cm wide, seemingly erupting from beneath the bark of the host tree; outer surface charcoal black, deeply and irregularly cracked; inner tissue dark golden to yellowish brown; this portion of the fungus is sterile; fertile portion (infrequently observed) a resupinate crust, approximately 1–5 cm across and up to 1 cm thick, at first whitish and becoming dark brown with age; pores angular to round, three to six per mm; stalk lacking; spores light to dark brown in mass, 7–10 × 3.5–7.5 µm, broadly ellipsoid to ovoid, smooth.

Habitat/Biological Role: Occurring on living or dead trees, most often birch; sterile portion usually solitary or several on a tree, but the reproductive portion reported as occurring beneath the bark of dead hosts; fruiting bodies can be found throughout the year. At first a parasite and eventually a decomposer.

Distribution: Found wherever birch trees occur and thus common in the Appalachian Mountains, particularly where black birch and yellow birch are present; widely distributed throughout North America and also known from Europe.

Comments: The deeply cracked black sterile structures of *Inonotus obliquus* are distinctive and resemble burn scars on a tree. Saucer-shaped scars on the trunks of birches are a good sign that the fungus may be present. It is unlikely this fungus would be confused for anything else occurring in similar situations; however, we have seen wood burls confused with it. In our region black birch and yellow birch are the primary hosts; however, it can be found on other species of birch. We once found it on hophornbeam, and

there are also reports from elm and alder. This fungus has numerous traditional uses, particularly in Russia, including as a tinder fungus; chaga is one of the most important mushroom species in Northern European traditional medicine. Modern medical studies have shown incredibly promising results for this fungus with respect to the immune system and in cancer treatment. A warm pot of *I. obliquus* tea is a great winter beverage for flavor and to fight off illness. Sustainable harvesting methods should be implemented to prevent overharvesting of this slow-growing fungus in our region.

Laeticutis cristata (Schaeffer) Audet

CRESTED POLYPORE

SYNONYM *Albatrellus cristatus*

FAMILY Albatrellaceae

Cap 4–20 cm wide, irregular in shape and often with two or more caps clustered or fused, convex to flat sometimes becoming upturned with age, brown to greenish sometimes dark yellow darkening with age; surface dry, velvety, becoming cracked, with occasional scales; pore-bearing surface usually white when young and then staining faintly yellowish green, pores often somewhat decurrent; stalk 3–7 cm long and 1–3 cm wide, centrally located or eccentric, similar in color to the surface of the cap; spores white in mass, 5–7 × 4–5 μm, elliptical, smooth, weakly amyloid.

Habitat/Biological Role: Occurring as solitary fruiting bodies or in clusters on the ground generally under broadleaf trees; typically fruiting during summer and fall. Forms mycorrhizal associations with trees.

Distribution: In our region most common in the Appalachian Mountains and primarily found in eastern North America.

Comments: Historically, this fungus was placed in *Albatrellus*, but the other members of that genus in our region are off-white to very pale in color, quite unlike the distinctive colors of *Laeticutis cristata*. This species is generally regarded as inedible but not toxic. Many species in the similar genus *Albatrellus* are too bitter to eat. *Albatrellus confluens* is occasionally found in the conifer forests of the Southeast; it has amyloid spores and is very pale in color. Another pale species with amyloid spores, *A. subrubescens*, is reported along the Gulf Coast under conifers. An additional pale species, with nonamyloid spores, is *A. ovinus*; it is generally reported from conifer forests in the Appalachians northward.

Laetiporus cincinnatus
(Morgan) Burdsall, Banik & T. J. Volk

WHITE-PORED SULPHUR SHELF

FAMILY Fomitopsidaceae

Rosette-shaped structure consisting of a series of overlapping caps, individual caps 3–25 cm wide, fan-shaped, fleshy to rubbery, the entire structure up to 60 cm wide, upper surface finely hairy to smooth, dry, radially wrinkled and concentrically zoned with age, pinkish orange to pinkish brown to pale pinkish white, margin when young generally pale pinkish to nearly cream and becoming the same color as the surface with age; pore-bearing surface white to pale cream, bruising pale brown, pores round, small, three or four per mm; stalk 4–7.5 cm long and 3–5 cm wide, consisting of complex conglomeration of fused cap bases, similar in color to the pore-bearing surface; spores white in mass, 5–8 × 4–5 µm, elliptical, smooth, nonamyloid.

Habitat/Biological Role: Occurring at the base of living or dead trees, usually oaks; primarily found as solitary fruiting bodies but sometimes with more than one fruiting body present; fruiting summer to fall, rarely in winter and spring. Parasite of living trees and decomposer of wood when the tree is no longer alive.

Distribution: Widely distributed in the Southeast and eastern North America.

Comments: Old faded specimens of *Laetiporus cincinnatus* can resemble the edible but less flavorful polypore *Bondarzewia berkeleyi*, which has much larger pores and is usually more brown in color but sometimes fading to off-white. *Laetiporus cincinnatus* has been considered by some authors to be a variety of the more widely known and similar *L. sulphureus*, but *L. sulphureus* is generally more orange, has a yellow pore-bearing surface, and usually occurs up on the sides of trees or along fallen logs, not only as rosettes at the base of a tree. Both *Laetiporus* species are regarded as choice edibles when young; however, there are a few reports of some individuals having gastrointestinal issues when alcohol is consumed along with the mushroom or when excessive quantities are consumed (see comments under *L. sulphureus*).

Laetiporus sulphureus
(Bulliard) Murrill

CHICKEN OF THE WOODS

FAMILY Fomitopsidaceae

Cap 5–30 cm across and 1–4 cm thick, semicircular to fan-shaped, usually occurring in overlapping clusters; orange-red to orange-yellow, upper surface smooth to slightly wrinkled; margin of cap usually bright yellow and wavy; pore-bearing surface bright sulphur yellow, pores very small and difficult to see, three to five per mm; spores white in mass, 5.5–7 × 3.5–5 µm, elliptical to ovoid, smooth.

Habitat/Biological Role: Occurring on living or dead broadleaf trees, fallen logs, and stumps; fruiting early summer to fall. Decomposer of wood but also a heart rot of living trees.

Distribution: Widely distributed throughout eastern North America.

Comments: The relatively large size and bright colors of *Laetiporus sulphureus* make it a very easy fungus to spot in nature. *Laetiporus cincinnatus* is somewhat similar in appearance but has a pale pinkish to pale peachy or salmon-colored upper surface, a white pore-bearing surface, and occurs only at the base of a tree, never up on the trunk. Both species are good edibles. If young fruiting bodies are collected or the tender outer edges of older specimens are trimmed and cooked well, they can taste a bit like chicken, hence the common name. Older specimens are flavorful but can make you feel like you ate soggy wood chips, so consider using the older individuals to make a vegetarian or vegan chicken broth. Like all mushrooms, *L. sulphureus* should be cooked well; occasionally, some people have minor gastrointestinal issues when excessive quantities are eaten or specimens are undercooked, too old, or harvested from conifers or cherry trees (see comments under *L. cincinnatus*).

Lenzites betulina (Linnaeus) Fries

GILLED POLYPORE

FAMILY Polyporaceae

Cap 2–10 cm across and 0.5–2 cm thick, semicircular, fan-shaped to somewhat kidney-shaped, tough and leathery; upper surface with concentric multicolored bands, hairy, pale buff to dingy yellowish brown to grayish brown; lower surface with what appear to be gills, these broad, widely spaced, cream-colored; stalk 1–2.5 cm long and 0.5–2 cm wide or lacking; spores white in mass, 5–6 × 2–3 µm, cylindrical, smooth.

Habitat/Biological Role: Occurring on the fallen branches and woody debris of broadleaf trees or more rarely conifers, usually found in overlapping clusters but sometimes scattered; fruiting from midsummer to fall. Decomposer of wood.

Distribution: Widely distributed throughout North America.

Comments: When viewed from above, *Lenzites betulina* resembles *Trametes versicolor* and several other polypores; however, the gill-like structures, which are actually elongated pores, make this species very distinctive. Also see *Gloeophyllum sepiarium*. *Daedaleopsis confragosa* is somewhat similar but has labyrinth-like pores, a smooth upper surface, and larger spores (7–11 × 2–3 µm). *Lenzites betulina* is too leathery to be of culinary interest, but it has shown some potential for medicinal applications.

Lenzites elegans (Sprengel)
Patouillard

ELEGANT TURKEY TAIL

SYNONYMS *Artolenzites elegans, Trametes elegans*

FAMILY Polyporaceae

Thick semicircular to shelf-like structure, 4–30 cm across, leathery to corky, more pliable when young or moist, upper surface white to buff when young, becoming gray to black at the base and green with algae as the specimen ages, finely hairy when young and becoming more bristly with age; lower surface poroid and white when young and yellowing with age, pores variable, typically rounded to angular; stalk usually absent but occasionally a stubby stalk-like base is present; spores white in mass, 5–7 × 2–3 μm, cylindrical to oblong-ellipsoid, smooth.

Habitat/Biological Role: Occurring as solitary fruiting bodies or in sparse groups on fallen branches, logs, stumps, or standing dead trees, usually on broadleaf trees; persisting throughout the year but primarily releasing spores late spring to fall. Believed to be a decomposer of wood.

Distribution: Very common in the Southeast and primarily occurring in eastern North America.

Comments: *Lenzites elegans* is relatively distinctive. The most similar species with which it could be confused is *Trametes cubensis*, primarily a Gulf Coast and Florida species, which differs in having multicolored zonation, a slightly reddish base with age, a thicker stature, very small pores, and slightly larger spores (7–9.5 × 3–3.5).

Meripilus sumstinei (Murrill)
M. J. Larsen & Lombard

BLACK-STAINING POLYPORE

SYNONYM *Polypilus sumstinei*

FAMILY Meripilaceae

Dense cluster or rosette of numerous irregular to fan-shaped lobes arising laterally from a thick-branched stalk, individual lobes 2–15 cm wide and the entire structure up to 80 cm across, leathery to rubbery in texture; upper surface of lobes fibrous, grayish yellow to grayish brown and pale to off-white toward margin, color somewhat zonate, staining black when bruised or sometimes with age; lower pore-bearing surface white to creamy, pores three to six per mm, round to angular; stalk convoluted and irregularly branching, usually central, white to reddish brown depending on age; spores white in mass, 5.5–7 × 4.5–6 μm, elliptical, smooth.

Habitat/Biological Role: Occurring in large clusters at the base of living and dead trees and stumps, usually broadleaf trees, particularly oaks; generally fruiting from late spring into winter. Believed to be a parasite of living trees and a decomposer of dead wood.

Distribution: Frequently encountered over much of the Southeast and most common throughout eastern North America.

Comments: *Meripilus sumstinei* is similar to *Bondarzewia berkeleyi* and *Grifola frondosa*, but neither stains black. Moreover, the individual caps of *G. frondosa* are usually smaller than those of this species, while the caps of *B. berkeleyi* are generally larger. All three fungi are edible when young. There have been some reports of *M. giganteus* from North America, but further study has shown that this species occurs only in Europe.

Merulius tremellosus Schrader

TREMBLING MERULIUS

SYNONYM *Phlebia tremellosa*

FAMILY Meruliaceae

Irregular, semicircular to fan-shaped structure projecting as a series of shelf-like caps, these 2–4 cm wide, often occurring in effused to overlapping clusters or in long contiguous rows, spongy to soft leathery or rubbery in texture; upper surface dry to moist, white to pale yellowish white, generally with irregular bumps and finely to densely hairy; pore surface irregularly wrinkled to nearly poroid, at first off-white but becoming pale yellowish brown to pale brown with age; stalk lacking; spores white in mass, 3–4 × 0.5–1.5 µm, sausage-shaped, smooth, nonamyloid.

Habitat/Biological Role: Occurring in confluent rows and overlapping clusters, usually on the wood of broadleaf trees but sometimes on that of conifers; fruiting early summer into winter. Decomposer of wood.

Distribution: Common in the Southeast and found throughout North America.

Comments: A few crust fungi can form similar-looking fertile surfaces; however, most of these do not form a shelf and instead are found completely appressed to the undersides of logs or boards. The crust fungus *Serpula incrassata* (dry rot fungus) can be similar in appearance; however, it is usually yellowish to dark orange-brown in color and often occurs on timbers in moist basements and on the aging or water-damaged wood of buildings. *Byssomerulius incarnatus* is similar in both stature and in the fertile surface, but the upper surface is pink. *Merulius tremellosus* is generally considered inedible.

Neofavolus alveolaris
(DeCandolle) Sotome & T. Hattori

HEXAGONAL-PORED POLYPORE

SYNONYMS *Favolus canadensis, Polyporus alveolaris, P. mori*

FAMILY Polyporaceae

Cap 1–8 cm wide, fan-shaped to nearly funnel-shaped, convex to flat, usually with a depression toward the stalk, pale yellow to orange or sometimes brick red but occasionally fading to pale yellow-orange; upper surface covered by appressed scale-like tufts that are generally darker in color than the rest of the surface, margin usually inrolled even with age; pore-bearing surface white to pale yellow, pores angular to nearly hexagonal, variable in size, 0.5–2 mm wide; stalk lacking or represented by a short lateral stub typically with decurrent pores; spores white in mass, 9–11 × 3–3.5 µm, elliptical to cylindrical, smooth, nonamyloid.

Habitat/Biological Role: Occurring on fallen branches of broadleaf trees; fruiting spring to summer. Decomposer of wood.

Distribution: Frequently encountered throughout the Southeast and widely distributed in North America but most common in the East.

Comments: The small fruiting bodies, smaller spores, and more orange color of *Neofavolus alveolaris* distinguish it from the edible *Polyporus squamosus*. The edible *P. craterellus* is also similar but generally differs in being ochre to tan in color, lacking or having only a few scales/tufts on the cap surface, and having a prominent stalk. The rare tropical and subtropical polypore *Hexagonia cucullata* (syn. *Pseudofavolus cucullatus*) is occasionally reported from the southern part of our region; it is generally more orange in color, lacks the scale-like tufts on the cap surface, and has larger spores (11.5–16 × 4–6 µm). *Neofavolus alveolaris* has been used as the source of a natural dye, is reported to be edible when young, and apparently has some poorly studied medicinal properties.

Phaeolus schweinitzii (Fries)
Patouillard

DYER'S POLYPORE

SYNONYM *Polyporus schweinitzii*

FAMILY Fomitopsidaceae

Cap 6–25 cm wide, round to oval, flat, usually forming a rosette of overlapping clusters, rubbery to spongy; upper surface irregularly bumpy, at first densely covered by fine hairs, reddish to brown often with bright yellow near margin, turning dark brown to almost black with age, zonate in both color and texture; pore-bearing surface decurrent, yellow to grayish brown, bruising dark rusty brown, sometimes exuding droplets of liquid from the pores, pores small, one to three per mm; stalk irregular, 10–75 mm long, sometimes rooting, usually the same color as the cap; spores white in mass, 5–9 × 3–5 µm, elliptical, smooth, nonamyloid.

Habitat/Biological Role: Occurring near the base of conifers that are dead or weakened by some stress factor, but sometimes fruiting bodies are attached directly to wood, typically pines in our region; fruiting summer to fall. Considered to be a parasitic butt rot and decomposer of wood.

Distribution: Widely distributed in North America.

Comments: This fungus is not eaten, but it is one of the best mushrooms for textile dyeing and can be used to create yellows, oranges, and browns. *Onnia tomentosa* is similar but differs in having a pale yellow to pale brown spore print and a smaller, thinner fruiting body.

Phellinus gilvus (Schweinitz) Patouillard

MUSTARD-YELLOW POLYPORE

SYNONYM *Polyporus gilvus*

FAMILY Hymenochaetaceae

Thick semicircular to fan-shaped structure, 3–12 cm across, leathery to corky when mature but more pliable when young or moist, upper surface very finely hairy or smooth, sometimes irregularly wrinkled; surface generally with several different colored zones, in young or fresh specimens the outer margin is mustard yellow and frequently has droplets of a brown liquid present, the next zone is usually dark brown and the innermost pale brown; lower surface dark purplish brown to dull brown, pores circular and small, six to eight per mm; stalk absent; spores white in mass, 4–5 × 3–3.5 µm, ellipsoid to oval, smooth.

Habitat/Biological Role: Occurring as solitary fruiting bodies or in groups on fallen logs, stumps, or standing dead trees, reported only from broadleaf trees; persisting throughout the year but primarily releasing spores from late spring to fall. Thought to be a decomposer of wood.

Distribution: Very common in the Southeast and found primarily in eastern North America.

Comments: The yellow margin in combination with the otherwise dark brown cap surface makes this species very distinctive. *Phaeolus schweinitzii* can have similar color features but is larger, found only on conifers, and is usually near the base of trees, not directly on the wood.

Phellinus robiniae (Murrill)
A. Ames

CRACKED-CAP POLYPORE

SYNONYMS *Fomes robiniae, Polyporus robiniae*

FAMILY Hymenochaetaceae

Cap 3–35 cm wide (occasionally larger), fan-shaped to shelf-like, 5–10 cm thick, texture tough and woody; upper surface pale brown to dark brown and often with zones of color apparent toward the attachment point of the fruiting body; surface breaking up into small blocky sections, margin of the cap usually pale brown; lower pore-bearing surface usually the same color as the margin but sometimes more yellow-brown, pores round, small and difficult to see, four to six per mm; stalk lacking; spores brown in mass, 4.5–6 × 3.5–5 μm, elliptical, smooth, nonamyloid.

Habitat/Biological Role: Occurring on living, standing dead, or fallen black locust trees; releasing spores during summer and fall but fruiting bodies can persist for many years. Decomposer of wood but considered parasitic when found on a living tree.

Distribution: Black locust and this fungus are particularly common in much of our region. Distributed throughout the range of black locust and the New Mexican locust.

Comments: Before harvesting a fruiting body of this species, it should be considered that the latter can be "old growth"; we have found specimens we believe to be more than 30 years old. This fungus is too hard to be eaten, but it can be carved like wood and works well as a tinder fungus to carry coals. There is some taxonomic confusion as to whether or not the nearly identical species *Phellinus rimosus*, which also occurs on locust, is actually the same species or possibly a synonym of *P. badius*. Several other morphologically similar fungi can be separated on the basis of their host tree species: *P. everhartii* occurs on oak (and usually has thicker fruiting bodies), *Sanghuangporus weirianus* (syn. *P. weirianus*) occurs on walnut, and *Porodaedalea pini* (syn. *Phellinus pini*) occurs on pine. All these species are too woody to be eaten, and information concerning their medicinal properties is limited.

Piptoporus betulinus (Bulliard) P. Karsten

BIRCH POLYPORE, RAZOR STROP FUNGUS

SYNONYM *Polyporus betulinus*

FAMILY Fomitopsidaceae

Cap 6–25 cm across, semicircular, convex, 20–75 mm thick, upper surface dry, smooth, leather-like, usually dirty white to pale tan but sometimes nearly gray-brown, tapering toward the attachment to the substrate, cap margin inrolled when young but becoming downturned in age; lower surface white to cream, pores small, three to five per mm, at first round but becoming irregular in age; stalk usually absent but very short if present; spores white in mass, 5–7 × 1.5–2 µm, sausage-shaped, smooth, nonamyloid.

Habitat/Biological Role: Occurring on birch trees or logs; usually releasing spores in the fall and sometimes persisting throughout the year. Decomposer of wood but considered parasitic when found on a living tree.

Distribution: In our region most common at higher elevations in the Appalachian Mountains and widely distributed in North America.

Comments: This distinctive fungus is unlikely to be confused with anything else in the Southeast. Some people have reported it to be edible when very young and tender, but it can have a bitter taste and is generally too tough to be eaten. It has long figured in traditional medicine, and some recent medical studies have shown a wide range of potential applications, including in cancer treatments and utilizing its antiviral and antibacterial properties. As one of its common names suggests, this fungus can serve as a substitute for a leather strop to sharpen steel-edged tools, and it has been used as a tinder fungus to transport coals.

Polyporus arcularius (Batsch) Fries

SPRING POLYPORE

FAMILY Polyporaceae

Cap 1–7.5 cm wide, convex to flat, usually with a small central depression, margin occasionally upturned, yellow-brown to dark brown, leathery; surface dry, covered by somewhat zoned appressed scales, margin fringed with fine bristly hairs; lower surface at first white to pale yellow and then darkening to brown with age, pores medium to large and irregularly hexagonal in shape, one or two pores per mm; stalk 2–6.5 cm long and 2–5 mm wide, equal to slightly enlarged at the base, centered, pores sometimes present near the apex of the stalk, overall stalk the same color as the cap surface, smooth to scruffy or scaly; spores white in mass, 7–11 × 2–3 µm, cylindrical, smooth.

Habitat/Biological Role: Sometimes occurring as an individual fruiting body but most commonly found in small groups, on fallen branches from broadleaf trees or partially buried wood; fruiting from spring to early summer. Decomposer of wood.

Distribution: Very common in our region and widely distributed in North America.

Comments: *Polyporus brumalis*, the most similar species in the Southeast, generally lacks the marginal bristles and prominent appressed scales, and its pores are somewhat smaller. Both species are generally regarded as inedible or too tough to be considered for the table. *Neofavolus alveolaris* is sometimes similar in appearance; however, it has a very short stalk, large pores, and the upper surface of the cap is generally orange when young, becoming pale buff with age.

Polyporus squamosus
(Hudson) Fries

DRYAD'S SADDLE, PHEASANT BACK

FAMILY Polyporaceae

Cap 5–30 cm across, 1–4 cm thick, semi-circular, kidney- or fan-shaped, broadly convex but becoming flat, shallowly depressed, or deeply depressed, dry, solitary or occurring in overlapping clusters, pale tan to creamy yellowish; upper surface of the cap with an overlay of large, flattened, brown to black scales, these more or less radially arranged, cap margin at first incurved and then becoming even, lower surface with large pores, these angular to frequently irregular, one or two per mm, pores extending some distance down the stalk; stalk 2–8 cm long and 1–4 cm wide, usually off-center or even lateral; spores white in mass, 11–15 × 4–5 µm, subcylindrical to long-ellipsoid, smooth.

Habitat/Biological Role: Occurring on decomposing broadleaf logs and stumps, especially those of elm and tulip poplar; fruiting in spring and early summer. Decomposer of wood but considered parasitic when found on a living tree.

Distribution: Widely distributed in North America but more common east of the Rocky Mountains.

Comments: The fruiting bodies of *Polyporus squamosus* commonly occur during the early spring and are not perennial, persisting for only a few months. Although they appear tough, the young fruiting bodies or the relatively tender edges of older caps are often collected for food.

Polyporus varius (Persoon) Fries

BLACK-FOOTED POLYPORE

SYNONYMS *Polyporus elegans,*
P. leptocephalus

FAMILY Polyporaceae

Cap 2.5–10 cm wide, semicircular, kidney-shaped, leathery, flat to occasionally upturned, sometimes white when young but becoming pale buff to pale yellowish brown with age; surface dry, smooth, lacking any zonation of color; lower surface white to grayish yellow when young and darkening with age, small pores that extend a short distance down the stalk, seven to nine pores per mm; stalk 5–80 mm long and 2–20 mm wide, centered to off-center or even lateral, upper portion of the stalk the same color as the cap and the lower portion black; spores white in mass, 9–12 × 2.5–3 µm, cylindrical to curved sausage-shaped, smooth.

Habitat/Biological Role: Occurring on decomposing broadleaf logs and stumps; fruiting in late spring and persisting into winter. Decomposer of wood.

Distribution: Very common in our region and widely distributed in North America.

Comments: Some taxonomists consider the two synonyms given here to be synonyms of each other and that they represent a separate species that can be distinguished from *Polyporus varius* by the lack of faint striations on the margin of the cap. Regardless of the nomenclature, these polypores are well named "black-footed" because of the black stalk base. They are too tough to be considered edible. The only species similar to the group in our region is *Royoporus badius* (syn. *P. badius*), but this fungus has a much larger cap (up to 25 cm wide) with a glossy dark reddish brown surface and smaller spores (6–9 × 3.3–5 µm).

Pycnoporus cinnabarinus
(Jacquin) P. Karsten

CINNABAR POLYPORE

FAMILY Polyporaceae

Semicircular to fan-shaped structure, 2–13 cm across; up to 2 cm thick, leathery to corky when mature but more pliable when young or moist, upper surface often covered with fine hairs, becoming finely bumpy or pocketed with age; lower surface bright orange with round pores at first but these becoming angular to irregular with age, two to four pores per mm; stalk absent or stub-like; spores whitish in mass, 6–8 × 2–3 µm, smooth, cylindrical to curved, nonamyloid.

Habitat/Biological Role: Occurring as solitary fruiting bodies or in groups on fallen logs, stumps, or standing dead trees, found most frequently in disturbed dry habitats with considerable sun exposure, including along roadsides or in clear-cuts; fruiting throughout the year but most vibrant in color during the summer and fall. Believed to be a decomposer of wood.

Distribution: Found frequently throughout the Southeast and East. There are reports of this fungus in other regions of North America and other parts of the world; however, there is some question about applying this name to morphologically similar species elsewhere.

Comments: The vibrant color of this fungus makes it distinctive in our region and unlikely to be confused with any other species. *Hapalopilus nidulans* can appear similar, but it differs in being smaller and duller in color, and its fruiting bodies turn bright purple if a drop of KOH is applied; this rare fungus contains toxins and is used as a source of organic dyes. *Pycnoporus sanguineus*, a look-alike found in the southern portion of our region, differs primarily in having a thinner fruiting body that looks seared on surface and smaller spores (5–6 × 2–2.5 µm). These species are too woody to be of culinary interest.

Stereum complicatum (Fries)
Fries

CROWDED PARCHMENT FUNGUS

FAMILY Stereaceae

Fan- to paddle-shaped structure, usually forming dense overlapping and laterally fused clusters, these often encircling a small branch or following the cracks in the bark of a larger log, sometimes appressed to the surface of the substrate and appearing like a crust; cap 2 cm or less across and up to 1.5 mm thick, upper surface hairy and with concentric bands of bright cinnamon-buff to cinnamon-brown, very leathery and capable of bending without breaking; margin of cap usually creamy buff; spore-bearing surface smooth, with no evidence of pores present, at first orange and then fading to cinnamon-buff to dull white; stalk lacking; spores white in mass, 5–7.5 × 2–3 µm, cylindrical, smooth.

Habitat/Biological Role: Occurring on dead branches, fallen logs, and stumps of broadleaf trees, especially common on oak; fruiting from midsummer to fall. Decomposer of wood.

Distribution: Widely distributed throughout eastern and central North America.

Comments: *Stereum complicatum* is both common and distinctive. It usually occurs in extensive fruitings, which are highly noticeable because of their bright color. This species could be mistaken for a polypore until the spore-bearing surface is examined and found to lack pores. *Stereum complicatum* could be mistaken for *Trametes versicolor*, but the smooth orange lower surface of the former is an easy way to tell them apart. Also see *S. ostrea*. All are too leathery to be of culinary interest.

Stereum ostrea (Blume & T. Nees) Fries

FALSE TURKEY TAIL

FAMILY Stereaceae

Shell- to petal-shaped structure, often forming overlapping clusters; cap 2.5–7.5 cm wide and up to 3 mm thick, upper surface finely hairy and with concentric bands of various shades of reddish brown, orange, gray, or yellow, leathery texture; margin of cap often white; spore-bearing surface buff to cinnamon-buff, smooth, with no evidence of pores present; stalk lacking; spores white in mass, 5.5–7.5 × 2–3 µm, cylindrical, smooth.

Habitat/Biological Role: Occurring on dead branches, fallen logs, and stumps of broadleaf trees; persisting throughout the year but releasing spores from summer to fall. Decomposer of wood.

Distribution: Widely distributed throughout North America and often exceedingly common.

Comments: This species is often confused with *Trametes versicolor*, but the spore-bearing surface of the latter is white and has numerous small pores present, while that of *Stereum ostrea* is smooth and not white. *Stereum complicatum* is quite similar but much smaller, and the fruiting bodies often occur in overlapping clusters. *Xylobolus subpileatus* is similar in fruiting body shape and thickness; however, it forms longer contiguous fruiting on logs and is dark brown on the upper surface and paler brown on the lower surface. All are too leathery to be of culinary interest.

Trametes versicolor (Linnaeus) Lloyd

TURKEY TAIL

SYNONYMS *Coriolus versicolor, Polyporus versicolor*

FAMILY Polyporaceae

Thin semicircular to fan-shaped or somewhat effused structure, leathery, up to 7 cm across, upper surface variable, ranging from velvety to finely hairy to smooth, concentrically zoned, color very variable and often with several colors present on one specimen, always arranged in concentric zones of color, some specimens have colors ranging from yellow to reddish brown, greenish gray, gray-blue, or almost black; lower surface white when young and yellowing with age, pores rounded to angular; stalk absent; spores cream in mass, 4–7 × 1.5–2 µm, cylindrical to sausage-shaped, smooth.

Habitat/Biological Role: Occurring in often large clusters on fallen branches, logs, stumps, or standing dead trees, usually on broadleaf trees; persisting throughout the year but primarily releasing spores in summer and fall. Reports on its role are mixed: it is either a weak parasite or solely a decomposer of wood.

Distribution: Widely distributed throughout North America.

Comments: *Trametes versicolor* is too tough to eat but is considered to be one of the most important medicinal mushrooms, with many applications in traditional medicine. It has antibacterial, antitumor, antiviral, and immune enhancement properties, and in clinical trials has demonstrated great potential as a treatment for cancer. *Trametes hirsuta* is similar but differs in having coarse hairs and duller colors on the upper surface. *Trametes suaveolens* is also similar but larger, paler in color, and smells like anise when fresh. *Trichaptum* species resemble *Trametes versicolor*, but they are lighter in color, with lilac to purple hues, have thinner fruiting bodies, and do not have true pores. *Stereum* species can be mistaken for *T. versicolor*; however, they have a completely smooth brownish orange lower surface.

Trichaptum biforme (Fries)
Ryvarden

VIOLET TOOTHED POLYPORE

FAMILY Polyporaceae

Thin effused semicircular to fan-shaped structure, leathery, up to 7.5 cm across, upper surface at first velvety but becoming smooth with age, concentrically zoned, when young faintly violet fading to off-white to faint gray-brown, later in the season becoming partially covered with green algae; lower surface deep violet when young and retaining faded violet hues with age, pores at first irregular to angular but maturing into hanging spike-like structures; stalk absent; spores white in mass, 5–8 × 2–2.5 μm, cylindrical, smooth.

Habitat/Biological Role: Occurring in large clusters on fallen branches from broadleaf trees, logs, stumps, or standing dead trees; persisting throughout the year. Decomposer of wood.

Distribution: Widely distributed throughout North America.

Comments: *Trichaptum abietinum* is very similar but has been reported to occur only on wood from conifers. *Cerrena unicolor* is one of the most similar look-alikes, particularly when compared to older fruiting bodies of *T. biforme*; however, it lacks the violet color and has a fascinating symbiotic relationship with some wasp species. *Trametes versicolor* is a similar fungus but does not have the violet coloration, and the pores are very white and regularly shaped. Some *Stereum* species can appear somewhat similar; however, they have a completely smooth lower surface and are generally more orange to brown in color. *Irpex lacteus* is similar but is always white and generally fused in habit. *Trichaptum biforme* is too leathery to be edible and has not been thoroughly studied for its medicinal properties. In some older specimens, the unusual fungus *Phaeocalicium polyporaeum* can be found fruiting on the upper surface of *T. biforme*.

Wolfiporia extensa (Peck) Ginns

TUCKAHOE, POOR MAN'S BREAD, INDIAN BREAD

SYNONYMS *Wolfiporia cocos, Macrohyporia extensa, Poria cocos, Sclerotium cocos*

FAMILY Polyporaceae

Crust-like structure associated with tree roots, resupinate, up to 10 × 20 cm in total extent, white to light buff, attached to a prominent sclerotium or to adjacent wood, pores up to 8 mm long and 5 mm across; sterile sclerotium oblong to globose, varying greatly in size, 7–104 cm across, gray to brownish, hard bark-like exterior, inside white, moist and pliable when fresh but becoming starchy and chalky as it dries out; spores light in color in mass, 7–9 × 3–4 μm, cylindrical to cylindrical-ellipsoid, often flattened on one side, smooth, hyaline.

Habitat/Biological Role: The sclerotium of this fungus almost always occurs underground, sometimes at a depth of more than a meter; persistent throughout the year. Decomposer of wood and possibly a root pathogen of pines and oaks.

Distribution: Mostly a southeastern species, but there are reports from as far north as New Jersey and Pennsylvania and as far west as Kansas and Texas.

Comments: *Wolfiporia extensa* has had a long and complex taxonomic history. In the 1740s, botanist John Clayton was likely the first scientist to collect it. The sclerotia are easiest to find when farming or land clearing has occurred; we have also found sclerotia where trees have been tipped over and root systems exposed. The crust-like fruiting bodies have almost never been seen. Supposedly sometimes the sclerotia fruit if incubated. According to early literature, sclerotia were an important food source for Native Americans and, later, slaves in the Southeast; specimens were either roasted fresh or pounded dry to produce flour for making bread. Specimens have been reported to weigh as much as 18 kg. Studies show that this fungus may inhibit the growth of tumors through boosting the immune system; however, the North American species may be shown to be different from the Asian medicinal species. *Polyporus tuberaster* forms similar sclerotia but is found in western North America, after fires. It is a mystery how Native Americans located this belowground fungus for food. Todd has pounded the dried sclerotia into flour and made *W. extensa* tortillas. These were mild pleasant and filling, similar to a corn tortilla.

Crust Fungi, Rusts, and Smuts

The crust fungi that are included in the following section are a small representative selection. Crust fungi are ubiquitous on wood in our region. They are very diverse, and most are impossible to identify unless a microscope is used. They are important decomposers.

Rusts and smuts are primarily plant pathogens. Many fungi within these groups are small, but they can cause serious economic damage. Some species—for example, corn smut (*Ustilago maydis*)—are actually important edible fungi, but most are interesting because of their unique roles in the ecosystem.

Although many rusts are some shade of "rusty" orange, members of the common rust fungus genus *Septobasidium* are frequently overlooked because of their drab color and appressed fruiting habits. Some of the crust fungi can appear similar; however, *Septobasidium* appears only on the outer bark of living trees and shrubs, not on dead or dying wood. This genus forms an association with scale insects in the order Hemiptera.

The fungi that are grouped together in this key are not necessarily described in this section, so follow the page numbers outlined in the key when they are given. Also check the genera *Craterellus* (pages 158–161) and *Thelephora* (pages 286–287).

KEY TO CRUST FUNGI, RUSTS, AND SMUTS

1. Fruiting body orangish or grayish, amorphous in shape, attached to living herbaceous plants or trees; often causing swelling or knots, sometimes in the fruits or seeds . . . .
. . . . *Cronartium, Gymnosporangium, Puccinia, Ustilago*
1. Fruiting body not as above 2

2. Fruiting body shelf-like but with a smooth or labyrinth-like lower surface 3
2. Fruiting body shaped like a flat crust or producing a burl-like structure on birch trees 4

3. Lower surface of the fruiting body labyrinth-like . . . .
. . . . *Byssomerulius incarnatus* (page 282), *Merulius tremellosus* (page 313)
3. Lower surface of the fruiting body smooth, some shade of yellowish to dull orange . . . .
. . . .*Stereum* (pages 323–324)

4. Black burl-like fruiting structure on birch and related trees with a golden color inside . . . . . .
. . . . *Inonotus* (pages 305–306)
4. Flat crust-like fruiting structure attached to wood 5

5. Fruiting body taking the form of an appressed crust on the bark of living trees . . . .
. . . .*Septobasidium ramorum*
5. Fruiting body on dead wood, on lower side or on cut ends of logs . . . .
. . . . *Terana coerulea, Xylobolus frustulatus*

Cronartium quercuum
(Berkeley) Miyabe ex Shirai

PINE-OAK RUST, EASTERN GALL RUST

FAMILY Cronartiaceae

Hemispherical to globose, gall-like structure occurring on the branches or trunk of various species of pine, 2–10 cm in diameter (or sometimes larger), at first reddish brown but becoming orange and then yellow as the surface breaks up and masses of spores appear; stalk lacking; spores yellow in mass, 22–33 × 12–17 µm, more or less oval to slightly elongated, strongly ornamented and with bright yellow inclusions.

Habitat/Biological Role: Occurring on the branches and trunks of living pine trees; new gall-like fruiting structures first develop in the spring but then persist throughout the rest of the year and often for many years thereafter. Parasite of the host pine tree.

Distribution: Especially common in the Southeast and found throughout North America, wherever the host pines are found.

Comments: As is the case for most rusts, *Cronartium quercuum* has a life cycle that involves two different host trees, in this case pine and oak. The presence of the fungus on an infected oak is not particularly conspicuous, but the gall-like structures that form on pines are rather obvious and not likely to be confused with anything else. *Cronartium quercuum* is one of several parasites of pines in our region that cause economic damage to the timber industry. Most pine knots are scars that result from parasitism by this fungus or related species. *Cronartium ribicola* is similar but occurs only on white pines. *Cronartium fusiforme* and *C. comandrae* are also similar; they differ in their alternate hosts and can be challenging to separate. *Cronartium strobilinum* is unusual in that it occurs only on the cones of pine trees.

Not considered edible but unlikely to be toxic. Taste and texture likely reminiscent of a pine board. The burls/knots caused by this fungus are rich in resin and can burn well if they are dead.

Gymnosporangium clavipes
Cooke & Peck

CEDAR HAWTHORN RUST

FAMILY Pucciniaceae

More or less globose structure studded with tube-like projections, the latter 7–12 mm long, at first white but darkening to rusty orange with age; the entire structure representing a fruit that has been infected by this fungus; spores orange in mass, 24–50 × 20–40 µm, globoid, warted.

Habitat/Biological Role: Occurring on the fruits, twigs, leaf petioles, and thorns of hawthorn and various other plants (e.g., apples, pears, serviceberry) in the family Rosaceae but usually noticed only when fruits are infected; infected fruits are most apparent during late spring and early summer, but the fungus can be present at any point during the year. Parasite of the aforementioned plants and also red cedar, which is the alternate host in the life cycle of this rust.

Distribution: Widely distributed throughout North America and present wherever the two host plants (cedar and appropriate members of the Rosaceae) occur.

Comments: Because some of the host plants that can be infected by *Gymnosporangium clavipes* are important as fruit trees, this fungus has considerable negative economic value. The infected fruits of these trees are conspicuous and easily noticed, but the presence of the fungus in other infected portions (which appear swollen) of the host plant are less obvious. In some situations we have seen this fungus wipe out an entire crop of serviceberries on an individual plant. This fungus is too small to be of any culinary interest.

Gymnosporangium juniperi-virginianae Schweinitz

CEDAR APPLE RUST

FAMILY Pucciniaceae

Spherical, brown, gall-like structure on the branches of red cedar, up to 3 cm in diameter; during wet spring weather producing a series of gelatinous orange "horns" that can be up to 4 cm long; spores (teliospores) yellow to golden in mass, two-celled, cylindrical-fusoid, 45–65 × 15–21 µm.

Habitat/Biological Role: Occurring on the branches of red cedar trees; usually apparent in late spring and early summer. Primarily a parasite of red cedars, with apple trees and other relatives as alternate hosts; however, the gall-like structures are found only on red cedar.

Distribution: Particularly common in populations of eastern red cedar in the Southeast but widely distributed throughout eastern North America.

Comments: When the gelatinous "horns" are present on the gall-like structures, this is a rather conspicuous fungus. In fact, a heavily infected tree can have the appearance of a decorated Christmas tree. *Gymnosporangium clavipes* is similar in shape and color but is generally smaller and parasitizes the fruits of woody members of the Rosaceae. The edibility of this fungus is not know, but it is unlikely to be toxic.

Puccinia podophylli Schweinitz

MAYAPPLE RUST

SYNONYM *Allodus podophylli*

FAMILY Pucciniaceae

Small discolored yellow spots on the leaf surface of mayapple (*Podophyllum peltatum*); undersides of leaves covered by clusters of small bright orange cup-shaped structures, these structures scattered to contiguous, forming irregular orange patches up to 7 cm across; producing two types of spores, the first type (teliospores) reddish brown, 37–59 × 16–27 μm, ellipsoid to clavate, non-catenulate with scattered spines, the second type (aeciospores) 25.5–32 × 22.5–29 μm, globoid to ellipsoid, smooth to roughened.

Habitat/Biological Role: Occurring on the leaves of mayapples; typically fruiting in the spring. Pathogen of mayapple.

Distribution: Found in most places where mayapples occur, from Louisiana and Arkansas east to the Carolinas and north to New York.

Comments: This is the only rust that is widely reported to grow on mayapples, so it is unlikely to be confused with any other species in this large group of fungi. The edibility of this fungus is unknown, but the compounds in the host plant are likely more potent than what is in the fungus. Most rusts have complex life cycles that often involve more than one plant species, so it is likely possible to find the species we discuss here on other plants. *Puccinia bolleyana* is common in our region and has similar fruiting bodies; however, it is typically reported on elderberry (*Sambucus*), where it deforms and enlarges the leaf petioles and forms similar minute orange cup-like fruiting structures. Another species, *P. recondita*, has similar fruiting structures but is found growing from jewelweed (*Impatiens*). None of these species are known to be edible.

Septobasidium ramorum
(Schweinitz) Donk

SCALE INSECT RUST

SYNONYM *Septobasidium curtisii*

FAMILY Septobasidiaceae

Thin, almost paper-like structure, approximately 1 mm thick and up to 5 cm broad, tightly appressed to the lower sides of horizontal branches and extending upward around the branch or sometimes on vertical sections of small saplings, often cracking in older specimens, occasionally oval to oblong, darkest at the center and generally becoming paler toward the margin, dark grayish to dark purplish gray to nearly black at the center and sometimes white at the margin; surface covered by erect irregular spikes (up to 1.5 mm long) of fertile fungal tissue; spikes single but sometimes forking irregularly; stalk absent; spores hyaline, 3–4 × 13–21 μm (occasionally up to 29 μm long), bent to elliptical, surface smooth to indistinct.

Habitat/Biological Role: Occurring on smooth portions of bark on the twigs of live broadleaf trees; fruiting throughout the year. Has a unique biological association with scale insects. Some mycologists consider this fungus a parasite of scale insects; others classify it as a mutualist. It is believed that some scale insects within the colony inhabiting a twig are killed, while others seem to benefit from living beneath the fruiting body of the fungus, where they are protected from predators.

Distribution: Widely distributed in the Southeast.

Comments: We encounter this fungus most frequently on the twigs of black gum (it has also been reported from ash, holly, honey locust, magnolia, oak, and pear). *Septobasidium* species are very similar to one another and can be rather difficult to differentiate. The tree upon whose bark *Septobasidium* fruits can be a somewhat useful character, although

some species can occur on a diversity of trees. It is unclear how many species in the genus are found in the Southeast, but there are between 300 and 350 described species worldwide, and to identify many of these species is well beyond the scope of this field guide. The similar *S. pinicola*, reported primarily from the mountains of the Carolinas northward and westward, is distinctive in part because it is found only on the smooth bark of white pines. *Septobasidium patouillardii* is frequent in our region, occurring on a diversity of hardwoods, but differs in being brown to yellowish brown and having shorter spores (4–6 × 11–17 μm). Another common brown-colored species in our region, *S. pseudopedicillatum*, has been reported on apple, orange, oak, gum (*Nyssa*), sweet gum, and dogwood; the fruiting body often has a white margin and curved spores that are 4–5 × 17–23 μm. This genus is poorly understood ecologically and certainly has not been studied for edibility. If a fungus that is associated with scale insects and has the texture of stiff paper appeals to your culinary desires, you are unlikely to find it to be toxic. Nevertheless, we do not recommend eating it or any of these species.

Terana coerulea (Lamarck) Kuntze

VELVET BLUE SPREAD, BLUE CRUST FUNGUS

SYNONYMS *Corticum caeruleum, Pulcherricium caeruleum*

FAMILY Phanerochaetaceae

Thin parchment-like or effused crust on wood, occurring in clusters up to 16 cm across, outer edge irregular, sometimes fusing with adjacent clusters, fertile surface dry, velvety, vibrant dark blue to nearly blackish blue, becoming more pale toward the margin; spores white, 6–10 × 4–5 µm, elliptical, smooth.

Habitat/Biological Role: Occurring almost exclusively on the undersides of fallen branches and logs; fruiting late summer into winter. Believed to be a decomposer of wood.

Distribution: Common in the Southeast and found primarily in eastern North America.

Comments: The bright blue color of this fungus makes it a very striking find and easy to identify. The edibility and possible medicinal properties of this fungus are not known.

Ustilago maydis (DeCandolle) Corda

CORN SMUT, CUITLACOCHE

FAMILY Ustilaginaceae

Gall- or tumor-like structure arising from ears of corn, 1–8 × 1–6 cm, silvery gray, glossy, smooth, becoming black and rupturing when mature, releasing dark spores; spores faintly olive-brown to nearly black in mass, 9–11 × 6.5–7.5 µm, nearly round, covered with prominent spines.

Habitat/Biological Role: Occurring on corn plants, where the fruiting structures essentially replace some of the kernels on an ear of corn; most apparent during the summer when the ears of corn are fully formed. Parasite of corn plants.

Distribution: In the Southeast this fungus is particularly common in small-scale home gardens and small farms, but it can be found almost everywhere in the world where corn is grown.

Comments: *Ustilago maydis* is a valued food in much of Latin America, often costing more than the corn itself, and it also has some promising medicinal properties. When firm and still silvery gray, it is frequently sautéed and added to traditional Latin American foods. The spores enter the silk of the corn, similarly to a grain of corn pollen, but instead of pollinating the corn, they parasitize an individual corn kernel. This is why an otherwise uniform ear of corn will occasionally have only one parasitized kernel and at other times the entire ear will consist of parasitized kernels. *Ustilago maydis* was one of the first recorded plant pathogens. Spanish conquistadores in the early 1500s reported it, and there are Mexican murals pre-dating the conquistadores in which this fungus is clearly depicted. *Ustilago maydis* is a relative of other species of grain smut that negatively impacted American food security prior to the advent of fungicides. To this day, some of the wheat smuts have devastating impacts on the grain industry in subsistence and small-scale farming situations worldwide.

Xylobolus frustulatus
(Persoon) P. Karsten

CRACKED PARCHMENT FUNGUS, CERAMIC FUNGUS

FAMILY Stereaceae

Flat parchment-like crust, on wood, in clusters up to 30 cm across, less than 3 mm thick, broken into individual sections up to 2 cm across, fertile surface smooth, pale pinkish gray, occasionally undulating; spores pinkish orange in mass, 3.5–7 × 2.5–3.5 µm, ellipsoid, smooth, amyloid.

Habitat/Biological Role: Occurring almost exclusively on large decorticated oak logs, often fruiting on the end-grain, where logs have been sawed. This fungus seems to be perennial and fruiting bodies persist for a long time; we have observed what appear to be the same fruiting bodies on certain logs for nearly a decade. A white pocket rot and thus a decomposer of wood.

Distribution: Particularly common in the Southeast but widely distributed in North America.

Comments: This fungus causes unusual white pockets in logs that average approximately 3 × 6 mm throughout. These odd-looking pockets are often noticed when oak firewood is split. *Xylobolus frustulatus* removes lignin, xylose, mannose, and a bit of cellulose from these "pockets" and leaves behind small hollows filled with the remaining cellulose as it moves through the wood. American chestnut logs were reportedly one of the primary hosts for this fungus, but it is now found primarily on oak logs. *Xylobolus frustulatus* contains possible antibiotic-like compounds but is not worth eating.

Puffballs, False Truffles, Earthstars, Stinkhorns, and Bird's Nest Fungi

All the species in this section share a common feature of being completely enclosed at some point in their development or for their entire development. Historically, fungi in this group were called gasteromycetes. Many different shapes, ecological roles, and reproductive strategies are represented by these fungi. Fruiting body morphologies range from round puffballs and star-shaped earthstars, which rely on rain to impact the outer surface of the fruiting body and thus eject their spores, to the phallic stinkhorns, who release unpleasant odors that attract flies and other insects to disperse their spores. Most fungi in this section are either decomposers of organic material or form mycorrhizal associations with trees. Some species of false truffles actually fruit below the ground and are important food sources for many animals. In order to find such hypogeous species, it is most effective to look for places where small animals have previously dug and then pull back the surrounding layer of leaf litter. Some species, such as the large puffballs, are favorite edibles among mushroom foragers in the Southeast. Compare some of these species with ascomycete fungi in the Truffles section (page 84). Occasionally, the "eggs" of *Amanita* (pages 121–138) can appear similar before they expand; however, cutting a specimen from top to bottom can reveal the outline of a developing agaric and resolve this question.

KEY TO PUFFBALLS, FALSE TRUFFLES, EARTHSTARS, STINKHORNS, AND BIRD'S NEST FUNGI

1. Fruiting body retaining a ball-like shape throughout its entire development 5
1. Fruiting body not retaining a ball-like shape throughout its entire development. 2

2. Fruiting body becoming star-shaped but not stinky . . . . *Astraeus, Geastrum, Myriostoma, Scleroderma*
2. Fruiting body not becoming star-shaped or retaining a ball-like shape. 3

3. Fruiting body short cylindrical, upper surface disappearing to reveal a small bird's-nest-like structure with spore packets that resemble eggs . . . . *Crucibulum laeve, Cyathus striatus*
3. Fruiting body phallic to club-shaped or forming a column-like structure or in some species having obvious masses of dark-colored smelly slime filled with spores 4

4. Fruiting body without masses of stinky slime; the apex with a small central orange pore; spores white, and sometimes with amphibian egg-like masses of jelly around the base . . . . *Calostoma cinnabarinum*
4. Fruiting body consisting of a column-like or phallic structure, often attracting flies and other insects; fetid odor apparent . . . . *Clathrus, Mutinus, Phallus, Pseudocolus*

5. Fruiting body off-white or pale in color when young (never having dark colors on inside when still firm), becoming dark and powdery (puffball-like) with age and maturation, not having thick skin, and the interior never having chambers . . . . *Calvatia cyathiformis, Lycoperdon*

5. Fruiting body not as above 6

6. Fruiting on the ground or below the leaf litter, firm and dark inside when young and developing powdery dark-colored spores with maturity . . . . *Pisolithus rhizus, Scleroderma*

6. Fruiting body typically below the ground or just emerging from the surface; either with chambers or solid 7

7. Fruiting body not apparent, but a hard, non-reproductive structure with a grayish to brownish bark-like outer layer and a white interior present, sometimes as large as a basketball, and located up to a meter below the surface of the ground in affiliation with tree roots . . . . *Wolfiporia extensa* (page 327)

7. Fruiting body at the surface or below the humus layer and chambered inside 8

8. Outer surface of the fruiting body often bruising reddish if young or at base; inside filled with chambers, white when young and becoming dark olive-green with age . . . . *Rhizopogon*

8. Outer surface of the fruiting body reddish brown; inside filled with chambers and producing pale-colored latex when cut . . . . *Zelleromyces cinnabarinus*

Astraeus hygrometricus
(Persoon) Morgan

BAROMETER EARTHSTAR

FAMILY Diplocystidiaceae

Spherical structure (spore case) surrounded by six to twelve star-like rays; spore case 10–25 mm wide, whitish to grayish or grayish brown; surface roughened, with a somewhat irregular apical pore; rays 25–50 mm long, yellow-brown to reddish brown or grayish to nearly black, rays variable depending on age, at first ray surface covered by irregular pale-colored cracked scaly patches, these patches lost with age, rays responding to changes in atmospheric humidity by closing around the spore case under dry conditions and expanding outward under moist conditions; spores at first white and then becoming brown and powdery in mass, 7–11 μm, round, warted.

Habitat/Biological Role: Occurring on the ground as solitary fruiting bodies or in small groups in sandy soils, often associated with conifer forests; fruiting in late summer and fall, sometimes the rays persisting for one or more years. Decomposer of litter and humus.

Distribution: Found throughout North America.

Comments: Earthstars are round and puffball-like at first, and with maturity the leathery outer layer splits into the rays, creating the star-like appearance. Immature unopened earthstars can be mistakenly identified as a puffball or false truffle. The rays of this earthstar respond to changes in atmospheric humidity (hence the common name); depending on age, the leathery rays can change greatly in appearance. Some species of earthstars are eaten in the young closed "egg" stage, but this is not widely done in North America. If the "stars" of this species are collected and dried, they will curl up into little balls; and if placed in water, these rays will expand. This can be repeated many times for years and serves as a great teaching tool or toy for children.

Calostoma cinnabarinum
Desvaux

STALKED PUFFBALL

FAMILY Calostomataceae

Distinctive structure consisting of a spherical, bright red "head" about 20 mm wide, surrounded by a semitransparent gelatinous layer and supported by a shaggy reddish to reddish brown stalk when mature but at first only the head is likely to be apparent, stalk 20–40 mm long and 10–20 mm wide; the apex of the head developing an apical pore with age; spores white at first and then becoming buff or yellowish in mass with age, 12–22 × 6–8.5 µm, oblong-elliptical, pitted and appearing reticulate.

Habitat/Biological Role: Occurring on the ground as solitary or clustered fruiting bodies in broadleaf forests, usually with oaks present and often associated with mosses, often found on the edges of forest trails; fruiting during late summer and fall. Forms mycorrhizal associations with trees.

Distribution: Found in eastern North America, usually at higher elevations in the Appalachian Mountains.

Comments: *Calostoma cinnabarinum* and other members of this genus are some of the most distinctive fungi found in the Southeast. All the species are generally considered inedible. *Calostoma lutescens* is similar but differs in having a yellow head, a longer stalk, and pitted globose spores that are smaller (5.5–8 × 5.5–8 µm). *Calostoma ravenelii* has a yellowish head whose outer surface breaks into fine scales; it lacks the gelatinous covering found in the other two species.

Calvatia cyathiformis (Bosc) Morgan

PURPLE-SPORED PUFFBALL

FAMILY Agaricaceae

Depressed globose to hemispherical structure that becomes somewhat pear-shaped with age, 9–20 × 7–16 cm; surface of peridium at first smooth and then developing distinct cracks, white to light pinkish tan when young and becoming brown with age; lower one-third of the fruiting body sterile and the upper two-thirds filled with a mass of spores (gleba); spores purple to deep purple-brown in mass, 3.5–7.5 µm, round, with minute spines.

Habitat/Biological Role: Occurring as solitary to scattered or sometimes numerous fruiting bodies in old fields, lawns, and other grassy areas; fruiting summer to fall and spore base sometimes lasting longer. Decomposer of organic debris associated with grasses.

Distribution: Most common in the Southeast and on the East Coast but widely distributed throughout North America.

Comments: In the Southeast the relatively large size of the fruiting body and color of the spores make this an easy fungus to identify. When fully mature, the upper peridium breaks apart, the spores are dispersed, and the base of the fruiting body persists as a deep purplish to purple-brown cup-like structure; this can remain intact for several months and be found even in mid-winter. When still immature and firm, and while the interior of the fruiting body is white, *Calvatia cyathiformis* is a popular edible. The mature powdery spores were used traditionally to coagulate blood. As one moves northward or westward from our region, there are several similar species. In the southeast *C. craniiformis* can be found in similar habitats, but it has spores that are greenish yellow in mass, not purple-brown, and the spores are smaller (2.5–4 µm). *Calvatia ruroflava* can appear similar at first; however, the outer surface bruises yellow to orange.

Clathrus columnatus Bosc

COLUMNED STINKHORN

SYNONYM *Linderia columnata*

FAMILY Phallaceae

Distinctive structure consisting of two to five stout, curved columns arising separately from an egg-shaped structure, columns fused together at the apex, the columns orange or red, spongy, and 50–75 mm long, inner surfaces covered with an olive-brown slimy mass that contains the spores; stalk lacking but the entire structure subtended by a white, sac-like volva; spores olive-brown in mass, 3.5–5 × 1.5–2.5 μm, elliptical, smooth.

Habitat/Biological Role: Occurring on the ground in lawns, wood chip/mulch piles, gardens, and forested areas where there is an accumulation of organic matter; fruiting from October until March. Decomposer of plant debris.

Distribution: Apparently restricted mostly to the Southeast, and we have frequently collected this species in North Florida in late winter. Known from several other regions of the world, including those as far away as Australia. It is possible that it was introduced to North America.

Comments: Like other stinkhorns, *Clathrus columnatus* develops from an "egg" stage that is usually not very apparent unless one examines the area immediately around already developed fruiting bodies. If the eggs are collected and placed on wet paper, they will usually "hatch" within a couple of days. Most stinkhorn eggs are considered edible, but there is some controversy relating to the edibility of the egg stage of this species, since it may actually contain some toxins. It has a rather fetid odor, which would discourage anyone from collecting mature specimens for the table.

Crucibulum laeve (Hudson)
Kambly

WHITE-EGG BIRD'S NEST FUNGUS
FAMILY Agaricaceae

Globose to short-cylindrical structure, 5–10 mm high and up to 10 mm across, tapering toward the base, when young cup-shaped and with an upper surface covered, this covering (lid) disintegrating with age and revealing numerous egg packets (the "eggs") in the cup ("nest"); surface of the lid ochraceous, velvety, sides of the cup roughened to finely wrinkled, buff-brown; inner surface of cup smooth, pale gray to light brown; eggs (peridioles) 1–1.5 mm in diameter, flattened, white to pallid, each egg connected to the inner surface of the cup by a thin cord (funiculus); stalk lacking; spores hyaline in mass, 6–9 × 3–5 μm, elliptical, smooth.

Habitat/Biological Role: Occurring on twigs, dead branches, fallen logs, mulch, and various types of organic debris, often found in small to large clusters; fruiting bodies releasing spores from spring to fall. Decomposer of wood and woody debris.

Distribution: Widely distributed throughout North America.

Comments: This is a common bird's nest fungus and the only one with white eggs found in the Southeast. The fruiting bodies are rather tough and resistant to decay. As such, it is possible to find "empty nests" at any time of the year. The spore packets are shot out of the "nest" when a rain drop hits inside. These packets can often be found adhering to the undersides of leaves up to a meter above the fruiting bodies. Since the spore packets resemble seeds, some authors have speculated that birds help with dispersal, but we have seen no indication of this in bird dietary studies. *Cyathus stercoreus* and *Nidula candida* are similar but darker in color and have dark-colored eggs and fine mats of "hairs" on the outer surface of the fruiting body; the former commonly occurs on dung. The fruiting bodies of *C. striatus* are darker in color and have prominent striations on the inside of the fruiting body. These fungi are too small and leathery to be of any culinary value, but some in this group have shown interesting medicinal properties for treatment of neurological conditions.

Cyathus striatus Hudson: Persoon

SPLASH CUPS

FAMILY Agaricaceae

Vase- or cup-shaped structure, 6–8 mm wide and 6–10 mm tall, tapering toward the base, upper surface covered at first, this covering disintegrating with age and revealing numerous spore packets in the base of cup; surface of the lid white, sides of the cup reddish brown to chocolate brown or grayish brown, shaggy-hairy or woolly and faintly to strongly grooved; inner wall of cup markedly grooved, grayish white, smooth, shiny; spore packets gray, disc-shaped, sometimes swollen slightly at center, 1–2 mm wide, each egg attached to the base of the cup with a tiny, coiled cord; stalk indistinct; spores 15–20 × 8–12 μm, color in mass not reported, elliptical, smooth but slightly notched at one end.

Habitat/Biological Role: Occurring on woody debris, twigs, and bark in broadleaf or conifer forests and occasionally on wood chips and mulch, fruiting bodies scattered or more often in dense clusters; fruiting from midsummer to fall, with fruiting bodies often persisting through the winter. Decomposer of wood.

Distribution: Widely distributed throughout North America.

Comments: This is the most common bird's nest fungus in the Southeast, and fruitings can be quite extensive. Like other bird's nest fungi, the fruiting body of *Cyathus striatus* uses the force of falling raindrops to disperse the spore packets, which can often be found adhering to the undersides of overhanging leaves. Inedible; see comments under *Crucibulum laeve*.

Geastrum saccatum Fries

ROUNDED EARTHSTAR

FAMILY Geastraceae

Spherical structure (spore case) surrounded by five to nine star-like rays; spore case 10–20 mm wide, broadly ovate to rounded, smooth, brownish to grayish brown or sometimes almost white, often has a pale-colored line and depression encircling the apical pore; rays 15–25 mm long, recurved in such a manner that the spore case appears to be sitting in a shallow bowl, ochre-brown to brownish pink, not changing shape substantially with changes in humidity; stalk lacking; spores brown in mass and becoming powdery, 3.5–6 µm, round, covered with blunt warts, nonamyloid.

Habitat/Biological Role: Occurring on the ground in broadleaf or conifer forests, fruiting bodies scattered to clustered and often occurring around stumps; fruiting from late summer until late fall. Decomposer of litter and humus.

Distribution: Found throughout North America.

Comments: Earthstars are round and puffball-like at first but with maturity the outer layer splits into the rays, thus creating the star-like appearance. Immature unopened earthstars can be mistakenly identified as puffballs or false truffles. *Geastrum saccatum* could be regarded as the "classic" earthstar and is likely the species represented in most images of this group of fungi. The distinguishing features are the apical pore surrounded by a depression and the fact that the spore case appears to be sitting in a shallow bowl. *Geastrum fimbriatum* is very similar but smaller. In some parts of the world certain species of earthstars are eaten when still in the puffball-like stage, but we do not know of a culinary tradition associated with any of our southeastern species.

Lycoperdon marginatum
Vittadini

PEELING PUFFBALL

FAMILY Agaricaceae

Spherical structure 10–50 mm wide, at first round but becoming flattened with age; surface at first white and covered with broad pyramid-shaped warts, warty outer layer flaking off in irregular patches with age, revealing the pale brown lower surface; gleba at first white and firm but becoming greenish yellow to grayish brown and powdery with age; stalk absent or a short stub at the base; spores brownish in mass, 3.5–4.5 µm, round, finely spiny to roughened.

Habitat/Biological Role: Occurring as solitary fruiting bodies or more commonly in scattered to dense clusters on the ground in cleared areas, often collected in pastures or edges of gravel driveways; fruiting summer to fall. Decomposer of organic material.

Distribution: Widely distributed throughout North America.

Comments: Several other species are morphologically similar, but these lose their surface spines individually instead of in patches as they mature. *Lycoperdon pulcherrimum* is smaller than *L. marginatum* and has longer hair-like spines covering the surface. *Vascellum curtisii* (syn. *L. curtisii*) is similar but almost always occurs in cespitose clusters, the fruiting bodies are usually much smaller (rarely larger than 20 mm across), and the spores are somewhat smaller (3–3.5 µm). All species in the genus *Lycoperdon* are considered to be edible when young, but care should be taken not to confuse them with unexpanded poisonous *Amanita* species in the "egg" stage: making a cut from the top to the bottom of an egg from an *Amanita* species will reveal the outline of a developing mushroom. The spores of dried puffballs have been used to coagulate blood on wounds.

Lycoperdon perlatum Persoon

GEM-STUDDED PUFFBALL

FAMILY Agaricaceae

Typically pear-shaped or globose structure, 2.5–6.5 wide and 3–7.5 cm tall; outer surface thin, white when young and becoming brown with age; surface studded with small, round, cone-shaped granules that are easily removed, when mature developing a small apical opening for spore release; upper two-thirds of gleba reproductive, white and fleshy when young but becoming olive-brown and powdery as the spores mature; lower third of the fruiting body sterile; spores olive-brown in mass, 3.5–4.5 µm, globose, thick-walled, covered by minute spines.

Habitat/Biological Role: Occurring on well-decomposed woody debris in both broadleaf and conifer forests, solitary to numerous, sometimes found in small clusters; fruiting throughout spring to fall and sometimes persisting into winter. Decomposer of litter and humus.

Distribution: Common throughout the Southeast as well as in other regions of North America.

Comments: *Lycoperdon perlatum* is edible when white throughout. It is possible to confuse this fungus with young members of the toxic genus *Scleroderma*. Not-yet-expanded *Amanita* species in the "egg" stage can resemble *Lycoperdon* species, but a cut from the top to the bottom of an egg from an *Amanita* species will show the outline of a developing mushroom. *Lycoperdon acuminatum* is similar but lacks the prominent stalk-like base and comes to a point at the apex. *Lycoperdon marginatum* also lacks the stalk-like base, is covered in pyramid-shaped warts, and the outer peridial layer ruptures into sections. *Lycoperdon pulcherrimum* is smaller than the other species and has long hair-like spines covering the surface. *Lycoperdon pyriforme* is the most similar in stature, but the granules near apex are smaller and the overall surface color is more greenish brown.

Lycoperdon pyriforme
Schaeffer

PEAR-SHAPED PUFFBALL

SYNONYM *Morganella pyriformis*

FAMILY Agaricaceae

Pear-shaped to spherical structure, 1.5–4.5 cm wide and 2–5 cm tall; surface covered by fine granular warts or spines, off-white when young but early in development becoming yellowish brown to dark brown, at maturity developing a single pore-like opening at the apex for spore release; tapering downward toward a short stalk-like base, base usually remaining white longer than the upper portion, usually several white cords of mycelium attached to the base; interior white when young but becoming greenish yellow and then powdery brown at maturity; spores brown in mass, 3–4.5 μm, round, smooth.

Habitat/Biological Role: Occurring in usually dense clusters on decomposing logs; fruiting from summer to winter, with fruiting bodies often persisting into spring. Decomposer of wood.

Distribution: Common in our region and widely distributed throughout North America.

Comments: *Lycoperdon pyriforme* is one of the few species in this genus that fruits on wood that is not highly decomposed. When still young and white inside, *L. pyriforme* can be eaten. The powdery mature spores of this and related puffballs have been used to coagulate blood from a bleeding wound. Also see *Scleroderma citrinum*.

Mutinus elegans (Montagne)
E. Fischer

ELEGANT STINKHORN

SYNONYMS *Mutinus bovinus*, *M. curtisii*

FAMILY Phallaceae

At first a small egg-shaped or puffball-like structure, gray to white, with a soft rubbery texture and white cord-like rhizomorphs present at the base; the egg-like structure ruptures at the apex, allowing the elongated stalk-like fruiting body to emerge; stalk 10–18 cm long and 1.2–2.5 cm wide, pink to reddish sometimes with orange tints, hollow, spongy in texture with a pitted surface, tapering evenly in both directions from the center, a small opening present at the apex of the stalk; fertile portion confined to the upper one-half to one-third of the stalk, at first covered by a dark olive-green slimy spore mass but the latter becoming increasingly sparse with age; spores dark greenish to gray-green in mass, 4–7 × 2–3 µm, elliptical to slightly oblong, smooth.

Habitat/Biological Role: Occurring as solitary fruiting bodies or in small to large groups, typically arising from thick layers of organic material; unopened "eggs" can often be found if the litter is raked away in close proximity to a fruiting body; fruiting in summer and early fall. Decomposer of organic matter and wood.

Distribution: Most common in the Southeast and East but widely distributed in North America.

Comments: This fungus is edible in the "egg" stage but is generally too stinky to consume when mature. The strong odor attracts flies and other insects, which help to disperse spores. *Mutinus ravenelii* is quite similar (and also edible in the egg stage) but differs in being more vivid in color and having a more pronounced head at the apex and smaller spores (1.5–2.5 × 3.5–5 µm). *Mutinus caninus*, believed by some to have been introduced to North

America, is also morphologically similar; however, it is more slender, generally more orange-white to pale yellowish in color, and has a more prominent head and slightly smaller spores (4–5 × 1.5–2.5 µm). If put in wet paper towels, the "eggs" of all these species will often hatch within a few hours or days.

Myriostoma coliforme
(Dickson) Corda

SALTSHAKER EARTHSTAR

FAMILY Geastraceae

Spherical structure (spore case) surrounded by five to twelve star-like rays; spore case 1–8 cm wide, rounded, upper surface often somewhat flattened, somewhat roughened to nearly smooth, brownish to grayish brown or sometimes silver-brown to almost white; surface with several pore openings across the surface of the spore case; spore case generally attached to the center of the rays by several short columns; rays 1–4.5 cm long, smooth, similar in color to the spore case or darker brown; basal stalk lacking; spores brown in mass and becoming powdery, 4–7.5 µm, round, warted to partially reticulated, nonamyloid.

Habitat/Biological Role: Occurring on the ground in sandy soil, fruiting bodies solitary or occurring in small groups; fruiting summer to fall, but often with the fruiting bodies persisting throughout the year. Believed to be a decomposer of organic material.

Distribution: Generally reported to be rare in the Southeast but sometimes regionally common; we find it most often in the extreme southern portion of our region, particularly in the sandy soils of northern Florida. Widely distributed in North America and also reported from other continents.

Comments: Earthstars are round and puffball-like at first, but with maturity the outer layer splits into rays, creating their star-like appearance. Immature unopened earthstars can be mistaken for puffballs or false truffles. *Myriostoma coliforme* is unique among the earthstars in our region because it has multiple pore openings to release spores. Similar multi-pored earthstars occur in Africa, Europe, and South America, but there is some question as to whether they all represent the same species. In certain parts of the world, some species of earthstars are eaten while still in the puffball-like stage, but we do not know of this being the case for any of the species found in the Southeast.

Phallus impudicus Linnaeus

NETTED STINKHORN

SYNONYM *Dictyophora duplicata*

FAMILY Phallaceae

At first an egg-shaped structure, gray to white, with a soft texture and white cord-like rhizomorphs present at the base; the egg-like structure rupturing at the apex and allowing the elongated fruiting body to emerge, the latter 12–17 cm long and 2–4 cm wide, upper portion consisting of a pitted, thimble-like cap, with a distinctly unpleasant (stinky) odor when young, covered by a greenish black mass of spore-filled slime; surface of the cap beneath the spores is off-white in color; a skirt-like netted veil usually hangs down from the cap in young specimens, the veil extending up to 5 cm from the lower edge of the cap; membranous cup present at the base of the fruiting body; spores greenish black in mass, 3.5–4.5 × 1–2 μm, elliptical, smooth.

Habitat/Biological Role: Fruiting bodies solitary or in small groups, occurring on accumulations of organic matter and thick layers of humus in broadleaf forests but occasionally attached directly to decomposing wood; unopened "eggs" can often be found if the litter is raked away in close proximity to a fruiting body; fruiting in summer and early fall. Decomposer of organic matter and wood.

Distribution: Rare in North America, but most records are from the Southeast or East.

Comments: This fungus is edible in the "egg" stage, but it is generally too stinky when mature. The name netted stinkhorn refers to several species found in the warmer temperate to tropical regions of the world, and they are culturally significant for everything from medicine to war charms. The taxonomy of this group of fungi is confusing, and some taxonomists suggest that the name *Phallus impudicus* does not apply to a stinkhorn with a veil/net. In our region, *Phallus hadriani* is similar, but the eggs have a pale purplish to rose color. *Phallus ravenelii* can resemble this species but generally has a smooth to slightly roughened cap. *Phallus rubicundus* is similar in stature but red to orange in color. If put in moist paper towels, the "eggs" of all these species will generally hatch in hours or days.

Pisolithus arhizus (Scopoli) Rauschert

DYEMAKER'S PUFFBALL, BOHEMIAN TRUFFLE

FAMILY Sclerodermataceae

Globose to nearly clavate structure, 3.5–25 × 4–30 cm, typically with a radiating base, when young the surface is smooth, glossy, and speckled olive-brown to nearly yellow; peridium very thin and disintegrating with age to reveal a powdery brown spore mass; interior of young fruiting bodies firm, composed of oval locules that are largest near the apex and become smaller toward base, varying in color from white to yellow to black to powdery brown; stalk usually represented by a hard, irregular radicating mass of hyphae; spores brown in mass, 7–12 µm, globose, with prominent spines.

Habitat/Biological Role: Occurring on compacted soil, road shoulders, ditches, and sometimes even cracking asphalt pavement, making it one of the toughest of all mycorrhizal fungi; fruiting summer and fall. Forms mycorrhizal associations with a wide range of trees.

Distribution: Often found in hard clay or sandy regions of the Southeast and widely distributed thoughout the world.

Comments: This distinctive fungus is commonly called *Pisolithus tinctorius*, but this name is currently believed to be a synonym. There is a suspiciously large range in both size and the variability of features in this species, and there are likely to be at least two different undescribed species in our region. For example, there is a distinctive small morphotype often found in the Deep South. This genus is an important mycorrhizal associate of tree which is sometimes used in restoration work. In North America, it can be used as a source of dye, producing rich browns to blacks. Most North American field guides list it as inedible; however, there are reports of what is believed the same or related species being eaten by people in Europe and by Australian Aborigines. *Pisolithus* is related to the genus *Scleroderma*, which is mildly toxic. As such, the former should be eaten only within a cultural context.

Pseudocolus fusiformis
(E. Fischer) Lloyd

STINKY SQUID STINKHORN

SYNONYMS *Pseudocolus javanicus,*
P. schellenbergiae

FAMILY Phallaceae

At first a small puffball- or egg-like structure, gray to white and soft in texture with
white cord-like rhizomorphs arising from
the base; the egg-like structure rupturing
at the apex, allowing the 2–6 × 1.5–3 cm
reproductive portion of the fruiting body
to emerge; the latter consisting of three
or four pink to red or sometimes yellow
arms; the arms spongy, tapering and
joined at apex, the lower surface of the
arms usually coated with a layer of gray-
green spore-filled slime; fruiting body
with a distinct unpleasant odor; spores
gray-green in mass, 4–5.5 × 2–2.5 μm,
cylindrical, smooth, and surrounded by a
transparent envelope.

Habitat/Biological Role: Occurring in
mulch beds or other areas with abundant

organic matter present, sometimes solitary
but usually fruiting in clusters; the "eggs"
can often be found if the litter is raked
away in close proximity to a fruiting body;
fruiting summer to fall. Decomposer of
organic matter.

Distribution: Particularly common in
the Southeast and reported elsewhere in
eastern North America.

Comments: This is believed to be an
invasive species, likely brought to North
America from Asia in the early 1900s.
Some stinkhorn eggs are eaten; however, this species is not recommended.
Pseudocolus fusiformis is similar to *Clathrus columnatus*, but the latter has thicker
arms. If stinkhorn eggs are collected and
placed on wet paper they will usually
"hatch" within a couple of days. This provides a great opportunity for an unusual
observation of natural history—or a way
in which to leave a friend a delayed-release
stink bomb.

Rhizopogon nigrescens Coker & Couch

BLACKENING RHIZOPOGON

FAMILY Rhizopogonaceae

Oblong to ball-shaped structure, 1–4 × 1–2 cm, off-white to yellow at first but becoming darker and mottled brownish orange to gray to black with age, staining dull reddish when bruised (particularly when young); peridium thin, sticky to dry, smooth to finely hairy, easily separable from interior, reddish cord-like rhizomorphs scattered across surface, these becoming black with age; interior white when immature but later becoming greenish brown, chambered; spores brown in mass, 6–7.5 × 2–3 μm, narrowly ellipsoid to oblong, smooth.

Habitat/Biological Role: Occurring under litter, generally hypogeous to partially emergent, fruiting bodies scattered to gregarious; fruiting throughout the year but most frequently found in the fall and early winter. Believed to form mycorrhizal associations with trees, primarily with pines.

Distribution: Commonly found in the pine forests of the Appalachian foothills to the extreme Southeast, but reported from as far north as New Jersey and as far south as the Dominican Republic, Mexico, and Nicaragua.

Comments: The genus *Rhizopogon* is common in the Southeast, with approximately a dozen species described. Many of these can be challenging to identify, even with the help of a microscope; however, *R. nigrescens* is relatively distinctive. It is somewhat similar to both *R. couchii* and *R. evadens*, but these species have larger spores and less mottling on the outer surface, and the peridium of young specimens does not peel away as readily. None of these species are reported to be eaten by humans, but they are not known to have toxins. They are important food sources for small mammals.

Rhizopogon truncatus Linder

YELLOW RHIZOPOGON

FAMILY Rhizopogonaceae

Oblong to ball-shaped structure, 1–4 × 1–2 cm, brilliant golden yellow to greenish yellow but becoming olive-green with age; peridium thin, dry, smooth, and with numerous tufts of hyphae; interior light-colored when immature but becoming dark olive-green to brown, chambered; spores brown in mass, 7–10 × 3.5–5 μm, truncate-ellipsoid, smooth.

Habitat/Biological Role: Occurring under leaf litter and almost always hypogeous, fruiting bodies scattered to gregarious; fruiting bodies can be found throughout the year. Believed to form mycorrhizal associations with true firs, hemlocks, and some pines.

Distribution: Reported from the Appalachians and the Pacific Northwest.

Comments: The genus *Rhizopogon* is common in the Southeast, and the dozen or so species that occur here are difficult to separate; however, the bright color of

R. truncatus is distinctive, and its hyphae, which are the same color as the peridium, are easy to see if the leaves are raked away. Nevertheless, its hypogeous habit makes this colorful fungus difficult to find; it is rarely reported or found in any quantity, and it has an unexciting flavor, so it is not a regularly consumed false truffle.

Scleroderma citrinum Persoon

COMMON EARTHBALL, PIGSKIN PUFFBALL

SYNONYMS *Scleroderma aurantium, S. vulgare*

FAMILY Sclerodermataceae

Globose to slightly flattened structure, 2–10 cm in diameter; surface characterized by a pattern of raised warts, yellow-brown to brown, peridium up to 2 mm thick, interior of fruiting body marbled white when really young but becoming deep violet-gray to purple and powdery with age; spores brown in mass, 8–13 µm, globose, covered with fine spines that form an incomplete reticulum.

Habitat/Biological Role: Occurring on the ground or occasionally in elevated situations, such as on stumps and decomposing logs; fruiting summer and fall. Forms mycorrhizal associations with trees.

Distribution: Widely distributed but most common in eastern North America.

Comments: *Scleroderma citrinum* belongs to a large genus of toxic puffballs that are found worldwide and distinguished from other puffball-like fungi by their thick outer peridium and dark solid interior (hence the common names). Within the genus, this species can be distinguished on the basis of the peridium and microscopic characters. *Scleroderma bovista* is somewhat similar but bruises light purplish and has a smooth or very finely cracked surface and a small irregular stalk. In Asia, some members of this genus are reported to be eaten while they are still white inside; however, most American literature regards this group as toxic.

Scleroderma polyrhizum
(J. F. Gmelin) Persoon

PIGSKIN PUFFBALL
SYNONYM *Scleroderma geaster*

FAMILY Sclerodermataceae

Globose to depressed structure, 4–14 cm in diameter; surface rough and covered with soil and thick hyphal cords, off-white to yellowish gray, peridium very thick (up to 5 mm), when young the interior of the fruiting body firm, filled with dark purplish black oval structures separated by white tissue; stalk is either a small mass of irregular hyphae or absent; when mature the peridium splits open into a large (up to 20 cm across) leathery black to dull yellowish orange star-shaped structure, revealing the dark brown powdery spore mass; spores dark brown in mass, 5–10 µm, globose, covered with warts and irregular ridges.

Habitat/Biological Role: Occurring in compacted soil, sometimes fruiting at the edges of dirt roads, parking lots, drainage ditches, or sports fields, sometimes even cracking asphalt, frequently nearly hypogeous or only partially emergent; fruiting summer and fall but the remnant star-like peridia can be found on the surface of the ground in the middle of winter. Forms mycorrhizal associations with trees.

Distribution: Most common in the Southeast but widely distributed in North America.

Comments: *Scleroderma polyrhizum* belongs to a large genus of toxic puffballs that are found worldwide and are distinguished from other puffball-like fungi by their thick outer peridium and dark solid interior. *Scleroderma floridanum* is neary identical but has slightly larger spores (9–12 µm) and possibly other subtly different characters; this species has likely been largely overlooked in the Southeast and lumped with *S. polyrhizum* by many mycologists. *Scleroderma cepa* is somewhat similar in size but has smaller spores (4–9 µm) and a smooth peridium that splits into smaller, more cup-shaped stars. *Mycenastrum corium* has occasionally been reported from the Southeast (common in the Great Plains), but it differs in having a peridium that splits into a stiff upturned star, finely reticulate spores, and spiny capillitium threads. Some *Bovista* species are somewhat similar but smaller in size.

Zelleromyces cinnabarinus
Singer & A. H. Smith

MILKING PUFFBALL

FAMILY Russulaceae

Oblong to ball-shaped structure, 1–4 × 1–3 cm, cinnamon to brown in color or sometimes nearly reddish, surface thin, dry, smooth, with occasional wrinkles, interior chambered, if cut when fresh white latex is present; spores light in color in mass, 13–18 × 12–16 µm, subglobose to short ellipsoid, ornamentation irregularly reticulate-ridged, amyloid.

Habitat/Biological Role: Hypogeous to partially emergent from soil, fruiting bodies scattered to gregarious and typically reported from pine forests; fruiting from late summer into fall. Believed to form mycorrhizal associations with pines and possibly broadleaf trees.

Distribution: Scattered reports from the Southeast.

Comments: Despite the macroscopic differences in growth form, genetic evidence will likely lead to this and other sequestrate latex-producing genera in the Russulaceae being combined with *Lactarius* and *Lactifluus*. In the Southeast, very few of the known truffle taxa produce latex; however, microscopic characters can help to separate *Zelleromyces cinnabarinus* from related species as well as other latex-producing truffle genera, including *Arcangeliella*, *Gastrolactarius*, and *Leucophleps*. Edibility is unknown.

Jelly Fungi

Jelly fungi come in a range of colors from white to bright yellow to brown. Many species in this distinctive group can shrivel and dry, becoming very brittle, and then rehydrate in a matter of minutes to a gelatinous or jelly-like structure. Some species are important medicinal species, and a few are worthwhile edibles. Most species are either decomposers or parasites, or they form a symbiotic relationship with surrounding trees. Because the diversity of common jelly fungi is limited in our region, and the small number that are found here are included in this guide, we do not include a key.

Auricularia fuscosuccinea
(Montagne) Hennings

WOOD EAR, JELLY EAR

FAMILY Auriculariaceae

Flattened ear- or cup-like fruiting body arising from a narrow base, usually 2.5–10 cm across and 3 mm thick, rubbery when moist but thin and brittle when dry; upper surface smooth to wrinkled and lower surface often appearing wrinkled or veined, both surfaces orange-brown to dark reddish brown; spores white in mass, 11–13.5 × 6.5–8.5 μm, sausage-shaped, smooth.

Habitat/Biological Role: Occurring in overlapping clusters on logs, stumps, and fallen branches of broadleaf trees; fruiting from late spring to fall. Decomposer of wood.

Distribution: Common in southeastern North America.

Comments: *Auricularia* species are an easily recognizable group of large edible jelly fungi, but figuring out which species you have can be more challenging. Most North American field guides list this and related species as *A. auricula* or *A. auricula-judae*, but it was recently shown these two species do not occur on this continent. *Auricularia americana* is similar but has not been reported south of New York state; it has larger spores (13–15 × 4.6–6 μm) and grows only on conifers (it may occur at high elevations in the Appalachian Mountains, but this has not been resolved). *Auricularia angiospermarum* is similar; however, it has larger spores (12–16 × 5–6 μm) and lacks a microscopic medulla (demarcated zone in cross section). *Auricularia nigricans* is found along the Gulf Coast; it is distinctive because it has a much hairier non-reproductive surface and larger spores (14.5–17 × 5–7 μm). There are reports from central Florida of the rare *A. scissa*, which has a reticulate-like lower surface. *Exidia recisa* is somewhat similar but has

a smaller, more globular fruiting body and smaller spores (10–15 × 3–5 μm). Most of these species have been reported to occasionally have whitish or pale color forms. This species and relatives have been eaten and used widely in traditional medicine in Europe, Asia, and North America; the closely related *A. polytricha*, for example, is cultivated and sold in markets throughout Asia. Their properties show promise for use in western medicine, particularly with heart health. Unlike most jelly fungi, the fruiting bodies are large enough to make a reasonable meal. One of the best ways to get the full flavor potential of these fungi is to dry specimens first and then reconstitute the fruiting bodies in a marinade before cooking.

Calocera cornea (Batsch) Fries

CLUB-LIKE TUNING FORK

FAMILY Dacrymycetaceae

Slender, cylindrical, unbranched to singly forked structure, 5–20 mm tall and 1–3 mm wide, tough gelatinous, orange-yellow to dull yellow, tip often becoming brown with age, viscid when moist; spores white to cream-yellow in mass, 7–10 × 3–4 µm, smooth, sausage-shaped.

Habitat/Biological Role: Occurring on decorticated logs of broadleaf trees, usually found in groups; typically fruiting during summer and fall. Decomposer of wood.

Distribution: Widely distributed throughout North America.

Comments: Following a period of rainy weather, this fungus can fruit prolifically on decomposing logs. It is much too small to be collected for the table, and its edibility is unknown. *Calocera viscosa* is similar, but it is larger (up to 10 cm), generally branches multiple times, and usually occurs on the ground.

Exidia recisa (Ditmar) Fries

AMBER JELLY ROLL

FAMILY Auriculariaceae

Irregular globular to brain-like structure, 1–3.5 cm wide and up to 2 cm high, wrinkled, jelly-like in texture when moist but thin and brittle when dry, drying out or rehydrating rapidly with changes in moisture, translucent pale brown to dark brown; sometimes with a short stalk attaching the upper portion to the substrate; upper portion sometimes having fine blackish dots present; spores hyaline in mass, 10–15 × 3–5 µm, sausage-shaped, smooth.

Habitat/Biological Role: Typically occurring in clusters, most often found on the lower sides of fallen branches from broadleaf trees or occasionally on other types of decomposing wood; fruiting from early spring to fall. Decomposer of wood.

Distribution: Widely distributed but found primarily in eastern North America.

Comments: *Exidia recisa* is one of the few brown jelly fungi in our region, and its globular form and smaller size make it easy to distinguish from *Auricularia fuscosuccinea* and related species. *Exidia glandulosa* is somewhat similar but has a rounder, less irregular shape, fewer wrinkles, and a much darker color (often black). *Tremella foliacea* shares a similar color, but it is much larger, with a broad leaf-like fruiting body, and has more elliptical to oval spores. Two ascomycete jelly fungi, *Ascocoryne cylichnium* and *A. sarcoides*, can appear similar to *E. recisa*, but, besides having asci, they are more purplish in color and not as wrinkled. The ascomycete jelly fungus *Ascotremella faginea* is also similar; however, in addition to having asci, it differs in having a fruiting body that can be larger (up to 10 cm), a more globular to brain-like form, and spores that are longitudinally striate and smaller (6–10 × 3.5–5 µm). The edibility of *E. recisa* has not been well studied; it is unlikely to be toxic, but if jelly fungi are your culinary desire, your time would be better spent in pursuit of *Auricularia* species.

Pseudohydnum gelatinosum (Scopoli) P. Karsten

JELLY TOOTH

FAMILY Auriculariaceae

Gelatinous, flattened spoon- or tongue-shaped structure, cap 2.5–7.5 cm across and 0.5–2.5 cm thick; upper surface translucent, smooth to somewhat downy, white to grayish brown; margin inrolled; lower surface covered by downward-pointed tooth-like spines, white to watery gray, 3–5 mm long; stalk varying from a short lateral extension of the cap to a distinct and upright structure, up to 4 cm long, same color as the cap; spores white in mass, 4.5–8 μm, globose, smooth.

Habitat/Biological Role: Occurring on decorticated logs, stumps, and fallen branches of conifers, sometimes appearing on moss-covered logs, solitary or in small groups; fruiting from summer into fall. Decomposer of wood.

Distribution: In our region most common in the Appalachian Mountains but found throughout North America.

Comments: This distinctive fungus shares features of both jelly fungi and tooth fungi (hence *Pseudohydnum*, "false tooth fungus"). It is edible but rarely collected for human consumption because of its small size and rather bland taste.

Sebacina pululahuana
(Patouillard) D. P. Rogers

WHITE JELLY FUNGUS

SYNONYMS *Bourdotia pululahuana, Ductifera pululahuana, Gloeotromera pululahuana, Tremella pululahuana*

FAMILY Tremellaceae

An irregularly folded gelatinous mass, up to 5 cm across but sometimes fusing into much longer structures, white to whitish yellow, smooth, translucent, gelatinous to rubbery when moist; spores light-colored, 9–12 × 4.5–7 µm, broadly elliptical to sausage-shaped, smooth.

Habitat/Biological Role: Occurring on fallen decorticated logs of broadleaf trees; fruiting summer to fall. Believed to be a decomposer of wood but insufficiently studied.

Distribution: Frequently encountered in the Appalachians and other parts of the Southeast. What is believed to be the same species is also collected in Central and South America.

Comments: Many aspects of this fungus are unknown, including its edibility. *Sebacina* was historically considered to be a saprotrophic genus, but DNA studies of roots have shown that it is mycorrhizal. Research is currently insufficient, but despite the fruiting habit, this fungus may be associated with plant roots. *Sebacina incrustans* (also found in our region), which occurs on the stems of living plants, is white in color, irregularly shaped, and has been shown to be mycorrhizal. *Tremella fuciformis* is somewhat similar, but the fruiting bodies are translucent to nearly clear, occur in small clumps, are more delicate in form, and have larger spores (7–14 × 5–8.5 µm). *Tremella concrescens* could be mistaken for this species on the basis of its irregular form, but it usually fruits on the ground and the fruiting body encloses portions of plants, stems, and leaves. *Tremella reticulata* is somewhat similar, but this is a terrestrial jelly fungus that has a more erect stature and smaller spores (9–11 × 5–7 µm).

Tremella mesenterica Retzius

WITCHES' BUTTER

FAMILY Tremellaceae

Irregularly folded, gelatinous structure, up to 10 cm across, orange to bright yellow, smooth, translucent, gelatinous to rubbery when moist, brittle when dry; spores light-colored in mass, 10–18 × 7.5–10 µm, elliptical, smooth.

Habitat/Biological Role: Occurring on the fallen branches of broadleaf trees, occasionally on logs and stumps; most commonly encountered in early spring to late fall but sometimes present throughout the year. Although it appears to occur on wood, this fungus is actually a parasite of the mycelium of wood decay fungi.

Distribution: Common in our region and found throughout North America and elsewhere in the world.

Comments: This fungus is one of the most colorful jelly fungi and, despite its delicate appearance, is relatively long-lasting and capable of drying out and rehydrating numerous times. Several other species in this genus are believed to parasitize the mycelia of various wood decomposing fungi; unfortunately, this parasitism is happening on a microscopic level in the wood and thus is not visible to the naked eye. The smaller yellow jelly fungus *Dacrymyces palmatus* is very similar but generally arises from white hyphae on conifer wood. Other *Tremella* species in our region are similar in structure, but they differ in color; these include *T. reticulata* and *T. fuciformis*, both of which are white, and *T. foliacea*, which is brown. *Tremella mesenterica* is edible but not noteworthy as an item for the table; there is some evidence of medicinal properties in this and related species of jelly fungi.

Tooth Fungi

Instead of having gills or pores as reproductive surfaces, this group of fungi has "teeth," which hang like icicles from the upper surface. The spores are produced along these downward-pointed spines, unlike coral fungi, whose branches point upward. Tooth fungi are relatively diverse; however, many of the species are infrequently encountered. Most species are believed to form symbiotic relationships with trees; a few are decomposers of wood. The sweet tooth or hedgehog mushrooms (*Hydnum* spp.) and lion's manes (*Hericium* spp.) are some of the best edible fungi in our region.

KEY TO TOOTH FUNGI

1. Fruiting body having a central stalk and cap . . . . . *Hydnellum, Hydnum, Phellodon, Sarcodon*
1. Fruiting body not having a central stalk and cap. 2

2. Fruiting body consisting of a ball-like structure with teeth and attached to a tree. . . . .
. . . . *Hericium*
2. Fruiting body either jelly-like or shelf-like, with teeth on the lower surface 3

3. Fruiting body with a stalk at the margin of the cap; entire structure jelly-like . . . .
. . . . *Pseudohydnum gelatinosum* (page 363)
3. Fruiting body a thin shelf-shaped structure. . . . . *Trichaptum biforme* (page 326)

Hericium americanum Ginns

BEAR'S HEAD TOOTH

FAMILY Hericiaceae

Irregularly globose structure with a mass of downward-pointed spines attached to horizontally projecting branches, the entire structure 10–30 cm broad, white at first but becoming yellowish with age; stalk usually absent, sometimes present as a short stalk-like base; spines 5–40 mm long; spores white in mass, 6–7 × 5–7 μm, elliptical to subglobose, smooth, amyloid.

Habitat/Biological Role: Associated with wounds on the trunks of living broadleaf trees or on dead wood, fruiting bodies solitary or sometimes several present on a single log; typically fruiting from late spring to fall. Decomposer and/or parasite of trees.

Distribution: Found throughout eastern North America.

Comments: This genus is very distinctive. Some coral fungi have similar growth forms, but their spines point upward. *Hericium coralloides* (syn. *H. ramosum*) is similar but has shorter spines attached to less densely occurring branches. *Hericium erinaceus* is also similar but has spines that all arise from a common base, not on individual branches. When young, all three species are very flavorful choice edibles (see comments under *H. erinaceus*).

Hericium erinaceus (Bulliard) Persoon

LION'S MANE, SATYR'S BEARD

FAMILY Hericiaceae

Globose to somewhat cushion-shaped structure consisting of what appears to be a solid mass of downward-pointed spines, the entire structure 5–25 cm in diameter, white at first but becoming dingy yellow with age; stalk usually absent, sometimes attached by a short stalk-like base; spines 2–4 cm long; spores white in mass, 4–5.5 × 5–6.5 μm, elliptical to subglobose, smooth or minutely roughened.

Habitat/Biological Role: Associated with wounds on the trunks of living broadleaf trees but can persist after the tree has died, fruiting bodies usually solitary; fruiting time highly variable, ranging from summer and fall to the middle of winter and into spring. Parasite of living broadleaf trees and decomposer of dead ones.

Distribution: Found throughout North America.

Comments: There are many traditional medicinal uses for this fungus, and clinical studies have shown its potential for treating neurological conditions ranging from Alzheimer's to Parkinson's. It is likely that this biochemical activity is shared across other species in this very distinctive genus. *Hericium coralloides* is similar but has shorter spines attached to branches instead of forming a single solid mass. *Hericium americanum* is also similar but has long spines that are located on densely packed branches. When young, all three species are very flavorful choice edibles. Occasionally, an individual fruiting body is bitter-tasting.

Hydnellum peckii Banker

RED-JUICE TOOTH FUNGUS

FAMILY Bankeraceae

Cap 2.5–15 cm wide, convex to flat, round to somewhat irregular in outline, surface more or less uneven, at first velvety but becoming smooth with age, white when immature but becoming brownish with age, with irregular dark brown to nearly black blotches where it is bruised, exuding drops of a reddish fluid; spore-bearing surface covered with downward-pointed spines, these 2–6 mm long, crowded and descending the stalk, pinkish white at first and then becoming brown; stalk thick, appearing very short but may extend into the ground for several centimeters; texture of entire fruiting body tough; spores brown in mass, 4.5–5.5 × 3.5–4.5 µm, subglobose, warted, nonamyloid.

Habitat/Biological Role: Occurring on the ground in conifer forests as solitary, scattered, or clustered fruiting bodies, often in association with mosses and in Virginia pine forests in our region; fruiting in late summer and fall. Forms mycorrhizal associations with trees.

Distribution: In our region most common in the Appalachian Mountains with some reports from the Piedmont of North Carolina, but generally rare, albeit widely distributed, in North America.

Comments: The drops of reddish fluid exuded from the cap of fresh fruiting bodies and the brown spines make it easy to separate this tooth fungus from most others. The uncommon *Hydnellum diabolus* also can exude the red droplets and is difficult to distinguish without genetics; it primarily differs in having a thicker cap. The fruiting bodies of *H. peckii* are generally very acrid in taste, and the edibility is not known. It has been used as a source of natural dyes.

Hydnellum scrobiculatum

(Fries) P. Karsten

RIGID TOOTH FUNGUS

FAMILY Bankeraceae

Cap 3–6 cm wide, at first flat and then becoming slightly funnel-shaped with age, leathery in texture, upper surface with concentric zones of color, pink at the margin and darker reddish brown or rusty cinnamon toward the center; spore-bearing surface covered with crowded, purplish brown downward-pointed spines, these 1–3 mm long, decurrent; stalk up to 40 mm long and 5–30 mm wide, usually becoming expanded to bulbous at base, color the same as the central portion of the cap; entire fruiting body tough and fibrous; spores dull brown in mass, 4.5–6.5 × 4–5 μm, irregularly ellipsoid to subglobose, with irregular spine-like warts, nonamyloid.

Habitat/Biological Role: Occurring as solitary or scattered fruiting bodies on the ground in conifer forests and sometimes in mixed broadleaf forests; fruiting during the fall. Forms mycorrhizal associations with trees, especially pine.

Distribution: Widely distributed throughout North America and also known from Europe.

Comments: *Hydnellum scrobiculatum* is part of a species complex that is very challenging to identify without molecular data. The very similar *H. concrescens* differs in having a stalk with a less bulbous base and flatter, spine-like warts on the spores. Other species in the complex, *H. ferrugineum*, *H. pineticola*, and *H. spongiosipes*, are very similar to each other but differ from *H. scrobiculatum* in being more fleshy, not having such prominent concentric zones, and exhibiting a darker color overall (sometimes white or pale tints but primarily only at the margin of the cap). None of these species are considered edible.

Hydnum repandum Linnaeus

HEDGEHOG MUSHROOM, SWEET TOOTH

SYNONYM *Dentinum repandum*

FAMILY Hydnaceae

Cap 3–10 cm wide, usually somewhat irregular in shape, buff to orange, bruising to dark orange; surface smooth to slightly scruffy, sometimes splitting, margin inrolled and often becoming wavy with age; spore-bearing surface consisting of numerous downward-pointed spines, these 3–10 mm long, cream-colored; stalk 2–6.5 cm long and 1–2 cm wide, often slightly off-center, white to pale yellow; spores white in mass, 6.5–9 × 5.5–8 µm, broadly elliptical to almost globose, smooth.

Habitat/Biological Role: Occurring as solitary fruiting bodies or in small groups on the ground in broadleaf or conifer forests; fruiting from midsummer into early winter. Forms mycorrhizal associations with trees.

Distribution: Widely distributed throughout North America.

Comments: *Hydnum repandum* has the general appearance of a typical agaric or bolete; however, the spore-bearing surface is very different, consisting of spines instead of gills or pores. DNA studies have shown that this is a species complex of multiple other taxa, including *H. rufescens* and *H. umbilicatum*; genetic studies and species complexes aside, these are all choice edibles. Genetic evidence seems to indicate that this group of tooth fungi may be more closely related to chanterelles than to other tooth fungi.

Phellodon confluens (Persoon) Pouzar

FUSED WHITE-TOOTH

FAMILY Bankeraceae

Cap 3–15 cm wide, irregular in shape, frequently several caps are fused together to form a more complex structure, flat to depressed, upper surface completely white in young specimens and white on margin in older specimens; surface becoming brown to black with age or bruising, cottony in texture, occasionally faintly zonate; inner tissue is the same color as outer tissue; lower spore-bearing surface consisting of crowded decurrent spines up to 4 mm long, at first white to grayish brown and then becoming black with age, bruising blackish; stalk variable, sometimes solitary and sometimes representing a composite structure, 10–45 mm long and 5–20 mm wide, generally tapering toward a point at base, similar in color to the upper or lower surface of the cap; spores white in mass, 3.5–6 × 3–4 µm, subglobose to globose, ornamentation prominent and spine-like.

Habitat/Biological Role: Occurring on the ground as solitary fruiting bodies or in groups in mixed broadleaf-conifer forests; fruiting in summer and fall. Forms mycorrhizal associations with trees.

Distribution: In our region most common in the southern Appalachians but found through much of eastern North America.

Comments: *Phellodon* is an infrequently encountered and poorly known genus of tooth fungi. *Phellodon niger* and *P. alboniger* are very similar to one another in having blackish inner tissue but differ from *P. confluens*, which has a gray inner tissue. *Phellodon fibulatus* is morphologically similar and can be difficult to separate, but it often has a tuft of orange hyphae at the base and an unusual abundance of clamp connections when tissue is examined under a microscope. Some *Sarcodon* species are similar in appearance, but their fruiting bodies have dark spines when mature. The edibility of *Phellodon* species is unknown.

Sarcodon atroviridis (Morgan)
Banker

BLACKISH GREEN SARCODON

SYNONYMS *Sarcodon bambusinus, S. blackfordiae, S. fumosus, Hydnum atroviride*

FAMILY Hydnaceae

Cap 3–12 cm wide, often somewhat irregular in shape, convex when young and becoming flat with age, margin often wavy and irregular with age; overall color varying from orange-gray to dark grayish green or dark grayish black, drying to olive-green; surface smooth to pubescent, with occasional cracks; lower surface consisting of crowded downward-pointing spines up to 1 cm long, white to light greenish brown; stalk variable in length, up to 11 cm long and 3 cm wide, generally tapering toward the base, smooth, off-white to gray-brown depending on age, color often similar to that of the cap surface or underside; spores brown in mass, 8–9 × 7–8 μm, subglobose, tuberculate ornamentation.

Habitat/Biological Role: Occurring on the ground in broadleaf or conifer forests, fruiting bodies solitary or in groups; fruiting summer to fall. Forms mycorrhizal associations with trees.

Distribution: Apparently most frequent in the southern Appalachians, but its full range is poorly understood.

Comments: *Sarcodon* is a relatively large genus of mycorrhizal tooth fungi. Most species in the genus are rarely collected and insufficiently studied. The edibility of *S. atroviridis* is not known.

Sarcodon underwoodii Banker

EASTERN SCALY-CAP SARCODON

SYNONYMS *Sarcodon fuligineoviolaceus, S. murrillii, S. radicatus, Hydnum underwoodii*

FAMILY Hydnaceae

Cap 3–14 cm wide, usually somewhat irregular in shape, convex to flat, sometimes depressed at the center, usually inrolled at the margin and becoming wavy with age, yellowish tan with slight pinkish orange tints; surface smooth when young and becoming squamulose with stiff tufts; spore-bearing surface consisting of small downward-pointed spines up to 3 mm long, white when young but becoming pale pinkish gray to dark gray with age; stalk variable in length, up to 9 cm long and 4 cm wide, sometimes enlarged toward the base and apex, similar but smaller tufts present, same to darker in color than the lower surface of cap, spines sometimes decurrent; spores brown in mass, 5–7 × 5–6 µm, subglobose, ornamentation tuberculate.

Habitat/Biological Role: Occurring on the ground in broadleaf or conifer forests, often under Canadian hemlock, fruiting bodies solitary or in groups; fruiting summer to fall. Forms mycorrhizal associations with trees.

Distribution: Frequently encountered in the Appalachian Mountains and found in much of eastern North America.

Comments: *Sarcodon scabrosus* is morphologically similar and also common in our region, but its spines are about twice as long and the overall color is usually darker brown. *Sarcodon underwoodii* is much more bitter than *S. scabrosus* when tasted raw. Neither species is recommended for human consumption.

Slime Molds (Myxomycetes)

Slime molds are a morphologically diverse group of organisms found on every continent, where they occur in many of the same ecological situations as true fungi. Historically, they were thought to be fungi, and in many respects they function in a manner similar to some of the true fungi covered in this field guide. But these organisms are not actually fungi: they are classified in the kingdom Protista, not the kingdom Fungi. Several hundred different species of slime molds are known from the Southeast, and they are very regularly mistaken for fungi, so we include a few of the most common species that are likely to be encountered by fungal enthusiasts. With a few exceptions, the individual fruiting body of a slime mold is quite small, but many species are colorful enough and occur in large enough groups to be easily seen in the field.

Slime molds produce spores in a single mass that is enclosed at first, but the covering involved eventually ruptures. Most myxomycetes have a system of sterile thread-like or elongated structures referred to as a capillitium or pseudocapillitium within the mass of spores; these microscopic structures can be incredibly intricate when viewed under a compound microscope. The life cycle of all slime molds includes a vegetative stage, in which the organism feeds upon the bacteria associated with decomposing plant material. Since these organisms are not true fungi and so few species are treated here, we do not include a key.

Arcyria denudata (Linnaeus) Wettstein

CARNIVAL CANDY SLIME MOLD

FAMILY Arcyriaceae

Ovate to cylindrical structure, 1.5–5 mm high and 0.5–1 mm wide, on a tiny stalk which may not be readily apparent in large fruitings, pinkish red to brick red but weathering to brown; stalk 0.5–1.5 mm long, dark red or red-brown, expanded at the apex to form a shallow cup; spores red or reddish brown in mass, 6–8 μm, with scattered pale warts.

Habitat/Biological Role: Occurring on decomposing wood or (less commonly) bark in broadleaf or conifer forests, often present in large groups; usually fruiting from midsummer until early fall. Feeds upon the bacteria associated with decomposing plant material.

Distribution: Found throughout the world.

Comments: Because of their bright red color, the fruiting bodies of *Arcyria denudata* are easily noticed. Large fruitings can be 15 cm or more in total extent. *Arcyria incarnata* is very similar morphologically, but the mass of threads making up the major part of the fruiting body is only loosely attached to the cup at the apex of the stalk. In *A. denudata*, the mass of threads is firmly attached. Fruiting bodies are too small to be of culinary interest.

Ceratiomyxa fruticulosa
(O. F. Müller) T. Macbride

CORAL SLIME MOLD

FAMILY Ceratiomyxaceae

Erect, simple or branched columns arising from a thin layer that extends over the substrate, usually slimy and translucent at first but then turning white (more rarely pink or pale yellow), often 10 cm or more in total extent and up to 1 cm high; stalk lacking; spores produced individually on tiny stalks; spores white in mass, 6–7 × 10–13 μm, ovoid to elliptical or rarely globose, smooth.

Habitat/Biological Role: Occurring on decomposing wood in broadleaf or conifer forests; less commonly on leaf litter or mosses; fruiting after rain in late spring and early summer. Feeds upon the bacteria associated with decomposing wood.

Distribution: Found throughout the world wherever decomposing wood is present and often exceedingly common after a period of wet weather.

Comments: *Ceratiomyxa fruticulosa* is unlike anything else likely to be encountered in the forests of eastern North America. Extensive fruitings can cover large areas of decomposing logs and stumps. It is not closely related to the other slime molds considered in this field guide.

Fuligo septica (Linnaeus) F. H. Wiggers

SCRAMBLED EGG SLIME, DOG VOMIT SLIME MOLD

FAMILY Physaraceae

Cushion-shaped to irregular structure, 4–25 cm wide and 1–3 cm thick, at first soft and slimy but becoming dry and brittle, yellow to orange when fresh but fading to pale tan on the outside, black on the inside; stalk lacking; spore-bearing surface lacking; spores black in mass, 6–9 μm, globose, nearly smooth to minutely spiny.

Habitat/Biological Role: Occurring on decomposing wood or litter in broadleaf or conifer forests; also frequent on wood chips and mulch beds in landscaped areas; fruiting from late spring to fall. Feeds upon the bacteria associated with decomposing plant material.

Distribution: Found throughout the world.

Comments: *Fuligo septica* is one of the largest of all slime molds and is often quite conspicuous because of its size and color. Although it might appear unappetizing, the developing fruiting bodies of *F. septica* are sometimes eaten by humans.

Hemitrichia calyculata
(Spegazzini) M. L. Farr

YELLOW-FUZZ SLIME MOLD

FAMILY Trichiaceae

Short-turbinate to globose structure on a tiny stalk, 1–2.5 mm high and 0.5–1 mm wide, bright to dark yellow; stalk usually at least one-half or more of the total height, slender, 0.5–2 mm long, reddish brown to black, expanded at the top to form a distinct funnel-shaped cup; spores dull to bright yellow in mass and located within a fuzzy mass of very small yellow threads, 6.5–7 µm, faintly reticulate.

Habitat/Biological Role: Occurring in small or large groups on decomposing wood or (less commonly) bark in broadleaf or conifer forests; fruiting from late summer to fall. Feeds upon the bacteria associated with decomposing plant material.

Distribution: Often common in the Southeast and found throughout the world, most frequently in the tropics.

Comments: *Hemitrichia calyculata* is one of the more common slime molds, and it is usually relatively easy to spot in the field because of the often bright yellow color of the fruiting bodies. *Trichia favoginea* is similar in color but has sessile, closely packed fruiting bodies.

Lycogala epidendrum
(J. C. Buxbaum ex Linnaeus) Fries

WOLF'S-MILK SLIME MOLD

SYNONYM *Lycoperdon epidendrum*

FAMILY Reticulariaceae

Globose to slightly flattened or somewhat angular structure, 0.3–1.5 cm wide and high, pinkish gray to yellow-brown or almost black; surface roughened or with scattered warts, often developing an opening at the top; spores at first pink in mass but changing to pale ochraceous or pallid, 6–8 μm, globose, reticulate.

Habitat/Biological Role: Occurring on decomposing wood or (less commonly) dead bark in broadleaf or conifer forests, solitary or in small or large groups; fruiting from late spring until fall. Feeds upon the bacteria associated with decomposing plant material.

Distribution: Found throughout the world.

Comments: *Lycogala epidendrum* is one of the most widely distributed and well-known slime molds. The fruiting bodies resemble small puffballs. If an immature fruiting body is squeezed or broken open, a slimy pink substance with the consistency of toothpaste oozes out.

Metatrichia vesparia (Batsch) Nannenga-Bremekamp ex G. W. Martin & Alexopoulos

WASP'S NEST SLIME MOLD

FAMILY Trichiaceae

Multi-headed structure (with each of the "heads" looking like a tiny goblet when the spores have been lost) sharing a common stalk, 1–4.5 mm tall and up to 0.4–0.7 mm wide, usually occurring in small clusters, wine red to dark maroon or sometimes nearly black; stalk 0.2–3.5 mm long, brick red in color; spore-bearing surface lacking; spores reddish brown in mass, 10–12 µm, globose, warted.

Habitat/Biological Role: Occurring on decomposing wood or bark in broadleaf or conifer forests; fruiting from midsummer to early fall. Feeds upon the bacteria associated with decomposing plant material.

Distribution: Found throughout North America and other temperate regions of the northern hemisphere, much less common in temperate regions of the southern hemisphere and in the tropics.

Comments: The fruiting bodies of this species, which resemble the nests of paper wasps, are truly distinctive and not likely to be confused with anything else. Specimens of *Metatrichia vesparia* that appear in fall can persist until the following spring. Because of their dark color, the clusters of fruiting bodies are often challenging to find.

Stemonitis fusca Roth

CHOCOLATE TUBE SLIME MOLD, TREE HAIR

FAMILY Stemonitidaceae

Slender, cylindrical structure, 0.5–2 cm tall and up to 1 mm wide, tufted, occurring in small or sometimes rather extensive clusters, deep fuscous to dark reddish brown; stalk black, shining, 0.3–1 cm long; spore-bearing surface lacking; spores fuscous in mass, 7.5–9 µm, globose, warted-reticulate.

Habitat/Biological Role: Occurring on decomposing wood or bark in broadleaf or conifer forests; fruiting summer to fall. Feeds upon the bacteria associated with decomposing plant material.

Distribution: Found throughout the world.

Comments: *Stemonitis fusca* is one of the more common and distinctive slime molds likely to be encountered in the forests of the Southeast. The tufts of fruiting bodies are somewhat hair-like in general appearance. This species and *S. axifera* are rather similar but can be distinguished on the basis of their overall color, with the fruiting bodies of the latter a bright rusty brown.

Trichia favoginea (Batsch) Persoon

YELLOW EGG-SHAPED SLIME MOLD

FAMILY Trichiaceae

Globose to egg-shaped or somewhat cylindrical structure, up 1.5 mm tall and 0.6–1 mm wide, crowded together in groups that can be 2.5–5 cm in total extent; surface bright yellow or yellow-brown and more or less shiny; spores yellow to ochraceous in mass, 13–15 µm, coarsely reticulate.

Habitat/Biological Role: Occurring on decomposing wood or bark in broadleaf or conifer forests, individual fruiting bodies crowded together in small or large groups; usually fruiting from midsummer until fall, but fruiting bodies can persist through the winter. Feeds upon the bacteria associated with decomposing plant material.

Distribution: Found throughout the world.

Comments: Because of the yellow color of the fruiting bodies, *Trichia favoginea* is relatively easy to spot against the darker wood or bark upon which it occurs. This is certainly the case for large fruitings, which are not uncommon. Several other yellow *Trichia* species occur in the Southeast; *T. varia* is one of the most common of these. It can be distinguished from *T. favoginea* in having fruiting bodies that are scattered and not crowded together; moreover, the fruiting bodies vary in shape but are never cylindrical.

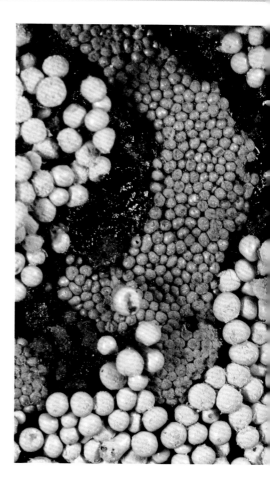

GLOSSARY

µm. See micrometer

acrid peppery or burning in taste

adnate having gills that are attached directly to the top of the stalk

adnexed having gills that are notched just as they reach the top of the stalk

aeciospore one of several different spore types found in rusts, generally having two nuclei and part of a chain of spores

agarics gilled mushrooms

aleuriospore a type of asexual spore produced by some fungi

amyloid reaction of spores to Melzer's reagent in which the spores stain purple to blue-green in color

annular zone area in which the stalk of a mushrooms has a ring of fibers present that is not defined well enough to be considered as an annulus

annulus ring-like structure found on the stalk of some mushrooms; it represents a remnant of the partial veil

apex top; usually referring to the top of the stalk or cap

apical pore distinct pore or opening at one end of a spore

ascospore sexual spore produced by members of the ascomycetes

ascus (plural: asci) the structure that holds the spores (ascospores) in the group of fungi called ascomycetes

basidiospore the sexual spore produced by basidiomycetes

basidium (plural: basidia) the structure on which spores are produced among basidiomycetes

butt rot a rot that impacts the base of a tree, the tree butt or trunk base

campanulate more or less bell-shaped

capillitium (plural: capillitia) a system of sterile elements found within the spore mass of many slime molds (myxomycetes) and some mushrooms

capitate describes a structure that ends in a distinct, compact head

cespitose condition in which several stalks are grouped together but not attached to one another

cheilocystidia cystidia that occur on the edges of the gills. Also see cystidia and pleurocystidia

chlamydospore a thick-walled and highly resistant spore that develops from hyphae in some groups of fungi; these spores enable the fungus in question to survive under unfavorable environmental conditions

clade a group of organisms considered to have evolved from a common ancestor

clavate club-shaped

confluent running together or merging

conidia (singular: conidium) asexual spores produced by ascomycetes

convex shaped like the exterior upper surface of a sphere

coriaceous leather-like in texture and appearance

cylindrical having the shape of a cylinder

cystidia (singular: cystidium) special sterile cells occurring in the hymenium of certain agarics

decorticated without bark; decomposing wood in which the covering of bark has been lost

decurrent condition in which the gills extend down the upper portion of the stalk

deliquescence an auto-digestion process that liquefies the gills of inky caps and other mushrooms to aid in spore dispersal

dendroid tree-like; branched like a tree

dextrinoid reaction of spores to Melzer's reagent in which the spores stain dark reddish brown in color

ectomycorrhiza a type of symbiotic association that forms between plants and fungi

endophyte a fungus that lives within the tissues of a plant for at least a portion of its life cycle

ferruginous rust-colored

fertile surface surface upon which the reproductive structures (asci or basidia) are located

fibrillose covered by hairs that typically adhere to each other

fuscous smoky brown

fusiform (fusoid) spindle-shaped, describing spores that taper at one or both ends

gills free condition in which the gills are not attached to the top of the stalk

glabrous smooth; lacking scales, hairs, or other structures

gleba the mass of spores and spore-producing tissue found inside some mushrooms

globose rounded or spherical; having a shape that resembles a globe

hemispherical having a shape suggestive of half a sphere

hyaline essentially clear; glass-like

hymenium the fertile surface of a fungus, e.g., the face/side of a gill, inside of a pore, inner surface of a cup fungus, etc.

hyphae (singular: hypha) microscopic, thread-like structures that make up both the mycelium and fruiting body of a mushroom

hypogeous below ground, usually used in reference to truffles or false truffles

KOH potassium hydroxide; a 3% solution of KOH is often used to moisten dried fungal tissue prior to microscopic study

macroscopic easily visible without magnification

Melzer's reagent a red-colored solution that is particularly important when using a microscope to identify species of fungi because it can produce different staining reactions

micrometer (μm) a metric unit (1,000th of a millimeter) used to measure microscopic characters under a microscope

morphological refers to the shape or form of a structure, including fruiting bodies

mycelium (plural: mycelia) a grouping of single strands of fungal tissue often found in the soil or wood

mycologist a person who studies mushrooms and other fungi

mycophagy/mycophagist eating fungi/ eater of fungi

mycorrhizae a symbiotic connection between plants and fungi that the majority of plants depend on for nutrient uptake and their overall health and survival

nonamyloid no readily apparent reaction of spores to Melzer's reagent

obovate inversely ovate, with the narrow end at the point of attachment

ovate shaped like an egg

partial veil a temporary covering that extends from the edge of the cap to the stalk in certain mushrooms

pellis the surface tissue of the fruiting body of a mushroom

perforated having a series of holes

perforation a hole or opening

peridiole the "eggs" in a bird's nest fungus or the spore-filled circular spots in some puffballs or false truffles

peridium the outer skin or rind of puffballs, false truffles, and truffles

perithecium (plural: perithecia) a flask-shaped structure found in many ascomycetes in which asci and spores are produced, often pimple-like

pleurocystidia cystidia that occur on the faces or sides of the gills. Also see cystidia and cheilocystidia

plicate folded or somewhat corrugated

pruinose covered with a fine powder

pulverulent powdery, consisting of fine particles

punctate covered by scattered dots or scales (although often more or less regularly distributed)

radial arranged like rays or spokes on a wheel

radicating generally referring to a stalk that projects into the soil or other substrate like a root

resupinate occurring flat on the substrate, usually on its lower surface

reticulate net-like; having a network of warts, spines, or ridges over the surface

rhizomorph cord or root-like masses usually found at the base of some species of fungi

saprotroph an organism that derives nutrients from decomposing organic matter

scabers short stiff hairs arranged in patches, often referring to the stalks of the genus *Leccinum*

sclerotium a hard, usually dark mass of fungal tissue, usually underground

scurfy coarse or rough, often feeling like sandpaper

setae pointed sterile cells that arise from surfaces of some mushrooms, particularly useful for identifying polypores (visible under a microscope)

sinuous having a number of curves or turns

striate having small radial or parallel lines or furrows

subdistant well spaced, often referring to gills that are well separated (between close and distant)

subfusiform somewhat tapered, not quite spindle-shaped. Also see fusiform

subglobose not quite globose (or round)

subovoid not quite ovoid

subpellis tissue of a fruiting body found just below the surface

subtended occurring in a position beneath or below a particular structure

teliospore generally a thick-walled resting spore formed at the late stages of a rust's or smut's life cycle

terete more or less round in cross section; slender, cylindrical

thallus a body that is not differentiated into stem, roots, leaves, etc.; commonly used in reference to lichens

translucent striate typically referring to lines on a cap surface created by gills

whose outlines are visible through the cap, creating the illusion of having ridges on the cap's surface

truncate blunt-ended, often describing a spore in which one end appears cut

turbinate shaped like a top or an inverted cone

umbilicate having a central depression or invagination

umbo a raised area in the center of the cap of a mushroom

undulate wavy

universal veil a temporary membranous covering that fully encloses the immature fruiting body of certain mushrooms (e.g., *Amanita*)

viscid sticky or slimy to the touch, a condition that sometimes disappears with age

volva cup-like structure found at the base of the stalk in some mushrooms; it represents a remnant of the universal veil

zonate with concentric bands/zones, usually of similar colors, on a cap surface

RECOMMENDED READING

Arora, D. 1986. *Mushrooms Demystified.* Berkeley: Ten Speed Press.

——. 1991. *All That the Rain Promises and More.* Berkeley: Ten Speed Press.

Baird, R., L. E. Wallace, G. Baker, and M. Scruggs. 2013. Stipitate hydnoid fungi of the temperate southeastern United States. *Fungal Diversity* 62(1):41–114.

Bessette, A., A. R. Bessette, and D. W. Fischer. 1997. *Mushrooms of Northeastern North America.* Syracuse, New York: Syracuse University Press.

Bessette, A., W. C. Roody, and A. R. Bessette. 2000. *North American Boletes.* Syracuse, New York: Syracuse University Press.

Bessette, A. E., W. C. Roody, A. R. Bessette, and D. L. Dunaway. 2007. *Mushrooms of the Southeastern United States.* Syracuse, New York: Syracuse University Press.

Bessette, A., D. B. Harris, and A. R. Bessette. 2009. *Milk Mushrooms of North America.* Syracuse, New York: Syracuse University Press.

Bessette, A., A. R. Bessette, and S. A. Trudell. 2013. *Tricholomas of North America.* Austin: University of Texas Press.

Beug, M. W., A. E. Bessette, and A. R. Bessette. 2014. *Ascomycete Fungi of North America.* Austin: University of Texas Press.

Binion, D. E., S. L. Stephenson, W. C. Roody, H. H. Burdsall, O. K. Miller, Jr., and L. N. Vasilyeva. 2007. *Macrofungi Associated with Oaks of Eastern North America.* Forest Health Technology Enterprise Team Publication 06-19, Morgantown, West Virginia.

Bonito, G. M. 2009. *Systematics and Ecology of Truffles (Tuber).* Duke University: Doctoral Dissertation.

Breitenbach, J., and F. Kränzlin. 1984–86. *Fungi of Switzerland.* 2 vols. Lucerne, Switzerland: Verlag Mykologia.

Coker, W. C., and A. H. Beers. 1943. *Boletaceae of North Carolina.* Chapel Hill: University of North Carolina Press.

Coker, W. C. 1974. *The Club and Coral Mushrooms (Clavarias) of the United States and Canada.* New York: Dover Publications.

Coker, W. C., and J. N. Couch. 1974. *The Gasteromycetes of the Eastern United States and Canada.* New York: Dover Publications.

Dennis, R. W. G. 1978. *British Ascomycetes.* Vaduz, Germany: J. Cramer.

Fortin, J. A., C. Plenchette, and Y. Piché. 2009. *Mycorrhizas: The New Green Revolution.* Quebec: MultiModes.

Hall, I., S. L. Stephenson, P. K. Buchanan, W. Yun, and A. L. J. Cole. 2003. *Edible and Poisonous Mushrooms of the World.* Portland, Oregon: Timber Press.

Hesler, L. R. 1960. *Mushrooms of the Great Smokies.* Knoxville: The University of Tennessee Press.

Hesler, L. R., and A. H. Smith. 1963. *North American Species of Hygrophorus.* Knoxville: The University of Tennessee Press.

Jenkins, D. T., 1986. *Amanita of North America.* Eureka, California: Mad River Press.

Kendrick, B., 1985. *The Fifth Kingdom.* 2nd ed. Newburyport, Massachusetts: Focus Information Group.

Kovacs, G. M., J. M. Trappe, A. M. Alsheikh, K. Bóka, and T. F. Elliott. 2008. Imaia, a new truffle genus to accommodate Terfezia gigantea. *Mycologia* 100(6):930–939.

Landvik, S., O. E. Eriksson, and M. L. Berbee. 2001. Neolecta: a fungal dinosaur? Evidence from β-tubulin amino acid sequences. *Mycologia* 93(6):1151–1163.

Largent, L., D. Johnson, and R. Walting. 1977. *How to Identify Mushrooms to Genus, III: Microscopic Features.* Eureka, California: Mad River Press.

Largent, D. L., and T. J. Baroni. 1988. *How to Identify Mushrooms to Genus, VI: The Modern Genera.* Eureka, California: Mad River Press.

Lincoff, G. H. 1989. *The Audubon Society Field Guide to North American Mushrooms*. New York: Knopf.

Mains, E. B. 1939. Cordyceps from the mountains of North Carolina and Tennessee. *Journal of the Elisha Mitchell Scientific Society* 55(1):117–129.

McIlvaine, C., and R. K. Macadam. 1973. *One Thousand American Fungi*. New York: Dover Publications.

Miller, O. K. 1977. *Mushrooms of North America*. New York: E. P. Dutton.

Miller, O. K., and H. H. Miller. 1988. *Gasteromycetes*. Eureka, California: Mad River Press.

———. 2006. *North American Mushrooms: A Field Guide to Edible and Inedible Fungi*. Guilford, Connecticut: Morris Book Publishing.

Miller, S. L. 1986. Hypogeous fungi from the southeastern United States I. The genus *Rhizopogon*. *Mycotaxon* 27:193–218.

Nuhn, M. E., M. Binder, A. F. Taylor, R. E. Halling, and D. S. Hibbett. 2013. Phylogenetic overview of the Boletineae. *Fungal Biology* 117(7):479–511.

Overholts, L. O. 1953. *The Polyporaceae of the United States, Alaska, and Canada*. Ann Arbor: University of Michigan Press.

Rogerson, C. T., and S. L. Stephenson. 1993. Myxomyceticolous fungi. *Mycologia* 85:456–469.

Rogers, R. 2011. *The Fungal Pharmacy: The Complete Guide to Medicinal Mushrooms and Lichens of North America*. Berkeley: North Atlantic Books.

Roody, W. C. 2015. *Mushrooms of West Virginia and the Central Appalachians*. Lexington: University Press of Kentucky.

Seaver, F. J. 1928. *The North American Cup-fungi (Operculates)*. New York: Seaver.

———. 1951. *The North American Cup-fungi (Inoperculates)*. New York: Hafner Publishing Company.

Smith, A. H., and L. R. Hesler. 1968. *The North American Species of Pholiota*. Monticello, New York: Lubrecht & Cramer.

Smith, A. H., H. V. Smith, and N. S. Weber. 1973. *How to Know the Non-gilled Mushrooms*. Dubuque, Iowa: William C. Brown.

———. 1979. *How to Know the Gilled Mushrooms*. Dubuque, Iowa: William C. Brown.

Stamets, P. 1996. *Psilocybin Mushrooms of the World*. Berkeley: Ten Speed Press.

Stephenson, S. L. 1989. Mushrooms and Other Fungi of West Virginia. Nongame Wildlife Program, West Virginia Department of Natural Resources.

———. 2010. *The Kingdom Fungi: The Biology of Mushrooms, Molds, and Lichens*. Portland, Oregon: Timber Press.

Stephenson, S. L., and H. Stempen. 1994. *Myxomycetes: A Handbook of Slime Molds*. Portland, Oregon: Timber Press.

Stephenson, S. L., and W. C. Roody. 1997. *Preliminary Checklist of Macrofungi and Myxomycetes of West Virginia*. Nongame and Natural Heritage Program, West Virginia Division of Natural Resources. Wildlife Resources Technical Bulletin 97-5.

Trappe, M., F. Evans, and J. M. Trappe. 2007. *Field Guide to North American Truffles*. Berkeley: Ten Speed Press.

Weber, N. S., A. H. Smith, and D. Guravich. 1985. *A Field Guide to Southern Mushrooms*. Ann Arbor: University of Michigan Press.

Wu, G., et al. 2014. Molecular phylogenetic analyses redefine seven major clades and reveal 22 new generic clades in the fungal family Boletaceae. *Fungal Diversity* 69(1):93–115.

PHOTO AND ILLUSTRATION CREDITS

All drawings are by Marjorie Leggitt.

All photographs are by Todd F. Elliott, except as noted here.

Kimberly R. Fleming, pages 381 and 383.

Dan Guravitch, pages 172 and 233.

Emily Johnson, pages 83, 151, 226, and 320.

Brian P. Looney, page 237.

John Plischke, page 96.

Bill Roody, pages 28, 45, 52, 56, 64, 66, 79, 122, 123, 132, 133, 142, 150, 153, 173, 180, 182, 224, 238, 254, 318, and 344.

Mary E. Smiley, page 209.

Steven L. Stephenson, pages 9, 10, and 379.

Armin Weise, pages 74, 141, 207, 285, 295, and 309.

INDEX

ABOUT THE AUTHORS

Todd F. Elliott is a freelance naturalist, biologist, and photographer from western North Carolina. Elliott picked his first edible mushrooms by age three, and by fourteen years old, he had coauthored his first peer-reviewed mycological publication. His research passions in the study of global biodiversity and interrelationships in nature have taken him to remote corners of the world to explore tropical rainforests, temperate woodlands, deserts, beaches, and high mountains on six continents. Elliott has authored or coauthored many peer-reviewed papers covering this research and has described fungi new to science. With a passion for spreading knowledge of the natural world, he regularly teaches nature-based programs in ecology, primitive skills, and foraging. Elliott holds a degree in interpretive natural history from Warren Wilson College. To read more, visit toddelliott.weebly.com.

Steven L. Stephenson is a research professor at the University of Arkansas. He has collected and studied fungi for more than thirty-five years, and his research program has taken him to all seven continents and every major type of terrestrial ecosystem. Stephenson is the author or coauthor of more than three hundred book chapters and papers in peer-reviewed journals and eleven books, including *Edible and Poisonous Mushrooms of the World*, *The Kingdom Fungi: The Biology of Mushrooms, Molds, and Lichens* (both with Timber Press), and the award-winning *A Natural History of the Central Appalachians* (West Virginia University Press, 2013).

DETAILED PARTS OF A MUSHROOM

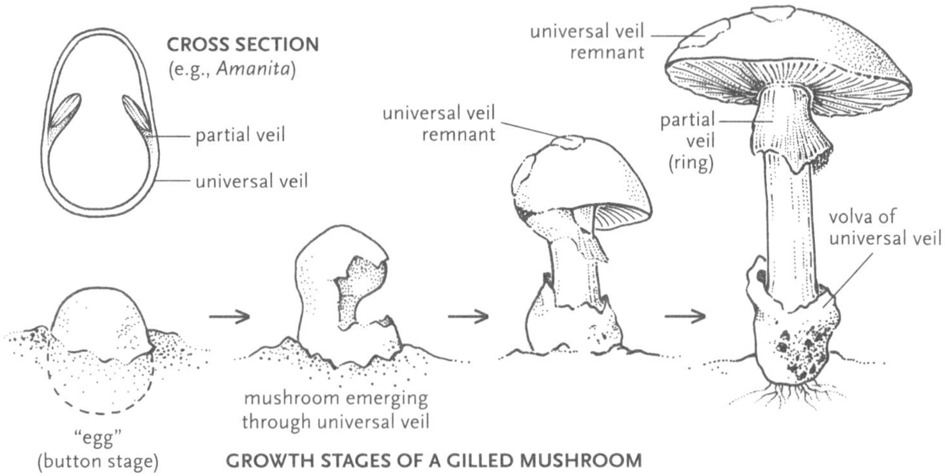
CROSS SECTION
(e.g., *Amanita*)
partial veil
universal veil
universal veil remnant
universal veil remnant
partial veil (ring)
volva of universal veil
"egg" (button stage)
mushroom emerging through universal veil

GROWTH STAGES OF A GILLED MUSHROOM

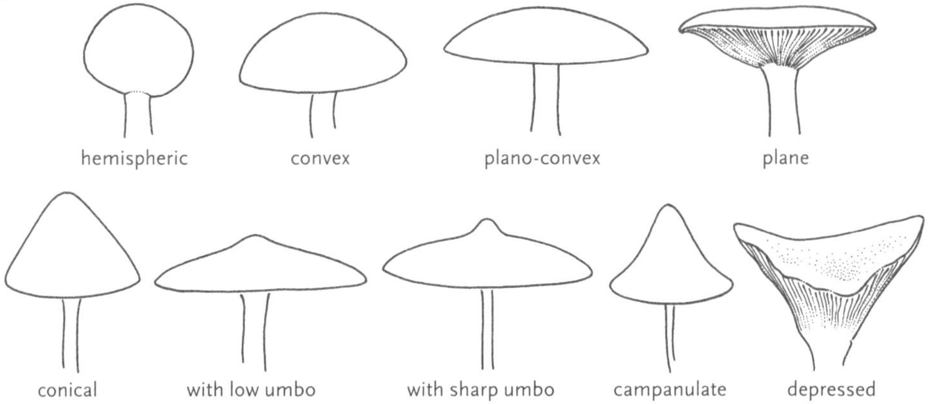
hemispheric
convex
plano-convex
plane
conical
with low umbo
with sharp umbo
campanulate
depressed

CAP SHAPES

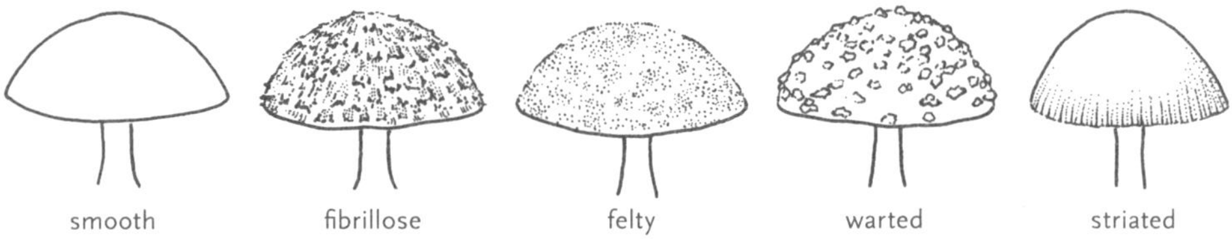
smooth
fibrillose
felty
warted
striated

CAP SURFACES

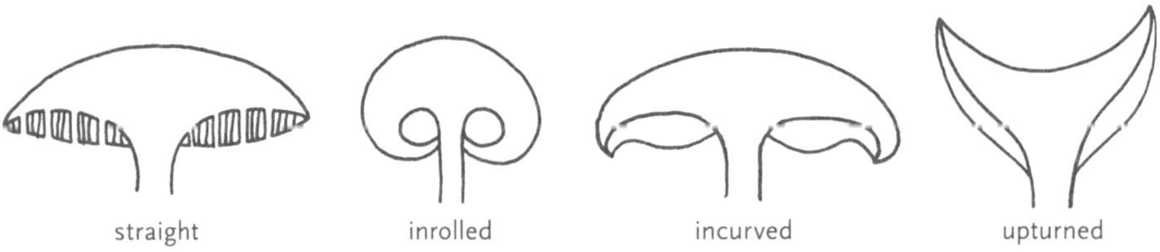
straight
inrolled
incurved
upturned

CAP MARGINS